PREFACE

This book, though based on Prof. J. P. Bose's 'An Outline Of Business Organisation and Management', is, as a matter of fact, a new one. The changes that have taken place in the new syllabus have called for a complete recast of the existing book. To make the book adapted to the revised and new syllabus, some topics have been completely discarded, some have been modified and updated and some new ones have been added.

As a teacher of the subject for over three decades, the experience that I have gathered has been fully utilised in making the book purposeful to the students for whom it is meant. I have taken all care to see that the book is not made voluminous and cumbersome with matters completely irrelevant to and unnecessary for the students and also unintended in the syllabus.

In spite of my best efforts, I feel there is yet enough scope for further improvement which I hope to do in future with the cooperation of my friends in the profession whose suggestions I shall thankfully accept.

To the publishers, particularly to Shri Amitabha Sen and to the proofreaders, I offer my heartfelt gratitude for the cooperation I have received from them.

I feel delighted to mention the name of Dr. S. Kr. Paul (Prafulla Chandra College) who has always been a source of my inspiration and encouragement.

Sivanata Bhawan
Calcutta 29
26th January 1992

S. Talukdar

Contents

CHAPTER ONE

NATURE AND SCOPE OF BUSINESS

MEANING, DEFINITION AND CHARACTERISTICS

Meaning — The dictionary meaning of 'business' is 'occupation', 'calling', 'personal concern', etc. Etymologically, the term business (busyness) comes from the word busy which means a state of being engaged in some work. Man may be busy in many kinds of activities – in reading, writing, playing, worshipping, politicking, earning money, etc. Since business means occupation or calling, the last kind of activity, i.e. earning money becomes very significant. Man may be busy in economic and non-economic activities. **By business, we normally refer to the economic or money-earning activities only.** Man wants money to buy goods and services to satisfy his numerous wants. Marshall, the founder of modern economics, wrote, "Political economy or Economics is a study of man's actions in the ordinary business of life. It enquires how he gets his income and how he spends it". Practically 'business' is related to that "ordinary business of life". Business, therefore, is income-oriented. Every individual chooses or enters into some occupation or calling to make income.

How can money be earned? **Money can be earned only by selling something,** either a goods or a service. No person can earn money by any other way, excepting a beggar and a thief. But 'earning' by begging or stealing cannot strictly be called earning because by begging or stealing no new income is generated but the income of one person is transferred from him to another. In case of begging, the transfer is voluntary from the side of the giver while in case of stealing it is against the will and even knowledge of the person robbed. Again, whenever a person wants to sell something there must be a buyer. Unless one person wants to buy something another person cannot sell it. **Buying and selling are reciprocal acts.** If earning is possible only by selling something then the whole process is a composite action of buying and selling. That is the ordinary business of life.

Definition — In the context of above, **business can be defined as 'repeated or recurring buying and selling of goods or services for the mutual benefits of the buyers and the sellers'.** In the definition, the word **repeated** or **recurring** is very significant. **One isolated transaction does not make business.** A student taking admission in a college buys his books and then after the completion of his course sells the books at reduced prices to another. Book-selling is not the business of the student. But the owner of a bookshop buys books from the publishers and sells them to the customers regularly keeping a margin of profit at each transaction. Book-selling is his business. The last part of the definition i.e. 'for the mutual benefits of the buyers and the sellers' also needs explanation. Man buys those goods or services which have utilities i.e. which can satisfy his wants. A seller can sell his goods or service only when there is some utility in it. When he sells his goods or service actually he sells the utility in it. For every buying-selling transaction, the buyer consumes the utility by which his want is satisfied and he is benefited and on the other hand the seller is also benefited as he earns some profit.

If goods or services are to be sold, they have to be produced or generated. **Business actually includes all the activities involved in the whole process of production to sale.** Functionally, business is divided into three types of activities – industry, trade and commerce. Industry means production, trade relates to the transfer of goods from the place of production to the place of consumption and commerce entails those activities which help trade. At every stage there are buying and selling activities, either of goods or of services.

Prof. Haney has defined business as "Business may be defined as human activity directed towards producing or acquiring wealth through buying or selling goods". He further writes, "On the one hand business rests on the technical process of trade and manufacture, on the other hand, it looks to the market. At the junction stands the businessman, either directing the technical process of production or gauging the market, or doing both; but always engaged in buying and selling for the purpose of gain". Actually, Prof. Haney sums up the functional characteristics of business in his definition and also adds the concept of market. Without a market, buying and selling functions cannot take place. Market is said to exist whenever and wherever buyers and sellers meet or when units of demand meet with units of supply.

It will not be an exaggeration to say that, in a broad sense, any money-earner is a businessman because he sells something, either any goods or any service. A publisher sells books after producing them, a book-seller sells books after procuring them from the publisher, a printer sells his printing service while printing the books, an author sells his knowledge, either general on technical, by writing a book, a coolie or porter sells his labour when he carries a load of books on his head reaching them from the binder to the book-seller, a tempo–owner sells transport service by carrying reams of paper to the press, a banker sells banking service at every point of payment, a binder sells his technical skill and so on. All these sellings (with corresponding buyings) make the world of book business. Everybody engaged in the process earns money in exchange of his ware or service. The economic world as a whole is composed of such smaller worlds of individual business. **This world is a business world.** Hooper nicely summarises all these concepts by saying, "The whole complex field of commerce and industry, the basic industry, processing and manufacturing industries and the network of ancilary services, distribution, banking, insurance, transport and so on, which serve and interpenetrate the world of business as a whole".

Characteristics — Business as a pattern of human behaviour has a number of characteristics. From the definitions ascribed to it the following characteristics can be sorted out :

(1) **Economic institution** — It is a kind of economic institution closely connected with Economics and is an organ of society. It is very often described as a practical application of economic theories related to production, consumption, distribution and exchange. Politics, a branch of social science, has much influence on business now-a-days. As such, business is a branch of social sciences.

(2) **Income-oriented** — It is income-oriented or gain-motivated. By transactions of buying and selling a businessman wants to make profit or earn income while the buyer also gains as he gets goods or services having utility to satisfy his wants.

(3) **Reciprocity** — There is a sense of reciprocity in every type of business. Whenever there is a seller there must be a buyer and *vice versa*. Both the sides gain something as a mutual consideration.

(4) **Concerning all** — Knowingly or unknowingly every member of a society is involved in it. Everybody may not be a businessman in a narrow sense. He may not belong to the business world but he belongs to the world of business. In a broad sense everybody has his own business, i.e., occupation or calling unless he is a parasite. Even a beggar or a thief has his own business. Everybody minds his own business.

(5) **Regularity or recurrence** — Another characteristic of business is its regularity or recurrence. One isolated transaction does not make business. Further, every type of business is interrelated with other types. No business can be carried out in an isolated manner. Hooper has said that all the business activities 'interpenetrate' to build up the world of business as a whole. Business, therefore, has a totality in its character.

(6) **Common features** — One important characteristic of business is that **every kind of business has some common or basic features.** They are: (a) Entrepreneurship: Every business must have some entrepreneur or entrepreneurs to promote it and to render leadership for its development. There may be State entrepreneurship as well. (b) Organisation: Every business must have an organisation made of human elements bound by authority relationship. A busi-

ness organisation has different forms of ownership and size. (c) Capital: Capital plays a vital role in every business. Business means rolling of capital for further gains. Capital is of different types: fixed and working. Capital has different sources: inside (or own) and outside (or loan). The amount of capital needed depends on the nature and size of the business. (d) Risk and uncertainty: Every business is concerned with different kinds of risks arising out of accidents and uncertainty whether there will be profit or not, whether the goods will be sold or not, whether the capital will be eaten up or not. (e) Surplus creation: The motive of every business is to create some surplus. This surplus is distributed among the risk-takers or investors as profit. Profit is the reward for uncertainty. For public sector enterprises the surplus is spent for the development of the country. (f) Objectives: A business has its objectives. There are individual motives as well as social objectives.

(7) **Area of operation** — Every business has its area of operation. That area may be big or small. The area may be local, confined to a State (like West Bengal only), spread over a region (say, Eastern Region of India) or the country as a whole or it may cross the boundary of the country and go for foreign market. The extent of the area depends on two major factors – (a) The nature of the business activity. Producers of perishable goods generally have a narrow market. (b) The size of the organisation. Unless the organisation is big, control over a large area of operation is not possible.

FUNCTIONS OF BUSINESS

Meaning — Function means characteristic action of a living or a created thing for which that thing is specially fitted and for which a thing exists. Business, as a created thing, has its functions. **In fact business as itself cannot function. The businessmen behind the business do it.** 'Economics is what economists do', said Pigou, the great economist. Echoing his statement we may say that business is what businessmen do. Business of business is to do business.

Functions — Functions of business can be of the following types: (1) **Utility creation – The main function of business is utility creation** in different forms by which the wants of man can be fulfilled. By industry, goods are produced which means creation of 'form' utility by changing the form of raw materials into finished products. By trade, 'place' utility is created by transferring the goods from the place of production to the place of consumption. By commerce, 'time' utility is created by moving the goods in time with the help of different commercial activities like transport, banking, warehousing, etc.

(2) **Buying and selling — Business means some form of buying and selling of goods or services.** The buyers and sellers may be businessmen themselves or the buyers may be ultimate consumers. Goods are of many types: movable or immovable, durable or perishable, production or consumption, etc. The services may be of different types: skilled or unskilled, regular or casual, technical or non-technical, etc. This buying-selling function is the external expression of business.

(3) **Exchange and cooperation — The essence of business is exchange** and exchange means cooperation. Through business, cooperation between individuals, between communities and finally between nations can be achieved.

(4) **Handling of money**– In the business world, at every step exchange is taking place. Such exchange was originally in the form of a direct barter. Now it is replaced by **use of money as medium of exchange.** Money in business also includes foreign money. Money denotes currency as well as negotiable instruments like promissory notes, bills of exchange and cheques.

(5) **Social development — Business has a big role to play for social development.**

In order to carry out the characteristic functions, a business has to undertake several operational, managerial and technical functions in the office and in the factory.

CLASSIFICATION OR COMPONENTS OF BUSINESS

Classification —Business can be classsified in three ways: functionally, structurally and entrepreneurally.

A. **Functional classification** — Business is a complex whole of various types of activities starting from production and ending into sale. At each stage there is a distinct type of activity. Accordingly, business is classified into industry, trade and commerce. Each can be called a component of business.

(1) **Industry — Industry means a process of converting raw materials into finished or semi-finished goods.** From iron ore (raw material), pig iron and steel is produced and from cast iron and steel different goods are produced. From bamboo, paper pulp is made, from paper pulp comes paper. Paper pulp is the semi-finished or intermediary goods while paper is the final product. Production may be carried out by manual labour or by machine or by automatic machine. Again, production can be carried out by muscular power or by mechanical power. Production may be by a simple process or by highly technical and sophisticated process. It can be done either in a small or a big scale. Industry itself can be sub-divided into many parts. Production involves machining, processing, hammering, heating, cooling, etc. and some other business functions like transport, warehousing, etc.; otherwise production is not possible. When a consumer pays a price for a product he pays for the raw material *plus* for all other services. Industry itself, therefore, is a composite function.

(2) **Trade — Trade denotes the transfer of goods from the place of production to the place of consumption** or from the producer to the consumer. It is a process by which exchange or sale or transfer of goods take place. This is perhaps the most important component of business because goods are produced for selling. Industry is a preliminary function while commerce is an auxiliary one. Trade has within it two distinct features. Outwardly, trade means the movement of the goods from the seller to the buyer. This is the physical part of the whole function. But inwardly there is a legal character. Through the movement of goods the title to or ownership of goods also passes from the seller to the buyer. There may be movement of goods in case of a contract of hire but there is no transfer of ownership. Hiring is a business transaction. Movement of goods together with transfer of ownership takes place when there is a gift. But it is not a business transaction. Trade can be further subdivided. Trade also means movement of goods from the surplus area to the deficit area.

(3) **Commerce** — There are many kinds of hindrances or obstacles standing in the way of trade or transfer of goods from the producers to the consumers. **Commerce denotes all the activities,** for example services of transport, bank, insurance, warehouse etc. **which remove all these hindrances for smooth and faster movement of the goods.** All these activities are auxiliary or helpful to trade. Goods must reach the right place, in right condition, at the right time and that against the right price. The function of commerce is to perform these. Commercial activities are divided into different functional parts.

Industry, trade and commerce are closely inter-linked. Trade and commerce are so closely inter-linked that some people consider that trade is a part of commerce.

B. **Structural classification — Business can also be classified structurally according to the size of the organisation.** A business becomes big when its volume of activities becomes big, a large number of people are employed, the organisation consists of a number of levels of authority and on the whole it becomes a 'tall' type organisation. On the other hand, if the organisation is small, the volume of activities is small, the number of employees are also small and on the whole it becomes a 'flat' type of organisation. Whether the business belongs to any of the three functions of industry, trade or commerce, the size of the business may be large or small.

There are various criteria by which the size is determined. For example, the amount of capital invested, the volume or value of output, the number of employees, the amount of raw material, power etc. consumed, the capacity of the plant etc. The most simple yardstick of measurement is the value of total investment. Accordingly, the Government of India considers three types of sizes : (1) Small size – involving investment up to Rs. 35 lakhs (Rs. 40 lakhs in case of ancillary industry). (2) Medium size – involving investment from Rs. 35 lakhs to Rs. 1 crore. (3) Large size – involving investment above Rs. 1 crore. Investment in plant is counted. The Companies Act of 1956 provides some special obligations on companies having paid-up capital above Rs. 25 lakhs.

C. **Entrepreneur classification** – There is still another basis of classification of business irrespective of its function. This is **on the pattern of entrepreneurship or ownership.** Broadly, business enterprises come under **two types of ownership :** Private and Public. Under private ownership we find Sole-proprietorship, Partnership, Joint Hindu Family, Cooperative Society and Company types. Under public ownership (or ownership of Government, either Central or State, or a combination of both) we find Departmental undertakings, Government Companies, Public or Statutory Corporations and other types (Board, Trust, etc.).

Structural classification and entrepreneural classification become identified for all practical purposes. A sole-proprietor's firm is hardly big while a company or a public undertaking is usually big or very big.

SUB-DIVISIONS OF INDUSTRY

Industries are classified according to the nature of the product. For example, jute industry, motor car industry etc. The word industry is used here to denote a group of firms engaged in the same line of production. In a different sense, industry also means production of goods itself out of some raw materials. For example, we say Tata Iron and Steel industry, i.e., by industry we mean a firm. Industry can be sub-divided into many types.

First of all **industry can be sub-divided into Primary and Secondary.** In the first group come Extractive and Genetic industries and in the second group Manufacturing and Construction. Manufacturing industries are again of different types :

(1) **Extractive** — These industries refer to drawing out of goods or materials from natural sources like lumbering (cutting of trees for wood), fishing, mining, fruit gathering etc. The products may be directly consumed or may be used as raw materials for further production. For example, fish or fruits are directly consumed but minerals are used as raw materials. Extractive industry may be of elementary type like fruit gathering or highly mechanised like mining. Extractive industry is one of the oldest types of industry practised by man. Today it has become highly sophisticated in respect of mining or even fishing. Agricultural farming is considered a kind of extractive industry which again is getting mechanised.

(2) **Genetic** — These industries are concerned with rearing and breeding of animals (piggery), of birds (poultry) and of plants (nursery). These industries largely depend on natural surroundings and usually plenty of land is necessary. This is also a very old type and simple type of industry. But in modern times, such industries also have been made sophisticated and highly mechanised with large scale operations. Refrigeration, pasteurisation etc. of animal products are the modern tendencies. Forestry and sericulture (growing of moth for silk) also come under this category of industries.

(3) **Manufacturing** – It means production of goods out of raw materials. Goods are of all descriptions, from semi-finished to finished stage. Manufacturing can be done with or without mechanical power, with or without machines, on a small or a big scale. It may be simple e.g. making of soaps or very sophisticated e.g. making of electronic goods. The product may be as tiny as a pin or as bulky as a locomotive. Generally when we think of industry we mean manufacturing.

Manufacturing industry is further sub-divided according to the processing or method of operation for production. The sub-division is as follows :

(a) **Continuous** — In this type of industry the raw material is fed at one end and then, through successive operations, with the help of different machines (or even one machine), the final product comes out at the other end. For example, cotton textile industry, paper industry, glass industry etc.

(b) **Assembly** — In this type of industry the different components of a product are separately produced with different types of raw materials and by different processings. After that, all the finished components are joined or assembled together to get the final product. For example, automobile industry, shoe-making industry, machine-making industry etc.

(c) **Analytical** — In this type of industry the same raw material is treated separately so that different products come out at different stages of treatment. For example, in an oil refinery the crude oil is brought under different processes or heat treatment so that from the same raw material different products like gasoline (oil for motor car), kerosene, diesel oil, lubricating oil, grease etc. come out continuously.

(d) **Synthetical** — In this type of industry different kinds of raw materials and ingredients are brought together and processed and out of mixing a completely new type of product comes out. For example, making of alloy steel, drugs, synthetic fabrics, cement etc.

(e) **Processing** — In this type of industry conversion of raw material into finished product does not take place but some qualitative change of a material is made. For example, printing, heat treatment, refrigerating etc.

(4) **Construction** — This type of industry consists of construction of buildings, roads, dams, bridges, pipelines, tunnels, ports etc. Various kinds of fabricated materials produced in other industries are used. Manpower is a big factor. Construction industry is essential for building up other industries. Nowadays, heavy machines like cranes, bulldozers, forks etc. are used in construction work. Power generation may be called a type of construction industry.

Conclusion — In manufacturing industry, capital plays the important role while in extractive and genetic industries man-power is the main factor. In construction industry, usually there is importance of both.

SUB-DIVISIONS OF TRADE

Trade can be sub-divided in two broad ways : Firstly, it can be sub-divided on the basis of area of operation. Accordingly we find inland or home trade and foreign trade. Secondly, the classification can be based on the unit of sale. Accordingly we find wholesale trade and retail trade. The sub-divisions are detailed below :

A. Area of Operation

(1) **Inland trade** — It means transfer of goods from the place of production to the place of consumption both belonging within the boundary of the same country. It is also known as home trade. The goods, not necessarily, will travel from the place of production directly to the place of consumption. The consignment may be received by intermediaries for further distribution.

The characteristics of inland trade are: (a) It takes place within the boundary of the same country. (b) It is more or less inevitable because every part of a country cannot produce all types of goods locally. (c) It has no problem of exchange of currency. Payment procedure is simple. (d) Large number of middlemen are not generally involved. (e) Government regulations are not varied and rigid. (f) Different types of transport and mostly land transport are used. (g) Both production and consumption goods are involved.

(2) **Foreign trade** — It means movement of goods from one country to another. Foreign trade takes place because of geographical division of labour and operation of the theory of comparative costs. Every country specialises in the production of those goods in which it has comparative advantage with regard to cost and then exchange these goods with the specialised products of other countries.

Foreign trade is **further sub-divided into** export trade and import trade but virtually they are reciprocal.

The characteristics of foreign trade are: (a) It is not inevitable. Trade between two countries can take place provided the Governments of both the countries agree. (b) The Government plays a dominant role in the matter and everything depends on the commercial policy of the Government of a country. (c) Political relations between countries also play an important role. (d) There is the problem of exchange rate determination between the currencies of the countries concerned. (e) Large number of intermediaries are involved in the process as various legal and trade formalities have to be observed and usually a long distance has to be covered. (f) The Government of every country imposes severe rules and regulations and controlling measures. (g) Generally, water transport is used though there may be foreign trade by land route. (h) The items involved in trade are divided into two groups — visible and invisible (capital, interest, services etc.) (i) International laws related to shipping, insurance, foreign exchange etc. have to be observed. (j) Generally, the goods are production goods as movement of consumption goods are restricted by the Governments.

(3) **Entrepot or Re-export trade** — Sometimes one country brings goods from another country then re-exports them to other countries after blending, processing, packaging or doing such other services. In the past, the Western powers used to do re-exporting of goods at a profit by bringing the goods at cheaper rates from their colonies. Now-a-days importance of re-export has largely declined. Even under-developed countries are developing their own industries.

Conclusion — Inland trade exists in every country while foreign trade is optional. Communist countries are recently entering into foreign trade discarding their old 'iron curtain' attitude.

B. Unit of Sale

(1) **Wholesale trade** — There are merchants called wholesalers who buy goods in bulk from the producers, hold the stock in their godowns and release the stock to the retailers as and when required. They **buy in bulk quantities but sell the goods to retailers in small units** by breaking the bulk. They take the risk of distribution and thereby producers are relieved and can devote more time for production work. A wholesaler may be of generalist type: keeping the stocks of many producers and many varieties of goods or, he may be of specialist type, keeping goods of limited variety, of limited number of producers. The business of wholesalers is known as wholesale trade and unit of sale is big. The wholesalers get discount on purchases from the producers out of which they offer a part to the retailers.

(2) **Retail trade** — Retail traders **buy goods from the wholesalers in small quantities and sell them to the ultimate consumers.** They get discount on their purchases from the wholesalers. Retailers generally have small shops where many varieties of goods are sold. There may be speciality shops too. For example, cloth shop, bookshop etc. There are varieties of retail trading through department stores, multiple shops, chain stores, tied shops, consumers' co-operative stores or mail order business.

Conclusion — It may be noted here that generally foreign trade is in the form of wholesale trade. After the goods have reached the importing country, they are locally distributed through retailers. Or, the goods are directly consumed by industries. On the other hand, in inland trade, both the wholesale trade and retail trade exist with equal importance.

SUB-DIVISIONS OF COMMERCE

Commerce is concerned with removal of hindrances standing in the way of trade. The hindrances are related to many aspects such as place, information, condition, price and exchange. **There are specific commercial activities to remove specific hindrances.** They are as follows :

(1) **Of place** — The first hindrance arises out of place as the producers and consumers are separated by distance. There is a gap which has to be covered. The distance depends on the nature of the trade, whether inland or foreign. Such hindrances are removed by a major commercial activity called transport.

(2) **Of information** — The gap between the producers and the consumers gives rise to another hindrance – the lack of knowledge of existence of each other. The consumer may not know the product. The producer may not know that he has a customer. This hindrance is removed by the commercial service of publicity.

(3) **Of condition** — Not only goods have to be transferred from the producers to the consumers, that shall be done in a manner so that the quality, quantity etc. of the goods are not affected. Goods may be damaged or lost while in transit. These hindrances are removed by warehouses and cold storages by providing safe storage and insurance business is there to compensate if there is any loss.

(4) **Of payment** — Payment of price is essential for transfer of goods. Such payment involves risk of carrying cash and also the hazards of handling cash. Banking service is there to remove the hindrance. Banks also provide credit facilities to facilitate payments without having actual money in possession of the buyers.

(5) **Of exchange** — In case of foreign trade there is one more hindrance as to conversion of one currency into another. The exchange banks render the necessary service. Moreover the Central Bank of the country is there to regulate and assist in the process of exchange.

Conclusion — In conclusion it can be said that the main hindrance that arise in the process of trade is **of persons.** Trade means contact between persons in various capacities. Commercial activities bring different persons together and then trade materialises and for that transport plays the predominant role. Other services like entertainment, recreation etc. also come in the process.

INTER-CONNECTION — INDUSTRY, TRADE AND COMMERCE

Industry, trade and commerce are described as components of business. **As the components make the whole, industry, trade and commerce are bound to merge into one.** Practically, **trade and commerce are inseparable.** If trade means movement or transfer of goods, there must be some transport, otherwise the movement cannot take place. There are writers who argue that business has two components, industry and commerce, trade being a part of commerce. On the other hand, if there is no industry or no production of goods, there cannot be any movement of goods.

The interconnection among the components of business can be studied from the following viewpoints :

(1) Industry presupposes existence of trade and commerce. Production means movement of men and material to the factory or place of production. Supply of raw materials itself is a case of trade, which needs transport. Similarly, the raw materials have surely been produced earlier, either by extraction or by manufacture or through rearing of animals. Therefore trade presupposes existence of industry too.

(2) All the three components have co-existence. Same industry may require the service of transport simultaneously for bringing in raw materials as well as carrying out the finished products. In the first case, the industry is a participant to trade as a buyer while in the second case the industry is a participant to trade as a seller. But for both the occasions the industry as a producer is a consumer of service of transport.

(3) Business means repeated buying and selling of goods or services. A businessman in industry buys goods as raw materials, adds his service of processing to produce the finished goods and then sells the goods. A businessman in trade buys goods from producers and then

sells them. A businessman in commerce produces his service and then sells it. Thus we find that the main characteristic of business is present in every component of it. Here lies an inter-connection.

(4) In the dictionary the inter-relation among the terms business, trade, commerce and industry has been established in the following manner : "Business may be an inclusive term but specifically designates the activities of those engaged in the purchase or sale of commodities or in related financial transactions : Commerce and Trade imply the exchange and transportation of commodities : Industry applies to the producing of commodities." From the above analysis it is clear how business includes trade and commerce and how trade and commerce are linked up. Industry, however, stands out as something different. But, unless goods are produced, trade and commerce become meaningless. In our academic life, Business Organisation and Industrial Organisation are treated as two distinct subjects.

BUSINESS MOTIVATION

Meaning — Motivation creates a will to do work. It is not enough that an individual knows a work. It does not mean that he will do it. There is something which encourages him or make him move for 'doing'. That something is motivation. Motivation is neither curiosity nor experimentation. To be motivated for something means to make the mind and action fully directed towards that. One has to be all out for it. Casually people think that allurement of profit motivates a man to go for business. But, in fact, profit is not the only source of motivation. There are other factors too.

Need of motivation — Man needs motivation for doing any kind of job. If he wants to join a service there also motivation is necessary. **Business motivation is something different** from motivation for accepting a job because business involves risk taking and uncertainty. In management science various techniques of motivation have been evolved. But managerial motivation is quite different from business motivation. In the former case a manager has to motivate his subordinates to work and to work with efficiency but in the latter case it is a kind of self-motivation. **Business motivation is a self-starter.**

There are people who go for business because they are born in business families. Apparently they cannot think of alternative occupations. It is not exactly a case of business motivation. Such people may or may not become successful businessmen. In business communities, like among the Marwaris in India, there is a general aptitude for business as heritage. On the other hand, there are people, who, after failing to get any job, go for business as a last resort. Some of them may come out as successful businessmen. This is not exactly a case for business motivation. But such people as once get the taste of success may feel the motivation. Some people may casually enter into business out of curiosity. But curiosity and motivation are not identical instincts.

Motivating factors – Real business motivation may arise out of the following situations :

(1) **Adventurous mind** — Some people are by nature adventurous. They are prone to take risks and can take risks. They find some pleasure in plunging into uncertainties. Such people find interest in going for business or risk-taking.

(2) **Independent spirit** — There are people who have independent spirit and do not want to serve as employees under others. Not that they have a spirit of risk-taking but as the only alternative to salaried jobs they go for business. Even though they may not be highly successful or earning a lot from business, they stick to it.

(3) **Post-retirement occupation** — After retirement some people want to keep themselves active and not be dependent on sons. Such people start small business out of the funds received by them by way of gratuity or provident fund accummulation. They are happy with small or limited earnings enough to maintain themselves.

(4) **Influenced by others' achievements** — There are people who hold salaried jobs and through that they learn the techniques of business. They look at the achievements of their

employers with aspirations. They slowly build up contacts in the market, accumulate funds or build up sources of funds and at the first opportunity leave the jobs and take to business. Some people, while in business, do part-time business as a supplementary source of income and ultimately leave the jobs and become full-fledged businessmen.

(5) **Out of allurement** — Some people, being allured by the wealth and status of businessmen enter into business without considering whether they have the necessary qualities or capabilities or not. Such people often fail in business and become frustrated. Allurement and motivation are not identical things.

(6) **Desire for achievement**— A businessman gets scope of achievement in life in many ways. If he gets the wealth he can command position and power and opportunities for enjoyment. There are ambitious people who go for business and try hard for such achievement.

Abraham Maslow in his famous Need Theory on motivation pointed out that man has a hierarchy of needs. It means that needs come one after another. When one need is fulfilled another need is felt. The Need Theory is partly applicable to business motivation. The first need is physiological need, i.e. man needs a job for his living. An individual may take to business for his livelihood. The last need is self-actualisation need i.e. culmination of all aspirations in life. The desire for achievement is akin to this self-actualisation need.

In India, the Government wants that people go for entrepreneurship, at least on small scale, to create self-employment. This will partly solve the problem of unemployment and at the same time shortage of goods will be reduced to bring down the price level. The Government is conducting several Entrepreneurship Development Training Programmes for business motivation, and has set up District Industrial Centres to guide the people, has set up many agencies like Small Industries Service Institute, has provisions for financial help on liberal terms from banks and other financial institutions, and has taken up such other steps. Frankly speaking, all these efforts of the Government have not yet attained the desired results because business motivation is primarily a self-starter.

BUSINESS AND OTHER DISCIPLINES

Meaning — Discipline means adhering to some rules or order or norms. But the word has a technical meaning too. **Discipline means "a subject that is taught or a field of study or a training** that corrects, moulds or perfects the mental faculties or moral character". Each discipline has its own norms and codes. It comes from the Latin word *disciplina* which means teaching or learning. Now-a-days the word is very much used to denote a field of study like Economics, Philosophy, Chemistry, Management etc. **In academic world discipline means a branch of a faculty or stream.** For example, Philosophy is a discipline under the Faculty of Arts. Accountancy can be described as a discipline under the Faculty of Commerce.

Can Business be called a discipline ? Is it a subject which can be taught ? If 'disciplina' means teaching or learning then **Business is certainly a discipline** which practically cannot be 'taught' but 'can be learnt'. What is taught is not really 'business' but some 'principles of business'. Business as a discipline can be learnt through experience. Experience means own experience though it may be supplemented by experience of others.

Business and other disciplines — It has been already discussed that business is a kind of economic institution of society. And, as such, it is a kind of social science. Social sciences are many, comprising Economics, Ethics, Sociology, Psychology, Political Science, Anthropology, Behaviourial Science, etc. **Business is definitely connected with the social sciences, either closely or remotely.** Some such relationship are discussed below :

(1) **Business and Economics** — These two disciplines, both being social science, are very closely related as both of them study the material aspect of human life. Both the disciplines enquire into the relationship between man and money. It has been already pointed out that Marshall has defined economics as the study of man in ordinary business of life. That ordinary life means earning and spending of money. Money is earned for spending to acquire

goods and services for satisfaction of wants. Business enquires into the process of earning money by selling some goods on services.

Business is often described as Applied Economics. Economics has more or less a theoretical approach. It has its theories and laws. In Business we find application of those theories and laws. In other words, Business has a practical bias in contrast to Economics. Businessmen very often use the tenets of Law of Demand, either consciously or unconsciously. Economic analysis has twin aspects – deductive and inductive. The deductive side of analysis draws much from the experience of the business world. Business itself is deducting its own norms and laws having impact on economic thoughts.

Though Business and Economics have close association **it will be wrong to call the study of Business a branch or outgrowth of the study of Economics,** just like it is wrong to state that Economics is a branch of Philosophy, the study of which has been the origin of the study of social sciences. Business has been accepted as a discipline only recently and long after Economics. Economics can claim seniority but not superiority. Business endeavours a deeper and closer study of human behaviour than Economics does. Though young in age, in respects of the extent and depth of study, Business, particularly its aspect of Management, has practically overtaken many of the other social sciences. The nature of business depends primarily on the economic system obtaining in a country. That brings Business and Economics closer.

(2) **Business and other Social Sciences** — Business is very much conditioned by political atmosphere. **Business, therefore, is very much concerned with Political Science** which discusses forms of Government and nature of State. Business needs forecasting and forecasting cannot be accurate unless the probable change in the political situation is anticipated.

Importance of Psychology is immense in business-life. Businessmen have to deal with human beings regularly and closely either as customers or employees or creditors or suppliers etc. Knowledge of psychology will help a businessman a lot to have perfect dealings by which his purpose is served without hurting others. Psychology today has an important branch called Industrial Psychology which is an important tool for efficient personnel management. **Modern Behavioural Science is assuming great importance** to make people conscious of 'group behaviour'. Business life is full of group life. Ethics, which deals with normal values in human conduct, has also a link with Business. A businessman must know how to respect the moral values. There are so many laws to regulate the actions of businessman. But law cannot itself mould our character unless we have the mental preparedness. Business develops its own moral values and norms. **Business Ethics is accepted to be a branch of Ethics.** Cultural branch of Anthropology (a science dealing in the origin and development of man) helps businessmen to understand human problems better and to find out remedies.

Business and Quantitative Sciences — Business needs continuous forecasting and decision-making. This is the managerial aspect of business. Forecasting and decision-making cannot be scientifically done by hunch or imagination, intelligence or intuition. They must be based on facts and data. There are so many variable factors which interact and have impact on the process of forecasting and decision-making. **Modern business has to rely much on quantitative sciences like Mathematics and Statistics.** Management techniques and event accounting have become largely mathematics oriented.

BUSINESS AND PROFESSIONS

Meaning — We have discussed the term business, but what is a **Profession** ? According to the dictionary, the term 'profession' means 'a calling requiring specialised knowledge and often long and intensive academic preparation'. **There are two distinct qualities of a profession :** (a) specialised knowledge and (b) academic preparation. The term 'business' means occupation or calling. Therefore, profession may appear to be business as a calling. But a **profession is not exactly a business because of the following reasons :** (1) Long and intensive academic preparation is necessary for a profession but, for ordinary business, preparation may be necessary but that preparation is not academic. (2) Professional men render specialised services to their clients individually and confidentially but generally in business customers are dealt with in general. (3) In most cases, a profession has its Institute or Association and a person intending to join the profession must be a member of that Institute or Association. For example, a practising chartered accountant must be a member of the Institute of Chartered Accountants of India. (4) A professional man charges 'fees' for his services, and he may charge his fees at different rates from different clients. In ordinary business there are fixed prices. (5) Unlike ordinary business, a professional man cannot make open publicity for his profession. Business, however, may be called a profession to a businessman.

Business and Professions — Business has very close relations with different kinds of professions like law, engineering, accountancy etc. Business has to comply with many legal formalities. Generally businessmen try to avoid law suits but sometimes they become unavoidable. Businessmen sue or are sued in business life. Therefore, they have to take the help of lawyers or men in the legal profession. For every kind of business, big or small, accounts have to be prepared and audited. In many cases, there are statutory obligations to prepare accounts and get them audited by qualified auditors. For example, according to the Company Law, every company must get its accounts audited by a qualified auditor, i.e. a member of the Institute of Chartered Accountants. Accounting and presentation of case is also necessary for different kinds of direct (e.g. income tax) or indirect (e.g. sales tax) taxes and duties. For each such occasion, businessmen need the services of chartered accountants who are professional men. Services of cost accountants are necessary for cost audit or for cost reduction or pricing. On the other hand, services of engineers, valuers, architects and others are necessary for construction work or for valuation of wealth.

Recently a new type of profession has cropped up to assist business in many ways. This is called 'management consultancy'. (The word consultancy is a peculiar word, though populary used but has no recognition in English language.) The management consultants advise and guide, on the basis of consultation fees, on various matters like costing, project making, cost reduction, tax planning etc. Many persons are practising as consultants in individual capacities or forming into firms or companies just like an audit firm.

Management itself is becoming a profession. Qualified people coming out from different management training institutes are known as professional managers. Big companies prefer to employ such people for key managerial posts. The Managing Agents in the past played the role of professional managers in Indian companies (Ref. 5.12). Even secretarial work is becoming professional. According to the Companies Act, 1956, every company having a paid up-capital of Rs. 25 lakhs or more must appoint a qualified secretary, i.e. a person who is a member of the Institute of Company Secretaries. Cost audit has become compulsory for certain categories of companies under the Companies Act, 1956, by a qualified cost accountant, i.e. a member of the Institute of Cost and Works Accountants of India.

From the above discussion it is clear that the relationship between business (at least big business) with professions is close.

IMPORTANCE OF THE FORMAL STUDY OF BUSINESS

The formal study of business has become a matter of necessity today. Business study was never a prerequisite for getting into a business. But now, as the concept of business has undergone changes and that various complexities have crept into the business world, there has been the need for the formal study of business. More and more people are entering into business and it has now become a very important branch of human activity. The changed concept on business is that business is both an economic and social activity. The social involvement of business has now assumed so much importance that business goal has got to be changed from money chasing and profit maximisation to the realisation of social objectes; the fulfilment of needs of the society, the maximisation of social satisfaction, the transformation of the dreams and the aspirations of the society to reality, have now become the integral components of business and it is not at all an exaggeration today that, to survive, business has to be, out and out, a social institution dedicated to the cause of the society.

To achieve these social objectives, business study in a formal way is a necessity. To achieve economic objective in these days of growing complexities in business, in the competitive market today, a formal study in business is the need that no successful businessman can avoid.

Business as it was and as it is today, will leave for us no room to doubt that the changes that have overtaken modern business consequent upon changes in other spheres – science, techonology etc. – have called upon businessmen to take to formal study of business. It is a plain truth that there was a time when one was pushed to get into business as a penalty for his nonacquisition of any formal education, not to speak of formal business study. Business, it was thought, was such an activity that needed no preparedness, no knowledge; rather the fact that one did not have any developed mental faculty was the strong argument for him to be in business.

But with the change of time, with the growth of complexities in business, with the development of international market, with the world economy being very much sensitive to even a minor economic disturbance in any pail of the world, because of the world becoming too small today owing to improved transport and communication system, the need for the formal study of business has all the more increased and its importance has now been beyond any doubt and question. It is no exaggeration to say that the successful businessman of today must be a man with adequate formal study of business – the study of the subjects allied to business activities such as economics, psychology, sociology, ethics etc.

The formal study of business is the study of the subjects which have a direct bearing on business.

ROLE OF BUSINESS IN SOCIAL DEVELOPMENT

Business and society — Fundamentally, **business from its functional aspect** can be described as a human behaviour because business is aimed at repeated buying and selling of goods or services for mutual gains. Since there are two reciprocal aspects of buying and selling, there must be a buyer and a seller in each business transaction who behave in a particular manner. Business cannot be one-way traffic. In other words, business is a group activity. Man by nature is gregarious, i.e. he wants to form a group or association with others with whom he has some affinity or like-mindedness. 'Man is' said Aristotle, the great Greek philosopher, 'a social animal'. Man lives in society. A society is nothing but a group, a very large group. Man's life is full of group activities. Business is a kind of group activity.

Business, from its structural aspect, means an organisation or a group, e.g. a partnership business. Whenever we think of business as a functioning group it consists of a number of persons having employer-employee, producer-customer and such other relations. Inside a business there are continuous activities and all are pertaining to group behaviour. In a community there are various types of group activities of which business activity is one.

The term society has a number of interpretations depending on the purpose and size of group formation. After all, the society is a group. Very often, by the term human society, we mean mankind as a whole. At the same time we call a nation a society. According to dictionary meaning, **society,** in its widest form, **can be defined** as "a community, nation or broad grouping of people having common traditions, institutions and collective activities and interests". The definition is big but comprehensive. It is observed that one of the elements of society is 'institutions'. There are different types of institutions – economic, political, and social. The term institution means 'a singificant practice, relationship or organisation in a society or culture'. For example, in India, joint family system of ownership is an economic institution; the kingship in the past was a political institution; the caste system is a social institution.

Business is applied economics. Therefore, **business** is a part of economic institutions and it **is a constituent of the society.** Business activities must have their impact on the society. For example, the caste system in India originally was meant for occupational division of labour. Later on it became a social institution having a direct bearing on the social structure. We have already seen (REF. 1.2) how, with the evolution of business, different production systems have grown – from the handicraft system to the factory system which has ultimately given rise to the capitalistic system of economy and the capitalistic society. On the other hand, in a socialistic society, all the economic activities are brought under the control of the State. **The nature of business activities is determined by the nature of the society.** Therefore, business and society are interrelated, one reacting on the other.

Karl Marx, the greatest sociologist of recent times, has propounded how the capitalistic system of production leads to exploitation of labour and class struggle and ultimately capitalistic society crumbles down to be replaced by a socialistic society. He divided society into four types : Asiatic, the ancient, the feudal, and the capitalist. He has shown how economic institutions have led to the formation of the different societies. While referring to unchangeable character of Asiatic society (including Indian), Karl Marx said because there was a kind of self-sufficient village economy it could overcome the forces of change. A self-sufficient village economy is based on barter type of exchange and there is quick adjustment between the forces of demand and supply. Such strong economy gives rise to a strong society. **Mahatma Gandhi** dreamt that independent India should have economically self-sufficient villages. During the British rule the villages were neglected breaking the very substratum of the society. Those who speak of industrialisation before revitalising the rural economy are fundamentally wrong. The premature bias for industry in the Second Five-Year Plan caused such an imbalance in our economy, leading to heavy deficit financing and inflation, that we have not even now been able to overcome it. The society is suffering.

Most of the advanced countries of the world are industrially advanced. Such societies are industrial societies. Drucker, the greatest exponent of management thoughts today, calls man an 'industrial man'. Whether capitalist or socialist, every advanced society runs after industrial growth. Industry runs after bigger scale, greater mechanisation and higher speed. Life of an 'industrial man' is also very fast, having greater 'needs' and bigger ambitions. This is the trend of general contribution of business to social development. The developing countries, being influenced by advanced and affluent societies, are running after industrialisation forgetting their objective conditions like the natural environment and traditional culture. They are running into debts and facing various social and economic confrontations. India is no exception to this.

Business and social development — If society means a nation then **social development means higher standard of living for a nation** by achieving higher national income. Since, income is earned through business or money-earning activities, business has a significant role to play for social development. In fact, economic activities are responsible for social development and business is applied economics. However, business plays its role for social development in the following manner :

(1) **Satisfaction of wants** — Business activities include industry or production (including agriculture). Business produces goods and services which are needed to satisfy human wants. By trade, goods and services reach the consumers for the satisfaction of their wants. Commercial activities hasten the movement of the goods and services by removing the hindrances standing in the way. With the passing of time, wants multiply in a society on account of (a) increase of the population, (b) rising standard of living and (c) a tendency to imitate affluent countries. Business activities have to be geared up to meet the situation. All these lead to social development.

(2) **Creation of employments** — Business creates employment opportunities. The entrepreneurs provide employment to others and get themselves self-employed. In public sector

the State as entrepreneur creates employments. Employments generate income on one side, resulting into effective demand for goods and services, and, on the other side, produce goods and services to meet the demand. Business also provides opportunities for different professional occupations like those of lawyers, accountants, consultants, etc. The primary tool of social development is employment creation.

(3) **Growth of business centres** — Business leads to the growth of business centres in the farms of industrial towns, terminals like ports, administrative headquarters etc. All these provide better living conditions and amenities and accommodation for the growing population.

(4) **Revenue of the Government** — The Government earns a major part of its revenue from the various kinds of taxes and duties collected from the business world. Moreover, the Government itself makes income from Government undertakings. Revenue is badly needed for administrative, developmental and defence expenditure. Business people also largely subscribe to Government securities.

(5) **Fruits of research** — Business people carry out research activities for the twin purposes of (a) improving the quality of the goods and services and (b) cost reduction. The society is benefited by addition to the total fund of utilities created and by lowering of prices.

(6) **The infra-structure** — The Government, particularly that of a developing country, has to create the infra-structure through (a) creation of capital, (b) construction of roads and other means of transport, (c) facilitating general and technical education and (d) generation of power. The society as a whole is benefited by all these developments and prospers.

(7) **General welfare** — Businessmen, by discharging their social responsibilities and largely contributing to various welfare funds, help general welfare of the society – which may increase productivity, improve health conditions, provide sustenance to the distressed, etc.

(8) **Utilisation of resources** — By business activities the natural resources of a country can be properly utilised and even the remote areas can be developed. Only business can lead to taking of risk for such utilisation and development.

(9) **Better relations** — Trade, particularly foreign trade, can establish relations between one group of people with the other belonging to the same country or between one nation and another. Such inter-relationship leads to better understanding between nations and exchange of culture for mutual benefits.

(10) **Investment opportunities** — Business opens up opportunities for channelising individual savings into productive investments. This is more true for company form of business organisations. Opportunities for investment encourage people to save and ultimately the society is benefited by faster and greater capital formation.

(11) **Art, culture etc.** — Social development also includes development of art, culture, literature, sports, religious activities and all such other aspects apart from wealth creation. The surplus funds of business are very often spent for the development of all these aspects of the society. Businessmen spend money on such activities for publicity or creation of goodwill.

(12) **Contribution of public sector** — The Government or the State enters into business not for profit motive but mainly to fulfil social objectives. Therefore, public sector undertakings are aimed at social development.

Business, however, becomes harmful and **deterimental to social development** when the businessmen take recourse to various malpractices or exert their influence through lobbying and pressure tacitcs on the Government or on the political party in power for personal gains and at the cost of the society. A society also suffers when there is a large - scale failure of business houses. There are cases where businessmen have been found making secret deals with enemy countries endangering the security of own countries and all that for personal gains. Production and sale of socially harmful goods like wine does not aid social development. All depends on the regulatory measures adopted and implemented by the Government and the watchful eye on business by the society itself.

GROWING COMPLEXITIES IN BUSINESS

The evolution of business from the early phase of the handicraft system to the modern phase of the factory system is a history of increasing complexities in business – trade, industry and commerce. Modern business is in a continuous process of evolution with more and more discoveries in the fields of science and technology. More and more production to meet the ever expanding human need is making business increasingly complicated. It is confronted with political systems of capitalism and socialism and accordingly assuming different organisational patterns. As a result and under both the types of political system, the actisans have lost their independent character, the means of production lie either in the hands of private entrepreneurs or the State controlled by a political party which holds the Government. Predate ownership today is generally in the form of a corporate body. Besides this, business is characterised today by large size, use of machines, high speed transport system, huge capital, existence of various regulatory laws, application of managerial techniques, peculiar human relationship called employer–employee relationship and overall supremacy of science and technology. These characterstics of modern business vary from one country to another depending upon the economic development of the country. So business is assuming more and more complex character through continuous experimentation for a better order and in this process it is confronting conflicting ideologies.

In primitive days, business was not a complex activity. A man's existence depended solely on his own exertions. He consumed what he produced and produced what he wanted to consume. There was no distance between the centres of production and consumption. There was, therefore, no obstacle of place, time or of person. With the passage of time and especially with the introduction of money economy in exchange of goods, men began to make it their business to provide people with things they needed and did not possess and to know where these things could be obtained. Today it is exactly the same. Civilisation has developed and conditions are far more complicated. Materials needed are to be procured from every corner of the world to be carried through long distance, to be converted through complicated processes, to place the finished products in the hands of those who are ready to pay for them.

The Industrial Revolution culminated in the factory system bringing in its wake far – reaching changes which has made business complicated and it is clearly visible that there is growing complexities in business. Today, the Scientific Revolution, according to Professor Condliffe, is taking place which is bringing about economic and social changes. These changes, in their turn, are calling upon business to go through complexities, to discharge its economic and social obligations.

Business is now an activity very much under the control and regulation of the State. Society today is no less vigilant as to the activities in which businessmen are indulging. In a competitive economy, business is to function with utmost efficiency to survive. Problems are there in production, marketing, finance and personnel management. These problems have to be tackled. Scientific management attitude has become cooperative in order to find out solutions to the complexities associated with the different aspects of business. Be it trade, industry or commerce – problems and complexities are inevitable. Right from the point of launching a business enterprise up to the point of effecting a suitable outlet for the jobs and services it deals with, numerous complications arise as to the procurement of raw materials, and quality of raw materials or goods, proocurement of finance, transportation of goods, management of personnel and these have been on increase every day. Local, national, international, small or big, trade, industry or commerce – no business is free from complexities; rather it is feeling the challenge of growing complexities in some form or other with every passing day .

SOCIAL RESPONSIBILITIES OF BUSINESS

Two aspects of business — It is a popular belief today that business has social responsibilities. In fact, the whole concept is misleading. Business, as it is, cannot have any responsibilities, whether individual or social. When we say business we actually mean the men, the businessmen to be precise, who are behind the business. They have social responsibilities.

In the same way it is said that business has **two aspects : motive and objective.** The motive is immediate and individual. It is something for which businessmen take to business ignoring the risks involved. **The motive is to make profit or to earn income.** Since there is enormous scope to make money out of business, people never fear to take risks. On the other hand, objective is ultimate and social. **The ultimate purpose of business,** from the point of view of the society, **is to produce some goods or services** for exchanging for money by which needs of man can be fulfilled. In short, it is doing of some social good. Business is an economic institution of a society and businessmen are members of the society. Therefore, a business is something which has social implication. A businessman must have the motivation for making money, otherwise, he shall not take risk, but that motivation must be subservient to the social need or objective. A businessman can do business in the society provided the society permits him to do so. The businessman is a producer but he is a consumer too. As some people depend on him for his goods or services, he has to depend on others for their goods or services. Therefore, he must be conscious of it and also cautious. He shall make profit but not at the cost of other members of the society. This consciousness gives rise to some reponsibilities for a businessman. **Unless he discharges the responsibilities to the society, the society will not permit him to make money out of the society.** This is the interpretation of 'social responsibilities of business'. Henry Ford, the greatest Captain of Industry for all time to come, once said that he wanted to make far more cars than profit. Mahatma Gandhi in his 'Theory of Trusteeship' said that businessmen should produce wealth and preserve them as trustees of the society. Peter Drucker makes a brilliant commentary when he says "the business enterprise should be so managed so as to make the public goods become the private goods of the enterprise".

It is very strange that only businessmen are asked to have social responsibilities. In fact, every member of the society who lives and earns in a society must have social responsibilities, it does not matter whether he is a professional man, a wage-earner, a political being etc. One can live and earn only by using some resource of the society and by taking part in social institutions.

Social responsibilities — As an economic institution of society a business is a complex entity. It has behind it either one or more businessmen or the enterpreneurs who are confronted with many other types of people interested in it. Social responsibilities are aimed at all such types of people as detailed below in a classfied manner.

(1) **To the customers or the consumers** — Peter Drucker says — "There is only one definition of business purpose : to create a customer". The customers or the consumers are the primary concern of a business. A business cannot thrive and grow unless the customers are satisfied. 'Sovereignty of the consumers' is one of the major criteria of competition. Even a monopolist has to satisfy the consumers, otherwise they may go for substitutes. The obligations or responsibilities of a businessman to his customers are as follows : (a) To supply goods of good quality. (b) To supply quality goods at reasonable and fair prices. (c) Not to mislead the customers by false advertisements. (d) Not to take recourse to any adulteration, hoarding, short weight or such other malpractices for higher profits. (e) To look into the complaints of the customers, if any.

In practical life, a businessman generally does not do anything which will cause dissatisfaction of customers. He knows that he cannot survive if he renders disservice to his customers. The Government also takes various regulatory measures to stop exploitation of customers by businessmen. The consumers themselves may form into Consumers' Association to establish their rights. When the market is sellers' market, i.e. there is short supply of goods, the businessmen may ignore the interests of the customers. On the other hand, when there is a buyers' market, i.e. there is excess supply, the situation becomes opposite. Sometimes the obligation appears to be contradictory. For example, quality goods cannot be supplied unless the price is proportionate. The term reasonable is vague.

(2) **To the workers or the employees** — A businessman has to engage employees. Manufacturers have to employ workers. As a whole, a businessman has the following responsibilities or obligations to his employees : (a) To pay reasonable remuneration, either salary or wages. (b) To provide various incentives in the forms of premium and also profit bonus. (c) To pay the remuneration in time. (d) To look after the welfare of the employees and to provide them fringe benefits. (e) To provide favourable working conditions to motivate them. (f) To provide them with opportunities for further education and training. (g) To maintain better employer-employee relations.

Normally, a businessman does not want to be unsympathetic to his employees but whaever he does for them is for getting higher productivity. Days of unilateral exploitation of labour by employers are gone. Almost in every country the Government passes legislations to regulate employers' behaviour and to maintain industrial peace. Trade Unions always keep watch on employers and fight for the employees' rights.

(3) **To the general suppliers** — A businessman has to purchase many things. As a trader he purchases goods for sale. As a manufacturer he has to buy raw materials, machines, tools etc. Besides, every businessman has to buy office equipment, stationery, vehicles and such other things. He has the following responsibilities and obligations to his suppliers : (a) To make proper payment and that in time. (b) Not to harass the suppliers unnecessarily with regard to the terms of supply. (c) Not to have any illegal gratification in the forms of secret commission, bribe etc. (d) Not to make unjustified discrimination betwen one supplier and another.

When there are a large number of suppliers, a businessman as a buyer takes the upperhand. But he is very careful as regards the quality and cost of his purchases because success of business largely depends on that. Here also the theories of buyers' market and sellers' market do apply. **Generally, a businessman does not want to spoil his reputation in the market by ill-treating the suppliers.**

(4) **To the suppliers of capital** — For a business there are **two types of capital :** Inside or own and Outside or loan. The **Inside capital** comes from the entrepreneur himself in case of a sole-proprietorship firm or from the partners in case of a partnership firm. In case of a company, capital is supplied by the members. Inside capital may also come from financial institutions. Those who supply the inside capital expect share in the profjts as return which is uncertain. **Outside capital** is supplied directly by banks and other financial institutions or bond holders (like debenture holders) and indirectly by trade creditors. They expect interests at fixed rates as returns. Trade creditors enjoy other benefits. Businessmen have the following responsibilities and obligations to the suppliers of capital : (a) To pay interests in full and in time. (b) To repay the debts in time. (c) To assure safety or security to the debts owed to the creditors. (d) To pay reasonable and fair share of profits to all the investors. (e) To prepare proper accounts for the purpose.

Profit is uncertain and depends on many factors beyond the control of a businessman. Payment of interest and repayment of debts also are often conditioned by factors beyond control. Sometimes the Government imposes restrictions on rates of dividend. What is needed is that a businessman must have the intention to pay. In most cases, a businessman does not want to deprive the suppliers of capital, for his own interest.

(5) **To the Society :** Apart from his responsibilities and obligations to the different classes of interested persons, **a businessman has some responsibilities and obligations to the socie-**

ty as a whole. Firstly, he has them to the Government as the custodian of the society. They are : (a) Payment of taxes and duties in full and in time. (b) Implementation of all the legal-formalities pertaining to business. (c) Observance of all the rules and directives issued by the Government from time to time. Secondly, he has the responsibilities and obligations to the society. They are : (a) Not to make any misuse of the resources of the country. (b) Not to encroach on the rights of others in order to establish or protect his own rights. (c) To take recourse to Court of Law when any dispute arises and not to take the law in his own hands. (d) Not to do anything which lowers the prestige of the country. (e) To contribute liberally for the development of social services, education, art and culture.

The responsibilities and obligations of a businessman to the society cannot be questioned. But it has to be remembered that **the society must also provide** the necessary infrastructure, facilities, security, opportunities etc. so that a businessman can carry out his business.

Conclusion — In conclusion, it has to be mentioned that, after all, **a businessman has responsibilities to his business itself.** He must see that the business thrives as a going concern and grows. It must have a market share or market standing, i.e. it must capture a definite portion of the total sales of the goods in the market so that the business can survive. According to Drucker, 'survival' is the primary objective of a business. It is rightly said that the business of business is to do business.

The word 'business' has been aptly used in three different senses in the above sentence. At first it has been used to mean function. Then it means a business concern and, lastly, it means to earn some minimum profit which is the immediate motive. But the profit motive must be blended with a sense of social responsibilities. Social responsibilities, however, can be treated as 'enlightened self-interest'. A businessman knows that by discharging his responsibilities to the society he earns his eligibility to make profit.

CHAPTER TWO

Environment Of Business

Physical and social conditions that influence an individual or a community can be called environment. So, environment is the sum total of conditions – economic and non-economic – that makes an individual what he is or a community as it is.

Business environment is the totality of conditions within which business operates. It is the total of all things external to firms that affect them.

Elements of environment :

The elements of environment are natural, social, economic and political. The overall situation of a region, where a business is carried on, is the sum total of its physical and non-physical factors. Environment, so far as it relates to business, consists of natural resources, social conditions, economic facilities and political situation or state policy. So, all these are environmental elements that create conditions favourable or unfavourable for a business to operate.

Need for identifying environmental facilities and constraints

Environmental facilities and constraints are matters that deserve serious consideration of all entrepreneurs. The entire structure and the component parts of a business are influenced by its environment. The significance of environment to a business can not be over-exaggerated. Business and its environment are inter-related and mutually dependent.

Effects of environment – favourable or adverse – should be carefully studied before launching the business. To study these, a clear identification of the facilities and the constraints of environment that would affect business is absolutely necessary. For example, the economic system prevailing in a country may be capitalist or socialist and, accordingly, business policies are framed. Systems of economic planning and controls; fiscal, monetary, commercial and industrial policies, and business laws influence business favourably or adversely. Economic and industrial policies of the Government regulate the growth of business in both the private and the public sectors. Monetary and fiscal policies affect initiative for business. Commercial policies affect import-export plans of business. Thus, we can see non-economic environment has its effects no less important than those of economic environment. The legal-political set up, ethical, moral and other social considerations, physical environment such as air, water pollution etc. have far – reaching effects on business. So, these factors have to be identified and there is the positive need for the identification of the favourable and unfavourable elements of environment.

Features of business environment in India :

Business environment in India after over four decades of Independence has changed considerably. A change from foreign rule to Independence has completely changed business environment in our country. Consequent upon the political change, there have been changes in the business environment in its physical as well as in non–physical factor. Since Independence, India has been passing through planned or controlled economy. An all–out effort is on to make the country economically developed. Substantial changes have also taken place and have been taking place in the social structure of the country. All factors, so to say, that constitute environment of business are being controlled by the state to create an environment favourable for development of business in the country.

Business environment in India today can be considered more or less favourable. The participation of the state in business activities has added a new dimension to the field of business environment. The system of mixed economy has also created atmosphere congenial for development of certain types of business. It will not be out of place to mention here that the concept of business having changed throughout the world, the environment of business has also changed in general everywhere and India is no exception. Society and business having admitted their mutual obligations have improved considerably business environment. Governement has been a very big contributory factor of the improvement of business environment. In India, all these factors are being played upon to ensure that all obstacles in the business environment are removed and favourable elements play a dominant role to help business to grow. It must be admitted that India, being a developing country, has environmental obstacles undoubtedly but a determined effort on the part of the Government to plug the loopholes in the environment of business has been kept unabated and we can say that India at present is in a much better environmental position than she has been during the British regime. Business is no more considered a concern of individuals but the concept of business system has received due acknowledgement and this has substantially changed the business environment of the country.

CHAPTER THREE

BUSINESS ORGANISATION AND BASIC FUNCTIONS

Nature pf business organisation

Business organisations are economic organisations. They are set up with a view to carrying on business activities – trade, industry and commerce. A business organisation "is a combination of necessary beings, materials, tools, equipment, working space and appurtenances, brought together in a systematic and effective correlation, to accomplish some desired object" (J. W. Schulza). Business organisations, as we understand from the above concept of organisation, are to make an assembly of men, machines, materials and other necessary things in a harmonious way to achieve business objectives. Business implies buying, manufacturing, selling and other allied activities.

Business organisations as economic institutions mainly concentrate on economic activities. In this recept they differ from social organisations. Social organisations such as charitable institutions, educational institutions or cultural organisations do not purchase or sell or manufacture in the sense in which these activities are undertaken by business organisations. Business organisations, today, are looked upon as social institutions to further the cause of the society and to serve public purpose in the best possible manner. But the nature of business organisations is such that they are to coordinate various economic activities such as buying and selling, financing, staffing etc. in such a way as to achieve the business objectives. A business organisation must have profit motive which is completely absent in a social organisation. But both business and social organisations are meant for society, but the former are to serve the society for their survival whereas the latter are set up only to serve the society. With economic considerations primarily in the mind, business organisations, continue their existence, carry on their activities but social organisations with deep feeling for the society, endeavour for its upliftment in a particular sphere and in its different spheres. So, business organisations are basically different from social organisations with the common there only in them being that society is a consideration in both the forms of organisations – business and social.

A broad outline of the different functional areas of business organisations :

Manufacturing : Manufacturing is one of the basic operating functions of business. It is concerned with the supply side of goods and services. Manufacturing activities constitute one of the most important functions of the top management. It is the production or manufacturing function around which the other activities of the organisation such as marketing, personnel and finance revolve. Manufacturing is concerned with the provision of goods and services for the satisfaction of human wants. The activities of manufacturing system must be closely related to the market demand and there will continue a constant endeavour of the management to ensure efficient and economic system of production for realisation of the enterprise objectives.

Manufacturing is a process and it is concerned with the conversion of raw materials into semi-finished and finished products. The manufacturing function is concerned with the organisation and control of production activities to ensure good quality products at minimum cost.

The scope of manufacturing function is very wide in the present era of competition. It is not only concerned with the proper and full use of manufacturing facilities but also the human factor, utilisation of latest techniques of production and production of quality goods. The top management of the organisation takes broad policy decisions about production activities. The various activities that form scope of manufacturing function can be separated into two broad areas design or formulation of manufacturing system and analysis and control of production operations after production system has been activated. The various decisions associated with these areas are – decisions to production system design, analysis and control of activities. Production system design relates to production engineering. Once the production system has been designed and activated, the management is to decide on production planning. Production control is another fundamental manufacturing managerial function that usually follows production planning.

To maximise production, there should be scientific and effective plant layout to facilitate the manufacturing process by maintaining balance in the process by minimising material handling, machine interference, employee hazards and by promoting effective utilisation of man – power and through increase in employee morale.

Through production planning and control, manufacturing function of a business organisation can reach optimum level of production by discarding all sorts of wastages. Routing, scheduling, despatching and follow up in production centre functions must be kept active in order to achieve desired results in the function of a manufacturing organisation.

Marketing function : Marketing is an operating function of business organisation. The importance of marketing cannot be over – exaggerated. In the words of Peter T. Drucker, "it is in marketing that we satisfy individual and social values, needs and works, be it through producing goods, supplying services, fostering innovation for creating satisfaction". Marketing generates revenue essential for the survival and growth of an organistion. The process of marketing involves delivery of new varieties, quality and beneficial goods to consumers enabling them to raise their standard of living. Not only to consumers, to the nation also, marketing has a significant role to play in a variety of ways. According to Drucker, "marketing occupies a critical role in respect of the development of developing nations". Integration of the various economic sectors of the nation, fullest utilisation of the existing assets and productive capacity, mobilisation of unknown and untapped economic energy and development of entrepreneur and managerial class of pepole are the ways through which marketing functions can contribute to the speedy development of a developing nation. Marketing function also helps in maintaining and creating employment opportunities, changing public opinion, creating norms of behaivour and standard of conduct and in expanding the home market to provide a more secure base for exports.

Marketing decisions precede marketing functions. These decisions have two major elements – marketing segmentation decisions and marketing mix decisions. Marketing mix decisions have, again, four strategy elements – (a) product strategy, (b) distribution strategy, (c) promotional strategy and (d) pricing strategy.

Marketing decisions are made after considering all the elements of marketing mix and the dyna mic nature of the environmental factors such as legal, economic, competitive and social.

The marketing decision process depends on marketing research which is a systematic search for an analysis of facts relating to a marketing problem. The marketing research process involves – (a) formulating the problem, (b) collecting relevant information and (c) preparing the research report.

In spite of marketing research being a key tool used by management, this activity is not given due importance. Limitations of marketing research are mainly three – limitation of accuracy, limitation of time and limitation of personnel. Since marketing research relates to human psychology, it is not an exact science but it cannot be denied that it contributes substantially to business management as it is based on scientific methods.

As a function of business organisations marketing is decidedly the most important function because goods and services are meant for marketing.

Financing : Financing as a function of business organisations can be compared to infusing blood to the life of a business. Finance is the life-blood of business. The significance of financing, so to say, financial management, has been increasing with the increase in the scale of operations in the modern money economy. Finance is necessary at every step – right from the birth of a business till its death i.e. from its 'cradle to its grave'.

The concept of business finance has changed. From different view – points finance has been described as cash only, raising of funds and raising and utilisation of funds. Literally speaking, the term 'business finance' connotes financing of business activities which presupposes both the procurement and the utilisation of funds.

Finance function is concerned with the proper planning, organising, directing and controlling of financial activities in a business enterprise.

The goal of finance function is to achieve the objective of the owners of business. Finance function cannot be confirmed to the fulfilment of the finance managers' own objectives which may include higher wages, earning reputation etc., but must be extended to the maximisation of the satisfaction of the owners of the business. Profit and wealth maximisation are, no doubt, objectives of financial management in the ultimate analysis.

As to the scope of finance function, we can say that the various functions should include estimation of financial requirements, investment of funds in long-term and short-term assets, determining the appropriate capital structure, identification of the various sources of finance, decision regarding retention of earnings and distribution of dividend and administrating proper financial controls.

On the correct estimation of financial requirement depends, to a great extent, the successful operation of a business enterprise. There are two bases of estimating financial requirements – length of time period and nature of assets. The long-term financial requirements are analysed under the heads – (a) production and formation expenses, (b) cost of fixed assets, (c) cost of current assets, (d) cost of financing, (e) operating losses and (f) cost of intangibles (goodwill, patent rights etc.).

After the assessment of the financial requirements of the enterprise, it is the responsibility of the financial management to decide about the pattern of financing such requirements. Decisions regarding the pattern of financing are reflected in capital structure. Capital structure decision aims at determining the types of funds necessary to finance the investment opportunity of the enterprise and the proportion in which these funds should be raised. While deciding capital structure, various factors are considered : (1) leverage or trading on equity; (2) sales position; (3) management attitudes; (4) assets structure; (5) cash flow ability of the enterprise; (6) external environment such as the state of capital market, taxation policy, state regulations etc.

Corporate finance is processed from different sources – long-term and short-term.

Long-term sources of finance are : (1) Issue of securities, (2) Borrowing from the special industrial financing institution, (3) Public deposits, (4) Retained earnings. Issue of securities constitutes – equity, preference share issue and debenture issue.

Short-term sources of finance include : (1) Trade credit, (2) Short-term loans such as Bank credit (Unsecured and Secured loans),. discounting of bills and loans from Finance Companies.

Besides, there are other miscellaneous sources.

While discussing the financing function of an organisation, one cannot ignore the significance of dividend policy decision of a company form of organisation. An effective dividend policy has positive effects on share prices, financing decisions, wealth of shareholders. The various dividend policies available to a firm are : (1) Stable dividend policy, (2) policy of regular and extra dividends, (3) policy of regular stock dividends, (4) policy of no immediate dividends, (5) policy of irregular dividends and (6) policy of regular dividends and stock.

Personnel function : Personnel function of the organisation means the dealings of the organisation with its people. This function of a modern organisation is, by far, the most important of all the functions. The human factor in all the factors of production merits utmost consideration because to make the modern techniques or management methods effective, competent employees are indispensable. Leadership, which is prerequisite for the success of an organisation, is a human factor and it is the personnel function of an organisation to help to develop leadership in an organisation.

Personnel function has to do with planning, organising and controlling various operative functions of procuring, developing, maintaining and utilising a labour force for the purpose of controlling to organisational goals.

It is generally agreed that personnel management (function) is a staff or advisory function where its major objective is to assist the line managers to do a better job in managing people.

The true nature of the personnel function, according to the Indian Institute of Personnel Management, is that the personnel department is a service department and none of its staff should ever forget this. The personnel officer must himself be responsible to the executive head of unit and all his recommendations should be made to him. When asked for advice by other executives he should give it, but he should be wary of offering advice when it is not sought.

Personnel function aims at maintaining an adequate organisational structure, integrating all the human constituents of the organisation with cordial and amicable relationship. It endeavours to ensure fair terms and conditions of work and congenial work environment. By providing maximum development of the employees, maximum efficiency through the minimum expenditure of time, money and energy is ensured. It is also the aim of personnel function to ensure social justice by uniform application of the rules and regulations and by effectively discharging the social responsibility of developing, maintaining and increasing the reservoir of scarce human resources.

The first operative function of personnel management is to determine manpower requirement which needs job analysis, nature and sources of recruitment, employee selection and induction and follow-up. After the selection of employees for their respective jobs, the next personnel function is training. On the completion of training, the employees are to be utilised in the organisation to the satisfaction of the employee and the organisation. Promotions and transfers are effected scientifically after job evaluation and merit-rating.

One of the most important personnel functions now-a-days is concerned with the determination of wages and salaries policy.

In the sequence of operative personnel functions, the organisation procures an employee, develops his skills and determines the manner and amount of monetary compensation. To these functions has been added the function of the personnel department to involve employees in organisational task and to sustain it through the provision of reasonably good working conditions.

CHAPTER FOUR

COMPANY

CORPORATE FORM

Concept — A corporate form of ownership is commonly found in the form of companies formed under the Company Law obtaining in different countries. To ascertain the meaning of the term reference has to be made to **Sec. 34(2) of the Companies Act, 1956 which defines a Body Corporate.** Accordingly, a body corporate means an association of persons who have contributed some money for some common purpose and with as much liability as determined by the body and that association has been registered or incorporated with a name and has a separate legal entity, perpetual succession and a common seal.

Features — From the above concept we find the following features of a 'body corporate' :

(1) **Association of persons — It is an association of persons.** Since it is an association these persons are called members. The first members are those who subscribe to the documents of the body corporate, i.e., who promote it. Afterwards other people join it as members by written application according to the rules of the body corporate. There is a contractual relationship between each member and the body corporate. There is no contractual relationship between one member and other (unlike partnership).

(2) **Common purpose** — A body corporate has **some common purpose** for which it is incorporated or formed. That purpose may be trading i.e. profit-making or non-trading i.e. non-profit making. (But in partnership there must be some business).

(3) **Incorporation** — It has **to be formed by incorporation** or registration according to the procedure given in the Company Law. (But registration is not compulsory in case of a partnership firm.)

(4) **Members' liability — Each member has to take some liability.** It means that every member has to contribute some money and his liability is limited up to that amount. The liability of the company may be larger than the liabilities taken by the members. This is the concept of limited liability. (Under partnership a member has unlimited personal liability.) There are, however, companies with unlimited liability of members, which are generally non-trading and rare.

(5) **Perpetual Succession** — A body corporate, once incorporated, **continues to exist** unless it is liquidated according to the provisions in the Law. It has perpetual succession. Its existence is not affected by the death, retirement or insolvency of any member. (A partnership is dissolved by the death, retirement or insolvency of a partner.)

(6) **Separate legal entity** — It has a **separate legal entity.** It means that it is separate from the members in the eye of law. A body corporate is considered as an artificial person or a person created by law. It can sue and can be sued in its own name. (Under partnership, all the partners are collectively called the firm. There is no separation between them. A partnership can sue or can be sued in the names of the partners and not in the name of the firm.)

A body corporate is a person in the eye of law. It has all the rights of a person granted by law. But it has no voting right in general election of the country. But it has voting rights at the meeting of another body corporate where it is a member. A company may be a member of another company and vote at its meetings. A company, being an artificial person, cannot act itself and so it needs human agents called directors.

(7) **Common seal** — **It has a common seal,** i.e., a rubber stamp bearing the name of the company which shall be imprinted on all documents of, and by, the body corporate as if it is signing its name.

Definition of company —According to Sec. 3(1) (i) of the Companies Act, 1956, "company means a company formed and registered under this Act".

According to Sec. 2(7) of the Companies Act, 1956 **a 'Body Corporate' or Corporation includes a company** incorporated outside India but does not include — (a) a corporation sole * (b) a cooperative society registered under any law relating to cooperative societies and (c) any other body corporate which the Central Government, by notification in the Official Gazette, specify in this behalf.

A company, when formed and registered under the Companies Act, 1956, becomes a body corporate. A society registered under the Societies Registration Act, 1961, is a body corporate. A cooperative society is a body corporate but under different Act.

Evolution

Historically, company form of organisation came into existence in Great Britain first and then spread in other countries of Europe. The company form of organisation itself has gone through an evolutionary change in Great Britain and in other countries, including India. **A short resume of the evolution is given below :**

The Indian Companies Act was first passed in 1850 in a scrappy way. By that time many British originated companies have been functioning in India known as 'sterling companies'. (Still some sterling companies are existing in India but they are gradually getting Indianised). In 1866, a new Act was passed in India containing comprehensive provisions for incorporation, regulation and winding up of a company. The Act was recast in 1882 and then was replaced by a more comprehensive Act in 1913. This Act continued to operate in India for a long time. In 1936 there were some major amendments, particularly to regulate the Managing Agency system, though with little success. Immediately after independence the national Government of India felt the need of having a company legislation suitable to Indian conditions and to cater to Indian interests. The Government **appointed a Committee in 1952, called the Bhabha Committee** for redrafting the legislation in the same line as Great Britain has appointed the Cohen Committee in 1948 for a comprehensive modification of British Company Law.

On the basis of the Draft Bill prepared by the Bhabha Committee, **the Companies Act was passed in 1956 after a prolonged deliberation** in Parliament. The Act was passed with the following objects : (1) to eliminate malpractices in company management so that general investors find interest in companies; (2) to safeguard the interests of the investing public; (3) to achieve social good through faster capital formation; (4) to empower the Government to have a greater control on company administration in the country. In the same year, the Securities Contracts (Regulation) Act was passed to control share markets.

It was thought that the new Companies Act would be comprehensive and enduring. But during 26 years of its functioning **amendments have been done 14 times,** of which the amendments of 1960, 1963, 1965, 1969 and 1976 are important. A number of amendments have been recommended by the Sachar Committee appointed in 1977. The Act applies to whole of India including the State of Jammu and Kashmir (by the first amendment of 1959).

Banking, insurance and electricity companies are governed by **the Companies Act and in addition by some special Acts** like Banking Regulations Act, 1949, the Reserve Bank of India Act, 1948, the Insurance Act, 1938 (also special Acts for nationalisation), Indian Electricity Act, 1910. The Monopolies Restrictive Trade Practices Act, 1969 (in short known as MRTO Act) and the Foreign Exchange Regulation Act, 1973 (in short known as FERA) have close link with the Companies Act. The Societies Registration Act, 1961, the Co-operative Societies Act, 1912 and the Trust Act, 1888 have many similarities with the Companies Act.

* 'Corporation sole' means a corporation made of only one person which has perpetual succession, e.g., the post of President of India. President of India cannot die but a person holding the position dies.

Advantages

The company form of organisation has a lot of advantages which make this form popular all over the world. The main advantages are as follows :

(1) **Large accumulation of finance** — A company form of organisation **can accumulate large finance because of the following reasons :** (a) In most of the cases there is limited liability of members and the risk is transferable as shares are transferable (with or without restrictions). Therefore, people come forward to buy shares. (b) The share value is generally payable in instalments which is an additional attraction. (c) There are different kinds of shares which attract different types of investors. (d) A company also takes loans in the forms of debentures and fixed deposits and this attracts a class of conservative investors. (e) Shares and debentures can be dealt in organised share markets adding greater liquidity and goodwill to the shares. (f) A company has greater credit – worthiness to banks and other financial institutions.

(2) **Limited liability** — Perhaps this is one of the most important advantages. **The investors know at the beginning what can be their maximum liabilities** and so they can make planned investment.

(3) **Spreading of risks** — A company has **a number of members who share the burden of the risks.** Bigger the company larger is the number of members and more is the spreading of the risks.

(4) **Stability** — A company as a body corporate has perpetual succession. **It continues to exist unless it is wound up according to the procedure** laid down in the Act. The Act also lists out preferential creditors and so every creditor knows what shall be his position in case a company is wound up. To safeguard the interest of the creditors at the winding up of a company, the court has responsibilities. A company cannot be easily liquidated by any group of members or directors or such other interested persons. **The Act provides many alternative arrangements** like compromise, amalgamation, etc., to save the company from liquidation.

(5) **Democratic management** — **The management of a company is carried on by democratic principles** and by elected representatives of the members called directors. At least two-third of the total number of directors must be elected by the members. The post of a director is not permanent. Every director has to retire after some time (at least one-third of the elected director must retire by rotation annually but are eligible for re-election) and so none can develop a vested interest in a company.

(6) **Democratic ownership** — As there is democratic management **there is democratic ownership** too. There may be a large number of members in a company, rich or poor, each contributing to the capital of the company according to his mite. They have voting rights, to exercise over-all control on the company, in proportion to their contribution.

(7) **Efficient management** — **Management of a company is expected to be efficient** for the following reasons : (a) Efficient persons can be elected as directors. (b) Inefficient directors can be removed by the members before the expiry of their appointment periods. (c) A company can afford to keep efficient and qualified managerial staff by paying handsome salaries. (d) In case of mismanagement, the Central Government may be approached for remedies. (e) A company can really go for efficient professional management.

(8) **Scope of expansion** — As a company **has scope for large capital** and efficient management, it **may go for expansion,** diversification and even trans-national extension to maximise wealth and profit (see below).

(9) **Public sector** — Public sector undertakings are **mostly in the form of Corporate bodies** because this form is better than other forms.

(10) **Accountability** — A company **has to maintain both statistical and statutory books,** i.e., books of account and registers giving full particulars about its workings. Besides, every

company has to get its accounts audited by a qualified auditor. Cost audit is compulsory in certain cases. A company **has to file many returns** and copies of final accounts with the Registrar of Companies and such returns and copies of accounts are open to public inspection, subject to exceptions. Accounts and reports of public sector bodies corporate are to be presented before Parliament or the State Assemblies as the case may be. All these generate public confidence in such form of organisations.

(11) **Control measures — The Companies Act contains many provisions for control over companies** by the Central Government and the court in the interests of the members and other interested persons, of the company itself, of the business to which the company belongs and of the public interest as a whole. All these generate further public confidence in this form of organisation.

(12) **Way of the business world** — This form of organisation has been **accepted as the common and most acceptable form of organisation** for large scale business in the present-day business world. Many partnership firms are very often found to be converted into companies to enjoy the advantages.

Disadvantages

The Company form of organisation is not an unmixed blessing. As a man-made system, it has some drawbacks and many of them are caused by the people who get involved in it. The disadvantages are :

(1) **Formalities** — The main inherent disadvantage of the company form of organisation is **too much burden of formalities.** From the very formation the formalities start. The formalities continue as a company continues to exist as a going concern. Even the process of winding up is very complex. It is not possible to expect of the businessmen to be capable of undergoing those formalities by themselves. Therefore, at every step, services of experts like lawyers, accountants, consultants and others have to be taken. All these formalities cause high cost. Day-by-day, formalities are increasing and also the resultant cost.

(2) **Separation between ownership and management** — As there is a **separation between ownership and management** the following complications arise: (a) Generally members do not find much interest in the management. They are happy with good dividends. (b) Those people who are in management, mainly the directors, may not have much financial stake and therefore they often become reckless and use the company as a tool for personal gains. This is partially true for a private company. (c) Management by experts or professionals make it very expensive. (d) The directors are liable to retirement and so they may not identify themselves with the interests of the company.

(3) **Malpractices — There are people who indulge in various kinds of malpractices** from the very promotion stage and particularly by participating in management. Taking advantage of callousness of the general members they try to make personal gains at the cost of the members. Secret profits, transferring of funds, manipulation of votes by controlling the proxies etc. are some of the methods of malpractices. Motivated people develop vested interest and by having controlling shares in their hands, or in the hands of their group, they always establish their grip and election of directors becomes almost a show only. Though the Companies Act incorporates various provisions to control malpractices and mismanagement, they can be skilfully avoided.

(4) **Speculation on shares — Speculation leading to gambling is very common with shares** of those companies which are enlisted in stock exchanges. Artificial fluctuation of prices of shares cause harmful reaction on the companies and people's faith may be lost. People in management indulge in such manipulations as they know all the inner affairs of the company. By deliberately lowering the price of shares in the market they may buy them underhand to gain control over the company.

(5) **No real democracy — Theoretically, it can be said that a company is a democratic organisation but in practice it may not be so.** A group of men from behind may control everything. The members get opportunity to have their say in general meetings only. It is very common that interested people manage to get proxy forms signed by non-attending members to their advantage.

(6) **Concentration of economic power — A few persons in groups** gradually capture a number of companies either through management or buying majority shares or by influencing members, and in this way they **develop a business empire** and there is concentration of economic power in the hands of a few. This is easy to establish when there is lack of consciousness among the investing public. In India, at the background of all big industrial houses there is the same story. To control it, the MRTP Act was passed in 1969 but it has not been that effective as desired. Both the Companies Act and the MRTP Act have their loopholes which are taken advantage of, at least temporarily.

(7) **Conflict of interests — There are many types of people who have interests in the same company** – the members, the managerial personnel, the employees as a whole, the creditors, the customers, the Government (with its different departments) and others. It is quite natural that **these interests are conflicting** and not common. There may be conflict of interests even among different classes of shareholders. In the circumstances, the inner hygiene is lost and a company cannot have a healthy growth.

(8) **Too many regulations — There are two many regulations** as found in the Companies Act and the Company Rules. The excessive regulations destroy the incentives of the promoters and managers. Flat rate of income-tax, whether the company is big or small, is a strong disincentive to investors. Some people think that because of such excessive regulations and control a tendency for malpractices grows.

(9) **No secrecy** — One strong point against the company form of organisation is **total absence of secrecy.** From the very inception stage till its winding up (if any) and during its continued existence there is always public disclosure about its functioning. Many people find no interest in a business which does not have its exclusiveness to the owners.

CLASSIFICATION OF COMPANY

Basis of classification — A company is a body corporate with the following major features: (a) It is an association. (b) It has members. (c) Members have liability to contribute. (d) It has some common purpose. From legal viewpoint, such an association has a separate legal entity and perpetual succession. From different characteristics **companies are classified: (A) Functionally** according to purpose, (B) **Constitutionally,** according to the nature of liability of members and their number, and (C) **Structurally,** according to the composition of membership. They are detailed below:

(A) Functional classification

Functionally, companies are classified into two parts: (1) **Trading** — Such companies carry out some business for earning profit. It can be involved in industry, trade or commercial activity and accordingly called industrial company, trading company, financing company etc. Most of the operating companies are trading companies.

(2) **Non-trading** — According to Sec. 25 of the Companies Act, 1956, a company can be formed to carry out some social, religious or philanthropical acts or for the development of art and culture. Such companies enjoy some privileges under the Act. The income earned by such companies are spent for their own development. Such companies are very rare. The aristocratic club in Calcutta – The Bengal Club or the Calcutta Stock Exchange Association are examples. Many businessmen are members of the Bengal Club but the club itself does not do business. Similarly, the members of the Calcutta Stock Exchange Association do business on shares but the Association itself is a non-trading body.

(B) Constitutional classification

Constitutional classification is based on **nature of liability and number of members. Every company must have capital but not necessarily share capital.** Every member has to contribute to the fund or capital of the company. Such contribution can be of the following types: (a) If the company has share capital, i.e., the capital of the company is divided into some equal parts called shares, then each member has to buy some shares. Shares are transferable from one person to another. Each member is a shareholder member and his liability is limited up to the full value of shares promised to be taken by him. Such companies are called Joint Stock Companies because 'stock' means a bunch of shares. **Company and Joint Stock Company are, therefore, not identical terms.** Joint Stock Company is a kind of company. (b) The capital of a company may be made of fixed minimum guarantee given by a member. There is a guarantee capital and not a share capital. The liability of a member is limited upto the amount of guarantee promised by him. Such companies have members but no shareholders. (c) There are companies where both guarantee capital and share capital exist. (d) There are companies having neither share capital nor guarantee capital but unlimited capital. Keeping all these points in mind, companies can be classified in the following manner:

(1) **Unlimited liability** — In such a company a member joins with a promise that he will personally be liable to meet proportionally with other members all the liabilities of the company. Such companies are very rare and are generally non-trading companies.

(2) **Limited by shares (Joint Stock Companies)** — In such a company there is a share capital divided into some equal parts or shares and the liability of a member will be limited up to the value of the shares taken by him. This is the most common type of company. All trading companies are generally companies limited by shares. Shares of a company may be of different types. Joint Stock Companies are further classified into: (a) **Private** – A private company has the following characteristics: (i) Its number of members cannot exceed 50 excluding the members of the staff, past or present, holding shares, (ii) It cannot invite the public to buy shares in it. (iii) Its shares cannot be transferred by the members freely. (The company specifies the rules for share transfer). (b) **Public** – A public company is that which is not a private company. It means that such a company can have any number of members, can invite the public to buy shares in it and the shares of such a company can be transferred by members freely. That public company which actually offers shares to the public is called a widely held public company. A public company which does not offer the shares to the public (although it can), is called a closely held public company. (e) **Private company deemed to be a public company** – (1) From the date when not less than 25% of its paid-up capital is held by one or more body corporate. (2) From the date when it holds not less than 25% of the paid-up capital of a public company. (3) After the expiry of three months from the date when the annual average turnover of it becomes not less than Rs. 1 crore. In spite of such change, the main characteristics of a private company may be kept unaffected but it loses many of its privileges. Such a deemed public company may be reverted to a private company if the conditions cease to exist.

(3) **Limited by guarantee** — Such a company has capital but not share capital. Each member, while joining the company, has to give guarantee that he shall bring that amount of capital as demanded by the company.

(4) **Limited by guarantee having share capital** — In such a company, a member has to buy shares as he likes but in addition he has to give guarantee that he shall bring that amount of guarantee capital as demanded by the company.

Such classification is called constitutional because what shall be the nature of capital, whether public will be invited to buy shares or not, how the shares can be transferred etc. are to be mentioned in the documents of company – the Memorandum of Association and the

Articles of Association which set out the constitution of the company. Such a company can be Private or Public.

(C) Structural Classification

This classification is **based on the composition or structure of the share holding.** The classification is as follows :

(1) **Holding and Subsidiary companies** — According to the Companies Act, a company is a holding company in relation to another company called its subsidiary if, but only if: (a) the former company controls the composition of the Board of Directors of the latter company; (b) the former company holds more than half, in nominal value, of the equity share capital of the latter company; (c) if the former company is a subsidiary of another company then the latter company is also a subsidiary of that 'another company'. The Act provides elaborate rules with regard to the presentation of accounts of a holding company together with the accounts of the subsidiary or subsidiaries.

(2) **Foreign company** — A foreign company is that which is incorporated outside India but has a place of business in India. The Act provides the following rules for a foreign company: (a) It must file with the Registrar of Companies of the State in which it has place of business, a copy of its Memorandum of Association and Articles of Association, particulars of its directors, address of its registered office in India as well as details of persons resident in India on behalf of the company to whom all communications are to be made by the Registrar. (b) It must file with the Registrar three copies of balance sheet and profit and loss account as well as annual return unless specially exempted. (c) It must display in English its name with the name of the country where it is incorporated on letters, documents etc. and to display its name in English and in local language on the signboard, at its registered office, mentioning the nature of liability of members. (d) It must maintain all the books, registers, accounts etc. as wanted by the Act. (e) If it invites the public to buy shares or debentures, then it has to issue a prospectus a copy of which has to be filed with the Registrar giving details of the company in its origin. (f) It shall be penalised if it makes any default in company law. (g) It can be liquidated under the Companies Act of India as an unregistered Company. Foreign companies are also subject to Foreign Exchange Regulation Act, 1973. A foreign company shall be fully under the Indian Companies Act if not less than 50% of its shares are held by a citizen or citizens of India or body or bodies corporate incorporated in India.

(3) **Unregistered company** — A partnership or any other association (except a railway company or a company registered under the Companies Act) having more than seven members is considered as an unregistered company for the purpose of winding up. There are special provisions under which an unregistered company can be wound up like a company.

(4) **Government company** — A Government company is that in which not less than 51% of the shares are held by the Central Government or by a State Government or by two or more State Governments or by the Central Government together with one or more than one State Government. It also includes a company subsidiary to a Government company. There are some special provisions in the Act for a Government company.

(5) **Companies under the same management** — Two bodies corporate shall be deemed to be under the same management if (a) the managing director or manager is the same person in both; (b) if the majority of directors of one body corporate form the majority of directors of the other body corporate; (c) if one-third or more of the total voting power is controlled by the same individual or body corporate in both the bodies corporate; (d) if the holding company of one body corporate is controlled by the same management as of the other body corporate; (e) if the directors of one body corporate themselves or with their relations hold majority shares of that body corporate as well as of the other body corporate. The Companies Act provide, some restrictions with regard to the transfer of funds from one body corporate to another under the same management.

PROMOTION, FORMATION AND COMMENCEMENT OF BUSINESS

Meaning

There are three terms — **promotion, formation and commencement of business, each of which has separate meaning** and significance though they are often used in the same sense. In fact, the three terms are used at three different stages of entrepreneural activities. Out of the three terms, promotion appears to be a comprehensive one and commencement is the result of the process. When all these stages are over, a joint stock company or a company limited by shares comes into being. The terms are explained below.

A. Promotion

The word 'promote' does not merely mean 'start'. **Promotion is mixed with imagination and action.** A company is conceptually born when the idea of it is conceived by a person or a group of persons, called promoters. It comes into its physical form after certain distinct commercial and legal steps have been completed. A living object also has a process of birth. Gerestenberg, a German expert on management, has defined promotion as "the discovery of business opportunities and the subsequent organisation of funds, property and managerial ability into a business concern for the purpose of making profits therefrom". From the definition **the components of promotion** are found to be : (a) discovery of business opportunities; (b) organisation of funds, property and managerial ability (in the process some legal formalities have to be observed); (c) setting up a business concern; (d) developing a situation of making profits out of the concern.

Promoter — A person who gets himself engaged in the process of promotion is called a promoter. It is a commercial term. In the Companies Act, 1956, some duties, obligations and liabilities of a promoter have been referred to but the word promoter has not been defined. A promoter has the following **functions** : (1) To visualise an idea of a prospective business. (2) To bring some other persons to co-operate with him since one promoter cannot promote a company. (3) To prepare a complete plan for the proposed company. (4) To secure advice from different experts in law, specially company law, to prepare the different relevant documents. (5) To procure sufficient finance to meet the preliminary expenses. (6) To undergo the legal formalities. (7) To get support from the investing public. To discharge all these functions a promoter must have the following two sets of **characteristics** : (a) imagination and initiative; (b) judgement and leadership. All people do not have these qualities and so all men cannot be promoters.

Types of promoters — There are different types of promoters depending on the nature of promotion work performed by them :

(1) **Particular promoters** — Such promoters are those who do the promotional work for a particular company only. Ordinarily businessmen going for a business just promote a company instead of a partnership because a company form of organisation has some advantages. For most of the private companies we find such type of promoters.

(2) **Occasional promoters** — Some promoters, after forming a company and running it for some time successfully, go for expansion and diversification and start some more companies as sister concerns practically under the same ownership and management. As a company has separate legal entity, different companies are formed to avoid pressures of income-tax law, factory law and such other laws. In India, in the big industrial houses or families, we find such promoters.

(3) **Professional promoters** — Such promoters are some specialists who make out plans for new companies, get them incorporated and take remuneration for their expert services. They are not interested to be involved in the business or in its ownership or profits. In advanced countries there are such professional promoters. In India, the Managing Agents used to play the role of professional promoters. Managing Agents as professional promoters also took the responsibility of managing the proposed company. After independence, the Government has

set up several institutions for promotional work directly or indirectly, e.g. National Industrial Development Corporation, Indian Investment Centre, Industrial Estates etc. Each State Government has set up an Industrial Development Corporation for the purpose. Even the different financial institutions do promotional work.

(4) **State as a promoter** — In a socialistic country the State is the promoter of all economic organisations. Under mixed economy the State is the promoter for the public sector undertakings. Obviously, the State as a promoter has many basic advantages. In a Joint Sector enterprise there are combined efforts of the private entrepreneurs and the Government.

Floatation — The term floatation is often used as synonymous of promotion. But to be precise, **the term floatation is mainly connected with raising of funds** by floating or offering for sale shares and debentures. To float means to offer a choice under the free interaction of the forces of demand and supply, e.g. floatation of a currency in the foreign exchange market allowing the rate of exchange to be settled according to the market conditions.

B. Formation

Formation is a part of the entire gamut of promotional functions. **More or less, it is the legal aspect of company promotion.** It has **two parts :** (1) Obtaining the Certificate of Incorporation from the Registrar of Companies. According to law, registration of a company is essential. This is also known as incorporation of the company by which a company becomes a body corporate. This is necessary for both types of joint stock company — private and public. (2) Obtaining the Certificate for Commencement of Business from the Registrar of Companies. In the mean time, there is floatation of shares to the public by a widely held public company. This second certificate is necessary only for a public company. From a narrow legal approach, formation of a company means promotion of a company.

C. Commencement of business

The word, meaning of **commencement is 'starting'.** But the word 'business' here has a special implication. The first business of a company, under law, is to allot shares. Shares can be allotted only when all the formalities for getting the Certificate of Commencement of Business have been completed. In case of a private company, such stage is set as soon as the company is incorporated. From commercial point of view, a company is in a position to commence its business when sufficient capital has come into its hands.

STEPS TO BE FOLLOWED FOR PROMOTION OF A COMPANY

Steps for promotion of a company has **two distinct aspects :** Commercial and Legal. Each aspect again is divided into stages. All the steps are to be followed by the promoters in consultation with experts. Minimum two promoters in case of a private company and minimum seven for a public company are necessary. A systematic discussion is made below on the basis of such aspects and stages :

A. Commercial aspects

This aspect exclusively belongs to the promoters as businessmen.

Stage I : Business planning

(1) **Conception or discovery of an idea** — At first **the idea of a business has to be discovered or conceived of** by one or a group of persons through discussion. Such idea comes up after proper market study and being inspired by the Government's policies and motivation. The conception may be of three types : a completely new business, expansion by diversification of an existing business and amalgamation with or absorption in or taking over of another business. Accordingly, subsequent modes of planning will differ.

(2) **Investigation — Thorough investigation has to be made in the market about the possibilities of success** or prospects of the proposed business or diversification. There are various sources of information – the Government, the market, the reports and accounts of existing

companies in the field, etc. Consultants may be engaged to prepare project reports. In case of amalgamation etc. the accounts and reports of the other company or companies have to be scrutinised. All the data and information collected require verification because there may be errors. Investigation includes search for a good site for the factory in case of a manufacturing company as well as search for sources of raw materials, availability of power, etc.

(3) **Assembling— All these data have to be assembled and arranged to prepare the blue-print** for the business. Side- by-side, the blue-print for the proposed factory, if any, also has to be prepared. A physical plan is meaningless unless side-by-side a financial plan is set out (see below). Man-power planning taking in view the skilled and unskilled labour as well as the technical personnel, if any, has to be drawn. All these will produce a comprehensive plan for the entire project in all its facets. It requires final discussion among the promoters to approve it. If necessary, advice of experts may be sought.

Stage II : Negotiation

Different forms of negotiation become necessary at this stage. **Negotiation has to be made with the Government** for getting an industrial licence under the Industries (Development and Regulation) Act, 1951, if the proposed business needs licence. There are other types of licences too, e.g. negotiation for obtaining Import Licence and clearance under Foreign Exchange Regulations Act, 1973, may also be required in case import of machinery, raw materials or technical know-how is needed. **Negotiation with foreign countries** becomes imperative for the same reasons. Different **financial institutions** may have to be approached for financial accommodation or participation if the promoters have such contemplation.

Stage III : Finance planning

One vital aspect of business promotion is finance planning. This is a formidable task. Finance planning includes **calculating the requirement of finance** both **long and short terms and ascertaining the sources.** There are two theories – Cost Theory and Earning Theory – for calculating the financial requirements. Finance includes finance for meeting the initial or preliminary expenses and cost of raising finance. The preliminary expenses are supposed to be met by the promoters themselves, initially.

B. Legal aspect

This aspect cannot be a function of the promoters as businessmen. They have to depend on some legal expert for the purpose. Generally, for big companies, a qualified secretary is appointed by the promoters at this stage for the purpose, who will be formally absorbed by the company after its incorporation.

Stage I : Getting the Certificate of incorporation

(1) **Informal letter to the Registrar** — An informal letter to is be written to the Registrar of Companies of the State concerned, suggesting at least three alternative names of the proposed company wanting to know which one will be available because no company can use the name of an existing company.

(2) **Preparation of documents** — Every company must prepare, i.e. print the matter, dividing into paragraphs with serial numbers, its Memorandum of Association containing : (1) the Name of the Company not using any word which makes it appear to have Government patronage. The name of a public company shall end with the word 'Limited' (unless exempted by the Central Government for a non-trading company) and the words 'Private Limited' in case of a private company. (2) Address, i.e. domicile or the name of the State where the company is going to be registered. (3) Objects, i.e. the purpose of the company. The objects shall be shown in three parts : main objects, ancillary objects and other objects. (4) Liability, i.e. whether the liability of the members of the company will be limited by shares, limited by guarantee, limited by guarantee and by shares or unlimited. In a limited company the liability of its directors, however, may be unlimited if so mentioned in the Memorandum or

subsequently decided. (5) Capital, i.e. the authorised capital of the company up to which the company can raise funds. If there is share capital then the division and classes of shares also will be mentioned.

A private company will prepare its own Articles of Association in full or in part and follow the Table A for the rest. A public company will prepare its own Articles of Association or follow the Table A in full or will prepare the Articles in part and follow the Table for the rest. This document also has to be printed and paragraphed with serial numbers containing all the internal affairs of the company like classification of shares, rights and duties of the members, rules regarding shares and meetings, accounts and audit etc.

The promoters, while preparing the documents, shall follow the models or Tables given in the Schedule I of the Companies Act.

Table A — a model of the Articles of Association of a company limited by shares.

Table B — a model of the Memorandum of Association of a company limited by shares.

Table C — a model of the Memorandum and Articles of Association of a company limited by guarantee.

Table D — a model of the Memorandum and Articles of Association of a company limited by guarantee and by shares.

Table E — a model of the Memorandum and Articles of Association of an unlimited liability company.

(3) **Filing of documents :** (a) One copy of Memorandum and one copy of Articles, together with necessary registration and filing fees, **have to be submitted to the Registrar** of Companies. The promoters will sign the documents giving their names, addresses and occupations and also the number of shares taken by each (at least one must be taken) and declare that all the legal formalities have been complied with. A lawyer, chartered accountant, engineer or such other person shall also sign as a witness authenticating the signature of the promoters.

(b) For a public company, filing of the following papers is also necessary : (i) A list of first directors. (ii) Directors' consent letters to act as directors and to take qualification shares, if any, (iii) A copy of the terms and conditions of appointment of the Managing Director, if any.

(4) **Filing of address of the registered office** — The promoters may **file with the Registrar the actual address** of the registered office of the company at this stage or may file it within 30 days from the date of incorporation.

The Registrar of Companies will examine the documents. He may accept them, reject them or may ask for some modifications. When satisfied, he will issue a **Certificate of Incorporation** with a serial number and date under his seal and signature.

The company is incorporated as a body corporate. A private company can commence business immediately.

Stage II : Getting the Certificate for Commencement of Business

A public company now has to decide whether it will be a closely held or a widely held company and accordingly will undergo the following steps:

(1) **Filing of Prospectus or a Statement in lieu of Prospectus:** (a) In case the company is a **widely held company:** (i) a document called Prospectus will be prepared i.e. printed with paragraphs serially numbered containing a full description of the Company, the names, addresses and occupations of the directors, the names and addresses of bankers, legal advisors, secretary, of the sharebrokers through whom the shares will be sold, of the auditors and of the financial institutions whose help will be or is being taken. The prospectus will contain a Share Application form. The Schedule II of the Act gives a model of a Prospectus. (ii) One copy of the prospectus is to be filed with the Registrar with necessary filing fees

and the remaining copies will be issued to the public for sale at a nominal price. (iii) **Newspaper advertisements** may be made according to the provisions of the Act. (iv) If the company wants to issue shares and/or debentures valued more than Rs. 50 lakhs a special **permission from the Controller of Capital Issue** shall have to be obtained before issuing the Prospectus. (b) In case of a **closely held company** a Statement in lieu of Prospectus has to be filed with the Registrar showing the allotment of shares at least 3 days before the allotment is made.

The Registrar will issue a Certificate for Commencement of Business with a serial number and date and under his seal and signature when he receives from the Company the following information: (i) That the minimum subscription, i.e. some minimum percentage of shares offered for sale as mentioned in the Prospectus but not below 5%, has been received by the company. (ii) The directors have paid for their shares.

Now the formation of a public company is complete and it can start its business.

DOCUMENTS OF A COMPANY

Importance

A company is an artificial person created by law. Such creation takes place through registration or incorporation of the company by a procedure mentioned in the Companies Act. The Act defines a Company as 'a company formed and registered under this Act'. The definition makes it clear that formation is a wider term and registration is a part of it. We have already seen how the formation and registration takes place. The main part in the legal aspect of the formation process is the preparation of the documents. It has to be remembered that the importance of the documents does not end as soon as the formation is over. **The documents continue to serve the company in many respects** and to a large variety of persons interested or want to be interested in the company, e.g. the members of the Company, the creditors, the banker, the Government authorities, persons entering into contract with the company for different reasons, etc. Because of their wide significance, the Act has provided models for drafting them.

Out of the three documents, **the Memorandum is the most important** and larger varieties of outsiders are interested in it. In the Articles, practically the members only are interested but bankers also are concerned. Prospectus has importance mainly to the potential investors. Although the documents have legal character, they have to be studied by businessmen for commercial purposes. Detailed discussion on the documents are given below.

A. Memorandum of Association

This is called the **fundamental document** or charter of the company by which the company is known to the outside world. It is meant for the outside world. Every company must prepare its own Memorandum. The clauses of a Memorandum are : name, address, object, liability, capital and subscription which describe a company. A company is a person (though artificial). Memorandum has the points to describe a person – name, address, objects (occupation), liability and capital (qualifications) and the subscribers to the Memorandum are the parents of the company.

Analysis of the clauses — Name and address clauses have mainly legal significance. Choice of name has restrictions. Address means the State i.e. the jurisdiction of the Registrar. Outsiders may be interested in it when they want to inspect some reports or accounts of a company. Liability clause mainly affects the members. Object and capital clauses have real commercial significance and affect the outsiders. From the legal sid,e object clause is ascribed highest significance because a company cannot do any act which is not expressly mentioned in the object clause. This is known as the doctrine of *ultra vires.* Any agreement made by a company with any outsider based on any matter which is not permitted by the object clause, is void. The outsider is helpless and cannot enforce the agreement. Therefore, for his own interest an outsider must go through the Memorandum of a company with which it intends to establish any business or contractual relation.

There is close connection between object and capital clauses. Obviously, the amount of capital must have co-relationship with the object. Normally an industrial company will require larger capital than a trading company. On the other hand, the volume of capital shall be exceedingly high for a finance company. Even the name of a company reflects its object or nature of business.

The Companies Act provides elaborate rules with regard to alteration of the clauses of a Memorandum. Out of them, the rules are strictest for the alteration of the Object clause. **The procedure** contains: (a) The decision of the members at a meeting by a special resolution (i.e. at least three-fourths of the votes cast are in favour of alteration). (b) No creditor shall have any objection or if any creditor has objection he must be paid off. (c) Opinion of the Registrar. (d) Final approval by the Company Law Board the highest authority in administration of companies in the country. The nature of the object has direct bearing on the extent of risks. For example, risk in manufacturing business is normally higher than that in trading business. Three-fourth majority of votes must be in favour of alteration of the object clause because it affects the members as risk-takers. Changing the object clause and thereby increasing the risk means indirectly making the investment less profitable and even less secured. Again, if the object is altered in such a manner that the risk becomes bigger, a creditor may rightfully object to it. A creditor, even as an outsider, has, therefore, a say in this matter. An individual, whether an insider or an outsider to a company, must know the facts.

The Name clause can be altered by (1) a special resolution by the members and (2) approval by the Central Government.

The Address clause can be altered by (1) a special resolution by the members and (2) approval by the Company Law Board.

The Capital clause can be altered by the members themselves, either by a special or an ordinary (simple majority of votes) resolution, as the Articles provide.

The Liability clause affects mainly the members. The Act specifically provides that a company cannot increase the liability of a member without his written consent. A prospective investor in a company is interested as an outsider, what shall be the nature of his liability. A would-be director is interested to know whether liability of directors in the company is unlimited.

B. Articles of Association

This is the secondary document for the internal affairs of a company. Preparation of it is not strictly compulsory as a public company may follow the Table A in full.

Analysis — It is concerned purely with the members of the company because it contains matters **related to the internal affairs of the company.** This document does not affect any outsider. The Articles include the conditions by which the different classes of shareholders can establish their relations with the company. Shareholders are very much interested in the transferability of shares. The Articles may provide restrictions for that and that is natural in case of a private company. It is one of the reasons why a private company must prepare its own Articles at least in part to state the restrictions with regard to share transfer. Clause on forfeiture of shares, if any, is of great importance to shareholders. Members are also interested in meetings as elaborated in the Articles. A private company has its own special rules with regard to meetings. Directors are also interested in Articles for their powers, rights, duties and obligations. Though these are specifically outlined by the Act, there may be some special points in the Articles. A private company can mention some special reasons for disqualification of its directors. Members are vitally interested in the matters of accounts and audit detailed in the Articles.

Any clause of the Articles can be altered by the members by passing a special resolution at a meeting. But no alteration is valid if it contradicts any clause of the Memorandum or it violates any provision of the Act. The Articles is subordinate to the Memorandum. An individual, whether an insider or an outsider to a company, requires this much knowledge about this document.

The Board of Directors of a company, in the process of day-to-day management, can do certain acts which are not permitted by the Articles of the company. But such act is not *ultra vires* because the Articles can be altered subsequently by the members to ratify the act of the Board. Therefore, an outsider entering into a contract with a company need not bother to consult the Articles. If the Board fails to get their act subsequently ratified by the members by that the Board is liable to the members but the outsider can enforce the contract. Articles are guided by the 'doctrine of indoor management' which means that the contents of the Articles are the inner affairs of the company. An act may be *ultra vires* (beyond the authority) of the Board but if it is *intra vires* (within the authority) of the company, i.e. its Memorandum; then it is valid.

C. Prospectus

This is a document to be prepared **only by a widely held public company.** Whenever such a company wants to offer shares and/or debentures for sale to the public, a Prospectus has to be issued. Prospectus is also necessary for inviting fixed deposits from the public. Thus, there are two types of Prospectus: (1) A Prospectus, to be issued **by a new company** immediately after incorporation. In such a Prospectus full description of the company and its business prospect together with full description of all the persons and institutions connected with the company, e.g. directors, bankers, auditors, legal advisor, secretary, sharebrokers, financial institutions, manager to the issue etc. are included. Besides, there is an Application Form for subscription.

(2) A Prospectus is to be issued **by an existing company** for issuing new shares for increasing the capital. In such a Prospectus, all the descriptions as in the other Prospectus must be given and in addition, a Report on the past performance of the company, up to five years back, showing the abstracts from balance sheets and trend of profits from the profit and loss accounts, has to be appended. Besides, there is an Application Form for subscription. Description of a company in a Prospectus means practically a reproduction of the Memorandum and Articles of it. Schedule II attached to the Companies Act provides models of both the types of Prospectus.

Incidentally, there is a third type of Prospectus called **Prospectus by Implication.** Any document inviting the public to buy shares in and/or debentures of the company shall be deemed to be a Prospectus. That is why, when an advertisement is published in newspapers in respect of sale of shares in or debentures of a company, it is written at the top – 'It is an announcement only and not a Prospectus'. Otherwise, such an advertisement shall be deemed as a Prospectus.

Analysis — Prospectus has an immediate value and not a permanent value like that of the Memorandum or Articles. Of course, it may take some long time for the sale of shares or debentures offered through a Prospectus. For a company with a good prospect or having some directors of repute, it is a matter of few days for the sale of all the shares or debentures. Importance of this document is to **two types of people:** (1) Those who issue them and (2) the potential subscribers to the issue. This is discussed below :

Generally, all the directors are responsible for the issue of Prospectus. They are the signatories to the document together with an expert authenticating the genuineness of the facts given in the document. These people shall be held liable for any deliberate misstatement or untrue statement either by concealing facts or by camouflaging by which the potential subscribers may be misled. There are two types of liabilities: (a) Civil – The persons responsible for the issue of the document shall be bound to compensate those subscribers who can prove that they have suffered loss being misled by the document. (b) Criminal – Every person who authorises the issue of the document containing misstatement shall be punishable with a fine not exceeding Rs. 5,000.00 or imprisonment for a period not exceeding 2 years, or both. The expert signing the document may, however, escape liability if he can prove that he had reasonable grounds to believe that the statement was true and apparently the statement means to be genuine. Generally a lawyer, a chartered accountant, an engineer or such other person acts as an expert.

A prospective subscriber or investor has to read a Prospectus carefully before he decides to buy shares in or debentures of the company. Generally, a Prospectus has publicity value and depicts a rosy picture of the company. That is not a misstatement. A statement can be construed as untrue when there is something which materially affects the position of the company. The potential investor may himself analyse the document if he knows the technique or he may take the help of an expert. However, **a Prospectus can be analysed or scrutinised or scanned on the following lines:**

(1) Whether the venture for which the company is incorporated (or existing), is itself **economically viable.** This can be judged from the following aspects: whether the product or service is of essential nature or it is a luxury or superfluous, whether all the factors of production are available, whether there is enough of supply already in the market, etc.

(2) The prospect of business can be ascertained by **comparing with the performance reports of other undertakings** already in that business. This will help verifying the rosy picture depicted in the Prospectus of the company under study.

(3) The **capital structure** of the company has to be thoroughly analysed to find out its adequacy, division into different sources like shares and debentures, if any, and also the different classes of shares, if any. Every investor by nature is either conservative or speculative. Accordingly he will make a choice of the securities offered by the company. An investor will try to estimate the extent of risk as well as the probable returns.

(4) It has to be seen how far the **management will be efficient** and effective. The full description of the directors, more or less, can provide an idea how far the management can be sound. Many of the directors are known in the business world being connected with other companies. Their reputation in those companies will provide an index. Name of names of a qualified technical director or directors also rouse confidence.

(5) A prospective investor also will look into **the voting rights, terms of repayment** of capital in case of debentures or redeemable preference shares as well as rights related to dividends.

(6) The **reputation of the bankers, auditors** etc. is also taken into consideration. If renowned share-brokers take the responsibility of marketing the securities or where financial institutions participate, the confidence of the prospective investor becomes solid.

(7) Now-a-days, **the policy of the Government** also has to be taken into account. If there is possibility of nationalising the business in future by the Government, very few persons will venture to invest. On the other hand, when the public financial institutions offer participation, there is positive Government patronage which enhances the goodwill of the company.

(8) In case of an existing company offering fresh shares, the Report part of the Prospectus giving the **past performance of the company** will be a very significant aspect of study.

(9) In case a company is formed to buy another company, or an existing company wants fresh capital to buy another company, then the description of the another company, i.e. **the vendor company** which wants to be sold, is given in the Prospectus. A prospective investor shall scrutinise the description as well as the terms of sale.

(10) The prospective buyer has to look into **the terms of payment** for the purchase of shares, whether with premium, whether by instalments etc. At the same time, the minimum number of shares, mentioned in the Prospectus, to be applied for.

(11) Another point may be watched. What is the **extent of investment made by the promoters-directors** themselves. When they have a good amount of financial stake, others may be inspired. On the other hand, if they together with or not financial institutions have in their hands bulk of the investment, then others may not find interest as the company is not really public or democratic. A stock exchange shall not enlist shares of a company unless it offers at least 49% of the shares to the public.

(12) Whether the company has applied for or promises to apply for **enlistment of shares in a stock exchange.** In case of an existing company, whether the shares are enlisted in a stock exchange. Such enlistment increases the liquidity, i.e. easy transferability of shares and the prospective investor is encouraged.

CAPITAL STRUCTURE

Meaning – Capital plays' a vital role in economic life. It is difficult to define capital. From the view of economists, as Bohm-Bawerk thinks, capital is 'produced means of production'. It is something produced by man from which further income can be generated through production. It has different forms – money, machines or capital goods or even labour, etc.

For every form of business capital is needed, big or small. A company needs capital. Its form of capital is quite different from the forms of organisation like sole-proprietorship or partnership. In the last two cases, capital creates ownership and ownership is identified with the right to management. In a company, capital gives rise to ownership but not a right to direct management. Moreover, with the investment of capital in a sole-proprietorship or partnership firm, business is carried on and assets are created and the sole-proprietor, or the partners as the case may be, acquires or acquire a right to the ownership of those assets. The reason is that the sole-proprietor is identified with his firm and the partners are identified with their firms. **In a company the position is different.** By using the capital primarily supplied by the members, the business of a company, an artificial person, is carried on. The assets which are created belong to the company and not to the members. The directors who are the elected representatives of the members look after the assets and property of the company as trustees. The Board of Directors neither can buy nor can sell the assets or property of a company without the sanction of the members.

Capital has a structure because it has its components or parts. In a company, capital is accumulated part by part from the members. The members may contribute to the capital in different proportions. Capital has parts because there are different types and sources of capital. It is more true for a company. Capital of a company has a structure because not only there are different sources or types of capital but **there is a hierarchy** too. Different types of capital ascribe different rights in order of preference to the investors. This is because of classification of shares and debentures according to the rights of the holders.

Functionally, a company, like any other organisation, has **two types of capital**, long term or fixed and short term or working or circulating. **Structurally**, capital of a company is divided into – own capital and loan capital. The main chunk of fixed capital comes from own capital and loan capital supplies working capital in general.

Own capital and loan capital — This is also known as owned capital and borrowed capital. Again, they can be known as inside and outside capital. Own Capital is further divided according to the preferential rights of the contributors. Loan capital is further divided into direct and indirect. The different types are detailed below :

A. Own or Inside Capital

This part or the main part of capital of a company is supplied by the members either in the form of shares or guarantee or both. In an unlimited company, there is neither share nor guarantee. In a joint stock company, the inside capital is in the form of shares. Own capital is inside capital because those who supply it enter inside the company and the return is dividend out of profits which is uncertain and fluctuating. It mainly provides the fixed capital.

Share Capital

Share has been defined by the Companies Act as 'share means share in the share capital'. It means that it is **a share or part in the total capital of the company which is divided into some equal parts and so the capital is called share capital.** The Authorised or Registered or Nominal capital of a company is the amount mentioned in the capital clause of the Memorandum of the company. Up to this amount the company can raise capital. If the company wants more capital then the capital clause has to be amended by the members by passing a special resolution at a meeting. Out of the total authorised capital, generally a substantial part is raised by the company by offering for sale a part of the total number of shares. This is called Issued capital. Out of the shares offered for sale either all or some of them are sold. The total value of such shares makes the subscribed capital. When the share value is payable by instalments, the actual amount paid by the shareholders on their shares is called the Paid-up capital. This is the actual money that the company can handle. As and when further instalment is asked for payment or a 'call' is made, the Paid-up capital increases with the further payment by the shareholders.

The **relationship between a shareholder and the company is contractual.** Therefore, a man without capacity to contract cannot hold shares in his own name. A share may be held jointly but the company recognises the first name of the joint holders as member.

Out of the contract, a **shareholder as a member gets the following rights :** (a) To get a Share Certificate as a proof of his share holding. (b) To get his name entered in the Register of Members as soon as the certificate is issued. (c) To get proportionate share in the profits, i.e. dividend. (d) To transfer his share. (e) Not to be burdened with greater liability without his written consent. (f) To get a notice of general meetings, as a member. (g) To vote at the meetings. (h) To become a director of the company if all the conditions are satisfied. (i) To get refund of capital, if possible, after the winding up of the company or earlier if the shares are redeemable.

A company is a democratic organisation owned by the shareholders as members. Every member has the voting rights in proportion to his contribution to the Paid-up capital. Therefore, **there are unequal voting rights.** A small number of persons holding majority shares can have control on the company and over the larger number of members. If a member fails to pay call money then his contribution to the Paid-up capital is proportionately reduced and consequently his voting rights are proportionately reduced. On the other hand, if a member pays call money in advance, his voting rights are not proportionately increased. This voting right of a member has great significance in the capital structure of a company. Under the Companies Act, there is **no restriction as to how many shares one individual can hold** in a company. One person can hold all the shares of a particular class. A body corporate can hold shares.

Classification of Shares

The importance of voting rights of shareholders is reflected in the mode of classification of shares. According to the Companies Act, **shares are classified on the basis of voting rights.** Accordingly, there are **two types of shares :** (1) Shares with proportionate voting rights or Equity Shares (formerly known as Ordinary shares). (2) Shares with disproportionate voting rights or Preference shares. This rigid classification is for public companies. The Act says that a private company can issue shares with disproportionate voting rights of any other variety. For example, the Articles of a private company may ascribe special voting rights for the founder members. Every company must have Equity Shares. Preference Shares are optional.

Preference Shares — Preference Shares are those holders of which have the following priorities – (a) They will get dividend out of the profits of the company at a fixed rate before dividend is paid to any other class of shareholders. (b) They will get repayment of capital first when the company goes to liquidation and in the process all the creditors have been fully repaid. On the other hand, they have disproportionate voting rights. It means that they cannot vote on all matters of the company but only on those matters which affect their interests, e.g. on a proposal for winding up of the company, and they vote in proportion to their contribution to the Paid-up capital.

Preference Shares are subdivided into following types : (1) **Cumulative** — In such kind of Preference shares, if, in any year, there is insufficient profit and the company is unable to pay fixed rate of dividend then the arrear dividend shall be paid from the profits of the subsequent year or years. Until all the arrears with current dividend are paid off, no other class of shareholders will get any dividend. If the holders of Cumulative Preference Shares do not get dividend for two consecutive years, they develop full voting rights. (2) **Non-cumulative** — In such kind of Preference share the arrear dividend is not payable from the profits of the subsequent year or years. The holders of Non-cumulative Preference Shares get full voting rights if they do not get dividend for three consecutive years. (3) **Participating** — When the Articles provide that the preference shareholders will get dividend second time along with the equity shareholders and will participate in the assets of the company with the participation of their capital when the company goes to liquidation, the preference shares are called Participating Preference Shares.

Preference shares can be **broadly classified** into two : (i) **Perpetual** – Generally shares are perpetual, i.e. shareholders do not get repayment of their capital until the company goes to liquidation. Preference shares are generally perpetual. (2) **Redeemable** – The Articles of a company may authorise the company to issue Redeemable Preference shares which will be refunded either after a fixed period of time or when the company wants to do it. Redeemable Preference shares can be redeemed at a premium (See below). The company builds up for the purpose a Redemption Fund out of the profits of the company or redemption can be by issue of fresh shares. Redeemable Preference shares must be fully paid-up. Perpetual Preference shares cannot be converted into Redeemable Preference Shares.

Preference Shares are **further classified** into groups like 'A' Group Preference Shares, 'B' Group Preference Shares according to the issue of the shares at different times. Each prior group has a preference over the next group.

Equity Shares — A company **must issue Equity Shares.** The holders of such shares really bear the burden or risk. They have full voting powers on all matters of the company. They will cast votes in proportion to their contribution to the Paid-up capital of the company. All Equity Shares are perpetual. There is no classification. The holders of Equity Shares **get dividend on the following principle :** (1) Out of the profits of the company the holders of Preference Shares, if any, will get dividend at a fixed rate including arrears in case there are Cumulative Preference Shares. (2) Out of the balance, the Board of Directors will recommend a percentage of dividend on Equity Shares. The Board may not recommend a high rate even if the balance is big because of two reasons : (a) The Board may want to maintain a standard rate of dividend for different years. (b) The Board may want to build up a big Dividend Equalisation Fund so that out of that dividend can be paid in some other year when the profit is very low. (3) The recommendation of the Board shall be placed at the annual general meeting. The Equity Shareholders may accept the recommended rate or may reduce it but they cannot increase it. They may want reduction to build up a big Reserve which can be subsequently capitalised to develop self-generating economy.

Bonus Shares or Ploughing back of profit — The profits of a company can be ploughed back to investment to develop self-generating economy by capitalisation of profit. This is done by issue of Bonus Shares by converting the Reserves into share capital. Such a decision is taken by the shareholders themselves at a general meeting and once a decision is taken no shareholder can refuse to accept Bouns Shares allotted to him. The allotment is made on pro rata basis. For example, suppose a company has a share capital of Rs. 10,00,000.00 divided into 10,000 shares of Rs. 100.00 each. The Company wants to capitalise a Reserve of Rs. 2,00,000.00 by issuing 2,000 Bonus Shares of Rs. 100.00 each. Each shareholder will get 1 share for each 5 shares held by him. He has not to pay anything. There will be only book adjustments. Permission of the Controller of Capital Issue may be necessary. The Central Government, time to time, makes Rules for Bonus Issue which have to be followed.

Benefits of ploughing back — There are so many benefits of ploughing back of profits enjoyed both by the company as well as the shareholders. They are : (a) The Company becomes self-reliant and develops a self-generating economy. It has not to go to others for loan. (b) This method of raising funds is very suitable for the expansion of the company. (c) The shareholders are benefited in the following way : In order to build up a big Reserve ,they might have made sacrifice in the past by accepting low rates of dividend. But once the Reserve is capitalised they get more shares and they will continue to get more dividend in future out of their larger shareholdings for which they have not to pay anything. Further, because of the expansion of the company, the profitability of the company increases followed by higher rates of dividend.

Bonus Shares and Rights Shares — According to the Companies Act, if a public company wants to issue fresh shares to increase its capital after one year from its first allotment of shares or after two years from the formation of a company, whichever is earlier, then the company must offer the new shares to the existing shareholders on a *pro rata* basis, unless a different intention is expressed by the shareholders by passing a special resolution (three-fourth majority). Such shares are called Rights Shares. The shareholders have to pay for such shares. A written offer is made to every shareholder. He has to decide within 15 days whether he will buy the shares or not. If he does not, he has to send a Letter of Renunciation or he may renounce the shares in favour of another. Those shares which are not taken by the existing shareholders can be offered to others.

Value of Shares

A share has got a value in terms of money. It has three aspects : (a) **Face value** – A share has a face value. It means the value of each share mentioned in the capital clause of the memorandum of the company. This value is written in the Share Certificate or Share Warrant issued as an evidence of shareholding. (b) **Market value** – It is the value of a share considered in the market depending on the position of the company judged by its profitability and solvency as well as liquidity of the share i.e. how easily the share is transferable. When the shares are enlisted in a stock exchange, the market value can be more equitably ascertained. (c) **Intrinsic value** – An accountant works out the intrinsic or inner value of a share of a company by dividing the difference between the total value of assets and the total value of liabilities by the total number of shares. Some fine adjustments of accounts have to be made in the process.

Shares are issued at a price or value in exchange. Such selling can be made in the following ways : (1) **Shares at a par value** – When the shares are sold at their face value, it is called shares at a par value. (2) **Shares at a premium** – When shares are sold at more than their face value, it is called shares at a premium. A company can sell its shares at a premium subject to some restrictions. Such premium money can be utilised to write off preliminary expenses, to issue bonus shares or to pay premium when Redeemable Preference shares are redeemed at a premium. (3) **Shares at a discount** – A company can sell shares at a discount provided the following conditions are fulfilled : (a) A resolution is passed at a general meeting. (b) Sanction is obtained from the Company Law Board. (c) The maximum rate of discount is specified in the resolution. (d) Not less than one year must have elapsed between the date when the company was entitled to commence business and the date of issue of share at a discount. (e) The shares must be offered for sale at discount within two months from the date of sanction by the Company Law Board or any extended time by the Board. (f) The maximum rate of discount cannot exceed 10 per cent. A company wants to sell the shares at discount for two reasons : (a) to attract investors and (b) the company is unable to sell the shares in normal course. (4) **Shares with interest** – Normally, a company cannot pay interest on the share capital. But under the following exceptional cases it can do so : (a) Where share capital has been raised to meet the expenses of a construction of a building or erection of plant which will not be profitable in a short time and the investors need some return in the meantime. (b) When it is authorised by the Articles or by a special resolution. (c) A permission is necessary from the Central Government. The Central Government shall fix the period for which interst will be payable. The rate of interest shall not be more than 4% per annum or as directed by the Central Government.

Evidence of shareholding

A shareholder wants an evidence of his shareholding to exercise his rights. A company must provide such evidence which can be done in the following two ways : (1) **Share Certificate** – the Companies Act provides that a company must issue a Share Certificate to every shareholder within 3 months from the allotment and within 2 months from the date of transfer. The Share Certificate contains the following : (a) The name of the company and its share capital. (b) The name of the shareholder. (c) The number and value of shares covered by the certificate. (d) A serial number. (e) A date. (f) The signature of directors with or without the signature of a secretary. A Share Certificate is transferable by endorsement and delivery by the shareholder to the transferee. A duly stamped and authenticated Share Transfer Deed has to be executed for the purpose. (2) **Share Warrant**– A company may issue a Share Warrant in place of a Share Certificate provided the following conditions are fulfilled : (a) There is such provision in the Articles. (b) Shares are fully paid. (c) the Central Government permits it. A Share Warrant contains all the matters as in a Share Certificate except the name of the shareholder. Therefore, his name cannot be entered in the Register of Members (See above). A Share Warrant holder is a shareholder but not a member. He can get dividend and transfer his share. He has no other rights. A Share Warrant is transferable by mere delivery. A Share Certificate and a Share Warrant are interchangeable.

In Sale of Goods Act shares have been described as goods since shares are saleable.

Alteration of Share Capital

Alteration of Share Capital can be made by the shareholders, i.e. the members of the company in the following manner : (a) They can increase the Share Capital beyond the amount mentioned in the Memorandum. (b) They can change the value of a share by decreasing it. (c) They can convert shares into Stocks. A **Stock** means a bunch of shares. A share cannot be transferred in part but a Stock can be transferred in part. Only fully paid shares can be converted into stock. A stock can be re-converted into fully paid shares. The members can do these if the Articles so provide.

The Companies Act empowers the Central Government to convert any loan advanced by any public financial institution (as recognised by the Act) into Equity Capital by making an order to that effect. If by that the authorised capital of the company is exceeded, then the capital clause in the Memorandum is automatically altered. This provision of the Act is very much criticised.

The shareholders, i.e. the members, can do **reduction of share capital** subject to the following conditions : (a) A provision has to be made in the Articles by a special resolution if Articles do not empower the shareholders to reduce the share capital. (b) A special resolution has to be passed on reduction of share capital. (c) Sanction of the Court has to be obtained. The Court will give sanction provided the Court is satisfied that no creditor has any objection to it. If any creditor has any objection then he must be paid off or secured. The Court may ask for public notification on such reduction and ask the company to use the words "(and reduced)" after its name for some specified period of time. (d) The Registrar shall be informed.

Reduction of share capital is wanted on account of the following reasons : (a) To reduce the liability of the shareholders. (b) To cancel any part of the Paid-up capital which is not supported by asset or is lost. (c) To refund any part of Paid-up capital which the company thinks excess. The shareholders are benefited because they can use this money for other purposes.

B. Loan or Outside Capital

The second main component of corporate capital structure is loan or borrowed or outside capital. This is called outside capital because those who supply it do not enter into the company and the return is interest at a fixed rate regardless whether the company makes any profit or not. Further, this capital is refundable after a fixed period of time, subject to exceptions.

Loan capital again can be broadly classified into two groups : Direct and Indirect. Direct loan capital comprises Debentures, Fixed deposits (called Public Deposits), different forms of bank accommodation and term loan from financial institutions. Indirect capital includes trade credit and deferred payment (even evasion) of direct and indirect taxes. Though officially it cannot be recognised, deferred payment or non-payment of direct and indirect taxes provide a good source of working and fixed capital, respectively, in practical life. Loan capital contributes mainly to working capital. The different types of loan capital are discussed below :

Debenture

The term debenture comes from the Latin word 'debere' which means "to owe'. By selling debentures, a company makes an acknowledgement of owing to the lenders with a promise to repay. 'A debenture is an admission of indebtedness'. The Companies Act defines debenture in the following language – "debenture includes debenture stock, bonds and any other securities of a company, whether constituting a charge on the assets of the company or not'. **The debentures have many similarities with shares.** As shares can be converted into stock, debentures are also consolidated into debenture stock. Like shares, debentures are also transferable. As share certificates are issued as evidence of shareholdings, debenture bonds are also issued. A debenture bond contains full description of it (like a share certificate) and contains the terms of issue such as : the date of repayment, the mode of repayment, the rate of interest, the class of debenture and whether they are secured by any charge or not. Like rights shares, rights debentures are also issued, Debenture holders are considered as second category of creditors in order of preference when a company goes to liquidation. According to law, debenture holders cannot have voting right. The Central Government makes out Rules with regard to issue of debentures.

Classification — Debentures are classified in many ways : (1) **Registered and Unregistered or Bearer** – When the name of the debenture-holder is written on the debenture bond and the name is recorded by the company in a Register, it is called a Registered Debenture. Such a debenture is transferable by endorsement and delivery. When the name of the debenture-holder is not written on the instrument, it is called Unregistered or Bearer Debenture. Such a debenture is transferable by mere delivery. (2) **Mortgage and Naked**— Some assets may be charged or earmarked against issue of debentures so that the loan is secured or/and those assets will be sold to repay the debentures if the company cannot repay from other means. The charge will 'crystallise', i.e. the debenture-holders will acquire claim on the charged assets only when the company has failed to repay the debentures by other means. That is the meaning of the term 'charge'. Charge may be fixed or floating. When the assets are specifically earmarked, it is called fixed charge. The company cannot dispose them so long the debentures have not been repaid. When the charge is floating, there are a number of assets listed and even if some of them are disposed off, the safety of the debenture-holders is not affected. (3) **Perpetual and Redeemable**— Perpetual Debentures are issued with the condition that they will not be repaid unless the company goes to liquidation. These are rare. Generally debentures are Redeemable. (4) **Convertible and Non-convertible**— Convertible debentures are those which are converted into equity shares after some fixed time.

Others are non-convertible ones. (5) **According to priority**— Debentures are often issued in series, e.g. 'A' Series, 'B' Series, and they will be repaid one series after another unless there is a *'pari passu'* clause which means that the debentures of different series will be repaid at a time. (6) **Debentures as Collateral** — Debentures are sometimes formally 'created' as security for taking loan from banks.

Repayment of debentures — Generally a company builds up a Debenture Redemption Fund annually out of profits for the repayment of debentures. These are the following **modes of repayment : (1) Redemption on a fixed future date** – The date of repayment is fixed and mentioned in the debenture bond. (2) **Redemption after a certain period** — The company has option to fix up the date of repayment after a fixed period is over. (3) **Repayment by annual instalments** – The company repays by equal annual instalments spread over a few years. (4) **Repayment by annual drawing** — Every year the company will repay some part of the total debentures, and by drawing or lottery, it will be fixed which ones will be repaid in that year. (5) **Redemption by re-purchase** – The company may reserve the right of purchasing the debentures back from the open market gradually. (6) **Redemption by conversion** – Redemption may be made in exchange of fresh debentures or converting the debentures into shares.

Public Deposits

Indian companies now-a-days have developed a tendency to raise funds by accepting Fixed Deposits from the public as well as from the members. Originally, it was a practice of the textile mills of Bombay and Ahmedabad regions but now it has become very popular for all companies. Companies receive deposits just like banks, offering high rates of interest and sometimes higher than what banks offer. In earlier days, the deposits were accepted for very short periods like several months but now comparatively longer period of a few years are preferred. **Companies accept deposits from the public as well as the members or employees or their relations.** In the latter case, the rate of interest offered is a little higher than that offered to the public. The cotton textile mills in the past has some bad experience with regard to public deposits. Whenever there was an economic crisis there was a rush for withdrawing deposits. Public deposits were used to be described as "fair – weather friends". But now-a-days, the situation is different. Public Deposit Certificates are not transferable but people like to invest in public deposits as the rates of interest are high and these are good as collateral security for loans.

Formerly, public deposits were controlled by the rules framed by the Reserve Bank of India but amendment of the Companies Act, in 1974, has incorporated the item and **the Government has been empowered to frame rules.** Accordingly, the Government issued in 1975 Companies (Acceptance of Deposits) Rules. These rules have been subsequently amended several times and have been made stricter. Prospectus has to be issued for inviting public deposits and all the rules regarding prospectus do apply. It is estimated that round about 10 to $12\frac{1}{2}\%$ of total capital of companies in India is covered by public deposits. Theoretically, this method of financing is not very dependable and economic because of heavy liability and high rate of interest. But, strangely enough, there is a high propensity among public companies to raise funds through public deposits. Even public undertakings are also accepting public deposits. A private company may accept fixed deposits.

3. Bank accommodation

Companies have to depend largely on banks for time to time accommodation. Banks in India are, by nature, commercial banks. Therefore, companies expect only short-term accommodation from them. But as the companies make long-term arrangement with banks, there is no dearth of bank accommodation on different counts. Such facilities are available continuously and recurrently. Every company develops some special understanding with one or more than one bank.

In the past, big industrialists in India also had control over big banks. Each industrial house had control over some big bank and so special favours could be obtained. For example, the Tatas had control over Central Bank of India Ltd. , the Birlas on United Commercial Bank Ltd., etc. Such system was helping concentration of economic power and indulging into misdirection of bank finance. A Social Control Order on bank credit was introduced in 1967 followed by nationalisation of major banks in 1969. Since then, the pattern of bank finance has changed.

A company gets bank accommodation in two distinct ways : (1) Overdraft, cash credit and loan. (2) Discounting of bills.

4. Institutional Finance

Since independence, **several financial institutions** have been established in our country like Industrial Development Bank of India, Industrial Finance Corporation of India, Industrial Credit and Investment Corporation of India, one State Financial Corporation in each State and Unit Trust of India. These corporations provide long-term loans known as term loans. Besides, Life Insurance Corporation of India extends help indirectly. The financial institutions also do underwriting function by guaranteeing sale of shares of a company at its formation stage. The Industrial Reconstruction Bank of India finances sick industries for their revitalisation. National Industrial Development Corporation and National Small Industries Corporation provide financial accommodation indirectly by assisting companies to buy machines on hire-purchase system.

5. Trade Credit

Whenever goods or services are bought on credit it means **use of others' capital** and it indirectly increases the working capital. Same can be said for all kinds of deferred payments. This is common fore every type of business concern including companies. Companies with reputation have greater credit-worthiness in the market.

CONTROL OF CAPITAL ISSUE

The control over the capital issue was introduced in India in 1943 under Defence of India Rules (a special measure introduced by the British rulers during the Second World War to safeguard their interest in War). The main purpose of the control order was to divert most of the capital available in India towards Government loans to help the War efforts. The order was replaced by a special Ordinance in 1946 and was finally replaced by Capital Issues (Continuance of Control) Act in 1947 which was amended several tIMes. At last, in 1956, the Act was passed in its final and permanent form. There are Rules also attached to the Act.

The Act is administered by the Ministry of Finance (Department of Economic Affairs) through a specially appointed officer called Controller of Capital Issues assisted by an Advisory Committee. **A company has to take permission of the Controller** before offering fresh securities in the market or issuing bonus shares under certain circumstances. The Controller will examine what for the capital is being raised. The main purpose of the whole control scheme is to see that the available capital resources are utilised in a balanced way and directed to agricultural, industrial and social developments as well as keeping a balance between production of capital and consumers goods. Another purpose of the Act is to see that there is neither over–capitalisation nor under-capitalisation and proper debt-equity ratio and other characteristics of capital planning are maintained.

Operation — Under the Act, a company has to take consent of the Controller of Capital Issues **under the following cases :** (a) Making an issue of capital outside India. (b) Making of issue of capital in India (subject to exceptions – see below), by a company whether incorporated in India or not. (c) Issuing in India any prospectus or other document inviting subscription or for publicity for sale of any securities. (d) Renewing or postponing the date of repayment of any security getting matured for repayment in India. (e) Accepting or giving any consideration for any securities in respect of any issue of capital.

But **there are some exceptions.** A company (other than a banking or an insurance company) need not take permission from the Controller of Capital Issues if it issues shares and/or debentures (other than bonus issues) the aggregate value of which does not exceed Rs. 50 lakhs in twelve months time. **In 1969, some relaxation has been made.** A public company has to submit a statement only to the Controller of Capital Issues within 30 days before the date of issue, provided the following conditions are fulfilled : (a) the debt equity ratio does not exceed 2 : 1 and equity-preference ratio does not exceed 3 : 1; (b) the shares are issued at par; (c) the rate of dividend does not exceed 9.5% and the rate of interest on debentures does not exceed 7.75% and (d) all calls are to be completed within 5 years. But companies coming under the Monopolies Restrictive Trade Practices Act will have to get permission of the Controller for any amount of issue.

Promoters of companies or people who are in the management of a company wanting to have fresh issue of shares, particularly as bonus issue, must be aware of the provisions of this Act.

CAPITAL GEARING AND CAPITAL PLANNING

A company needs capital at the time of its formation and continuously during its operations. At the initial stage, company needs both the fixed capital and the working capital. During its continuance, mostly working capital is necessary but fixed capital is also necessary for expansion. Generally, fixed capital is derived from inside capital while working capital from outside capital. But, at the initial stage both the fixed capital and the working capital would come from the inside capital because at the very beginning borrowing is difficult. A company needs very careful planning for its capital. The promoters make the planning at the time of formation and subsequently annual or periodical planning is done by the managerial people, mainly directors. Capital planning is a continuous process.

While planning for capital is taken up, **the following points have to be kept in mind :** (a) There shall not be over-capitalisation and under-capitalisation. If there is overcapitalisation, then capital will remain unnecessarily blocked and the volume of profit compared to the volume of investment becomes less. If there is under-capitalisation, the company may be ruined for want of funds.

(b) There must be proper provision for fixed and working capital. A good company with good amount of total capital may become bad of want for working capital. Again, what shall be the proportion between the two depends on the nature of the business. A manufacturing company obviously will require more fixed capital than that of a trading company.

(c) There must be a judicious mixture of inside capital and outside capital or between shares and debentures. Shares are generally equity shares, therefore, the ratio between the outside capital and inside capital is called the **debt-equity ratio.** The Central Government makes rules with regard to the debt-equity ratio. The capital planning is done primarily by the promoters (who become the first directors) and then by the directors. Both the groups prefer more of outside capital because of the following two reasons : (1) Interest is payable on such capital as is an admissible expense before calculating profit and then income-tax on it. (ii) The lenders have no voting rights and so the promoters (and directors), can have control over the company by having controlling amount of shares and voting rights. The position may be diluted by in – coming of more shareholders.

(d) Shares are of two types : Equity and Preference. A judicious mixture between the two is also necessary to attract different types of investors; speculative and conservative. Preference shareholders have restricted voting rights. The promoters (and directors) will like to sell a good amount preference shares so that they themselves can take control of equity shares and control of the company.

Capital gearing means to find out a correct proportion between these two types of shares. A company is like a motor car. A motor car really runs by rear wheels (equity shares) and not by the front wheels (preference shares). The function of the gear is to make the connection between the rear wheels and the front wheels so that both the sets of wheels rotate at the same rate and the car moves faster.

According to experts of financial management, three principles have to be followed for a scientific financial planning : (1) Debentures shall be issued only when the company is sure about constant future earnings so that the interest does not become a burden; (2) Preference shares are preferable when the earnings are not irregular but there is a standard average margin of profit; (3) Equity shares will depend on the expected earnings which are low and uncertain.

Mechanism of capital gearing — It is true that the promoters and the directors of a company will try to keep the share of equity capital as low as possible in the total capital, but it is not always practicable. There are many factors which influence the capital gearing. The whole mechanism depends on the following factors :

(1) **Trading on equity** — It means the strategy of keeping the share of equity capital as low as possible. If the share is kept low, then the existing equity shareholders can get maximum return on their investments. They will be eager to buy equity shares and the equity shares will be quickly sold. There will be satisfactory 'trading' on equity shares. When the proportion of borrowed capital is relatively large, it is called 'trading on thin equity'. Again, when the proportion of borrowed capital is relatively small, it is called 'trading on thick equity'.

The mechanism of 'trading on equity' can be explained by an example. Suppose a company needs a capital of Rs. 10,00,000.00. The expected profit is 10% or Rs. 1,00,000.00. The composition of the capital can be varied in different ways to maximise the gains of the equity shareholders. The promoters (and the directors) hold equity shares. If the company issues only equity shares, the rate of dividend is 10%. It is a very common or rather marginal return on investment. The composition can be made in the following proportions : (a) Preference shares of Rs. 1,00,000.00. at 6%. (b) Equity shares of Rs. 7,00,000.00. (c) Debentures of Rs. 2,00,000.00 at 6%. Then the profit is reduced to Rs. 88,000.00 because Rs. 12,000.00 is paid by way of interest to the debenture holders. Out of Rs. 88,000.00, Rs. 8,000.00 goes to the preference shareholders and Rs. 80,000.00 remains for the equity shareholders. The percentage of dividend on equity shareholders will be about 11.5%.

Trading on equity, however, has some **limitations** : (a) This mechanism can be adopted when there is possibility of good and steady earning; otherwise the interest will become a heavy burden. Repayment of the capital money also becomes a problem. If the company is in a competitive market, and the goods of the company have elastic demand, then any time sales may fall, stock may remain unsold and the company is at a tight corner. (b) The company must have good amount of assets and specially fixed assets which can be offered as security against debentures or any kind of loan. It pre-supposes that the company has a good amount of inside capital. (c) The nature of the business must not be of speculative type but of some steady type. (d) By general rule, the rates of interest become gradually higher for successive borrowings as the risk becomes bigger. Under no circumstances the rate of interest shall be allowed to be higher than the expected rate of profit. According to experts, the total interests payable by a company must not be more than 20% of its gross earnings.

(2) **Elasticity of capital structure** — The capital structure must be elastic. If there is predominance of preference share or debenture, the capital structure becomes rigid because they

cannot be increased as and when required as the commitments of the company will be higher and higher.

(3) **Keeping of control** — The promoters want to keep the proportion of equity shares high for retaining their control over the company. In that case the public character of the company is much lost. Preference shares cannot be easily sold in large numbers.

(4) **Need and mood of the investors** — For raising a large capital largest number of investors have to be tapped. There are people of different temperaments, some speculative, some conservative and some very conservative. Equity shares, preference shares and debentures are meant for them respectively. Some want good return, some prefer solvency. Some people want to take part in management while some are indifferent. The main criterion for the composition of the capital structure is to draw all types of investors.

(5) **Market condition** — Market condition is also another important factor. When the general economic condition is bad, the capital market becomes tight. Investors become shy and less speculative. On the other hand, when the general economic condition is good people become somewhat speculative as more money comes into the hands. The Bank Rate plays a big role as it determines the market rate of interest.

(6) **Period of investment** — For fixed capital, shares, both equity and preference, depending on the nature of the investors are the sources while for working and medium term capital debentures or public deposits are the better sources.

(7) **Cost of financing** — Cost is less to raise funds by selling of debentures or by public deposits than by selling shares. Interest or dividend are both considered as cost of raising funds because a company as a separate legal entity looks at interest or dividend as cost because both have to be paid.

(8) **Government's policies** — The Government may impose some rules with regard to debt-equity ratio. This has been already explained with Capital Issue Control. A banking company cannot issue any share other than equity shares.

COMPARISON OF DIFFERENT SECURITIES

A. By characteristics

(1) **Period of investment** — Equity shares are for long-term investment rather fixed since the money is not refundable until the company goes to liquidation. Preference shares are mainly for long-term or fixed but occasionally for medium term because some preference shares are redeemable. Debentures are for medium and short periods depending on their dates of repayment. Very rarely they are for long or fixed period when perpetual debentures are issued.

(2) **Price** — Equity and preference shares are of different denominations. But generally preference shares are of higher denomination like Rs. 100.00. Equity shares may be of Rs. 100.00, Rs. 10.00, Rs. 5.00 etc. Debentures are of higher denominations like Rs. 1000.00, Rs. 100.00 etc.

(3) **Mode of payment**— The price of equity shraes are generally payable by instalments. The price of preference shares and debentures are payable in full.

(4) **Expected returns** — Returns on equity shares are most uncertain and fluctuating. But the rate of return may be very high too. Preference shares have returns at fixed rate but not certain because profit is uncertain. Returns on debentures, are fixed and more or less certain. When a company is unable to pay interests on debentures there is a possibility of its liquidation and then the debenture-holders have a claim on the assets of the company.

(5) **Solvency** — No assets are charged against equity shares or preference shares but debentures may be of secured or mortgage type when there is fixed or floating charge on the assets of the company.

(6) **Ranking** — From ownership and management point of view, the equity shareholders belong to the owners group with full voting rights. Preference shareholders belong to the owners group with restricted voting rights. Debenture-holders have nothing to do with ownership and management. At the time of liquidation of a company, the equity shareholders rank last for refund of their money, the preference shareholders rank last but one and the debenture-holders second to the Government and unpaid employees.

(7) **Credit-worthiness**— Bigger the amount of equity capital, bigger is the credit-worthiness of the company. Preference cpital does not create any significant effect. Bigger the amount of debenture capital less is the credit-worthiness because the company is already overburdened and assets are charged.

(8) **Flexibility**— Capital raised through equity shares cannot be reduced except under special conditions. Capital raised through preference shares can be partially reduced by redemption of redeemable preference shares, if any. Unless there is any perpetual debenture, capital raised by debentures shall be reduced after some time.

(9) **Popularity** — Debentures are not very popular because of the following reasons : **From the side of lenders**— (a) The face value is generally high. (b) The amount is payable at a time. (c) The stamp duty for transfer is high. (d) The rate of interest is not very attractive. **From the side of companies**— Companies do not prefer debentures because (a) the subsequent credit-worthiness of the company is reduced and (b) there is a heavy commitment on the company. (c) There are strict rules made by the Central Government. Between equity and preference shares the choice depends on the temperament of the investors and how far the company can do trading on equity.

B. By advantages and disadvantages

Different types of shares and debentures have their advantages and disadvantages judged from the viewpoints of the company, the investors and the promoters.

Equity shares

Advantages — (1) Equity shares provide the main part of the inside capital and also the total capital of a company. It has the greatest significance in the capital structure. The Act makes compulsory for every joint stock company to issue such shares.

(2) This is the permanent source of capital of a company as it is non-refundable so long the company is in running condition. This part of capital provides the real financial strength of a company.

(3) Unless a company has a good volume of equity capital, the lenders will hesitate to afford any financial accommodation. Equity capital is the indicator of the credit-worthiness of a company.

(4) The equity shareholders bear the real risk and so it is possible to form companies with the help of genuine investors.

(5) Return on equity shares is not only fluctuating but uncertain. The equity shareholders, within the limits of the recommendation of the Board of Directors, themselves decide what shall be the rate of dividend or even whether dividend shall be at all declared or not. The decisions are taken in the interest of the company and to generate its inner financial strength. So, such shareholders are the real friends of the company. They not only take risk but also make sacrifice.

(6) Such shares do not create any charge on the assets of the company nor a company has to make any provision for redemption of such shares. Thus, these shares are absolutely free from any encumbrance to the company.

Disadvantages— (1) The equity shareholders have real control over the company. Various manipulations can be made by the group holding majority of the equity capital which may affect the interest of the company.

(2) Speculation on shares of a company in a stock exchange virtually means speculation on equity shares. It may be harmful to the company.

(3) A company cannot depend on equity shares only, otherwise the benefits of 'trading on equity' cannot be enjoyed.

(4) Over-capitalisation is generally caused through issue of excessive equity shares.

(5) When a small group of men hold the majority of equity shares, the real democratic character of a company is lost.

Preference Shares

Advantages — (1) These shares can be considered as safe investments because normally a company is able to pay the fixed rate of dividend which is low. Moreover, preference shares may be cumulative.

(2) The promoters gain because by issuing such shares of disproportionate voting rights some capital is raised but at the same time control of the company is not affected. The promoters take equity shares mostly.

(3) By issue of such shares the benefits of 'trading on equity' can be enjoyed.

(4) Such shares increase the capital of the company and its credit – worthiness though control of company is not affected.

(5) Such shares are rarely redeemable and so practically they do not create any charge on the assets of the company nor any responsibility for creating redemption funds.

(6) The conservative type of investors can be tapped to increase the share capital of the company. Redeemable preference shares are very attractive to them.

(7) Evils of over-capitalisation and under-capitalisation can be avoided by issuing redeemable preference shares.

Disadvantages — (1) The rate of dividend, though fixed, is very low; so generally such shares are not very attractive.

(2) Restrictive voting rights make such shareholders almost outsiders. Much of the attraction of investment in a body corporate is lost. They get full voting rights when they do not get dividend regularly. But at that stage the position of the company seems not to be happy.

(3) Priority over equity shareholders in respect of refund of capital at the time of liquidation of the company has practically no importance because when a company goes to liquidation it is not solvent and even unable to repay its creditors.

(4) In a private company such shares have practically no appeal because the number of shareholders is limited and there is little scope for classification of shares, equity shares being compulsory.

Debentures

Advantages— (1) Debentures are meant for the rentier class and to them debentures are good sources of investment.

(2) The money is not refundable and at the same time debentures are transferable like shares. Therefore, there is high liquidity.

(3) Investment is safe as most of the debentures are secured or mortgage debentures.

(4) Even people from longer distance can invest in a company through debentures as there is no question of attending meetings unless the company goes to liquidation.

(5) Companies are benefited by raising extra capital without any long term commitment nor by sacrifice of control on the company.

(6) Very conservative types of investors can be tapped for raising capital of a company.

(7) The benefits of 'trading on equity' can be fully enjoyed by issuing debentures.

Disadvantages —(1) Debentures create burden on the company because of liabilities for payment of regular interest irrespective of profits and repayment of the principal.

(2) Some assets of the company are generally charged affecting further credit-worthiness of the company.

(3) The face value of a debenture is generally high and the full amount is payable at a time and so investors may not like them.

(4) The stamp duty for transfer of debentures is also high making debentures unpopular.

(5) The rentier class now-a-days has many other better avenues of safe investments, e.g. units of the Unit Trust, Capital Bonds, etc.

STRUCTURE OF MANAGEMENT

Meaning— A company as an organisation is not a self-starter. It has to be managed. Since a company is an artificial person, it cannot manage itself. A company needs some human agency for its management. The Companies Act provides elaborate rules for the management of a company. As there are various components of company management there is a structure with a hierarchy. There are **different levels in the structure of company management.** Bigger the organisation larger will be the number of levels.

Provisions in the Act— What shall be the pattern of company management has been clearly and precisely given in the Companies Act. Accordingly, the structure is as follows :

A. Directors— Every company **must appoint directors** for its management. There shall be minimum two directors in a private company and minimum three in case of a public company. The Articles of every company shall provide what shall be the maximum number of directors in it. But if the number exceeds 12, in case of a public company, permission of the Central Government is necessary.

B. Others— In addition to directors, a company may appoint either a managing director or a manager. It means that if a company appoints a managing director then it cannot appoint a manager and vice versa. The term manager under the Companies Act has a special meaning which is different from the ordinary meaning of it.

In the past, India had a system of company management by appointing Managing Agents and subsequently also by Secretaries and Treasurers. From 1970, such system has been abolished because of various reasons.

In addition to directors and managing director or manager, a company appoints a large number of **executive staff** with managers (in ordinary sense) including general manager and area managers and their assistants to carry out the day-to-day managerial work. Besides, a secretary is appointed to look after the legal formalities of a company. According to the Companies Act, a company having paid-up capital of Rs. 25 lakhs or more **must appoint a qualified secretary** (i.e., a person who is a member of the Institute of Company Secretaries of India). In modern times, directors also function as executives and are called executive directors.

Overall management— The overall managerial powers are in the hands of the members of the company who are virtually the owners. All others are subordinate to them in a scalar chain.

4-Tier system— In short, the management structure of a company is a 4-tier system based on levels of authority. It is as follows :

Tier I — The members of the company, either shareholder members or otherwise. They exercise their authority through holding of meetings and taking decisions in the forms of resolutions by majority votes. They appoint the directors.

Tier II — The directors with or without managing director or manager as the case may be. The directors are entrusted to make policy decisions through holding of meetings and by majority votes and a substantial part of their powers is delegated to the managing director or the manager, if any.

Tier III — The general management staff including the general manager, departmental or area managers and the deputies. They get the decisions of the directors carried out or executed. They have some decision-making powers within limits but not policy-making decisions.

Tier IV — The junior level executives or supervisors taking charge of some sections or cells with further limitation of authority.

Under these managerial and executive personnel there are the clerical staff and the workers who really do the work physically. People belonging to this category and to Tier III and Tier IV are common with other forms of organisation like sole-proprietorship and partnership.

The structure of management of a (big) co-operative as a corporate body is the same.

In the Companies Act, the term 'Officer of a company' has a special meaning. The directors, the manager, the secretary, and even occasionally the auditor of the company come under this group. Such people are personally liable for any default of legal provision. The Act is very particular about the legal obligations of a company.

Further, **the Act uses the terms 'office' and 'place of profit' with special meaning** with regard to company management. 'Office' means any employment directly under the company while place of profit' is a position which is not directly under the company but the remuneration comes from the company itself directly or indirectly. A manager holds an office of profit but a supervisor appointed by a contractor, to look after day-to-day construction work – holds a 'place of profit' whose salary is paid by the contractor out of the payments made by the company to the contractor.

The Companies Act further provides that no public company can pay annually as managerial remuneration more than 11% of the net profits or maximum Rs. 50,000.00 when there is insufficient profit. Managerial remuneration means here remuneration paid to the directors and managing director or manager, if any. This remuneration is called commission. In addition, they can get monthly salaries, perquisites, provident fund and gratuity and medical benefits like other employees, if they render regular services like employees.

NATURE AND PROBLEMS OF COMPANY MANAGEMENT

A. Nature

Meaning— Nature of company management is studied from **two aspects : (a) the characteristics and (b) the procedure.** In short, the main characteristic of company management is that **by nature it is democratic.** As a company is an association of persons and is composed of members whose number may be as minimum as 2 (in case of a private company) and may be hundreds or even thousands (in case of a large widely – held public company). The management is carried out by majority decisions. The procedure of company management again has two aspects : **(a) taking of decision and (b) execution of the policies.** These are discussed below in detail.

Characteristics — The nature of democratic management of a company is indirect. The members of a company delegate their powers of management to their elected representatives called directors. For all practical purposes the directors are all-powerful in a company for day-to-day management of a company. Moreover, those people who hold majority shares or control the majority voting rights become directors and control the company. A chairman is elected for the Board of Directors. He seems to be the most influential person and has a command over the Board.

In a very small private company consisting of two or three members, all the members generally become directors. In such a case there is direct democracy. The members themselves vote for their directorship. Election becomes a formality only. Moreover, by special restrictive provisions in the Articles, the situation is made such that only a few persons get the opportunities to get elected.

Procedure — The main aspect of the procedure of management is **holding of meetings** for the purpose of taking decisions. There are many kinds of meetings in a company : (1) The meetings of the Board of Directors. (2) The meetings of different functional committees like Production Committee, Finance Committee etc. as well as Sub-committees, formed by the Board consisting of directors and also some senior members of the executive staff. (3) The meetings of the creditors at the time of winding-up of a company. (4) The meetings of a particular class of shareholders. (5) The company meetings or the general meetings of the members of the company. The last type of meeting is the most important. The Companies Act provides elaborate rules as to when and how different types of meetings shall be held. The Articles of a company may authorise a member to send his proxy instead of attending a general meeting personally.

Legal significance of meetings — At meetings, decisions are taken through passing resolutions by majority votes. Resolutions of general meetings are broadly of two types : (1) Ordinary — when the resolution has to be passed by simple majority of votes, even by the margin of one vote. Most of the resolutions are passed in this manner. (2) Special — when three-fourths of the total votes cast at a meeting are in favour of the motion. Any decision which affects the constitution of the company needs special resolution, e.g. alteration of the object clause in the Memorandum. At a Board meeting or a Committee meeting every resolution is an ordinary resolution. But there are cases where every director present at a meeting must agree.

Voting is done either by show of hands, one member casting one vote or by poll, i.e. each member casting his votes in proportion to his contribution to the paid-up capital. There are different voting rights for different members. When voting is by poll then it is cast with the help of ballot papers. At a Board meeting, however, each director has only one vote and that is cast by show of hands.

A meeting of a company must be **lawful and valid.** For a valid meeting the following conditions must be fulfilled — (1) A notice containing the date, time, place and agenda (items to be discussed at the meeting) of the meeting must be sent to each person entitled to receive it. (2) Quorum, i.e. the minimum number of members who must be present in person (not by proxy). The Articles shall provide what shall be the quorum of a company meeting or a Board meeting. The Act provides minimum acceptable quorum for a company meeting — two for a private company and any five for a public company. Proxies are not counted. At a Board meeting the quorum shall be one-third of the total number of directors or 2, whichever is bigger. (3) There must be a chairman at every meeting. (4) Proper minutes have to prepared in a Minute Book as evidence of the meeting.

For every meeting there shall be a chairman. Generally the chairman of the Board of Directors becomes chairman of all types of meetings of the company.

Rules regarding Board meetings

(1) There shall be at least one meeting in 3 calendar months or minimum four meetings in a year.

(2) Any director can call a meeting by giving written notice to every other director.

(3) Generally 7 days' notice is enough. The Act does not provide any definite rule.

(4) If there is want of quorum, the meeting is automatically adjourned to the next week, same day, same place and time for which no notice is necessary. Whoever is present at the adjourned meeting will make quorum.

(5) A resolution may be passed by circulating a matter among the directors at their residence for opinion without holding a meeting.

(6) Any matter concerning the business of the company can be discussed at a meeting.

(7) A director loses directorship if he does not attend a minimum number of meetings as specified.

Rules regarding members' or company or general meetings

(1) General meetings are **classified** in the following manner : (a) Annual General Meeting – every company must hold one AGM within six months from the date of year ending. (b) Extraordinary General Meeting – it means any other general meeting held in between two annual general meetings. Such a meeting can be called by the directors or by members themselves. (c) Statutory Meeting – every public company must hold a statutory meeting after one month and not later than six months from the date of commencement of business to discuss some matters as specified in the Act. This is practically an introductory meeting of the members who may be unknown to one another.

(2) The Act provides what shall be discussed at an annual general meeting. Any other business must be mentioned as Special Business with Explanatory Notes in the agenda of the notice.

(3) A notice must be sent to every member at least 21 days before the meeting. The notice is signed by the Chairman of the Board or by any director or the secretary authorised by the Board. Together with the notice, an Annual Report and a copy of audited Balance Sheet and Profit and Loss Account in case of annual general meeting and a Statutory Report together with a copy of audited up-to-date Statement of Account shalll be sent in case of annual general meeting and statutory meeting respectively. A proxy form, by which a member may authorise another person to attend the meeting on his behalf, also may be sent if there is provision for proxy in the Articles.

(4) The meeting must be held on a working day and during business hours.

(5) The meeting shall be held in the city or town or village where the registered office of the company is situated.

(6) If there is want of quorum at the meeting, the meeting will be adjourned next week, same day, same place and time (if that is a public holiday then on the day following). No fresh notice is necessary. Whoever present at the adjourned meeting will make the quorum.

(7) Within 30 days of the meeting, minutes must be prepared and confirmed by the Chairman (in his absence by any other director authorised by the Board) and the Minute Book shall be kept ready for inspection by the members during some fixed office hours at the registered office of the company.

(8) Some returns and copies of some specific types of resolutions have to be filed with the Registrar within a specific time.

Annual General Meeting – This meeting is vital for a company from the point of view of its management. At the meeting there are four types of business : (1) Consideration of the Annual Report and audited Final Accounts. (2) Declaration of dividend. (3) Election of director or directors to fill up vacancy or vacancies caused by the annual rotational retirement of director or directors. (4) Appointment and fixing of remuneration of the auditor. At the meeting the members get ample opportunities to criticise the performance of the company in the previous year and accordingly may or may not adopt the Report or the Accounts. They may replace the directors through election. Three copies of the Balance Sheet and three copies of the Profit and Loss Account together with a copy of Annual Return (containing the names, addresses of the members and directors as on the date of the annual general meeting) must be filed with the Registrar within 30 days and 60 days of the meeting, respectively.

B. Problems

Any democratic process has its own problems. **Democracy may not be based on equality.** In a company, different members may have different numbers of shareholdings and corresponding voting rights. As a result, a group of majority shareholders or voting right holders may oppress the minority group. Even one single person may exercise control. Election of directors or passing of resolutions become mere shows. It is rightly said that in many cases directors are elected, i.e. supported by majority votes but not chosen i.e. less number of members having larger number of votes elect their candidates though it may not be the choice of the majority of members.

Another great problem of company management is that it is full of very complicated and **rigid legal formalities.** It appears to be very expensive and very time-consuming. For small companies the whole procedure becomes a burden.

All the persons who become directors may not have educational background or academic qualifications to understand the complications and fineries of law and may make defaults which are punishable, sometimes very highly punishable. They have to depend on legal experts and to spend money for that. Here comes the importance of a qualified secretary. But he has to be paid a high remuneration. Holding of AGM for a big company is highly expensive.

ORGANS OF COMPANY MANAGEMENT

A. Director

Definition — The Companies Act defines a director as "director includes any person occupying the position of director, by whatever name called". Again, "any person in accordance with whose directions or instructions, the Board of Directors is accustomed to act shall be deemed to be a director of the company". A director is an 'officer' of the company. From the above statements it is clear the word 'director' is of little significance. It is the function of a director which is really important. Further, a single director has nothing to do unless authority is specially delegated to him (as a managing director). A company is managed by a Board of Directors.

Qualifications — A director must be a person (an individual and not a firm or a body corporate which is a person in the eye of law) having capacity to contract since the relationship between a company and its directors is contractual. A director is a member of the company. The Articles may provide that a director has to buy some minimum number of shares as qualification shares, but not exceeding Rs. 5,000.00 in case of a public company. The Act provides under what circumstances a person becomes disqualified to be a director, e.g. when a person is punished for any criminal offence. The Articles of a private company may provide additional reasons of disqualification, e.g. if he does similar business elsewhere.

Power — The powers lie in the hands of the Board. The Act provides how the powers can be exercised : (1) There are certain powers which can be exercised by Board meetings, e.g. approval of transfer of shares, making calls etc. (2) There are certain powers which can be exercised by the Board subject to the approval by the members, e.g. to buy or to sell any property of the company. (3) There are certain powers which require sanction by the Central Government, e.g. appointment of sole selling agent for the products of the company. Powers of directors are collective.

Position — Legally, the position of directors is partly of agent and partly of trustee. A company is an artificial person and so requires human agents for its running. The directors are the agents. On the other hand, the directors have the duty to protect the assets and property of the company and to that extent the directors are trustees. But they have more the characteristics of the agent because an agent is bound by the provisions of the Contract Act as are directors. In addition, directors have some powers given in the Companies Act.

The position of a director is low than that of a trustee. A trustee can buy or sell the trust property. Directors cannot without the approval of the members.

Duties — Each director has the duty to attend Board meetings regularly and to act honestly and diligently, and to disclose whether he has any personal interest in any contract with the company, whether he holds any office or place of profit in the company etc. One person cannot be director of more than 20 public companies at a time. He has to disclose to every company in how many other companies he is a director. Private companies are not counted. The duties are individual.

Rights — Every director has the right to attend Board meeting and to get sitting fees and to get any other remuneration for any extra service rendered by him. He can claim compensation if he is a wholetime or executive director and removed from his post not for his fault or not for liquidation of the company. Rights are individual.

Liabilities — In a limited liability company the liability of its directors may be made unlimited. A director is liable for his legal faults knowingly made, by which the company suffers. Liabilities are individual.

Types — There are two types of directors : (1) **Elected** — by the members. According to the Act, every company must have elected directors – minimum 2 in case of a private company and minimum 3 in case of a public company. At least two-thirds of the total number of directors of a company must be elected. At least one-third of elected directors must retire annually by rotation and the vacancies shall be filled up by elections at annual general meetings. The retiring directors are eligible for re-election. (2) **Nominated** — A company may appoint directors, nominated by (a) the Board of Directors temporarily, (b) the financial institutions as a condition of loan and (c) by the Central Government under different circumstances, e.g. when the Central Government receives complaint of oppression of minority group of members by majority group. The nominated directors are optional, non-retiring [except (a) above] and their number cannot exceed one-third of the total number of directors.

Remuneration — Every director shall get sitting fee for attending Board meeting, not exceeding Rs. 250.00 for one meeting. A director will get share in the commission out of the net profit. A director is not an employee of the company and he is not supposed to attend office regularly but an employee can be taken in the Board as a nominated director. In the latter case or when a director does some executive or technical work and attends office regularly he is entitled to get salaries, perquisites (free quarters, car, attendants etc.) provident fund, gratuity, medical benefits etc. The Central Government fixes the limits of salaries and perquisites of a director from time to time and every company has to follow the order. The Income-tax authorities may not allow all such expenses as deductible expenses.

B. Managing Director

Definition — The Companies Act defines a managing director as "managing director means a director, who, by virtue of an agreement with the company or of a resolution passed by the company in general meeting or by its Board of Directors or by virtue of its memorandum or articles of association, is entrusted with substantial powers of management which would not otherwise be exercisable by him, and includes a director occupying the position of a managing director, by whatever name called'. The Act further provides that "substantial powers" means more than mere office duties and a managing director has to function "subject to the superintendence, control and direction of its Board of Directors'.

Appointment becomes effective only when the terms and conditions of the agreement are approved by the Central Government. Whenever any change is made with regard to any of the terms and conditions, fresh approval of the Central Government is necessary. The approval is not necessary in case of a private company.

From the above statements **the following points come up** : (1) A managing director after all is a director and so all the points with regard to the qualifications, rights, duties and liabilities of a director shall apply to a managing director. (2) He can be appointed in many ways as mentioned in the Articles of the company : (a) By an agreement with the company. This is generally done in a public company. (b) By a resolution at a general meeting or a Board meeting. Generally these are the procedures of appointment in private company. (c) He has substantial powers which otherwise would not be exercisable. This is so because a single director has ordinarily no powers. 'Substantial powers' means not office duties, e.g. signing of cheques but sole charge of account. (d) By whatever name called – a managing director may be called Whole time Director, Governing Director or Resident Director etc. (e) Under the superintendence, control and direction of the Board of Directors – a managing director exercises substantial powers as much delegated to him by the Board. He is accountable to the Board for his performance of duties. (f) He alone can get maximum 5% of the net profits as his remuneration out of the maximum 11% of the net profits payable.

Because he has extra responsibilities, a managing director can get a big share in the total commission payable out of the 11% of net profits to the managerial personnel. In addition he can get salary, perquisites etc. The Act does not specify how many managing directors one company can appoint. Obviously, the number is 'one'. But the Act provides that one person cannot be managing director of more than two companies at a time unless permitted by the Central Government. He has to disclose to the second company that he is already a managing director of another company. If the appointment is by a Board resolution then all the directors present at the Board meeting of the second company must agree. The Act provides that one person cannot be appointed managing director for more than five years at a time. But he may be re-appointed.

A managing director is a **wholetime director** with substantial powers. There may be other wholetime or executive directors who do not have substantial powers.

C. Manager

Definition — The Companies Act defines a manager as "manager means an individual (not being the managing agent) who, subject to the superintendence, control and direction of the Board of Directors, has the management of the whole, or substantially the whole, of the affairs of a company and includes a director or any other person occupying the position of a manager, by whatever name called and whether under a contract of service or not".

The definition of a manager is **complicated.** The following points come up from the definition : (a) A manager is an individual and not necessarily a director (as in case of a managing director). But a director also may be a manager. He is not the managing agent. This is specifically mentioned because managing agency system has been abolished and there shall not be any confusion. (b) He has whole of the management or a substantial part of it. It has to be noted that a managing director cannot have the whole of the management. This is so because the Board of Directors empower the managing director with special authority who is himself a member of the Board having equal status with other directors. But an individual who has high managerial ability and special qualifications may be appointed as manager. This is a tendency today when professional management is coming into importance. (c) The manager is appointed either by virtue of a contract service or not. When an outsider as an expert is appointed as manager generally it is by a service contract. In case a director is appointed manager it may be by a resolution of the Board. The appointment of a manager in a public company or any change in its terms of appointment are subject to approval of the Central Government. (d) A manager alone can get maximum 5% of the net profits as his remuneration out of the maximum 11% of the net profits payable. In addition he can get salary, perquisites etc.

A manager must have capacity to contract. Disqualifications applicable to a director shall also apply. Ordinarily, one person cannot be manager of more than one company. But in case he is appointed manager of a second or more companies same rules, as related to the managing director, shall apply. Any change in the rules of the company with regard to appointment of manager requires approval by the Central Government. A manager is an 'officer' of the company as understood by the Act. In the commercial world, a manager holds a high executive position but after all his powers are limited. He carries out, with the help of others, the decisions of the top level management people – the proprietor, the partners or Board of Directors. But a manager under the Companies Act himself takes decisions.

D. Chief Executive

Generally, the managing director or the manager is the Chief Executive of a company, if there is such officer. In a company where there is no such officer the salaried General Manager may be the chief executive. There is no such specific term like Chief Executive in the Companies Act.

E. The Secretary

A company has to undergo various legal formalities. It is neither possible nor desirable that the directors shall do these though they have the formal responsibility for it. It is also not convenient to go to legal advisors at every step. For convenience, a company appoints a Secretary who has all the necessary qualifications and expertise. The Act provides that a company having paid-up capital of Rs. 25 lakhs or more must appoint a qualified secretary. A person has that qualification if he is a member of the Institute of Company Secretaries by passing the examinations conducted by the Institute. He is a high ranking executive and gets high remuneration. In many companies the secretary is taken in as a director. Or, a director may be the secretary particularly when he has the qualifications. He is an 'officer' of the company as understood in the Act. The Companies Act defines a secretary as "an individual possessing the prescribed qualifications appointed to perform the duties which may be performed by a Secretary under this Act and any other ministerial or administrative duties". Since a secretary can do administrative duties he may be entrusted with some decision-making authority.

REGULATORY MEASURES

Necessity — A company is a democratic organisation and everything is done there by the support of the majority. But according to the structure and composition of company legislation **majority in a company does not necessarily mean majority of the members.** As a result, there are ample cases where **manipulation by a few** is practised for personal gains at the cost of the company and of a large number of innocent members. In this context, necessity arises for some regulatory measures for keeping the democratic character of a company and to rouse public faith in such form of organisation. **This can be studied from the following aspects :**

(1) **Capturing majority shares** — The promoters are the first directors of a company and as such empowered to allot shares. The allotment of shares is done to such share applicants who are the friends or relations of the promoters or their "benamdars'. In this way control over the company is established having larger group holding of shares. Majority shares means at least 51% of the shares.

(2) **Capturing majority votes** — Capturing of majority shares is wanted to have control over majority votes. But majority votes can be captured without having majority shareholding. A large number of members do not come to general meetings. They can send proxies according to Law. The interested members get the proxy forms signed by the non-interested members in their favour.

(3) **Capturing controlling shares** — It has been found by experience that as a large number of members are disinterested in meetings (they are happy if good dividend is paid and the market value of shares remains high), it is enough for a group to serve their interests if they directly or indirectly have control over about 30 to 40 per cent of the total number of shares or voting rights. This is not very difficult.

(4) **Transferring funds of the company** — Funds of a company can be transferred by way of loan to or purchasing shares in other companies or firms in which directors are interested. In this way with the help of the money of a company personal businesses of the people in management in the forms of partnership firms or private companies can be flourished.

(5) **Entry of unscrupulous men** — By virtue of control over voting rights and taking advantage of democratic process, unscrupulous men may enter into the management of a company for the purpose of exploiting it.

(6) **Filling up remunerative positions** — Remunerative positions or 'offices' are being filled up by own men of the directors, like near relations for monetary gains as well as executive control over the company.

(7) **Gambling on shares** — People who are in the management of a company know many secrets. Taking advantage of that, they speculate on the shares of the company and even resort to gambling in stock exchanges.

(8) **Exploiting the loopholes of law** — Though company legislation is elaborate and comprehensive, there are loopholes in it and interested people take advantage of these loopholes.

Measures taken

Meaning — Exploitation of companies by interested men is not new. This has been existing for a long time. The Companies Act has been amended many times in India (also in U.K. and in other countries) to plug the loopholes and to impose regulatory measures on company management. During the British rule the major complaints for exploitation were levelled against the managing agents. In 1936, a major amendment was made of the Companies Act, 1913 to restrict the powers of the managing agents. It was also felt that directors were also not fully innocent. As a result the Companies Act, 1956, was enacted with great care introducing various regulatory measures in the interests of companies and their members as well as of the business as a whole and the public. The measures covered all the different aspects of company management from offering and allotting shares to day-to-day management and even winding up.

Types — The regulatory measures can be classified into two parts : (a) **Negative** — There are so many sections or provisions by which some restrictions are imposed on the managerial personnel of a company – the directors, the managing agents, and others. (Now, managing agents do not exist.) (b) **Positive** — Some alternative methods of management have been introduced. For example, as an alternative to the managing agents, a system of appointing secretaries and treasurers was introduced in the British model. (Now this system also is abolished.) Apart from the Companies Act, the Government sponsors or subsidises different management training institutes to produce professional managers to take the responsibility of company management in the country. It was thought in 1956 that the Act was comprehensive but, within a short time, many of its shortcomings and loopholes could be exposed mainly through the unscrupulous acts of insincere men in the field of company management. A number of amendments have been made already.

Some of the important regulatory measures are :

(1) **Allotment and transfer of shares** — Certain provisions have been made in the Act with regard to receiving subscriptions and making allotments when a company is formed so that no manipulation can be made at this stage. A chronological record of the applications of shares has to be made so that allotment can be made correctly on priority basis. No allotment can be started till at least 5 days pass from the date of issue of the prospectus so that fair opportunities can be available for the general public to buy shares. Moreover, some rigid restrictions have been introduced by the MRTP Act of 1969 to check transfer of shares to the hands of a group. If a company wants to issue fresh shares, the existing shareholders must be offered the shares first, proportionate to their share-holdings.

(2) **Shares with disproportionate voting rights** — In the past a company could issue shares with disproportionate voting rights (e.g. Deferred Shares) other than preference shares. Such shares with larger voting rights used to be taken by the promoters or their friends or relatives. Now, a public company cannot issue shares with disproportionate voting rights other than preference shares.

(3) **Loan by companies** — Under the present Act, an approval by special resolution by members is necessary if a public company wants to give loan to other companies under the same management and the total loan exceeds 10% of the aggregate of the subscribed capital and the free reserves of the lending company. Further, approval of the Central Government will be necessary if aggregate of the loans given to all companies exceeds 30% of the aggregate of the subscribed capital and free reserves of the lending company or exceeds 20% where all the borrowing companies are under the same management. There are, however, some exempted companies like a banking company. By this inter-company transfer of funds for some ulterior motive of the managerial people, if any, can be checked.

(4) **Investment by companies** — If a public company wants to invest in other companies by passing a resolution at a Board meeting, then all the directors present at the meeting must agree to it. Further, the whole scheme must be sanctioned by a resolution at a general meeting and approved by the Central Government when (a) the total investment exceeds 10% of the subscribed capital of the company where the investment is made or (b) the amount exceeds 30% of the investing company's subscribed capital or (c) exceeds 20% when all the companies where investment is made belong to the same group. Some companies are exempted from such restrictions like a banking company. By this restriction any attempt of concentration of economic powers through inter-company investment is checked.

(5) **Holding of remunerative positions** — Sanction by members by a special resolution is necessary for holding any office or place of profit carrying a monthly remuneration of Rs. 500 or more, by (a) a director (in any other capacity than a director or managing director); (b) by a partner of a director in any other firm; (c) a firm in which a director or his relative is a partner; (d) a private company in which a director is a member or a director; (e) a manager if there is any, of such private company; and (f) a relative of a director of the company. The Act provides a list showing 22 types of relatives. Permission of the Central Government is also necessary, if the monthly remuneration exceeds Rs. 3,000.00. If a director conceals the fact, the holder of the position loses his post when the fact is disclosed and all moneys received have to be refunded.

(6) **Disclosure of interests by a director** — If a director is interested directly or indirectly in any contract with the company concerned, he must disclose it at a Board meeting for approval and he has no voting right when the matter is discussed. Of course, there are some exceptions. A director loses directorship if he hides the fact.

(7) **Loan to directors** — If a director of a public company takes loan from the company without approval of the Central Government, he loses directorship.

(8) **Unlimited liability of directors** — The liability of directors in a limited liability company may be made unlimited by mentioning the fact in the Memorandum or by altering the liability clause of the Memorandum subsequently.

(9) **Unwanted persons in management** — The Act provides categorically the disqualifications of a person by which he is debarred from entering into the management of a company as a director, managing director or manager. He loses his post if he subsequently suffers from such disqualification.

(10) **Direct controlling measures** — The Act provides some direct steps for controlling mismanagement in a company : (A) **The Registrar** — The Registrar is empowered to ask for some additional information from the company other than the usual returns and reports, if he has any doubts and he may refer the matter to the Central Government for necessary action.

(B) **The Central Government** — (a) the Central government may ask for special audit of a company's accounts for such period or periods as wanted by the Government if the Government thinks that the company is managed not on sound business policy or against public interest. (b) The Central Government may appoint one or more inspectors to investigate in the affairs of a company when an application is made to the Government by some required number of members or the Registrar or the company itself passes a resolution in that respect or the Court makes such order. (c) The Central Government may make enquiry to find out who are the actual owners of a company when there are sufficient reasons for such enquiry. (d) The Government may send non-retiring nominated director on the Board of a company or may enforce a system of proportional representation on the Board when the Government receives complaints of oppression from a required number of members belonging to the minority group. (e) The Government may order that no change in the ownership of a company or its constitution of the Board of Directors will be effective unless the Government sanctions it when the Government receives a complaint from required number of members or even from a director. This, however, does not apply to a private company. (f) The Central Government may order for compulsory amalgamation of companies for their interests. (g) The terms of appointment or reappointment of a managing director of a public company require approval of the Central Government. (h) The Government may convert loan by public financial institutions into equity capital having full voting rights. (C) **The Court** — On receiving complaint from required number of members or from the Central Government the Court, if satisfied of the complaints, may order for (a) regulation of the company's conduct in future ; (b) the purchase of the shares or interests of any members by other members or by the company (leading to reduction of capital); (c) termination or modification of any agreement with managing director or manager or any director; (d) setting aside any transfer, delivery, execution of any act, payment, etc. by the company; (e) any other just and equitable provision. The Court may also order for any compromise when there is any dispute among members to save the company from liquidation. The Court may also order for reconstruction of a company or amalgamation with any other company. The Act empowers the Central Government and the Court to take necessary measures for so many reasons : (a) if some minority group of members of a company suffer in the hands of a majority group; (b) if the company is managed in such a manner which is against its interest or against the interest of the business to which the company belongs or against the interest of the public.

(11) **Making of Rules** — In addition to the provisions of the Companies Act, the Central Government is empowered to make Rules in connection with functioning of a company. For example, rules regarding the remuneration of directors or acceptance of public deposits etc. Besides, there are other Act which have bearing on the Companies Act, e.g. the Capital Issues (Control) Act, Monopolies Restrictive Trade Practices Act, etc. The Companies Act empowers the Superme Court to make rules in respect of winding up of companies, after consulting the High Court.

(12) **Penal measures** — The Act refers to various penal measures as punishments for violation of the provisions of the Act by the promoters, directors, managers and such other 'officers' of companies. The punishments include fines on daily basis like Rs. 50.00 per day or lump sum of money up to Rs. 5,000.00 and imprisonment running up to 7 years. Fine and imprisonment may run together. Maximum punishments are provided for any attempt to defraud the general public either by making untrue statement in prospectus or inducing anybody to give credit to a company knowingly that the company is going to be wound up. Severe punishments are provided for defaults, misfeasance, fraud, etc. during the process of winding up of a company. Even the promoters can be brought to book. Law can disqualify an offender not to enter into management of any company for some time. The Court can, however, order for relief.

(13) **Other measures** — There are various other measures for regulating the company affairs. The Company Law Board, which is a new development in company legislation for reg-

ulating company affairs, is entrusted with powers of a court. Foreign companies are increasingly brought under the control of Indian Companies Act.

Conclusion — In India, the regulatory measures on companies have great importance because a large section of the investors in companies lack the necessary educational background and knowledge about company law administration falling easy prey to unscrupulous and designing promoters and directors or their associates. Further, we do not find in India any strong organisation of the investing public. There is no attempt on behalf of the Government to educate the general public in this respect. Some critics are of the opinion that members of the public should be allowed to participate in the equity capital of public sector bodies corporate for a healthy growth of investment practice. The concept of Joint Sector is a step towards that direction.

CHANGING PROFILE OF COMPANY MANAGEMENT

Background — The concept of corporate form is a recent affair. Through the process of evolution and growth of large-scale business with proportionate large risks the concept of company with limited liability **has come into existence hardly 150 years back** The origin has historical significance. At the early stage there was no codification of the structure, operation and management of companies. Gradually legislations on companies have come into existence first in U.K. and then in other countries. Company form of organisation **is a non-traditional form of organisation. Therefore, its pattern of management has no basis on any social custom or institution. It is mostly formal as codified in statutes.**

The second important factor influencing the pattern of company management is 'experience'. The experience has two aspects : (a) The people in the process felt the need of certain definite rules for the day-to-day affairs of a company. (b) The Government realised that certain rules were necessary for company management as public money would be involved.

The company form of management basically is a product of the capitalistic system of economy. With the passing of time, the capitalistic system of economy has been facing criticisms and challenges. If one of the major drawbacks of the system is exploitation of many by a limited few with economic power, the company form of organisation itself can be reckoned as a tool of exploitation. Therefore, **changes in the pattern of company management are being brought about all over the capitalistic world to give it more and more a democratic shape.** Thus, amendments of company law is a common feature in evey country where such law prevails. U.K. gives the lead in this respect, followed by others. A similar state of affairs we find in India. In our country our company law is very much influenced by the English law.

A CASE FOR INDIA

The Past — The concept of company was **introduced by the British rulers** in India as early as in 1850 when Indian Companies Act was passed. The main motive of the British people behind formation of companies in India was **to exploit Indian resources** through such organisations. They could do it by encouraging Indians to invest capital in companies as far as possible but keeping the control of the companies in their own hands. For this purpose the Britishers introduced a unique system of company management through the Managing Agency system. Under this system a company is managed by an individual or a firm or a body corporate, appointed by virtue of a contract to manage the company against some consideration. The consideration includes a share in the profits of the company or a lump–sum monthly remuneration or both. The Managing Agency firm has the expertise and experience in management by which a company can be benefited.

The Managing Agency system conceptually sounds nice. In fact, whatever industrial development that could take place in India before independence was mainly due to the efficient services of the managing agents. **They served Indian companies in three distinct capacities :**

(1) **Manager** — The Managing Agents took **charge of management of companies** on behalf of the directors who did not have the knowledge of the technicalities of company management. This was very natural because, to them, the company form of organisation was purely non-traditional form.

One Managing Agent used to manage a number of companies at a time and by that economies of concentration could be enjoyed. The office of each of the company under the same managing agent could be located at the same place for greater economy and control.

(2) **Financier — The Managing agents could provide finance to companies directly and indirectly.** (a) **Directly** — They used to participate into equity capital of the managed companies and also provided loans at a rate of interest lower than the bank rate. (b) **Indirectly** — They stood as guarantors to loans given by banks. At that time, banks in India were mostly foreign banks who did not advance money to Indian companies unless some foreign Managing Agent stood as guarantor. The Imperial Bank of India, as the biggest bank, was a British bank wanting such guarantee and that is one of the reasons for which it was nationalised in 1955 to form the State Bank of India. Further, if any Indian company could have a renowned foreign Managing Agent, the goodwill of the company would enhance immediately and shares could be sold quickly. This was the indirect support to the equity capital by a Managing Agent.

(3) **Promoter** — The Managing Agents also took the initiative of promoting companies. They played the role of professional promoters in India, taking, simultaneously, responsibility of management. The Managing Agents wanted to promote companies for their own interests because they would get opportunities for more contracts of management. India, however, was benefited in the process as more companies were formed for industry or trade or commerce.

At the beginning, all the Managing Agents were foreigners. **Gradually, some Indian businessmen entered the field.** Calcutta was the centre of activities of foreign Managing Agents. All the big merchant offices like Bird & Co., Balmer Lawrie & Co., Andrew Yule & Co., Mcleod & Co., Shaw Wallace & Co., Duncan Brothers & Co., Martin Burn & Co., etc. all were Managing Agency companies concentrating their business in Jute, Coal, Tea and Engineering and Shipping industries. Indian Managing Agents were mainly Bombay-based, concentrating in Cotton Textile industry. The Iron and Steel Industry was divided. Tata & Sons, Birla Brothers, etc. were the leading names among Indian Managing Agency houses.

Although the Managing Agents have contributed a lot in the process of industrial growth in India, they have exploited the Indian companies indiscriminately and have amassed huge wealth. Thousands of crores of rupees have been taken away by the foreigners from India, either openly or secretly, as Managing Agents. The main source of wealth of the big Indian industrialists has been such exploitation. It is a matter of pity and shame that Indian Managing Agents were worse in comparison with their foreign counterparts in respect of exploitation. **Some of the modes of exploitation were :**

(1) Making secret profits by setting up firms in other names as sole selling agents of the products of the companies or as main suppliers of goods to the companies.

(2) Filling up the remunerative posts in the companies by friends and relatives.

(3) Taking loan at a low rate of interest from one company having surplus fund, and lending it to another company at a higher rate of interest and thereby making margin of profit.

(4) Capturing the Board of Directors of a managed company by sending nominee directors as a condition of contract as well as by winning of some seats through election.

(5) Speculating on shares of the managed companies in the stock exchanges.

(6) Managing a large number of companies (even 20, 30, 40) at a time and thereby developing an economic empire.

(7) Charging a high rate of commission out of the net profits as remuneration together with office and other allowances.

(8) Entering into almost permanent contracts with companies for their management, turning them into own properties.

For a long time severe criticism was being levelled against the Managing Agents and there was a continuous demand for regulating their powers. In 1936, an amendment was made to the Companies Act of 1913 to regulate the powers of the Managing Agents. Such amendments were not very effective because of the advent of the Second World War diverting the interests of the British rulers. Moreover, the Managing Agents renewed their activities by setting up many new industries for war supplies. In fact, this was the time when the Managing Agents practically minted money.

The Present — Since independence, things have changed a lot. **The Bhabha Committee, appointed to draft the new Companies Bill,** had to exert much to find out suitable provisions for company management. The Bill was discussed threadbare for about two years in Parliament before **the Companies Act was finally enacted and made effective from 1.4.1956.** The main debate was on regard to the future of the Managing Agency system. Some were of the opinion that the system should be abolished forthwith. Sri C.D. Deshmukh, the then Finance Minister, made a very valuable comment on the issue. He said, 'The Managing Agency system should be mended and not ended'. That was really the only way out. If the system was abolished forthwith a vacuum would have been created in the field of company management in India, there being no immediate alternative to fill it up. In principle, it was accepted that companies, in their interests, should be managed by the directors directly. But Indian businessmen at that time did not have that educational background nor they had the experience to take up the responsibility. In the meantime, one important event happened. Foreign Managing Agency companies were largely Indianised.

There was no denying the fact that even the directors of Companies were not above – board. A tendency of exploiting companies also had gripped the directors, specially through the practice of common directorship between managing and managed companies. Majority of Indian companies were (and even today are) private companies. The main reasons are : (a) most of the companies in India are of small size and (b) the shareholders prefer to form private companies instead of partnership firms as the company form of organisation is a better tool for exploitation without personal liabilities of the owners. Even in public companies, directors come from a group or coterie holding majority or at least controlling amount of shares and the directors behave like proprietors.

The pattern of company management in India, as envisaged in the Companies Act, is as follows :

(1) **In respect of directors :** The Act provides 72 Sections to define the powers, rights, duties and liabilities of directors. Perhaps the largest number of Sections have been devoted to directors alone. Restrictions have been imposed on the powers of the directors, their rates of remuneration and their exploiting tendencies, control over allotment and transfer of shares, through use of company funds and offices or places of profit. Not only the directors but their relations or partners or firms and private companies in which they are interested have been brought under the purview of the restrictive provisions.

(2) **In respect of Managing Agents :** Two types of provisions in 54 Sections were there : negative and positive. **Negative provisions** – (a) Restrictions were imposed on the period of appointment, rate of remuneration, number of companie, one Managing Agent could manage at a time, the extent of representation of the Board of Directors of the managed company, taking of loans from the managed company etc. (b) The Government was empowered to abolish the system gradually as and when found necessary. **Positive** — An alternative system of management was introduced like appointment of Secretaries and Treasurers (in the British model) or Manager to break the monopoly of the Managing Agents in the field of company man-

agement. The Act contained restrictive measures for them but the restrictions were somewhat liberal compared to those for the Managing Agents.

The new Act was partially successful in curbing the powers of the Managing Agents. But many of them wanted to take advantage of the alternative system of appointing Secretaries and Treasurers, by changing their formal appointments. In the meantime, however, socio-economic changes could be witnessed in the country. Big public sector undertakings came into existence. Management training institutes, sponsored or supported by the Government, started producing professional managers. The business community got the coming generation entering into the fields of higher and technical education. The educated section of the community found increasing interest in business, taking advantage of various State incentives and subsidies. Companies were found to prefer management directly by directors and trained personnel. The importance of the Managing Agents receded much and finally the system together with the newly introduced system of appointing Secretaries and Treasurers were abolished with effect from 3.4.1970.

During the early seventies, the Government took certain drastic measures like nationalisation of big banks, setting up of large public companies and corporations, tightening up of the position of big industrial houses, introduction of the Joint Sector system, nationalisation of general insurance business etc. and all these in the name of socialism. In fact, some big industrial houses, being favoured by the ruling party, got richer expanding their business empire. The loopholes of the socialistic economy have become the main sources of exploitation. **Lobbying by the big industrial houses in the administration** has become a significant feature in India. Political parties and individual political leaders have to depend on the **funds of businessmen**. Though there is total ban on contribution by companies to political parties, such contributions in secret forms cannot be avoided. Businessmen doing favour ask for favour in exchange. There is a tug-of-war between the legislators who try to plug the loopholes of the Companies Act (and other allied Acts) to curtail the manipulations by the management of companies and the people in the management representing the vested interest class who try to hoodwink legal provisions. As a result, the Companies Act is becoming fabulously voluminous and complicated, much to the benefit of the legal practitioners and allied professionals. The public sector having failed to achieve the desired success, the management in private sector companies are getting an upper hand. The rich multinational companies are playing their tricks. Theoretically, more and more widening of the gap between ownership and management is envisaged.

The Future — The future is uncertain and virtually unpredictable but the present casts its influence on future and puts up some indicators by which the future trend can be anticipated. With the spread of education, both general and technical, **the investors are getting more and more conscious of their position. Educated people are entering into companies** either by virtue of share – holdings or as professional managers. Companies managed by the professional managers have much objective rationality in its management process achieving near full separation between the ownership and management. **A new profession is going to flourish in the market which is Management Consultancy.** Groups are organised with engineers, accountants, cost accountants, management experts and others to advise companies on various related management matters. Many big companies are having a separate division for management services of its own. The Association of Management Consultants of America (AMCA) defines Management Consultants as "Individuals qualified by education, experience, technical ability and temperament to advise and assist on a professional basis in identifying defining and solving specific management problems involving the organisation, planning, direction, control and operation of enterprise. They serve the enterprise as impartial, objective advisors and are not employees of the enterprise". There are basically four kinds of relationship existing between an enterprise and the management consultant : (a) supplying information; (b) providing technical service; (c) managing with objective point of view ; (d) diagnosing problems and suggesting remedies. **Management is recognised as**

a separate discipline through the management consultancy services. The system is fast becoming popular. The Government also is seeking the help of professional Management Consultants. At the same time, the Government itself has started consultancy business in the public sector, e.g. MECON, WEBCON etc.

With the expansion of the number of **management training centres** scattered in almost all the cities in the country, more and more professional managers will be available. Most of the institutes, however, imitate the American techniques of management not suited to Indian concerns. Management training suited to Indian condition has become highly imperative. Concurrently, all attempts have to be made for checking all kinds of malpractices in the field. But law cannot make man perfect. No amount of legislative control can stop the malpractices. Self-control is the best control.

FUNCTIONS OF A BOARD OF DIRECTORS

Significance — It is desirable that a company should be managed directly by its Board of Directors and the directors must be really chosen by the members in a democratic way as their true representatives and not merely be formally elected by votes. **Modern time is a time of administration by committees or 'plural executives'.** In the Government, the cabinet of ministers, in educational institutions the governing bodies, in every association the managing committee, and, similarly, the Board of Directors in a company hold the position of the plural executives. Since a number of members of a company may be very big and they may be scattered at different places, they have to elect the directors who will assemble together and manage the company.

Composition of a Board — George Terry defines a Board of Directors as "A board of directors is legally created by the papers of incorporation of a corporation, and by them it is given the authority to exercise the powers of the corporation, limited by any conditions set forth in the corporation's by-laws". A Board is constituted by elected as well as nominated directors. "At the one extreme is the Functional Board and at the other Policy Board." A **Functional Board** consists of full – time members who are geneally directors by profession having the expertise and experience to take charge of day-to-day management of companies. They are good executives but may not be competent for policy making. They are generally professional managers nominated on the Board. A **Policy Board** generally consists of a few part-timers whose function is determination of policy and creation of leadership. They delegate the executive authority to the full-time executives. In most of the Indian companies the Boards are Policy Boards consisting of directors representing the members and owners deciding the policies of the company without having the technical knowledge of actual execution or operative management although they do the day-to-day executive jobs. This is specially true in private companies. A Policy Board is more subjective in outlook while a Functional Board is supposed to be objective. **An Ideal Board** is that which makes a combination of both types of elements because neither a pure Functional Board nor a pure Policy Board can be effective. The former type cannot formulate policies correctly and so perfect execution has no value. The latter type gets biased with self-interest while trying to execute the policies. The size of a Board also must not be very big. In public sector companies or corporations, the Board is generally a Functional Board because the policies are determined by the Government from behind.

Functions — Brech has summarised the functions of a Board of Directors as "To determine policy and check up on progress towards its fulfilment; to ensure that the company's legal obligations are carried out; to watch over the interests of the shareholders." Accoring to Drucker – "A business enterprise must have a government. In fact, it needs both an organ of overall leadership and final decision and an organ of overall review and appraisal." The Board of Directors is that organ.

Taking into consideration of all the different views, the functions of a Board of Directors are as follows :

(1) **Determination of enterprise objectives** — The Board shall determine the objectives as well as the broad policies within the framework of which the objectives will be achieved.

(2) **Selection of executives** — The Board shall appoint the executive officers by following a proper course of selection, so that the objective of the company can be achieved within the policies or guidelines set up by the Board. The Board may also appoint the Chief Executive or the Managing Director. In USA he is called the President and is followed by Vice-Presidents each of whom takes charge of a particular division.

(3) **Approval of budgets** — Budgets have to be prepared for the different plans or programmes taken up. The departmental heads as senior executives prepare their departmental budgets which have to be co-ordinated and finalised by the Board. The Board is assisted by the finance manager or such other expert staff.

(4) **Checking results** — The Board shall check up the performance periodically and verify the actual performance with the plan. This is the control function of the Board.

(5) **Recommendation of dividend** — The Board shall recommend the rate of dividend payable on equity capital. Such recommendation shall be made after considering the net financial position of the company, looking at its solvency. The main object shall be maximisation of wealth.

(6) **Securing long range stability** — A company shall continue to exist and prosper. This should be the main object of management by the Board. Nothing can be done knowingly which hampers the stability of the company. The Board shall steer the company through the waves of changing circumstances. Koontz and O'Donnel have described the functions of the Board as "husbanding of the assets of the corporation for the benefit of the stockholders".

Gradual erosion of the Board

A company is an artificial person and a contemplation of law. It requires some human agents as directors (by whatever name called) under whose instructions and by whom it shall function. The legal necessity of a Board cannot be refuted. The question arises how far does a Board actually manage a company. Usually the Board relies much upon the executive officers and outside agencies or advisors. As day-by-day opportunities for management training are being increasingly available, **the Boards are depending on more and more professional managers.** A Board is, therefore, often called "a legal sham" or "a mere showcase", or "a rubber stamp", or "ciphers" or "puppets".

Drucker has aptly said, "To the law, the Board of directors is the only organ of the enterprise. And in one form or another such a 'Board' exists in every industrial country, even in Soviet Russian law. In reality, the Board, as conceived by the law maker, is at best a tried fiction." It is perhaps not too much to say that **it has become a shadow king.** This is really what is meant by a "gradual erosion" of the directors. **The causes of the gradual erosion are as follows :**

(1) There is a separation between ownership and management and so the shareholders who have no opportunity to look after the company elect directors for its management. But the directors depend mostly on the executives.

(2) Holding of Board meetings is expensive and takes time to arrange it and so the directors avoid meetings.

(3) Modern management is so complicated that it is not possible for ordinary people to do it. Therefore, the Board has to depend on outsiders.

(4) A Policy Board, which is most common, cannot carry out management in its true form.

Conclusion — The whole problem can be solved by making the Board a combination of Policy Board and Functional Board. That is the future trend.

Summary

Promotion, formation and commencement of business — Promotion is not mere starting. It includes imagination and action. Business promotion has four components : (a) discovery of business opportunities; (b) organisation of funds property and managerial ability; (c) setting up a business concern ; (d) developing a situation of making profits out of the concern. The term promoter is a commercial term. Functions of a promoter are : (a) to visualise a business; (b) to bring some other persons with him; (c) to get advice from experts; (d) to get finance for promotion; (e) to get support from the investing public. He needs imagination, initiative, judgement and leadership. Promoters are of three types : (a) Particular – such a promoter promotes one particular business. (b) Occasional – He, after promoting one business, promotes sister concerns. (c) Professional – He always makes plans for new business. In modern times the State itself plays the role of a promoter. **Floatation** is used to mean promotion, though precise meaning of it is raising of funds for business. **Formation** – More or less it includes the legal formalities for promoting a business. **Commencement** — of business to start the actual business activities.

Promotion of a company : It has two aspects, commercial and legal. The Commercial aspect includes : discovery of an idea, investigation in the market about the possibilities of success of the business, assembling of all information and date about the business and then preparing the plan, negotiating with the Government for licence, if any, negotiation with financial institutions and foreigners in case of foreign financial or technical assistance, and procurement of initial finance. The legal aspect includes : preparation and filing of documents like the Memorandum and the Articles of the company, with the Registrar of companies, payment of filing and registration fees, submission to the Registrar actual address of the registered office, filing by a public company (i) a list of first directors, (ii) their consent letters to take qualification shares, if any, and to act as directors and a copy of the terms and conditions of the appointment of managing director, if any. The Registrar issues the Certificate of Incorporation. A private company can start business immediately. A widely held public company has to issue a Prospectus inviting the public to buy shares in and/or debentures of the company and a copy of Prospectus has to be filed with the Registrar. A closely held public company has to submit a Statement in lieu of Prospectus showing the allotment of shares at least 3 days before the allotment. Permission of the Controller of Capital Issue may have to be obtained. The Registrar will issue the Certificate for commencement of Business when he is informed that (a) the minimum subscription (as mentioned in the Prospectus) has been raised and the directors have paid for their shares. Now a public company can start business.

Documents of a company — A company has to prepare some documents the models of which are attached to the Companies Act as Tables. (1) **Menorandum of Association** — This is the fundamental document by which a company is known to the outside world. Every company must prepare its own Memorandum. It has five clauses : (a) Name – A company cannot use a name which is similar to that of an existing company or containing any words meaning Government patronage. A public company must end its name with 'Limited' and a private company with 'Private Limited'. (b) Address – It means the name of the State where the company is registered, (c) Objects – The purposes for which the company is formed. The objects shall be shown in two parts : main and others. This is the most vital clause. A company cannot do any act which is not mentioned in the object clause. (d) Liability – The nature of liability of members whether limited by shares or by guarantee or by shares and guarantee or unlimited liability. (e) Capital – This clause will depend on the nature of the company whether having share capital or guarantee capital etc. (f) Subscription – The promoters will sign with their description and number of shares taken and the signature of a witness. The first three clauses are called condition clauses which can be altered by a special resolution (three-fourth majority) and sanction by the Central Government (name), and the Company Law Board (address object). Liability and capital clauses can be altered by the members by special resolution but for reduction of share capital permission of the Court is necessary. (2) **Articles of Association** – It contains all the internal affairs of a company — shares and their classifications, rights of shareholders, powers of directors, meetings, accounts etc. The directors can do what is not mentioned in the Articles but they have to be ratified by the members. Any clause in the Articles can be altered by a special resolution provided it does not go against the Memorandum and the Act. Outsiders are not interested in this document. (3) **Prospectus** – Whenever a widely held public company wants to issue shares and/or debentures, this document has to be issued. In contains the summary of the Memorandum and the Articles, the commercial aspects of the company, the names and descriptions of the directors, bankers, auditors, sharebrokers etc. and a share application form. Prospective investors are interested in this document and will scan the document before deciding to invest, from the following viewpoints : (a) Whether the company is economically viable. (b) The performance report of the company when an existing company wants to raise fresh capital. (c) The Capital structure of the company – different classes of shares and debentures. (d) How far the management will be efficient and effective. (e) Voting rights of members, terms of repayment of debentures etc. (f) Reputation of the bankers, auditors, sharebrokers etc. concerned. (g) Any chance of nationalisation of the business. (h) Position of other company if there is a proposal for amalgamation, merger etc. (i) Terms of payment of share price. (j) Investment by promoters and directors. (k) Whether shares are to be enlisted in a stock exchange.

Capital structure — Every company needs capital. Primarily the members supply the capital with which the company as an artificial person carries on business and acquires property which do not belong to the members but to the company itself. The members contribute to the capital in different proportions. A company needs both long-term and short-term capital. The capital structure is made of two components : Own or inside capital and loan or outside capital. **Inside Capital** is supplied by members who enter into the company's ownership and get share in the profits as dividend. This is called share capital for a company limited by shares. Shares are transferable. Share price is payable in instalments — application allotment and calls. A share certificate is issued to every shareholder and his name appears in the Register of Members to be maintained by a company. Then a shareholder become a member and gets voting rights at meetings. Shares are broadly divided into two parts : (a) **With disproportionate voting rights or Preference Shares** – Such shareholders get dividend first at a fixed rate out of the profits, get repayment of capital before other shareholders when the company goes to liquidation and have voting rights only on matters which concern their interests. It is optional for a company to issue such shares. Preference Shares can be classified into – Cumulative, non-cumulative, participating and redeemable. (b) **With proportionate voting rights or Equity Shares** – Such shares are compulsory. Such shareholders get dividend at fluctuating rates out of the profits after the Preference Shares have been paid, repayment of share capital after the Preference shareholders have been repaid but they have full voting rights on all matters of the company. The Board of Directors recommend the rate of dividend but the members of a company may accept the rate or may reduce the rate but cannot increase the rate. Sometimes accumulated profits of a company are capitalised by offering **Bonus Shares** to the members in proportion to their holding of shares. This is called ploughing back of profit. Normally, when an existing company issues fresh shares they are offered to the existing shareholders on pro rata basis to make their acceptance within 15 days. Such shares are called **Right Shares.** Ploughing back of profit is good because it generates self-sufficiency in capital. **Value of shares** – Shares have three types of value. **Face Value** as written on the share certificate. **Intrinsic value** – as calculated by deducting the total liabilities of the company from its total assets and dividing the difference by the number of shares. **Market value** —is the value at which it can be sold or purchased in the market. **Evidence of shareholding** – A company must issue **Share Certificates** as evidence of shareholding by a shareholder. A share certificate contains the number and value of shares, other particulars and the name of the shareholder. A share certificate can be transferred by endorsement and delivery subject to the rules of transfer given in the Act and in the Articles of the company. Alternatively, a company may issue a **Share Warrant** provided it is mentioned in the Articles and the shares are fully paid. A share warrant contains all the details as in a share certificate except the name of the shareholder. A share warrant can be transferred by mere delivery. A share warrant holder is not a member of the company. Shares can be issued at par, i.e. at its face value or at a premiun, i.e. higher than its face value and at a discount, i.e. lower than its face value. In the last case, permission of the Company Law Board is necessary. Normally no interest is payable on share capital but it may be allowed by the Central Government when the business is such that dividend can be payable after a long time. **Outside Capital** — is supplied by outsiders like banks or financial institutions in the forms of short or long term loans, the debenture-holders by buying debentures and the public by keeping fixed deposits in the company. All these people do enter in the ownership of the company and get fixed rates of interest as well as repayment of capital after the agreed period. **Debentures** are like shares and are transferable. Debenture bonds look like share certificates. Debentures are of many types : Registered – When the names of the debenture-holders are written on the debenture bonds. Such bonds are transferable by endorsement and delivery. Unregistered – When the names of the debenture-holders are not written on the bonds. Such debentures are transferable by mere delivery. Mortgage or Secured – When some assets of the company are charged against the debentures. Naked or unsecured — when no such assets are charged. Perpetual – debentures are mostly redeemable but exceptionally there are perpetual debentures repayable only when the company goes to liquidation. Debentures can be repaid in many ways : redemption on a fixed future date, repayment by annual instalments, repayment by annual drawing, i.e. by lottery. Some debentures are repaid every year, redemption by re-purchase of the debentures by the company and redemption by converting them into shares. **Public deposits** — a company may accept fixed deposits for few years from the public by paying high rate or interest, even higher than bank interest. The Companies Act has recently imposed some restrictions on public deposits. **Bank accommodation** — a company can get short term financial accommodation from banks in the forms of overdraft, cash credit and loan as well as by discounting or bills. **Financial institutions** — provide long-term loans or even subscribe to the equity capital. The Central Government is empowered to convert by order any loan given by a public financial institution into equity capital and by that total capital of the capital clause can be increased.

Control of Capital Issue —The Ministry of Finance, Government of India, appoints an officer called the Controller of Capital Issues to watch the Capital composition of public companies made by contribution by the public. According to the Capital Issues (Continuance of Control) Act, 1947, a public company has to obtain permission of the Capital Issue Controller if the company wants to issue shares and/or debentures more than Rs. 50 lakhs in twelve months time. There are other restrictions too under the Act.

Capital Gearing and Capital Planning — Capital gearing means striking a suitable ratio between the equity capital and debt capital of a company. If equity capital is kept low and the company can manage its capital from other sources like the preference capital and debenture capital, then the equity shareholders will get higher rates of dividend because rates of return on preference capital and debenture capital are low. This is called 'trading on equity'. While **planning for capital** the following points have to be considered : (a) There shall be neither over-capitalisation nor under-capitalisation. (b) There must be proper provision for fixed and working capital. (c) There must be a judicious mixture of inside or own capital and outside or loan capital. (d) The principle of 'trading on equity' has to be followed. This shall be done by (a) maintaining proper elasticity of capital structure which is possible if equity capital is big; (b) maintaining control on the capital (and also corresponding voting rights) by the promoters; (c) catering the need and mood of the investors; (d) conforming to the condition of the capital market; (e) considering the period of investment; (f) cost of raising the capital, and (g) the policies of the Government. Every kind of security

– equity share, preference share and debenture – has its own advantages and disadvantages. Comparison has to be made by an investor before making any choice.

Structure of Management — A company as an artificial person needs human agents for its management. According to the Companies Act, the **structure** of company management is as follows : (A) Every company must appoint directors. Minimum 2 in case of a private company and minimum 3 in case of a public company. (B) In addition to directors, a company may appoint either managing director or a manager. The overall control is in the hands of the members of the company. Actual work is done by the executive officers. A public company can pay by way of managerial remuneration maximum 11% of net profits in a year or a maximum lump sum of Rs. 50,000 in case of insufficient profit. There is no such restriction for a private company. The **nature** of company management is democratic. The members elect directors as their representatives. In a very small private company all the members may be directors. Decisions are taken by passing resolutions at **meetings.** For that purpose, meetings of the Board of Directors and of the members must be regularly held according to the regulations provided by the Companies Act. Members have voting rights in proportion to their contribution to the paid-up capital. Decisions are recorded in Minute Books and are binding if the meeting is valid, i.e. held according to the rules. The Board of Directors shall hold at least one meeting in 3 calendar months. The members must hold at least one general meeting in a year, i.e. the annual general meeting to approve the report and accounts of the last year, to declare dividend to elect directors and to appoint auditors. **Problems** in company management : (1) In practice the management is not democratic because some interested group of members generally hold majority shares and majority voting rights and thereby exploit the company. (2) There are very rigid legal formalities in respect of management. (3) The management is expensive. In a company, **the Board of Directors** have powers of management and not one single director. But substantial power may be delegated on a single director called managing or whole-time director. Such substantial power may be delegated on a manager. The term manager has different meaning in the Companies Act from its ordinary word meaning. Directors are partly agents and partly trustees of the company to manage the company on its behalf and to look after the assets of the company in the interests of the members. Any person competent to contract and a member of the company can become a director. He may have to buy some qualification or minimum number of shares in the company. At least one-third of the **elected directors** must retire annually by rotation but they are eligible for re-election. The Government or any lending financial institution may send an outsider as **nominated director.** The main duty of a director is to attend Board meetings. A director may render additional services like an executive offiver. He gets extra remuneration for that in the form of salary, perquisites, provident fund and other benefits. The Government by order fixes what shall be the limits of such remuneration. The managing director or manager gets high remuneration. They are also called the **the Chief Executive.** The terms of appointment of a managing director in a public company must be approved by the Central Government. A company appoints a qualified secretary to look after the legal formalities. It is compulsory for a company having paid-up capital of Rs. 25 lakhs or more. **Functions of the Board** of Directors are : (a) Determination of enterprise objectives. (b) Selection of executives. (c) Approval of budgets. (d) Checking results. (e) Recommendation of dividend. (f) Secuing long range stability. **Gradual erosion of the Board** – Companies are now-a-days managed mostly with the help of professional managers. The directors depend much upon them. That is why the importance of the Board is eroding.

Regulatory measures—There is a tendency of a group of interested persons to **exploit companies** through management. This is done by different methods : (a) Capturing majority shares, i.e. at least 51% of the shares and thereby capturing majority votes. Generally, the promoters do this. (b) Capturing controlling (and not necessarily majority) shares, i.e. 30 to 40% shares is enough because a large number of members do not come to meetings. (c) Funds of a company are transferred by the directors to other companies or firms in which they are interested. (d) By manipulating election unscrupulous men may enter into the Board of Directors. (e) Remunerative posts in the company are filled up by friends and relations of the directors. (f) Gains are made by speculating on the shares of the company in a share market taking advantage of knowledge of secrets of the company. (g) The loopholes of Law are exploited to advantage. Various **measures** have been taken in the Companies Act to control such drawbacks. Strict regulations have been imposed in respects of (a) allotment and transfer of shares; (b) restriction on issue of shares with disproportionate voting rights; (c) restrictions or limits on the amount of loan to be given by a company to other companies or firms in which directors are interested; (d) restrictions or limits on the amount of investments to be made by a company in other companies in which directors are interested; (e) restrictions on filling up office or place of profit in the company by directors or their relatives or associates; (f) disclosure of interests by directors in the contracts made by the company; (g) making the liability of directors unlimited in a limited company; (h) disqualifying unwanted persons to be directors; (i) direct controlling measures in the hands of (1) Registrar who can ask for additional information, (2) the Central Government which can alter the composition of the Board of Directors, and (3) the Court which can change the constitution of a company or ask for amalgamation, reconstruction etc. (j) the Central Government is empowered to make rules for companies time to time; (k) several penal measures in the forms of fine or imprisonment or both have been provided in the Act for violation of the Act; other measures like formation of the Company Law Board with powers of Court to regulate the administration of companies in India.

Changing Profile of Company Management — The corporate form of organisation has come into existence almost 150 years back. The form is non-traditional and so its pattern of management is fully codified and in the process of evolution. It is largely based on experience. Changes are obvious as found in every country. In India, the Britishers introduced a peculiar system of company management by appointing Managing Agents on contract basis. The Managing Agents were mostly British or foreign at the beginning and later on Indians joined the system. The managing agents played the triple role of Manager, Financier, and Promoter. They did much good to Indian industries and were mainly instrumental for the industrial growth. But they used to exploit the managed companies in different ways by making secret profits out of the buying and selling transactions, capturing majority seats in the Board of Directors, speculating on shares, filling up remunerating posts by friends and relations, transferring funds from one company to another for secret personal gains, managing many companies and thereby establishing business empire etc. Indian managing agents were worse than the foreign counter-parts in this respect. Foreigners took away hundreds of crores of rupees in this way. All the big industrial houses in India had made money in this way. There was much criticism of the system and in 1936 some amendments were made of the old Companies Act to restrict the powers of the managing agents but it was not much effective. During the Second World War managing agents flourished and promoted many companies for war supplies. **After independence,** most of the foreign managing agency houses were Indianised. The Companies Act, 1956 had brought many restrictions : (a) Positive – Introducing alternative systems of management by appointing Secretaries and Treasurers or Manager. (b) Negative – Imposing restrictions on appointment, remuneration, powers etc. of the managing agents. The Central Government, being empowered by the Act, has abolished managing agents and secretaries and treasurers systems from April 1970. At present, Indian companies are being managed by the directors. Many educated people have entered into the field. Some management training institutes have been set up to train professional managers. Management consultancy services are developing fast in the country to assist the directors in various managerial capacities.

Composition and Functions of Board : Composition — A Board may be a **Policy Board** when it consists of directors who decide policies to be executed by salaried executives. It is a **Functional Board** when the directors themselves also carry out the executive functions. An **Ideal Board** is that which consists of both the types of directors.

COOPERATIVE SECTOR

Definition — A cooperative society or conveniently called a cooperative can be defined as "an enterprise or organisation **owned by and operated for the benefit of those using its services.** It is marked by a willingness and ability to work with others". "It is a form of organisation wherein the persons voluntarily associate together as human beings on the basis of equality for the promotion of economic interests of themselves". Concept of cooperative society has added a new dimension to forms of business. Though it has apparent similarities with the company form with regard to its capital structure, membership, management, registration etc., a cooperative society has some distinctive features of its own and has assumed a great significance in the economic world both in advanced and developing countries, particularly in the latter. Therefore, a separate sector, called the cooperative sector, is conceived of. The details are discussed below under classified heads.

Features

(1) **Ownership** — **It is owned by a group of persons generally residing in the same locality or working at the same place.** Since the whole system is based on the principle of mutual help, it is not practicable to build up a cooperative with scattered people. There must be some form of nearness. The ownership is determined by contributing to the capital of the cooperative as a member. There may be a minimum number of members by law but there is no limit.

(2) **Control** — **The control is in the hands of some elected representatives** from among and by the members forming a Managing Committee just like the Board of Directors of a company. The members on the Managing Committee retire annually by rotation and fresh election takes place at the annual general meeting to fill up the vacancies. The retiring members are eligible for re-election. A cooperative must have a secretary who has the main responsibility. He acts on honorary basis. A big cooperative may keep paid office or executive secretary. There is overall control by all the members through holding of meetings. Usually the management is carried on without any remuneration by the members of the Managing Committee. They may take conveyance allowance.

(3) **Size** — Usually the size of a cooperative **is small to medium.** But there are examples of large cooperatives having widespread activities. It depends mainly on the type of the cooperative.

(4) **Legal status** — A cooperative **has to be registered under the specific Act** prevalent in a country. In India, there is the Cooperative Societies Act, 1912. Cooperatives are controlled in India by State Governments. There is a Registrar of Cooperative Societies in each State. By registration a cooperative becomes a body corporate.

(5) **Risk** — **Generally a cooperative has a share capital and the liability of each member is limited** up to the value of his shareholdings. The value of each share is small and there are restrictions with regard to extent of shareholdings by one individual member (See below). Therefore, the liability of a member is not at all high. But, it has to be remembered that cooperatives are generally formed by the weaker section of the community. A cooperative can be formed with unlimited liability of members, e.g. primary level credit society.

(6) **Profit-sharing** — **The profit is distributed among the members** by way of dividend in proportion to their contribution to capital. A good part of the profit is transferred to reserve funds to be capitalised later for the development of the society itself. The rate of profit is not very high but the members are benefited indirectly through the services rendered by the society.

(7) **Stability** — Like any other body corporate **a cooperative has a perpetual succession.** It is not affected by the death, retirement or insolvency of a member. The Act provides the process of winding up of a cooperative. In India, cooperatives often break up due to disputes among the members.

Principles

The Cooperative system has been described as 'a religion applied to business'. Cooperatives are formed and conducted on **the dual principles of democracy and equality.** This statement can be justified in the following manner : (1) There is a limit of individual shareholding. One member cannot hold more than ten shares or more than one-tenth of the total share-holdings, whichever is bigger. By this principle, it is not possible for any member to have any form of controlling shares in the society.

(2) **Every member has one vote** irrespective of his share holdings. This justifies a spirit of equality and discourages holding of large number of shares by those who have the intention of dominating.

(3) **The management is in the hands of an elected body** called the Managing Committee. So, the management is purely democratic. There is rotational retirement of the committee members.

(4) The objective is based on the **principle of mutual help.** The source of cooperative principles is the 'Rochdale Principles' enumerated by the Rochdale Pioneers when the first Consumers' Cooperative was formed at Rochdale of U.K. in 1844.

Objectives

Cooperatives are **not formed with profit objective but with service objective.** Besides, such objective is based on the principle of mutual help and by that, indirectly, self – help is achieved. Indirectly, there is an objective of achieving self-sufficiency in certain line by the members. The definition of cooperative points out that "it is marked by willingness and ability to work with others". This willingness is a part of the objective. But ability to work with others is altogether a different thing. It largely depends on national character. In case there is a strong sense of individualism in the minds of the people by nature, the cooperatives will fail. Individualism is a characteristic of feudal economy and also of capitalistic economy. It is very strange that cooperative movement originated in Denmark and really blossomed in U.K. and then spread in other countries. Both these countries belonged to capitalistic economy. One of the reasons of failure of cooperative movement in India is a strong sense of individualism among the people which is a common outcome of feudal economy.

Formation of cooperatives, therefore, primarily depends on the willingness and ability to work with others. If there is such ability, willingness will automatically grow. This willingness may be described as the motivation. Again, if there is strong willingness or motivation, ability will grow.

Motivation

We have already seen what motivation is. Ability is not enough. There must be some motivating factors. Cooperative motivation is something different from business motivation. The motivating factors are discussed below :

(1) **Persons belonging to the weaker section of the community feel motivated to form into cooperatives** for some economic activities for mutual gains as they realise that such econoimic activities cannot be done by them individually. This is the cause of formation of industrial cooperatives like weavers' cooperatives or cooperative housing societies. Cooperative housing societies have become very popular among urban middle class people (See below).

(2) But such motivation was not self-generating at the early phase of cooperative movement. The word 'movement' is very aptly used with the cooperative organisation because **it has gained momentum by the efforts of some leaders** like Raiffisien of Germany or Robert Owen of England.

(3) Sometimes cooperatives are formed **to fight out common difficulty.** For example, cooperative credit societies have become popular in India as an alternative to oppressive money

lenders. Consumers' Co-operative Stores are set up to fight against hoarding and other malpractices by a section of the trading community.

(4) Recently, the **State comes out to be a great motivator.** Cooperative farming has developed very fast in Israel and Mexico by virtue of State encouragement. In India, development of coopertives has been accepted as a part of the economic policy by the State. Cooperative sector is considered to be a powerful sector under the Industrial Policy, Industrial Licensing Policy and Bank Nationalisation Policy.

Measures taken by our Government for cooperative motivation — The Government of India has taken several steps for vitalising the cooperative movement in the country. Some of the important steps are discussed below :

(1) **Finance** — Cooperatiave Credit Societies are more common out of other forms of cooperatives. The Government has adopted an integrated credit scheme, on the recommendations of the. All India Rural Credit Survey Committee or the Gorwala Committee, to help such societies. For that purpose, the State Bank of India has been established (by nationalising the Imperial Bank of India in 1955) and several funds like National Agricultural Credit (Long-term Operations) Fund and the National Agricultural Credit (Satabilization) Fund have been set up to supply necessary funds.

(2) **Storage** — The National Cooperative Development and Warehousing Board, the Central Warehousing Corporation and several State Warehousing Corporations have been established for the improvement of storing facilities.

(3) **Processing and marketing** — To assist in diversification and expansion of the cooperative processing and marketing, the National Agricultural Marketing Federation and several State Marketing Federations as well as central and primary marketing societies have been set up.

(4) **Cooperative farming** — With a view to popularising cooperative farming, National Cooperative Farming Advisory Board has been set up. Model cooperative farms have been established to encourage the people.

(5) **Cooperative distribution** — The National Cooperative Consumers' Federation and a large number of wholesale and retail stores have been established for the distribution of consumer goods at fair prices.

(6) **Personnel training** — For the purpose of training cooperative personnel who can take the responsibility of managing cooperatives, the Government has established the National Cooperative Union of India and a large number of special training centres at different places like Pune, Ranchi, Indore, Madras etc.

(7) **Other measures** — (a) Special financial assistance offered to different producers' unions by weavers, small traders, artisans etc. (b) Subsidies to management expenses of new cooperatives. (c) Concessions with regard to different taxes and duties. Exemption of income tax. (d) Liberal industrial licensing for cooperative sector.

On the whole, the Government is spending huge amount of money under the Five-Year Plans for the development of cooperatives.

For the development of Cooperatives the **International Cooperative Alliance** was established in 1895. It has membership for more than 50 countries. According to the Alliance, the principles and objectives of the cooperative shall be : (a) Open membership. (b) Democratic control. (c) Dividend on purchase. (d) Limited interest on capital. (e) Political and religious neutrality. (f) Cash trading. (g) Promotion of education.

Formation

A cooperative is established by registration. The steps for the formation of a cooperative are as follows :

(1) **Planning** — At first a group of promoters must prepare a plan for the prospective society. According to the Cooperative Societies Act, 1912, a minimum of ten promoters are necessary for the formation of a Cooperative.

(2) **Preparation of documents** — Documents comprising memorandum and bye-laws have to be prepared containing the description of the cooperative with name, address, object, capital and liability of members as well as rules for its management, meeting, accounts, audit etc.

(3) Filing — A copy of each of the documents signed by the promoters must be filed with the Registrar of Cooperative Societies of the State concerned.

(4) **Incorporation** — The society is incorporated when the Registrar issues a Certificate with a serial number and date with his signature under his seal. Now the society is born as a body corporate.

Classification

(1) **Credit Cooperatives** — People living in the same village or locality or working at the same place form such cooperatives by accumulating their savings and thereby building up a loanable fund out of which loans are given to members. The terms of payment and the rates of interest as well as the securities wanted against the loans are liberal. Loans are given even against life insurance policies. The members can take loan to meet their personal liabilities or expenses. The members buy share in the society or keep fixed deposits. Outsiders are also allowed to keep fixed deposits to increase the loanable fund. Such cooperatives are very popular in our country, particularly among the rural people as an action against high-handed money–lenders. The State Bank of India assists such rural societies with funds through Cooperative banks. There is a cooperative bank in every State with its branches in the districts. In all big mercantile or educational concerns we find credit cooperatives by, and for, the members of the staff.

(2) **Producers' Cooperatives** — These are also known as industrial cooperatives formed by small industrialists or artisans. Producers' Cooperatives by artisans like weavers, shoemakers, etc. are very successful. The products are sold among the members as well as to outsiders for profit. The whole system works in a co-partnership system. There is no question of workers or employees on wage basis. The members of the cooperatives themselves are workers. They get their remuneration in the form of share in profits. The workers can show their best abilities as there is no employer-employee relationship. It becomes possible for the artisans to produce goods and to show their talents collectively which individually is not possible for lack of funds. Once a Producers' Cooperative is formed with the limited resources of the members, financial help becomes available from banks and other Governmental agencies. Producers' Cooperatives are very suitable for the development of small-scale and village industries. Producers' cooperatives are, however, not always successful mainly because of marketing difficulties. Such Cooperatives, however, can take the help of marketing cooperatives, for this purpose. The failure is also for lack of managerial efficiency.

(3) **Consumers' Cooperatives** — Some people living in the same village or locality or working in some organisation may set up Consumers' Cooperative Stores for the purpose of eliminating middlemen from the process of distribution or for protesting against black marketing or hoarding by a section of dishonest traders. There are Wholesale Cooperatives to procure the goods from the producers and to supply them to the Consumers' Cooperatives. Through Consumers' Cooperative Stores the members can get regular supply of consumer goods which are fresh from the producers and at reduced prices because middlemen are eliminated. Goods can also be sold to outsiders. Such stores are very common in industrial towns.

(4) **Marketing Cooperatives** — Such cooperatives are generally formed in villages to facilitate the marketing of products of the fields or of small and village industries. As each cultivator produces a small quantity of crops, it is not possible for him to sell the crops at a

good margin of profit for lack of his organising capacity. Marketing Cooperatives purchase the products in small quantities from the rural producers, agriculturists or non-agriculturists, and then sell them from common counters. The producers get reasonable prices and at the same time they are relieved of risks.

(5) **Housing Cooperatives** — A Housing Cooperative is formed by a group of members intending to build their residential houses or flats. The members make a common pool of their savings and, together with Government or bank assistance, buy a big plot of land which individually they could not buy. The big plot of land is divided into smaller plots for the members. Or a multi-storied building is constructed with flats and each member gets one. The payment of price of the land or flat or even building is made in easy instalments and with a low rate of interest. Housing Cooperatives have become very popular among the urban people in recent times.

(6) **Multi-purpose Cooperatives** — A multi-purpose society can be formed with a number of objectives together and rendering a number of services simultaneously like processing, storaging and marketing of products.

(7) **Other types** — There are other types of service cooperatives, e.g. Transport Cooperative by which a bus service is maintained in a village. There are insurance societies also. A cooperative farm is established by consolidating small land – holdings of a number of cultivators so that large-scale mechanised farming can be done.

Significance

Significance of cooperatives is great in the economy of a country as they render various services. There are so many advantages of cooperative sector and practically no disadvantages. There are, however, limitations for which cooperative movement cannot always be very successful. In India, the movement has not achieved what was expected of it in spite of the Government's all-out assistance.

Advantages — (1) By cooperatives the members (and even outsiders) get the supply of goods (through consumers' stores) or services (through credit cooperatives) at a reasonable price or service charge. Cooperatives are utility-oriented.

(2) Much of the establishment or management costs is reduced by the voluntary services rendered by the members in these respects.

(3) A spirit of fellow-feeling develops among a group of persons which may reflect in other spheres of life too.

(4) Supply of goods and services can be vastly increased through cooperatives which has an effect on the general price level.

(5) Many achievements are possible and many talents can be unfolded through cooperatives which could not be possible by individual efforts.

(6) In many cases some uneconomic expenses e.g., unnecessary advertisement cost, middlemen's commissions or profits etc. can be eliminated leading to reduction of price.

(7) Cooperatives can offer a challenge to the exploiting class of industrialists and traders.

(8) The movement fosters employment through setting up of small industries or commercial or trading enterprises.

Limitations

(1) It is difficult to carry on an enterprise with a spirit of cooperation for a long time.

(2) Very often a cooperative is formed with great enthusiasm but after a period of time it is closed as the enthusiasm dies out. This causes economic waste.

(3) Cooperatives suffer from lack of managerial efficiency and as a result there is diseconomy.

(4) Some members develop vested interest in a society and try to exploit it for personal gains. The very spirit of cooperation is thereby destroyed.

(5) Fake cooperatives are registered to get various kinds of State assistance in money and in kind. This is a common feature of the cooperative movement in India.

It is evident that the advantages of cooperatives outweigh the limitations. The limitations can be easily overcome by better organisation and by better administration from the side of the Government. Unfortunately, it is also a fact that cooperatives have not prospered in India becuse of too much interference by the Government's departments.

G. Company and Cooperative

(1) **Ownership** — In a company, the ownership is in the hands of the members, either shareholder members or otherwise if the company is unlimited type or limited by guarantee.

In a cooperative, the ownership is in the hands of the members who are invariably shareholder members.

(2) **Relation** — In a company, every member has a contractual relation with the company. There is no contract among members. Their inter-relationship is of status belonging to the same association.

In cooperatives the position is the same.

(3) **Number of members** — In a company : (a) in case of a private company the minimum number is 2 and the maximum number is 50, excluding the members of the staff, past or present, holding shares ; (b) in case of a public company the minimum number is 7 and – (i) in case of a company limited by shares, the maximum number is (theoretically the number of shares the company has if one member holds only one share practically which is not) not fixed; (ii) in case of guarantee or unlimited company it is mentioned in the Memorandum and Articles of the company and the Board of Directors is empowered to increase the number when required.

In a cooperative the minimum number of members is 10 and the maximum number (theoretically the number of shares the cooperative has if one member holds only one share, practically which is not) is not fixed. A cooperative wants to increase the number of members by issuing new shares which are not required to be offered to the existing members (as required in a company).

(4) **Share in the business** — In a company, each member has share in the profits of the company (not in the property which belongs to the company which has separate legal entity) in proportion to his contribution to the capital of the company.

In a cooperative it is same as in a company.

(5) **Classification** — Companies are classified in many ways. The broad classification : (a) functionally – trading and non-trading. (b) Constitutionally – unlimited company, company limited by shares (Joint Stock Company) company limited by guarantee and company limited by guarantee and by shares. A company can be private or public. Besides, shareholders are classified according to class of shares – equity and preference.

Cooperatives are classified functionally into credit, producers', consumers', marketing, multi-purpose, housing, transport etc. There is no classification of shares. But, structurally, a cooperative can be primary, rural, and urban.

(6) **Legal status** — A company is a body corporate having a separate legal entity.

Cooperative is same as company.

(7) **Registration** — Company needs compulsory registration by which it is born as a body corporate. The Central Government appoints a Registrar of Companies in each State for the purpose.

A cooperative needs compulsory registration by which it is born as a body corporate. Each State Government appoints a Registrar of Cooperative Societies for the purpose.

(8) **Liability** — In a company, the liability of a member may be unlimited, limited by shares, limited by guarantee or limited by guarantee and by share. In a limited company, the liability of directors may be made unlimited.

In a cooperative, the liability of a member may be unlimited or limited.

(9) **Management** — In a Company, the management is in the hands of a Board of Directors consisting of elected representatives of the members and the Board may have nominated members not exceeding one-third of the total number of directors. The Board of Directors function by meetings. The overall control is in the hands of the members functioning through meetings.

In a cooperative, the management is in the hands of a Managing Committee consisting of elected representatives of the members. The Managing Committee functions through meetings. The overall control is in the hands of the members functioning through meetings.

(10) **Accounts** — In a company, accounts are to be annually audited by a Charatered Accountant appointed by the company and the accounts to be filed with the Registrar of Companies.

In a cooperative, accounts are to be annually audited by a Chartered Accountant appointed by the State Government and accounts are to be filed to the Registrar of Cooperative Societies.

(11) **Objectives** — In a company the objectives are either trading or non-trading and they are meant for the company.

In a cooperatives the objectives are mainly some services to the members.

(12) **Rights of Members** — In a Company one shareholder member may buy as many shares as he likes (provided the company allots them) and he has proportionate voting rights.

In a Cooperative, one shareholder member cannot buy more than ten shares or more than one-tenth of the total number of shares. Every member has one vote irrespective of the number of shares held by him.

(13) **Dissolution** — A company as a body corporate has perpetual succession. It can be dissolved voluntarily by members as a solvent or insolvent company or compulsorily by the court at the claim of a creditor for more than Rs. 500.00 and when a company makes any default to the legal formalities. Voluntary winding up may be subject to the supervision of the court. The Companies Act provides elaborate procedure of liquidation ending into dissolution.

A Cooperative as a body corporate has perpetual succession. It can be dissolved voluntarily by the members.

(14) **Regulation** — Companies are regulated by the Companies Act, 1956, and rules to be set out by the Central Government. Besides, other Acts like the MRTP Act, 1969, the Securities Contracts (Regulation) Act, 1956 etc. have effects on it. The Companies Act is vast and exhaustive with wider powers in the hands of the Central Government to regulate companies in the interests of the members, of the company, of the business to which the company belongs, and of the public.

A Cooperative is regulated by the Cooperative Societies Act, 1912. It is not a vast and exhaustive Act. The Act is intended to make the system popular. The Government provides many concessions with regard to taxes, fees, licencing etc. to cooperatives.

D. Private and Public Companies

Companies limited by shares or joint stock companies can be broadly classified into Private and Public, based upon three main characteristics. There are many other points of difference between the two. A private company enjoys some privileges or advantages granted by the Companies Act. In fact, a private company has the limited liability of members but at the same time it has many characteristics, specially secrecy, as those of a partnership firm. The points of difference between a private and a public company are enumerated below :

(1) **Name** — A private company must use the words 'Private Limited' at the end of its name so that from its very name its character is clear. A public company has to use only the word'Limited' at the end of its name unless the Central Government does not allow it to use the word when the company is a non-trading one.

(2) **Number of members** — The minimum number of members for a private company is 2 while that of a public company is 7. The maximum number of members of a private company is 50 excluding the members of the staff, past or present, holding shares in the company. In case of a public company, no maximum number is fixed for a company limited by shares. Theoretically, the number is same as the number of shares the company has, assuming that one member holds only one share but in practice such does not happen. In case of a guarantee or unlimited company the maximum number is given in the documents but the Board of Directors are empowered to increase it.

(3) **Shares** — There are so many points of difference in respect of shares :

(a) A private company must issue shares with proportionate voting rights, i.e. equity shares and in addition may issue shares with disproportionate voting rights like preference shares as well as some other types. A public company must issue equity shares and, in addition, may issue preference shares.

(b) A private company can start allotment of shares immediately after incorporation of the company but a public company has to file with the Registrar of Companies a Prospectus (in case of a widely held company) or a Statement in lieu of Prospectus (in case of a closely held company) in connection with shares.

(c) In a private company, shares are transferable under restrictions as provided in the Articles of the Company. In a public company, shares are freely transferable.

(d) In a private company, if the directors refuse a share transfer then nothing can be done by the Central Government. In a public company the transferor may make an appeal to the Central Government.

(e) A private company cannot issue share warrants against its full-paid shares but a public company can do so if the Articles so provides and the Central Government permits.

(f) A private company can give financial assistance for purchasing shares in itself or in its holding company. A public company cannot provide such assistance.

(g) When new shares are issued by a private company, it is not obligatory for it to offer the shares to its existing shareholders but it is obligatory for a public company.

(6) **Formation** — There are a number of points of difference in this respect : (a) A private company can start its business immediately after getting the Certificate of Incorporation, but a public company has to obtain a second certificate called the Certificate for Commencement of Business.

(b) A private company must prepare its own Memorandum and the Articles in part. It cannot follow Table A in full. A public company must prepare its own Memorandum, may not prepare its own Articles as it can follow Table A in full and must prepare its Prospectus when it wants to offer shares and/or debentures to the public.

(c) In case of a private company, consent letters of directors need not be filed but it is necessary in case of a public company.

(5) **Management** — A private company can appoint a firm or a body corporate for office or place of profit in the company but a public company cannot do so. It can appoint only an individual.

A private company can pay any percentage of its annual net profit by way of managerial remuneration but a public company can pay maximum 11% of the net profit or a maximum lump sum of Rs. 50,000.00 in case of insufficient profit.

Restrictions on the Board of Directors with regard to buying and selling of properties of the company or to borrowings beyond limits, do not apply to a private company.

(6) **Directors** — There are a number of points of difference in this respect : (a) The minimum number of directors for a private company is 2 and the maximum number shall be mentioned in the Articles. For a public company, the minimum number is 3 and the maximum number shall be mentioned in the Articles but if that number exceeds 12, permission of the Central Government is necessary.

(b) If there is provision in the Articles for director's qualification shares, there is no limit for the amount in case of a private company but for a public company the amount cannot exceed Rs. 5,000.00.

(c) One person can be director for any number of private companies at a time but one person cannot be director of more than 20 public companies at a time.

(d) In case of a private company a director has not to file his consent letter to the Registrar of Companies but a director of a public company has to do it.

(e) In a private company there is no compulsory retirement for one-third of the total number of directors annually but it is compulsory for a public company.

(f) A private company may mention in its Articles special disqualifications or special grounds for vacation of office of a director other than what are provided in the Act but it is not possible for a public company.

(g) For a public company there are special provisions and procedure to grant loan to a director or his associate but such restrictions do not apply to a director of a private company.

(h) A director in a private company can participate in a Board meeting where any contract in which he is interested is to be discussed but in a public company a director cannot.

(i) For a private company, no approval from the Central Government is necessary for the terms of appointment of a managing director but approval is necessary for a public company. Restrictions with regard to manner of appointment of manager, applicable to a public company do not apply to a private company.

(7) **Financing** — A private company can give loan of any amount to or can invest any amount of money in other companies either under different or under the same management. Of course, such investment may cause a private company to be deemed to be a public company and thereby losing its privileges. For a public company, there are various restrictions in this respect.

(8) **Meetings** — A private company need not hold a Statutory Meeting which a public company must hold after one month and not later than six months from the date of its commencement of business.

A private company may provide its own rules with regard to general meetings, e.g., longer or shorter period of notice, different rules for voting and appointment of proxies etc.

(9) **Returns** — Like a public company, a private company has to file with the Registrar of Companies three copies of its Balance Sheet and three copies of its Profit and Loss Account but it has to submit the copies of Profit and Loss Account separately, which, unlike the case of a public company, cannot be inspected by the public in the office of the Registrar.

(10) **Government's interference** — Power of the Government to interfere in the management of a private company is less than that of a public company. The Government cannot prevent change in the Board of Directors of a private company.

PUBLIC ENTERPRISES

Meaning — The Dictionary meaning of public enterprise is **'economic activity undertaken by the State or locial authorities'.** The word "public" aims at general welfare of the people. In other words, a publc enterprise means a State enteprise or public undertaking or Government undertaking. A public enterprise means an enterprise belonging to the public sector. Under a democratic system it is believed that the greatest good to the greatest number of people can be achieved through 'freedom of enterprise' with equal opportunities for all. The experience, however, says that such greatest good could not be achieved as expected through freedom of enterprise and competition. Inequality of wealth and exploitation by monopolistic concerns have become a natural outcome. **As an alternative to the sytem of freedom of enterprise, public enterprise has emerged.**

The emergence has two sources : (a) State ownership is a result of a doctrinaire approach in a totalitarian or communisitic State. Under the communistic thought, the State alone has the power to own and to control all the economic activities and no individual has any right to exploit any resource of the country. Therefore, all economic activities shall be under State or public ownership. In a communistic State, every enterprise is a public enterprise. (b) State ownership or public enterprise has become an alternative to private ownership for the good of the people. It is limited in certain spheres of the ecomomic life and not engulfing all the economic activities. Some essential services known as public utilities (see below) have been from old days in the hands of the Government, e.g. power supply, water supply, transport and communication, in every free economy country. With the passing of time **more and more types of economic activities are coming under the control of the State** as public enterprises to make the nation more and more self-sufficient. This can be done in two ways : (a) The State establishes a number of public enterprises in a planned manner. (b) Existing private sector enterprises are taken over or nationalised.

Objectives — Public enterprises are increasingly being set up on account of the following objectives :

(1) To accelerate and maximise the rate of economic growth of the country in the interest of the people and to increase the rate of growth and volume of the national income.

(2) To provide an infra-structure for the economic activities to be carried out by the private enterprises as well.

(3) To create new employment opportunities irrespective of profitability of the enterprises.

(4) To remove inequality of wealth by breaking the concentration of economic power in the hands of the few controlling the major economic activities related to industry, trade and commerce.

(5) To widen the sphere of ecomomic activities by taking up ventures which require heavy capital investments which the private sector finds difficult.

(6) To supply or to render better goods or services to the consuming public in respect of quality and regularity and that without any discrimination and at reasonable prices.

(7) To ensure better living conditions to the people as a whole and better working conditions to the working class. This is possible as the organisations are service-oriented and not profit-oriented.

(8) To cooperate with the private sector is to make the rate of economic growth faster. This is a major objective when a policy of mixed economy is followed.

Characteristics — Public enterprises have some characteristics or distinctive features different from private enterprises. They are as follows :

(1) **Under a planned economy** — Existence of public enterprises **presupposes existence of a planned economy.** In a communistic country, every kind of economic activity from production to consumption is under some economic plan and rigid control. In a country under mixed economy there is existence of some economic plan in which the public and the private sector have their respective roles to play. Planning relieves the economy from the evil effects of trade cycles, uneconomic speculation and such other evils of the capitalistic system.

(2) **Selected industries** — Generally public enterprises are meant for **the key and heavy industries** which require huge capital and provide the foundation for other industries. This is particularly true for the public enterprises under a mixed economy. In fact, such public enterprises help the private enterprises for their establishment and growth. The strategic industries like making of arms and ammunitions are invariably public enterprises in the interest of the nation.

(3) **Management** — Management of public enterprises **primarily goes into the hands of the Government** servants or bureaucrats. Such a system may cause of some evils. But the public enterprises are now increasingly coming into the hands of trained professional managers. The management is supposed to be service-oriented and not profit-oriented. The nature of management largely depends on the form of ownership.

(4) **Unusually heavy investment** — Since the public enterprises are engaged in key, heavy and strategic industries and also in public utility services, the initial capital as well as working **capital requirements are unusually high.** Such large volumes of capital can be procured by the State only. Sometimes arrangements have to be made with international financial institutions or with other advanced countries which can be possible only at the Governmental levels.

(5) **At different levels** — The ownership of public enterprises can lie **at different levels of authority,** e.g. owned by the Central Government, any State Government, a combination of the Central and one or more than one State Government, a combination of a few State Governments, a local authority like a municipality. The area of operation and size of a public enterprise will depend on the pattern of its ownership.

(6) **Forms** — The ownership of a public enterprise may assume **different forms** — Departmental undertaking, Government Company, Public or Statutory corporation, others.

(7) **Monopoly** — Generally a public enterprise is a **legalised monopoly** in its respective field of economic activity, e.g. the Coal India Limited (CIL). Again, it may compete with the private enterprises, e.g. the Steel Authority of India Ltd. (SAIL) competing with the Tata Iron and Steel Co. Ltd. (TISCO).

PUBLIC UTILITIES

Meaning — The dictionary meaning of the term public utility is **"a business organisation performing some public service and subject to special governmental regulation".** From the definition, it is clear that a public utility has two distinct aspects – (a) It performs some public service. It means that it supplies some essential goods or services, e.g. supply of gas, electricity, water, etc. or rendering services of transport or communication. **All such services are meant for serving and protecting 'public interest'.** It is very difficult to define 'public interest'. It can be said, however, that public interest means anything that brings benefit to a community as a whole. Every member of a community is interested to get the supply of essential goods and services at reasonable prices. Public utilities, by supplying those essential goods and services, protect and satisfy public interest. (b) The public utilities function under special Governmental regulation. **The reasons for such regulations** are as follows : (i) Every such goods or service has a definite area of operation but the scale of operation of a public utility is generally large which needs proper control. (ii) It is necessary that the goods or service must be supplied or rendered to every member of the community without any discrimination. A public utility, therefore, functions as a legalised monopoly, may be in the private sector (e.g. The Calcutta Electric Supply Corporation (India) Ltd. was given monopoly to supply electricity in the city of Calcutta) or in the public sector (e.g. the Indian Railways). (iii) It has been found by experience that competition in a public utility is futile, wasteful and uneconomic. It needs to be a monopoly but at the same time it shall not charge high price or exploit the consumers in any way. (iv) The doctrine of public interest has to be properly observed. (v) There must be uniformity of standard with regard to the quality, rate and type of the goods supplied or the services rendered.

Characteristics — A public utility is somewhat different from an ordinary business concern and has some special characteristics. The main characteristics are described below :

(1) **Essential goods or services — A public utility supplies some goods or renders some service which is essential or indispensable** to the members of a community. If such goods or services are not available in the desired manner, community life becomes disorganised and there is great suffering of the public. For example, if there is dislocation in the supply of power then the domestic life of individuals, production in factories, movement of trains, etc. are affected. Life may be paralysed.

(2) **Special nature of demand** — The demand for the goods or services under public utilities has some specialities : (i) The demand is **highly inelastic** and so there is every possibility that the supplier will charge very heavy prices or rates unless there is regulation and controls. (ii) The demand is **not transferable.** Since a public utility is generally monopolistic or semi-monopolistic in nature, the demand for its goods or service is not transferable. In other words, there is practically no substitute for the goods or the service. If the consumer is not satisfied with the quality, quantity, price or rate, he has no remedy.

(3) **Limited area of operation** — In many cases, the public utilities have limited areas of operation. For example, electricity or water cannot be supplied to a very long distance. It must remain **confined within some fixed area** and under some well-defined authority (e.g. a municipality).

(4) **Unusually heavy investment**— Generally, the scale of operation of a public utility is large and it requires **heavy fixed capital investment** for the installation of plant and machinery, construction work (roads, railways, conveyors, etc.). Besides, the costs of operation and maintenance are also quite high, necessitating huge working capital. A public utility has to continuously plan for expansion and extension and to make provisions to meet suddenly higher demands, emergencies, etc. There is huge cost for financing by way of interest or otherwise.

(5) **Legalised monopoly** — Almost in all cases, a public utility concern is granted monopoly in that particular line of activity. **In public interest** it is desirable that a public utility **shall have monopoly** in the service rendered by it. Then only can it satisfy a large number of consumers in a definite or limited area. **Competition in** such cases will lead to unnecessary duplication of plants, constructions, etc. leading to **social waste** and diseconomy. For example, it is absurd to think of laying a number of railway lines with a number of duplicate stations to connect two places. Public utility concerns are also granted some **'franchise'**, i.e. right to use public properties to carry out their activities. For example, in Calcutta, The Calcutta Electric Supply Corporation can dig the roads and lay the cables.

(6) **Government regulation** — Public utilities are legalised monopolies but at the same time they have to function **under strict Government regulations.** Monopoly does not mean absolute freedom to use monopoly power. The Government will see that the public utilities render services or supply goods of standard quality and at reasonable prices. There shall be neither exploitation nor harassment of the general public. Flow of supply shall never be halted to cause hardship and inconvenience of the public. There are special legal provisions

for strikes and lockouts in such concerns. Strikes and lockouts require notices well in advance and only when they are really unavoidable.

(7) **Ownership** — Most of the public utilities are owned by the Government or local authorities like a municipality. By the nature of such organisations it is desirable that they should be **under public ownership** but there are examples of private ownership.

(8) **Management** — The nature of management of public utilities also has its own speciality. The **management is more service-oriented** than profit-oriented. Even if it is under private ownership, the price fixation is subject to Government regulation restricting any tendency to monopoly gains. Emoployees' representation in the management is a common feature. But, generally, public utilities are public enterprises (see below) and as such they have all the characteristics of a public enterprise.

RELATION BETWEEN PUBLIC ENTERPRISES AND PUBLIC UTILITIES

One of the objectives of public enterprises is to supply or render better goods or services to the consuming public in respect of quality and regularity and that without any discrimination and at reasonable prices. Public utilities are meant for supplying essential goods or rendering essential services. Such goods or services must be available in better quality, at regular time, without any discrimination and at reasonable prices. Therefore, public utilities should be run as public enterprises. In fact, **the objectives of public enterprise could be effective primarily in the forms of public utilities.** Power generation, water supply, communication service, railway transportation, etc. are found as public enterprises in almost all countries of the world including leading capitalistic countries. Competition in public utilities is futile, wasteful and uneconomic. They must be legalised monopolies. Public enterprises only can be dependable for the purpose. Some public utilities are essential for maintaining Government administration, e.g. communication, i.e. postal service or railways. The Government will prefer to keep such services under its direct control for better service. Public utilities at national level require perfect coordination which can be achieved through Government ownership and control. Therefore, public enterprises should be most suitable.

Let us take the example of the communication service, i.e. the postal system. The postal services are required by every individual in the country, every business concern, every other organisation and the Government itself. The service is required at every corner of the country, however remote it may be and the service must be cheap, within the reach of the common man. Regularity of service, as far as possible, must be perfect. There must be absolute uniformity and no discrimination from person to person or place to place. As it is essential for our daily life, it comes under public utility group. As it must be well-coordinated, it cannot but be a monopoly. In order to satisfy all the requirements it has to be a public enterprise.

FORMS

Form entrepreneural view-point, organisations can be classified according to the nature of ownership. Broadly speaking, there are **two types of ownership – individual and corporate.** Under the former type, there is identification of the owner or owners and the enterprise and in the latter case there is a separation between the owners and the enterprise. Sole-proprietorship and partnership forms come under the first category while the company form is the corporate form. Private enterprises belong to either of these two broad groups.

Public enterprises belong to the State. They also fall into the two broad categories. Accordingly, **public enterprises can be classified** in the following manner :

(1) **Departmental organisation** — such an organisation belongs directly to the Government as a department and under respective Ministries, e.g. railways. There is identification of the Government with the enterprise.

(2) **Government Company** — such companies with separate legal entities under the Companies Act with major or all the shares held by the Central Government or a State Govern-

ment or a combination of them. There is legal separation between the Government and the company.

(3) **Public or Statutory Corporation** — such a corporation is just like a Government Company but formed not under the Companies Act but under a special statute made for the purpose.

(4) **Other forms** — like Board, Trust, etc. formed as statutory bodies for some specific purposes and having autonomy, i.e. separate from the Government.

The details of the different forms of public enterprises are given below :

A. Departmental organisation

Meaning — This is the oldest form of public enterprise. Originally, the Government did not recognise what is called a public enterprise but **carried out certain functions as a part of traditional functions of the Government** as sources of revenue. The Departments of Posts and Telegraphs and the Railways come under this purview. Before independence, the Government of India had only the Posts and Telegraphs Department under its direct departmental control. After independence, private railway companies were nationalised and integrated under the Railway Board. The Indian Railways not only run transport services but also large-scale repairing workshops and two engineering units — the Chittaranjan Locomotive Works and the Integral Coach Factory.

Characteristics

(1) Departmental organisations are planned, owned and managed by the Government under a Ministry and there is a Minister in charge of it.

(2) The annual budget is presented and approved by the Parliament. The budget may be separately prepared as in the case of Railways or appropriated through the general budget as in the case of Posts and Telegraphs. The revenues earned are transferred to the general exchequer.

(3) The personnel are recruited in the same manner as in other departments of the Government. For all practical purposes the employees are Government employees and the conditions of their services are same as those of other civil servants.

(4) These are subject to accounting and audit as applicable to other departments of the Government.

(5) Any suit to be brought against any such organisation, the same legal restrictions and procedure shall apply which are applicable in case of a suit against the Government.

Merits

(1) It enjoys all the benefits and immunities as the Government itself enjoys.

(2) There is maximum control over its functioning and accounting as the Government itself has.

(3) If there is any complaint or grievance, directly the matter can be raised in the Parliament for necessary action. Public opinion has some command on each such unit.

(4) The Government can use such departmental organisations as tools for implementing its policies and exercising control.

Demerits or limitations

(1) Departmental organisations are under ultimate control of ministers who are political beings knowing little of management. It is difficult for them to take business decisions. Same is applicable to the other civil servants who take part in the management.

(2) Such organisations are different from the other ordinary departments of the Government. But this fact is not kept in mind and so business principles are ignored.

(3) All the evils of bureaucratic administration like red-tapism, delay in decision-making, ignoring the public, etc. creep in the management of such organisations. These are highly detrimental to business undertakings.

(4) Same department may have to look after many matters other than the undertaking and so there is lack of attention and concentration.

(5) Such organisations are very slow-moving compared to the organisations under private sector because of the following reasons : (a) It takes much time to obtain sanctions from higher authorities. (b) There is lack of incentives for the staff. (c) The accounting and audit systems are lengthy and complicated. (d) The terms of employment, promotion, etc. for the staff are conventional and not conducive to business outlook. (e) Shortage of properly trained personnel.

(6) The civil servants are not business-minded nor are they trained in that line. Therefore, a kind of insensitivity to consumer needs develops and so consumers do not get satisfaction.

(7) Sometimes too much interference by the Ministers or Members of Parliament or the political party in power retards the progress of the organisations and creates dissatisfaction in the minds of the personnel.

(8) Policies often face sudden change with the change in the Government. A business cannot prosper unless there is consistency of policy.

B. Government Company

Meaning — A Government Company is that in which **not less than 51% of the shares are held by the Central Government or by any State Government or by two or more State Governments or by the Central Government together with one or more State Governments.** Sec. 617 of the Companies Act, 1956, provides the definition. The Act also provides that (1) A company subsidiary of a Government Company is a Government Company. (2) A foreign company in which 51% or more shares are held by the Government is a Government Company. (3) All the provisions of the Companies Act shall apply to a Government Company with the following special points : (a) The auditor of a Government Company is to be appointed by the Central Government on the advice of the Comptroller and Auditor– General of India and he can direct how the accounts will be audited. He can ask for supplementary test audit by his department. (b) The accounts of a Government Company shall be presented before the Parliament or the State Assembly or Assemblies as the case may be. (c) The Central Government by notification may direct, subject to approval of the Parliament, that some provisions of the Act shall not apply to Government Companies.

Characteristics

(1) It is a body corporate as understood by the Companies Act and can sue and can be sued in its own name. It holds all the assets and investments in its own name and they do not belong to the Government.

(2) The Government (either one or in combination) supplies majority of or all the capital. A part of the capital may be supplied by the public, even foreigners. The Government holds the shares in the name of the President of India or in the names of high officials, not as persons but by virtue of their posts.

(3) A Government Company is not subject to the rules and procedure of accounting, audit or personnel recruitment.

(4) The employees of a Government Company are not civil servants but the directors nominated by the Government from among its officials continue to be civil servants.

(5) All or majority of the directors are nominated by the Government according to its holding of shares. But, from the legal point of view, the Board of Directors of a Government Company has autonomy in respect of day-to-day affairs.

(6) It is more like a private limited company since the number of members is very small. Majority of the Government companies are still in the form of private companies. But it is not proper since the Government represents the public.

(7) Generally a Government Company is formed (a) when the Government takes over an existing company in the private sector and (b) when the Government wants to do any revenue-earning departmental activity on business footing and in competition with private sector units.

Merits

(1) The Government can run any revenue-earning function on business footing but at the same time it is financed, managed and taxed as a private enterprise.

(2) There can be better management, particularly when it is in competition with the private enterprises. Much of the slow-going process of departmental organisation can be avoided.

(3) There is autonomy in day-to-day management and, at least theoretically, the evils of bureaucratic administration and political interference can be avoided.

(4) The private sector very often provides standards of performance to encourage the management. The Government inducts professional managers from the private sector to such companies.

(5) The documents of a Government Company like the Memorandum of Association or the Articles of Association can be altered by the Government according to necessity and, for that, approval of the Parliament is not necessary (as in case of a Public Corporation – see below). There is necessary latitude and flexibility.

Demerits

(1) That a Government Company is, as a body corporate, an autonomous body separate from the Government itself becomes, for all practical purposes, a myth because of the following reasons : (a) the Government is the major shareholder or the holder of all the shares and so virtually it becomes a subsidiary of the Government. The Company functions according to the desire of the Government. (b) The meetings of the Board of Directors or of the shareholders become merely paper-work. All decisions are virtually taken by the Government itself, i.e. the department concerned, depending on the nature of the business.

(2) As the Board is full of Government officials, the entire management is designed in a bureaucratic model and all the evils like red-tapism, delay in decision-making and execution, etc. enter into it.

(3) Even when a Government Company has to face competition with the private enterprises, the management remains callous because there is hardly any fear of extinction or liquidation as the Government is there at the back.

(4) The Government nominates the directors from among its high officials who do not have the acumen or experience in running a business. In spite of their best efforts they may not achieve success. Further, they are not in a position to do manipulations which are very common in a private enterprise and sometimes are necessary in the interest of the business itself.

(5) There is lack of incentive among the directors as they have hardly any personal gains to make. On the other hand, some unscrupulous persons indulge in dishonesty and malpractices causing ruin to the Company and thereby making personal gains.

(6) As there is lack of profit-motive, the overhead expenses are generally high in a Government Company compared to its counterpart in the private sector. The productivity becomes low.

(7) It takes a long time to take remedial measures when defects are discovered or when any organisational change or managerial change has to be brought about. Changes are seldom made. Therefore, the so-called flexibility becomes a myth.

In fact, most of the demerits are common to the Governmental set-up as a whole and not to Government Companies in particular. Since a Government Company is autonomous, the callousness of the staff becomes more pronounced. The sense of responsibility reduces as accountability is not rigidly imposed. A Government Company functions more as a department of the Government than as a company as evidenced in India.

C. Public Corporation

Meaning — A Public Corporation is **a form of business organisation created by a special Act or statute enacted in Parliament.** It is also known as a Statutory Corporation. The statute defines its objects, powers, duties and obligations, indicates the sources of finance and prescribes the pattern of management. It is a powerful and suitable instrument to run big public enterprises without much Government regulation and control and with the flexibility of private enterprise. Since it is created by Parliament, it is really a public institution and it is answerable to Parliament though the relevant Ministries have authority and responsibility for them. This form has a long process of evolution.

Characteristics

(1) A Public Corporation is a body corporate **created by a special Act or statute** enacted in Parliament. It can sue or can be sued and hold property in its own name.

(2) **The statute is comprehensive** making all the provisions with regard to its objects, finance, operation, management and relation with the Government.

(3) It has **independence in every respect** as an autonomous body and is answerable to Parliament because it is created by a statute passed in Parliament.

(4) The relevant Ministry of the **Government has some rights and obligations** in relation to a Public Corporation because the Government drafts the Bill with a view to achieving some objective using the Corporation.

(5) It raises **finance through** public subscription and borrowing, from financial institutions, banks, etc. as detemined by the statute. The Government, by way of appropriation, provide capital initially or to cover losses or for its expansion as sanctioned by the Parliament from time to time.

(6) The **management is by a Board of Directors** constituted according to the provisions in the statute taking representatives from the contributories, the Government and other interested parties. The supreme authority vests in a whole-time Chairman assisted by a Managing Director or Chief Executive.

(7) The **employees** of a Public Corporation **are not civil servants.** They are appointed according to the terms and conditions fixed by the Corporation itself.

(8) The objective of a Public Corporation is **service-oriented** and not profit-oriented though it is supposed to earn some surplus because returns are expected on the capital contribution which is sometimes guaranteed by the Government. **It can use and re-use the revenues** earned by it.

(9) A Public Corporation is generally formed to operate any business **on a large scale** and **on a monopoly basis** spreading over a large area and preferably the whole country. It is often formed when an industry as a whole is nationalised so that all the constituents can be incorporated into it.

(10) Originated in UK as "the chosen instrument of administering the nationalised industries", this form of organisation has become **very popular** all over the world.

Merits

(1) The greatest merit of a Public Corporation is its autonomous character in the real sense. Every specific Corporation is formed by a specific statute. The statute is drafted and enacted befitting the objects of the proposed Corporation. It is not regulated by any general Act.

(2) It is the best instrument to run a large scale public enterprise with monopolistic operation but with service-oriented outlook.

(3) It can structure and re-structure its capital according to its time-to-time requirements. There are varied sources of finance.

(4) It makes an admirable combination of the characteristics of giant joint stock company of the private sector enjoying all its privileges and the outlook of a service-oriented public enterprise. According to Herbert Morrison, it is a "combination of public ownership, public accountability and business management for public ends".

(5) It is a powerful agency of the Government to carry out economic activities on a gigantic scale without having the evils of the Government machinery. The Administrative Reforms Commission in its Report has remarked that "statutory corporations are set up after full public debate and with the approval and sanction of Parliament. This leads to a clear and precise definition of their objectives and obligations. It also results in a clear demarcation of power between the Government and the public undertaking".

The history of commercial evolution reveals how giant joint stock companies have played significant role in the economic development of the free world in the nineteenth century in particular. The emergence of totalitarian or communistic States in the twentieth century have created glamour for the State-owned enterprises. But total restriction of individual freedom in the process of economic growth robs from it much of its charm. The public corporations come as a relief. Prof. Robson aptly observes that a public corporation is 'destined to play, as important a part in the field of nationalised industries in the twentieth century as the privately-owned corporation played in the realm of capitalist organisation in the nineteenth century'.

Demerits

(1) Though it has a greater autonomy than other forms of public enterprise in practice a Public Corporation cannot avoid the influence of the Government and the political elements in power.

(2) The very constitution of a Public Corporation makes it very rigid. Any change will require approval by the Parliament which is not always easy or at least cannot be prompt.

(3) The Board of Directors is composed of people representing varied interests. It is difficult for them to come to a concrete decision soon. The Corporation cannot take progressive steps easily. The heterogeneous character of the Board also hampers efficient working.

(4) A Public Corporation is generally of a very big size having a very wide area of operation. It needs effective decentralisation and at the same time proper coordination and control. It becomes increasingly difficult to maintain coordination and control.

(5) It takes considerable time to prepare a plan for a Public Corporation and to give it a practical shape and to set-up the entire organisation.

(6) It is difficult to get men with expertise and experience to manage such giant concerns. Training of the managerial personnel is essential but not easy. Much depends on the whole-time Chairman or the Managing Director or the Chief Executive.

(7) The evils of bureaucratic administration very often creep in Public Corporations since the initiative in setting up such organisations lies with the Government.

D. Other forms

Public enterprises are also managed by specially constituted bodies, which may be statutory or not. **Trust** is a common form constituted by the Government with varied representations including the Government nominees to run any particular establishment of public interest. For example, a Port Trust. The Chairman has the highest authority who is assisted by Secretaries, Deputy Secretaries and Assistant Secretaries and others. The Trust is constituted for a particular period. The Chairman is a salaried person appointed for a definite period. In the same line, **Boards** can be set up. For example, the Tea Board, the Coir Board, etc.

COMPARISON AMONG DIFFERENT FORMS

Public enterprises have different structural forms. They also differ in the procedure of their formation as well as their sources of finance and methods of management. **Each form has its merits and demerits.** The Government chooses the form according to its convenience and the object of the proposed undertaking as to what should be the form. The difference among the different forms can be studied in the following manner and on the following viewpoints as found in India :

(1) **Procedure of formation**—A Departmental Organisation is formed by setting up a separate wing for the purpose under a Ministry or a separate Ministry may be set up for the purpose. (In practice this type of organisation is hardly set up now-a-days.) A Government Company is established by getting it registered under the Companies Act. It is an executive function only. It does not require any approval of the legislature. For establishing a Public Corporation, a Bill is drafted first which has to be passed in the Parliament. It is a time-consuming and elaborate procedure.

(2) **Area of operation**—A Departmental Organisation is generally for public utility service and its area of operation covers the country as a whole. A Government Company is usually a trading concern competing in the market with other private sector units. It has its area of operation within the field of that particular trade whether in industrial or commercial field. A Public Corporation is ordinarily a giant organisation having monopoly in its field of operation and in some cases it is a public utility.

(3) **Legal status**—A Departmental Organisation is identified with the Government itself as it is a wing of a particular Ministry. A Government Company is a body corporate having a separate legal entity as understood by the Companies Act. A Public Corporation is also a body corporate as determined by the special Act under which it is constituted. A Departmental Organisation enjoys the immunity under law as the Government does but neither a Government Company nor a Public Corporation enjoys such immunity. (Immunity in law means that a special procedure has to be followed if any suit has to be brought against it in the Court.)

(4) **Sources of finance**— A Departmental Organisation is directly financed by the Government through budget appropriation and the entire revenue goes to the treasury of the Government. In case of Railways, however, a separate budget is prepared and presented in Parliament. In case of a Government Company or a Public Corporation the finance is raised independently through equity shares and borrowings. The Government supplies the equity capital and the loans but, in addition to the Government, funds are raised from financial institutions, from the public and even from foreign sources. Both of them can use or re-use their earnings. They have to pay taxes like other trading bodies corporate unlike a Departmental organisation.

(5) **Mode of management** — A Departmental Organisation is managed, just like any department of the Government, by a Minister with the executive officers. A Government Company is managed by a Board of directors in the line as provided in the Companies Act. A

Public Corporation is also managed by a Board of Directors which is constituted in the manner as provided in the special Act by which the Corporation has been formed. In both the cases, however, the members are practically Government nominees taken from the high officials. In case of a Public Corporation, the Board may have a wider representation on behalf of other interests.

(6) **Staffing** — The staff of a Departmental Organisation are just like the personnel of the Government. Their procedure of recruitment and terms of service are same as those of the civil servants. They are Government employees. But a Government Company or a Public Corporation has its own system of recruitment and terms of service. The employees of these organisation have job security like the Government employees but they are not in par with the Government employees in the strict sense.

(7) **Autonomy and flexibility** — A Departmental Organisation is under the total control of the Government and does not have any autonomy. Its mode of functioning is rigid, as the Government as a whole maintains rigidity. It takes a long time to introduce any organisational change. A Government Company has autonomy as much as it is a body corporate having a separate legal entity as understood by the Companies Act. It can introduce organisational changes by altering its documents. At least theoretically it can do so. A Public Corporation has a greatest autonomy which is conferred on it by the special statute by which it is formed. But it has less flexibility because any change to be brought about must be passed by Parliament which has enacted the special statute.

(8) **Working and accountability** — A Departmental Organisation functions just like a department of the Government or a part of it under a bureaucratic system and with secrecy. There is obligation of the Ministry concerned to answer questions in Parliament raised by the members. The public accountability is limited upto that stage. Of course, enquiry may be made by the Public Undertakings Committee. A Government Company or a Public Corporation is supposed to function like any other body corporate under a business– like managerial set-up. But the public accountability is great. The Annual Reports and Accounts have to be placed before Parliament for consideration. No secrecy can be maintained. Besides, they have to face exposure to the Public Undertakings Committee more rigorously. All the reports and accounts are discussed and criticised by the public through the Press and other media.

Choice of form

The choice of form out of the three alternatives is not an easy task. Actually, **there is no open competition among the three alternatives.** The Government makes the **choice taking into consideration the following aspects :** (1) What is the purpose behind setting up the organisation? In other words, what are the functional objects of the organisation ? Whether it is a business undertaking or a public utility ? (2) What shall be the scale of its operation and the size of the organisation ? (3) What shall be the area of its operation and what shall be the extent of its impact on the people and on the ecomomy of the country ? (4) Whether it shall have a monopoly in its field of operation ? (5) How much direct control, in the interest of the nation, the Government intends to exercise on it ? (6) How much public accountability is desirable.

It can be mentioned, however, that **Departmental Organisation as a form is getting obsolete now-a-days.** Whatever may be the form, some amount of autonomy and flexibility must be granted to it for its efficient and progressive functioning. In the Industrial Policy announced in 1948 it was declared that "the management of State enterprise will, as a rule, be through the medium of public corporations under the statutory control of the Central Government". No change towards this attitude has been made when the Industrial Policy was revised subsequently. In practice, however, **the Government has preferred to form Government Companies** more to Public Corporations. Perhaps the main reason behind such practice is the high flexibility of the company form.

PROBLEMS

The public enterprises and the public utilities in particular **pose some special problems** because of their specialised character. The problems are discussed below in a classified manner :

(1) **Location** — In case of a manufacturing unit, the choice of location of the plant becomes the first problem. Such a manufacturing unit is established under a planned economy and the location is determined accordingly in the greater interest of the people. In case of local public utility unit the plant must be situated in the **local area.** Normally **a big area is required** as the size of the plant will be large. It is difficult to get large and compact land at a convenient place. Public enterprises, however, have the franchise right to acquire any suitable land overriding individual objection of the owner or owners. For the Railways the problem is gigantic because land is required throughout the length of the track for laying the rails and setting up stations, repair centres, quarters, etc. For a service type of organisation with its area of operation all over the country the problem is how to open service stations or branch offices in evey important cities or towns and even in rural areas.

(2) **Size** — The size itself is a problem as the size is big. A big size confronts with **the problems of finance and control.** Finance is not really a problem for a public enterprise as the Government backing is there. This is, however, concerning the procurement but **proper management of the finance is a formidable task.** It needs recruitment of efficient personnel for the purpose. The civil servants may not cope with the problem as finance management is a highly specialised job. Apart from finances **efficient management and control is required in every area** like purchasing, marketing, personnel, production, etc. The over-all control is still more problematic. Another problem is that there may not be opportunity for the gradual growth of the size. **The scale of operation shall be big from the very beginning** for the utilisation of the plant capacity to avoid diseconomy. This is more true for a manufacturing unit and specially when it is a public utility for power generation, water supply, etc.

(3) **Ownership and management**—There are different forms of ownership for public enterprises and accordingly the mode of management varies. **A proper choice of form has to be made after taking into consideration various aspects.** A public utility may be entrusted with a private enterprise subject to regulation. It needs serious thinking before such step is taken because a public utility means a monopoly with franchise right (Ref. 8.2). The general belief is that only a public enterprise is capable of handling any public utility service because of the vastness of its opertion and the need for service-oriented functioning. **It is risky to depend on a private enterprise for any public utility service.** It loses its public character. In spite of the fact that autonomy and flexibility are granted to a Government Company or to a Public Corporation the influence of the bureaurcacy and the interference by the Government in the management of public enterprises cannot be totally eliminated. **Management of a public enterprise lacks dynamism and business character.** Red-tapism and even nepotism are very common. Lack of motivation is evident. Keeping pace with the changing circumstances is rarely found in public enterprises. In case of a public utility under a local authority like a municipality local politics gets involved as the **representatives of the political parties** must be included in the management. Consistency in the management policy cannot be maintained as there may be change of the ruling political party. **Lobbying and pressure tactics** by political elements and by business and other interests (foreign interests cannot be ruled out) in the management process of public enterprises have become an unavoidable and regular feature. **Malpractices and manipulations by the staff at different levels** for their personal gains often make the management weak and uneconomic.

(4) **Pricing technique** — Public enterprises are not purely profit-oriented concerns. **They are predominantly service-oriented.** This is specially applicable to public utilities. But that does not mean that they should be uneconomic and run in deficit. Surpluc creation is one

of the characteristics of an enterprise. **A public enterprise should generate surplus** for the betterment of the unit itself. Many of the public enterprises and the Departmental Organisations in particular, like the Railways, are meant for revenue earning. Determination of price plays the most significant role in the quest of earning profit or surplus. Under competition, the private enterprises adjust their costs of production with the market price but under monopoly the monopolist goes for profit maximisation. Public enterprises are mostly legalised or social monopolies. They can adopt the line of a monopolist but a public enterprise has to pay due respect to other social considerations.

The various factors to be considered by a public enterprise for price determination : (a) The consumers shall get the supply of goods or services at fair and reasonable prices. (b) The marginal cost of production shall not be higher than the price. In the long run, the overhead cost also has to be covered. Since the scale of operation is generally large, the average cost can be reduced to a lower level by full utilisation of the productive or plant capacity. The pricing policy of a public enterprise should aim at operating at the lowest cost possible and maximising efficiency. A cost-benefit analysis shall be continuously carried on. (c) In case of public utilities the people expect the supply of the essential goods or services at the minimum possible prices. It is the duty of the Welfare State to honour such expectations. The Government, very often grants subsidies to public utilities to maintain lower prices. (d) As a monopolist a public enterprise may adopt a policy of price discrimination on the principle of 'what the traffic can bear'. The State-controlled Railways maintains different 'classes' for the passengers from different earning groups. (e) A fair return on the capital must be ensured. Capital of a public enterprise may be supplied by others and not the government alone. (f) There is a popular belief that public enterprises (and specially public utilities) may have to run at a deficit because they are meant for employment creation and so the number of employees and consequently the remuneration bill is bound to be unusually high. But this cannot be allowed to continue indefinitely as the accumulated deficits ultimately become the burden on the society as a whole. Therefore, at the time of calculating the overhead cost, it has to be seen that uncessary employments are avoided. (g) The problem of pricing becomes more acute when a public enterprise has to compete in the open market with private enterprises and when it aspires for a foreign market. The only consideration in such cases shall be business consideration. (h) Pricing of goods under key and basic industries shall have to be made very carefully. If the prices of basic products are high it will have adverse impact on the prices of the final products made with the help of them. (i) Prices must be as far as possible uniform throughout the country for the same goods or services.

(5) **Marketing policy** — Every public enterprise requires to develop a sound marketing policy. A public enterprise generally has **a wide coverage of market.** In case of a public utility, there are large numbers of individual customers spread over a wide area requiring **door-to-door individual service.** Maintaining good public relations therefore is a fundamental aspect in developing a sound marketing policy. Through satisfactory services by public enterprises the importance of a Welfare State can be realised by the general mass. The success of a business enterprise largely depends on efficient marketing. A public enterprise generally lacks motivation and incentives from the side of the staff. In that case, marketing ought to be a failure. Organising of the sales force must be on a business outlook. This outlook is from the side of the enterprise as a whole and not from any individual. **An enterprise must have some market standing, otherwise it cannot survive,** it does not matter whether the enterprise is public or private. Public enterprises generally enjoy a sellers' market which makes them complacent. This attitude is harmful for the society and has to be shunned. Sometimes the Government creates confusion by establishing **a number of enterprises engaged in the same business,** e.g. a number of Fertiliser Corporations or Oil Companies. The nationalised banks are still competing each other in the same market. A rational view has to be taken of the situation and the duplication of units has to be removed. On the other hand, the competing steel plants have been rightly brought under one holding company — SAIL.

EVOLUTION

Origin — The concept of public enterprise **practically originated in UK.** The first Public Corporation in UK was the Port of London Authority established in 1908. Before the World War I, in UK, there were three other public corporations – the Central Electricity Board, the British Broadcasting Corporation (BBC), and the London Passenger Transport Board. After the War, many more corporations were added, such as the Bank of England, the National Coal Board, the British Overseas Airways Corporation (BOAC), the Iron and Steel Corporation, etc. It is to be noted that in India, after independence, we are having public corporations more or less of the British model. Before independence, India had two public corporations — The Damodar Valley Corporation (DVC) formed in the manner of the Tennessee Valley Authority (TVA) of USA (to control the floodwaters of R. Tennessee) and the Bombay State Transport Corporation (BSTC). In a socialist country, all the economic activities are carried out by the State and, as such, there is nothing like public enterprises in a strict sense. The public enterprises exist in contrast with the private enterprises but in a socialist country there is no private enterprise. This idea, however, is applicable to a fully or unmixed socialist or communist country like USSR or China. In Europe today we find many socialist States, even they are called communist States but in fact they largely differ from a communist State like USSR. (A concept of Euro-communism has cropped up). Many people do not know that public sectors exist in the Western countries like UK, France, Italy, Sweden, etc. and even in USA in a very large way, larger than people generally think of. In UK there are some nationalised industries like steel, coal, railways, power an so on, arising out of taking over by the State from the private sector.

Evolution — There has been a wave of nationalisation of industries in many Western countries after the Second World War. It continued upto the 1950s. At the early stage, nationalisation was found necessary to salvage or rescue failing private enterprises. This is called the **first-generation nationalisation.** The substitution of public ownership for private ownership, however, did not cause any major change in the structure of the industries nor in workers– management relationship.

From the early 1960s, the socialists in Western countries have developed what is called **the second-generation nationalisation,** trying to pull out the public enterprises from stagnation. (India is passing through the same stage now what the European countries experienced about 20 years back). The public enterprises are getting influenced by the private enterprises. The public enterprises are now **more market-oriented than plan-oriented,** throwing a challenge to the private enterprises. Such change of attitude has been revealed in the famous Nora Report of 1967 of France. In 1970, a new type of state-holding company, called the States Fortag, has been established in Sweden having a wide range of activities with a view to making public enterprises more competitive in nature. The same can be said of the IRI of Italy.

A Case for India

Origin — Before independence the public enterprises in India were restricted to the following areas — the Railways, the Posts and Telegraphs (Prof. Galbraith, the US Ambassador to India, called Indian socialism during the British rule as 'Post Office Socialism'), the Port Trusts, the ordnance Factories and some State-managed small factories like salt factories, quinine factories, etc. Though the Indian National Congress stressed the need of economic planning (even planning was adovcated by the private sector — Bombay Plan) but large-scale growth of public enterprises was not much advocated.

After independence, **in the Industrial Policy of 1948,** the importance of the public sector first came into forc. In the Industrial Policy Resolution it was announced that "The State will progressively assume predominance and direct responsibility for setting up new industrial undertakings and for developing transport facilities". It has to be noted that development of transport facilities was given special importance as an area of infra-structure.

There are accepted objectives behind the formation and growth of public enterprises. **For India there are some special reasons and some of them are unusual.** The reasons are :

(1) **Conventional** — The conventional reasons are definitely present for India. The single major reason was that there were many fields of business where the private sector did not have the financial competence nor had the private sector willingness to venture on account of absence of immediate returns on investments.

(2) **Special** — Another major reason was mis-exploitation of natural resources by a number of private sector agencies. If this was allowed to continue, great damage could be caused to the national economy. Further, there were large-scale manipulations in import-export transaction for personal gains to Indian and foreign businessmen which had to be stopped. Another reason was to provide some competition to private enterprises as a check against monopolistic tendencies. It was believed that only giant public sector undertakings could introduce large scale R and D (Research and Development) programmes to inspire the big industrial houses in the private sector.

(3) **Unusual** — Of late, a significant but unusual (and uneconomic) reason for taking over of private enterprises has set in – that is 'sickness', either because of mismanagement or economic difficulties. The State is often compelled, on public demand, to take-over sick units in order to save thousands of employees from being thrown out of employment. In most of the cases the sick units continue to be sick but the State cannot close them down and thereby doing enormous harm to the society as a whole. Sometimes, State take-over is done **without giving reasons.** For example, the nationalisation of 6 banks by an Ordinance of 15.4.80.

Growth of public enterprises in India

During the last few decades, the public sector in India has passed through a remarkable fantastic growth in terms of number of units, capital invested and range of activities. But the growth has not been with stability and efficiency.

Number — At the beginning of the First Plan the total number of Central Government undertakings was 5. By the end of the Second, Third and Fourth Plans the numbers stood at 21, 48 and 85, respectively. After that, the number increased at a very fast rate and by 1983-84 the number has become 214.

Investment — At the beginning of the First Plan the total investment was Rs. 29 crores. By the end of the Second, Third, Fourth and Fifth Plans the figures shot up to Rs. 81, Rs. 953 and Rs. 3,902 crores and Rs. 13,389 crores, respectively. By the end of 1983-84 the figure has gone up to Rs. 35,411 crores for 214 enterprises excluding the investment of Rs. 1,355 crores in 11 enterprises not under direct managerial responsibility of the Central Government and three financial insitutions. The Public Sector outlay in the Seventh Plan has been fixed at Rs. 1,86,000 crores (Centre – Rs. 95,734 crores, States – Rs. 80,498, crores, Union Territories – Rs. 3,768 crores). According to the latest report of the Bureau of Public Enterprise; the investments (in Rs. crores) in the first 10 public sector enterprises are as follows : Steel Authority of India (5,334), Coal India (4,057), Oil and Natural Gas Commission (2,031), Fertiliser Corporation of India (1,013), Rural Electrification Corporation (1,341), Shipping Corporation of India (748), Kudremukh Iron Ore Co. (748), National Fertilisers (780), Hindusthan Fertiliser Corporation (775), Food Corporation of India (524). The total investment in Railways, Posts and Telegraphs and other departmental undertakings stands at Rs. 5,000 crores (approx.) Besides, the total investment by the State Governments in their undertakings amount to Rs. 5,000 crores (approx.).

The industrywise break-up of Rs. 35,411 crores of investment stands at : Construction — Rs. 1,747 crores, Production (including metals, minerals, consumer goods etc.) – Rs. 26,369 crores, Service – Rs. 5,429 crores and Insurance – Rs. 121 crores.

Range of activities — The public sector has today a very wide range of activities classified into four basic categories : (1) Production (basic raw materials, capital goods, consumer goods and agrobased industries). (2) Service (trading, marketing, transport service, technical consultancy services, tourist services, etc.) (c) Financial (public financial institutions engaged in long term financing and underwriting, banking and insurance). (4) Promotional or Developmental (institutions for helping small industries, construction units, research units, etc.) (5) Rehabilitation (corporation for helping sick industries).

Employment creation — The total numbe of employees in various groups of public enterprises was about 19 lakhs by 1978-79. The annual average growth rate of employment is higher than that in the private sector. It provides about 68% of the total employments.

Contribution to national exchequer — The public enterprises contribute to national exchequer in the form of interests on loans given by the Government, dividends as well as direct and indirect duties. During the year 1977-78, the total contribution was to the tune of Rs. 1,802 crores.

Performance — Performance of business units is judged mainly from the point of view of profitability or the rates of dividend. But the public enterprises are not solely guided by profitability, particularly when they are public utilities. The rate of social return and not the rate of return on capital shall be the main criterion. The public enterprises have to offer better rates of remuneration to the employees, to offer goods or services at subsidised prices and to create such other social values through appointing larger number of employees than what the private enterprises would have done at similar situations, creation of townships with better living conditions, etc. During the year 1977-78, the over-all net profits of 81 public enterprises amounted to Rs. 628 crores which was offset by a loss of Rs. 392 crores in 41 enterprises. After deducting income-tax on the profits of profitable units, there was a net loss of Rs. 14 crores. In 1978-79, 159 public sector enterprises made a net profit of Rs. 193.45 crores before tax. After providing tax, the figure recedes to a net loss of Rs. 32 crores. According to the Annual Report submitted to Parliament by the Bureau of Public Enterprises (BPE) there was a total profit of Rs. 484.75 crores in 88 units in 1978-79 while 69 units suffered a loss of Rs. 516.71 crores. The public sector enterprises have paid to the employees — by way of remuneration of all kinds – Rs. 2,064 crores during 1978-79. In the same year, the public sector enterprises have helped the growth of 805 ancillary industries employing over 18,000 people and have purchased from the ancillary industries and small-scale industries goods worth Rs. 96.5 crores.

According to the latest report of the BPE, during 1980-81 the turnover of 168 operating enterprises has reached a record figure of Rs. 28,645 crores. Out of which Rs. 18,625 crores came from manufacturing units and Rs. 10,020 crores from service and trading units. The rise in total turnover, however, was mainly due to the rise in prices. Capacity utilisation rates in 1980-81 were : (a) 75% or more in 150 units ; (b) 50 to 75% in 133 units and (c) below 50% in 131 units.

According to the **latest report** of the Bureau of Public Enterprises, during 1983-84, while the net profit declined to Rs. 245.67 crores from Rs. 613. 51 crores of previous year as the loss-making units increased their losses by Rs. 507 crores taking the net total losses to Rs. 1,533 crores. But during 1983-84, wages went up by Rs. 350 crores and interest charges by Rs. 161.91 crores. The leading profit-making units were ONGG, OIL, IOC, Air India, Indian Airlines, STC, etc. The leading loss-making units were SAIL, Bharat Coking Coal, Eastern Coalfields, Delhi Transport Corpn., Fertiliser Corporation, Heavy Engineering etc. The export earnings were quite high – Rs. 5,418 crores (Rs. 4,747 crores in 1982-83). There has been no improvement in capacity utilisation from old rates : (a) 75% or more in 150 units ; (b) 50 to 75% in 133 units and (c) below 50% in 131 units.

OWNERSHIP AND MANAGEMENT

The patterns of ownership of public sector enterprises are different and have been already discussed. With regard to management, **the whole system is in the process of an evo-**

lution. The departmentally owned units have been and still are in the hands of the civil servants, i.e. the bureaucracy. At the initial stage the management of autonomous enterprises in the forms of Government company, public corporation or any other form of statutory body was vested in the hands of the civil servants and mostly by the IAS officers and as such all the necessary evils like red-tapism, delay in decision-making, too much rigidity of rules, absence of cost consciousness, lack of initiative, etc. have been very much pronounced. The Government did not have any alternative at that time. With the establishment of management training institutes and with the growing availability of **professional managers** things have started changing. **Experienced managers in the private sector** also could be transferred to the public sector. Further, the Government adopted a policy tht the same civil servants should not be sent on deputation to the public sector managerial positions for more than two to three years at a time. In the meantime, opportunities for managerial training for the civil servants were made available at the Administrative Staff College, Hyderabad. Most of the big public sectors gradually started opening their own in-plan management training centres.

It has been observed that most of the civil servants do not like to hold managerial positions in the public sector because they are not accustomed to business-oriented administration. The public sector is often considered by them as a convenient and temporary 'parking ground' without having any roots.

At the beginning, there was no definite and scientific policy of recruitment for the topmost positions like salaried and executive directors. An Action Committee on Public Enterprises was appointed and on its recommendations the **Public Enterprises Selection Board** (PESB) **has been set up** for the selection of topmost management personnel. Below the Board level, all recuritments are done by the units themselves. In addition to this, **a bio-data bank has been created** comprising of people from the Central and the State Governments as well as from the private sector and defence services. The PESB makes attractive offers to such people.

Theoretically, the shareholders of a company are the virtual owners of it and as such they have the right to elect the directors to look after the management of the company. In case of a public enterprise, the Government (either the Central or any State) is the only or major shareholder and so it must have the right to appoint the Chairman, the full-time directors and the chief executive. **The management of a public enterprise has a special feature.** Every such enterprise is tagged with a particular department or Ministry of the Government and it is essential that a close contact be maintained between the two. After all, the Government is answerable to the people for the performance of the public enterprises. Therefore, it is suggested that the civil servants must occupy executive and directoral positions in public enterprises. At the same time public sector professional managers may be sent to the Government on deputation temporarily.

The Boards of Directors of public enterprises generally have representatives of at least two Ministries — One from the finance and the other from the department with which the particular enterprise is concerned. The representative from the finance department plays a predominant role because enerything depends on financial assistance granted by the finance department as and when required. He may agree at the expansion programme of an enterprise at its Board meeting but may turn down the proposal when it comes to the finance department for sanction on account of non-availability of resources or such other reasons. This is quite natural because the two decisions are taken under two different environments.

AILMENTS — REMEDIES

The public sector enterprises suffer from various ailments and shortcomings resulting into diseconomy. Remedial measures are taken but not before much loss have been caused. Some of the ailments are inherent in the very nature of the public sector and cannot be easily cured.

There are, however, some ailments which can be prevented. The ailments are discussed below:

(1) **Inadequate planning** — It has been the sad experience in many cases that the planning for a public enterprise has been inadequate and faulty without taking into consideration all the probable eventualities. As a result, it takes a **longer time for completion** of the project leading to **higher investments and recurring costs** which are not productive. Inadequate planning upsets the budget. This might be accepted as one of the contributory causes to inflation as the Government has to take recourse to higher level deficit financing to meet the additional expenditure.

(2) **Over-capitalisation** — According to the findings of the Study Team on Public Sector Undertakings (1967), many of the public sector enterprises suffer from over-capitalisation which means **wastage of financial resources** (which are already limited) and **low rate of profitability.** Over-capitalisation takes place on account of faulty planning, delay in completion, extravagant expenditure during the period of construction of establishment, expensive turn-key projects, wrong selection of site, etc.

(3) **Non-utilisation of full capacity** — One of the major ailments is non-utilistion of the full capacity of the plant making overheads high and leading to various kinds of wastages. In most of the plants the average rate of capacity utilisation is between 50 and 75 per cent. This is highly uneconomic because giant and sophisticated plants, mostly imported or installed with foreign collaboration, cannot run economically unless there is full capacity utilisation. Under-utilisation of full plant capacity is **socially harmful leading to higher prices and affecting other industries** which depend on such industries. This is specially true for basic and key industries in which the public sector is mainly involved. Faulty production-planning results into non-utilisation of capacity.

(4) **Inefficient management — Inefficiency in the management in public enterprises has become almost proverbial.** Management is a comprehensive task and it pervades the organisation as well as over its different areas. An analytical discussion is given below :

(a) The Government is yet undecided as to what should be the form of management. There has been a lot of controversy on the extent of autonomy a public enterprise should enjoy. Even in government companies or public corporations the Government exercises unwanted control and interference.

(b) The public enterprises are supposed to function with a commercial outlook, particularly when the enterprise is in competition with the private sector. But this hardly takes place. Bureaucratic administration stands in the way.

(c) The Government does not follow any scientific recruitment policy. There is much politicalisation of higher posts. Very often the posts of the chairman or topmost executives are filled up by political persons (and even defeated legislators rejected by the people). On the other hand, because of comparatively lower rates of remuneration and perks, efficient men prefer to join the private sector or leave the public sector as soon as they get better offers from the private sector. Such frequent changes do not allow grow of deep – rooted interest of the professional managers in the public enterprises.

(d) Perhaps the greatest weakness lies in the man-management. Lack of discipline has become a common and regular feature in almost every public enterprise. Reckless trade unionism, being guided more by political considerations than by labour interests, is the constant cause of failure of the public sector. Even the attempt of the government to appoint retired army officers or labour leaders as the topmost executive has not been successful. Full job security like that of a Government servant encourages the employees to go for extreme indiscipline. It is really strange that industrial unrests take place in public enterprises and the trade unions take recourse to destructive policies. Because of lack of proper man-power budgeting, most of the concerns are over-staffed.

(e) In the field of marketing, there is inefficiency as there is lack of incentive on the part of the marketing manager and his people.

(f) With regard to finance, there are two extreme sides. Rigid formalities are demanded by the departmental audit but at the same time there is usual extravagance as witnessed under bureaucracy. Misfeasance and misappropriation of funds are common. Complaints of manipulation and bribing are rampant.

(g) Of late,the Government is thinking of some positive steps for the improvement of the management of public enterprises. They are : (i) Professionalisation of management, as far as possible, granting greater autonomy which will, in turn, result in greater accountabilty. (ii) Greater autonomy to be signed to giant organisations like SAIL, CIL, BHEL, NTPC, ONGC etc. by signing Memorandum of Understanding (MOU) for each which is a 'critical instrument providing the parameters where the Government would act and where the unit's chief executive would have autonomy. A very unfortunate state of affairs is that very often the post of the chief executive remains vacant for a long time for the inability of the Government to select a competent person. (iii) The Government may set up five or six 'super holding companies' (in Italian model) to take over a number of enterprises.

(5) **Lack of social consciousness** — By far the greatest ailment is the lack of social consciousness among the people as a whole. We are yet to recognise the public enterprises to be the properties of the people as a whole. About three hundred years of foreign rule makes us feel even today that the Government is an outsider, if not an alien. We do not realise that any loss to a public enterprise is ultimately our personal loss. We forget that any diseconomy in the public sector means a step towards rising price. **The citizens of India, the Indian public, have not identified themselves with the public enterprises.** The public enterprises are not 'public' in true sense. Socialism in India is only lip-deep.

Remedies

The Government, in its usual way, has set up a number of Committees, Bureaus, Study Teams, etc. to find out ways and means to overcome the shortcomings and to adopt remedial measures. Heaps of report have been published but the implementation of the recommendations have not been commensurate. Innumerable speeches have been delivered by the Ministers, political leaders and trade unionists. Whenever a new Government comes, fresh assurances are given for the improvement of the public sector. The election manifesto of every recognised political party makes promises to bring in socialism. In practice, the public enterprises (at least most of them) continue as white elephants. In the name of socialism we more and more takes side with "state capitalism". The public sector cannot prosper economically so long as, in the name of democracy, we indulge in indiscipline and, while professing socialism, we deliberately forget that every citizen has certain reponsibilities to the society.

GOVERNMENT POLICIES AND CONTROL

The need — The Government, in a Welfare State like India, has the responsibility to see that the resources of the country are properly utilised, in the interest of the people as whole. Such responsibility is equally aimed at by both the private and public sectors. But the responsibility in the field of the public sector is reasonably more as the Government itself takes the risks on behalf of the public. The Government must show the way. It is really deplorable that the public enterprises are charged with inefficiency, misuse of resources, inability to avoid industrial unrest, failure to secure consumer satisfaction, etc. Apprehending such irregularities and shortcomings, the Constitution of India makes some provisions for control of the public undertaking through Parliament on behalf of the people. The Governmental control over the public enterprises is primarily Parliamentary control. But there is usual financial control through the Government audit.

On the whole, the control over the public enterprises is exercised by virtue of the **guidelines provided in the Constitution and the policies time to time determined by the political**

party in power. The different types of control and the Government policies in respect of that are discussed below :

(1) **Questions in Parliament** — The members are entitled to ask questions on the workings of the different public enterprises during the question hours in Parliament and the Ministers concerned have to supply satisfactory and relevant answers.

(2) **Debate in Parliament** — Public enterprises have to submit accounts and reports before Parliament (or State Assembly) as there is the question of public accountability. The President in his inaugural speech in Parliament (the Governor in the State Assembly) makes reference to public enterprises. Reference to public enterprises is also made in budget allocations. These provide opportunities for debate on public enterprises. Sometimes, Committees are appointed on the basis of such debates for further investigations and recommendations.

(3) **Special Committees** — In the past, there was a provision to appoint two committees called the Public Estimates Committee and the Public Accounts Committee with some MP's (MLA's in case of States) belonging to different parties as members and a Chairman from the Opposition Party, to look into the functions of the public enterprises. In 1964, a system of appointing a special committee called the Public Undertakings Committee has been introduced instead of the aforesaid two committees. The function of the Committee is to examine the reports and accounts, including the reports of the Comptroller and Auditor General, on the public undertakings and to see whether in the context of the autonomy of the public undertakings they have been "managed with sound business principles and prudent commercial practices". On the basis of reports of the Committee, the Government takes various actions. Though, theoretically, it is an effective method of control, it is complained that the Committee is often influenced by political motivations.

(4) **Direct Government control** — The Government companies or public corporation have to prepare documents like the Memorandum and the Articles. By virtue of such documents the Government exercises direct control over the public enterprises because the Government is generally empowered (a) to appoint the chairman, the directors, the chief executive, etc., (b) to sanction capital expenditure, borrowings beyond certain limits, etc.; (c) to issue directives keeping line with the plans and programmes taken up by the Government in general; (d) to determine terms and conditions of employment, etc. The Government as the only or the majority shareholder has the right to have such control. Indirectly, the Ministry concerned exerts influence on each enterprise.

(5) **The Bureau of Public Enterprise** — The government has set up **a number of Divisions in different Ministries and in the Planning Commission** to have better coordination among the public enterprises and to have Governmental control over them. **The Bureau of Public enterprises set up under the Ministry of Finance** is by far the most effective agency for the purpose. It has the following main functions : (a) to provide consultation and advice for coordinated functioning of public undertakings : (b) to suggest ways and means to improve the productivity and profitability of the public enterprises; (c) to make periodical review of the working of individual units; (d) to apprise the Government with their findings; (e) to carry out research and to make publication of books and journals related to the public enterprises, etc.

(6) **Project Planning** — In 1971, after two decades from launching the Five-Year Plans, the Planning Commission realised the importance of project planning in the public sectors. The Government appointed in 1972 a Project Appraisal Board (PAD) in the Planning Commission with the following objects : (a) to suggest a standard format for submitting projects; (b) to carry out cost – benefit analysis of the projects; (c) to help the Central and State Governments in the matters of project evaluation. The Government also set up a special committee called the Public Investment board (PIB) for scrutinising public sector investment projects involving Rs. 5 crores or more. The suggestions of PAD pass through PIB for final decisions by the Government.

THE JOINT SECTOR

Meaning — In simple words, the term Joint Sector means a **partnership between the private entrepreneurs and the Government,** whether Central or State. Joint Sector is also defined as application of the concept of **mixed economy at the micro – level.** The Industrial Policy of 1956 referred to mixed economy at the macro – level but the **Industrial Policy of 1956 indirectly hinted to Joint Sector.** The Industrial Policy of 1956 divided the industries into three categories or in three Schedules – A. B and C. With regard to industries belonging to Schedule B, it has been stated that "Private enterprise will also have the opportunity to develop in this field, either on its own or with state participation". With regard to industries belonging to Schedule C, it has been stated that "In suitable cases, the State may also grant financial assistance to the private sector. Such assistance especially when the amount involved is substantial, will preferably be in the form of participation of equity capital, though it may also be in part in the form of debenture capital".

On the basis of the Industrial Policy of 1956, Joint Sector enterprises cropped up at different parts of the country with partnership between the State and private entrepreneurs even together with or exclusively with foreign collaboration. Some important examples are Madras Fertilisers, Madras Refineries, Cochin Refineries, Gujarat State Fertiliser Corporation, etc.

The Industrial Licensing Policy Enquiry Committee of 1969 for the first time made categorical reference to 'joint sector' and advocated for it. According to the Committee, there can be the **following alternative forms of 'joint sector' :**

(1) Existing private enterprises belonging to large industrial house, should be brought under the joint sector by converting the loans given by public financial institutions into equity capital.

(2) Those private undertakings where already the State has made participation in the equity capital shall be called joint sector enterprises.

(3) In order to prevent economic concentration of power large size industrial units, belonging to the categories of **Schedule B and Schedule C,** shall be under joint sector.

The Committee wanted that a joint sector enterprise shall be more inclined to a public sector enterprise with the State as a partner playing predominant role.

The Tata Memorandum — Sri J. R. D. Tata, in a memorandum, called the Tata Memorandum and submitted to the Government, defined joint sector as partnership between the private sector and the Government where (a) the Government should hold 26% of the capital and (b) the day-to-day management should normally be in the hands of the private sector but the Government should have adequate representation in the Board of Directors. It is interesting to note that before the idea of joint sector could be floated by the Industrial Policy of 1956, the Tatas had created the Air India International jointly with the Government.

Areas of operation

The joint sector, because of its various interpretations, is found in operation in different forms in the public as well as in the private sectors.

The Dutt Committee Report and the Tata Memorandum have defined the scope of 'Joint Sector' in different ways. However, we can say that, keeping in view the objectives for the creation of the joint sector, the operation of this sector has been over an wide area.

Joint sector operates in the Refineries and the Fertilizers company areas since the Industrial Policy Resolution of 1956.

Since the Dutt Committee Report appeared in 1969, a number of State Governments and State Industries Development Corporations have participated in industrial projects with private participation in ownership and management.

According to the Tata Memorandum, the areas of operation of the joint sector may be existing private enterprises, Centrally sponsered new companies, existing public sector companies, newly sponsored State Government enterprises. In all these areas, the Central and the State Governments will mainly look after the financial requirements of the Joint Ventures. The financial aspect of the joint sector being the primary consideration of the comments, it can be said that the areas of operation of the joint sector are wide open where the private sector is either operating but languishing for lack of funds, or the public sector is operating but lacking in Managerial efficiency.

So, where there is need for the economic development of the country, a joint effort – better financial and managerial combination – is attempted. The confinement of the joint sector to the core sector of the economy as envisaged by the Dutt Committee has not been conducive to the overall development of the economy of the country. This narrow concept of joint sector frustrates the very object of the joint sector effort. The development of the core sector alone cannot lead the country to the desired economic development.

So, the areas of operation of the Joint Sector are in the Public enterprises with private participation and in the private enterprises with public participation. With a happy marriage between capital and management, a joint sector venture in any area of our economy is expected to bring in the desired objective of the joint sector concept.

Government Policy on the Joint Sector

The Government policy on the Joint Sector can be ascertained from its industrial policy decision of February, 1973.

The policy enunciates :

(1) Joint Sector would conform to Governments' social and economic objective.

(2) The areas left void by the private sector because of the existing policy will be filled in by the Joint Sector.

(3) New and medium entrepreneurs would use the Joint Sector as a promotional instrument.

(4) Policies, management and operation of the Joint Sector would be controlled effectively by the Government.

The Government had accepted in principle the concept of joint sector long ago but wanted to implement it after the recommendations of the Industrial Licensing Policy Enquiry Committee were presented. **The Government issued some guidelines with regard to the composition** of joint sector enterprises with participation of State Governments or State Industrial Development Corporations. It can be presumed that the Government wants to have specific rules for respective joint sector enterprises at the Central Government level. **The guidelines are :** (a) When there is **no foreign participation :** (i) 26% of the equity shares to be held by the State Government or State Industrial Development Corporation. (ii) 25% of the equity shares by the private entrepreneurs. (iii) 49% of the equity shares by the investing public and financial institutions. (b) When there is **foreign participation :** (i) 25% of the equity share to be held by the State Government or State Industrial Development Corporation. (ii) 20% by the Indian entrepreneur. (iii) 20% by the foreign investor. (iv) 30% by the investing public. (c) In no case a single party (private) is allowed to hold more than 25% of the paid-up capital without previous permission of the Central Government. (d) Permission to form a joint sector undertaking is necessary from the Central Government if the private entrepreneur belongs to a big industrial house or a foreign majority company.

Nature and Importance of Joint Sector— By nature a Joint Sector appears to be **a compromise between nationalisation and economy of free enterprise.** By Joint Sector the Government avoids to take full responsibility of the undertaking. The whole approach is for faster economic growth and not breaking of concentration of economic power. There is a general trend in all States towards establishment of Joint Sector enterprises. This is quite so because after the failure of the public sector to a great extent and financial shortage faced by the private sector, the Joint Sector appears to be a way out.

The **importance of Joint Sector** can be understood from the following viewpoints :

(1) **The findings of the Industrial Licensing Policy Enquiry Committee adequately justify** the importance of Joint Sector. The Government is not in a position to nationalise a large number of industries. The private sector, enjoying financial assistance on a large scale from the financial institutions, cannot be asked for repayment immediately. On the other hand, such financial assistance has been largely responsible for the creation of big industrial houses. The only solution for all such problems is the Joint Sector.

(2) **The rate of investment in the private sector is on the decline** on account of various reasons. Private investment is not expected for basic or heavy industries but they need be developed with heavy capital expenditure. The Joint Sector may be the best form.

(3) The private sector has managerial efficeincy but does not have adequate capital to invest. Through Joint Sector, **the managerial efficiency can be fully utilised.** There is, however, no definite direction with regard to the pattern of management. The Tata Memorandum demanded that the control on day-to-day management should be in the hands of the private entrepreneur. The Government is not finally committed to this idea. Some are of the opinion that the representation on the Board of Directors should be in proportion to share–holdings. But it is doubtful that the Government or the participating financial institutions have enough qualified people to sent nominee directors to a large number of concerns. **Appointment of professional managers might be a good solution.**

(4) Generally, the public sector is meant for such industry where heavy investments are necessary though there is no guarantee of good or immediate returns. The Government cannot continue business under such circumstances for an endless period. Through Joint Sector, **the Government may enter into more profitable businesses** which so far remained with the private sector.

(5) The Joint Sector shall provide **opportunities for good investment** of the corporate and household savings.

(6) The Government, through Joint Sector, can also **direct private entrepreneurs to go for those desirable industries** development of which is wanted for the over–all interest of the nation and from the social point of view.

CHAPTER FIVE

BUSINESS COMBINATIONS

DEFINITION

Combination—Prof. Haney writes, "to combine is simply to become one of the parts of a whole, and a combination is merely a union of persons to make a whole or group for the prosecution of some common purpose". **Different business units combine together and become a bigger unit.** Such a unit is called a Combine. Combination is a state of affairs—a kind of relationship among some business units. The combined unit or a combine is also called a combination. There are **two aspects** of a combination: (a) There shall be a number of business units. (b) There shall be a common purpose for which they combine.

There are many **types and forms** of combinations. Types are considered from the **purpose** for which the combination is formed. Forms are considered from the **method** by which the combination is formed. The former is a classification from the nature of the combining units and the latter is a classification from the structure of the combine. It is a development in the last quarter of the nineteenth century, **originating in USA** and then spreading in other parts of the world. **Combination is also known as integration.**

Concentration—The word concentration in business is normally used to denote **centralisation of industries at one particular place.** There may be concentration of a number of industries at any particular region because of economic and geographical facilities or there may be concentration of a particular industry at a particular place because of special, mainly geographical, factors. For example, concentration of industries is found in and around Calcutta, particularly jute industry, to take the advantage of the port.

Concentration or centralisation is also used **to mean concentration of economic power** through ownership of a number of businesses. This may take place directly through combination or through holding of majority shares in number of companies or indirectly or even secretly through various kinds of manipulations by holding controlling amount of shares or voting rights, transfer of funds from one company to another, benami ownership etc. **A combination is generally a concentration but a concentration is not necessarily a combination.**

The main characteristic is that a group of persons having an intention to possess more wealth take some steps to control a number of business units.

No Government of a country likes concentration or any combination if it is with a motive of concentration. There are legislations all over the capitalistic world to control such combinations and straightway concentration. In socialistic countries, all economic powers are concentrated in the hands of the State for social good. But whether the heads of the ruling political party exploit the situation for personal or 'party' gains is a matter of great doubts.

In a sense, a **partnership is a combination of persons** in business for some common purpose. But a company or a body corporate is not a combination because it is a person in the eye of law. **A few busines, units, however, may combine.** This is the most common form of combines.

In USA, there are laws to check combinations, e.g. the Anti-Trust Act or the Sherman Act. In India, there is law to check concentration, e.g. the MRTP Act.

CAUSE

Really speaking, there cannot be any 'cause' for a combination, there are causes. But there is **a root cause** no doubt. The root cause is defective competition. Prof. Clay has said "Competition leads to combination". When it 'leads' there must be some obvious and latent cause. That cause is excessive and defective competition.

Adam Smith, the father of Economics, had absolute faith in competition. Competition is based on the principle of 'survival of the fittest'. That leads to incentive to better production by which consumers are benefited and the society as a whole prospers. Competition pre-supposes self – interest. Prof. Clay has unrefutably argued that so long the interests of the competitors are of conflicting nature, there is competition. Conflict of interest starts from the very stage of procuring the factors of production, men and materials, and continues to exist till the products are sold and the customers are satisfied. Whenever the interests become common, the competing firms combine. Interests become common because of various reasons : (a) because of cut-throat competition by which nobody gains but everybody loses his capital slowly; (b) there is some common enemy, e.g. imported goods of better quality or cheaper price, discovery of a substitute etc.; (c) a few giant firms which survive cut-throat competition form a monopolistic combination. All these **situations** arise when competition is acute and excessive. Liefmann says, "This intensification of competition, which became a universal phenomenon of modern economy, led to the formation of combinations". Such condition was prevailing in the last quarter of the nineteenth century. All these factors are described as 'original, driving, beckoning and facilitating forces of combination'.

Further analysis — Every firm wants to grow in size for greater economy and higher profits. Competition becomes cut-throat when a firm fixes the price at a lower level even suffering loss but with the hope that some of the competitiors will be forced out of the market and then the former will have a commanding position and may even achieve monopoly. On the other hand, a few small firms may voluntarily combine to become jointly big in size and by that greater economy is achieved for higher profits. Therefore, behind combination there is **a motive for higher profit either with a monopolistic tendency or not.** If there is pure monopoly motive, the price is made high while if there is ecomomy motive, price is made low because of reduction of cost.

Taking all the views and situations together, the following **causes** (and not cause) or combination can be enumerated :

(1) **Wasteful competition** — Competition, a characteristic feature of capitalistic economy, gradually became defective, excessive and unfair. Freedom of enterprise led to mushroom growth of large firms with wastage of resources. Cut-throat competition led to nobody's gain. Competitors, once enemies, agreed to shake hands as competition became 'futile, obsolete and sterile'. Conflicting interests were replaced by common interests. Competition led to combination.

(2) **Economies of scale** — Smaller concerns cannot enjoy the benefits of large scale, cannot reduce cost and offer goods at the market price at profit, cannot engage in expensive research work for reduction of cost of improvement of quality and cannot buy better and bigger machines which are costly. Such firms may combine to gain the advantages of scale which individually they cannot. This is a **facilitating cause** of combination. This is a common cause for vertical combination.

(3) **Lust for power** — The lust for power and to build business empire often encourage some businessmen to join hands and to form a monopolistic combine even on international basis. 'Ambition for superlatives in all spheres of life' make competitors as cooperators who form combines. This can be done by groups of interested men capturing secretly the majority shares of companies and thereby creating a concentration. It is a **driving force** for combination.

(4) **Advantages of companies** — The constitution and operation of joint stock companies are such that by capturing majority shares secretly business empires can be built. If one company is captured, through that company another company can be captured by purchase of majority shares in the latter company by the former one. This is also a case of concentration by the same driving force as in lust for power.

(5) **Influence of tariffs** — Competing domestic producers may combine to compel the Government to impose duties on imported goods of better quality or cheaper price. Otherwise, all the domestic units will liquidate. Against such protective tariff wall, domestic firms thrive and at the same time mushroom weak firms also grow. These mushroom firms may

merge into combines for survival as none of them is economically viable. This is a facilitating force.

(6) **Trade cycle** — In a capitalistic economy where competition exists, there are cyclical movements of good time and bad time or prosperity and depression. These are called trade or business cycles. During depression, many firms have to suffer because of fall of demand for goods and falling of prices below economic levels. At this time, many firms combine for survival. This is an original force.

(7) **Organising ability** — People with organising ability are inelastic in supply. It is very common that some common individuals promote a number of companies and hold managerial posts. In this way, indirectly, concentrations take place which are akin to combinations. This can also be described as a driving force.

(8) **Rationalisation** — Rationalisation means putting reason to industry. In other words, it means introduction of scientific management for higher productivity not in one single firm but in an industry as a whole by introducing better production techniques and greater mechanisation. A part of reationalisation programme is combination of inefficient firms for their survival. This is one of the beckoning forces.

(9) **Nationalisation** — When there is nationalisation of an industry as a whole, all the firms under it are taken over by the State and brought under unified State control and ownership. In fact, a combination is created. This is a beckoning force. This is done either to save the industry or to save the society from the exploitation by the industry which itself has turned out to be a monopolistic combine or a case of monopolistic competition.

(10) **Cult for colossal** — There is a great respect, if not awe, for big business. This inspires some firms to combine to become a colossal or a giant so that all others are respectful or fearful of the unit. Big industrial houses are motivated by this driving force which leads to not only combination but also concentration. By influencing other companies, such interested people bring those companies under their fold or resort to clever manipulations to achieve the goal.

(11) **Government's policy** — Recently in India, the Government is wanting combination to save sick firms. Instead of providing financial assistance to sick units through Industrial Reconstruction Bank of India, the Government wants that one sick company may be taken over by an efficient company. The latter will get benefit of set-off in income-tax by adjusting the losses of the sick unit with its profits. This can be called a facilitating force.

TYPES

Combinations or integrations are classified into different types **according to the nature of functions of the combining units.** Accordingly, **there are four types of combinations :** Horizontal, Vertical, Lateral, and Diagonal. Sometimes a combination may be of a mixed type and cannot be placed in any of the above types. Each type of combination can be further classified according to their **structures** or forms. Thus, combinations are classified on the **basis of two questions :** Who are combining ? How are they combining ?

(1) **Horizontal combination — When some business units doing the same business and being on the same plane or level combine together,** it is called a 'horizontal' or 'trade' or 'parallel' or 'unit' combination. For example, two or three cotton mills may combine, a few transport service companies may combine, or a number of retail shops may combine.

Purpose — There are many purposes behind such combination : (1) To enjoy benefits of large scale. (2) To fight a common enemy. (3) To survive during depression time. (4) To reduce cost of production and earn more profits. (5) To establish monopoly.

Effects — Whatever may be the purpose behind such combining, there are some economic effects. Competition, at least cut-throat competition, is eliminated. If they are manufacturing units then production can be standarised and quality can be improved by joint research.

Similarly, marketing becomes less expensive through joint publicity. Economy can be achieved in every respect leading to reduction of cost. In practice, however, such combinations have **monopolistic tendency.** By combining they want to avoid wasteful competition, restrict entry of others in the business and enjoy maximum profits by raising prices.

Forms — The combining units are basically rivals to one another. They combine on the point of some common interest. Generally they choose **loose forms** of combination, so that the identity of the combining units is not totally lost. Such combinations may not be very durable. Such integrations are called **external type integration.**

(2) **Vertical combination — When some business units, engaged in various successive stages of a line of production or trade, combine,** it is called a 'vertical' or 'process' or 'sequence' combination. As the units do not stand on the same plane but at different levels of a productive activity, it is called vertical combination. As they belong to different processes which are successive or sequential, such combinations are also called process or sequence combinations. For example, when extraction of iron ore, making of pig or pure iron out of the iron ore, making of steel, making of steel goods out of steel by fabrication are all combined under one organisation, it is a case of vertical combination. Similarly, if cotton curing, spinning, weaving, dyeing, garment-making all are combined, there is vertical combination. Vertical combination also takes place when a manufacturer also opens own shops for selling the products and thereby integrating production and distribution. for example, the Bata (India) Ltd.

Purpose — There are some purposes behind such combination : (1) To gain economies by combining allied activities. (2) To get a sure market of the product or service as it will be consumed by another part of the unit. (3) To eliminate intermediate profits. (4) To establish a total control on the final product. (5) To have a very big size business and concentration of power.

Effects — It brings great economy by elimination of intermediate profits and the quality of the product is improved. In fact, vertical combination is suitable in that industry where the quality largely depends on the standard of the raw materials which again have to be processed through different stages or steps. It is suitable when the processes are complementary to one another and a balancing among them is necessary. Thus, there is a general tendency of such types of combination to achieve **overall economy** and higher profits through cost reduction.

Forms — The combining units are not competitive but complementary to one another and so it is obvious that the common interest is very strong. Generally, vertical combinations are of more durable and **strong type** and the combining units may lose their identities. This is an example of **internal type of integration.** The combination may take shape either **by forward or backward movement.** Suppose an iron mining firm combines with a pig iron making firm and then with a steel making firm and so on, then it is a case of forward movement. On the other hand, a steel making firm combines with a pig iron making firm and then with a mining firm, it is a case of backward movement.

(3) **Lateral combination** — When business units producing different but allied types of goods combine together it is called 'lateral' or 'allied' combination. It is a kind of 'Circular' combination in a broad sense. Lateral combination is of **two types :** (a) Convergent lateral combination and (b) Divergent lateral combination.

(a) **Convergent type** — When business units producing different goods or services but supplying them to a common industry combine, it is called convergent lateral combination. We may take the example of building construction industry. Different materials are produced by different units made of altogether different types of raw materials and using altogether different processes for the purpose, e.g. cement, iron rods, bricks, aluminium fabrications, steel fabrications, sanitary wares made of china clay, wooden fittings, electrical goods etc. But all these converge into common supplies to building construction. Business units producing those different goods may combine.

(b) **Divergent type** — This is a combination of different units producing different goods but each of them gets the raw material from the same source or they use the same raw material. The supplier of the common raw material may combine with other units producing the different final goods. For example, steel industry. From steel so many kinds of products can be made like engineering goods, vehicles of different types, machines, locomotives etc. If a steel mill combines with all these industries there is a divergent lateral combination.

Purpose — A convergent type of lateral combination is formed (1) To have assured market for its products. (2) To have improvement of quality in the interest of the common buyer and for self-interest. A divergent type of lateral combination is formed : (1) To get an assured market as there are so many definite openings. (2) Different grades of raw materials can be produced for different kinds of consumption and by that the plant can be run with full capacity. There may be a tendency towards monopoly or concentration.

Effects — In case of convergent combinations, the buyer industry is highly benefited because of regular supply and in accordance with demand. In case of divergent combinations it is a kind of vertical expansion. It is very difficult to control so many divergent units.

Form — The firms are of different nature but they have some common link. Generally they are of loose forms in case of convergent and strong forms in case of divergent combinations.

(4) **Diagonal combination** — When a main producer combines with those units which either supply some ancillary parts or other services required by himit is a diagonal combination. For example, a big manufacturer may combine with its power generating and supplying concern. Suppose a manufacturer sells his products in tin containers which are supplied by another concern. The manufacturer may combine with the container supplier. Such a combination is also known as service combination. It is a kind of circular combination in a broad sense.

Purposes : The purposes of such combination are : (1) To have greater economy by reduction of cost of ancillary service. (2) To have assurance of supply of some essential part or service. (3) To gain advantage in the competitive market.

Effects : By such combination generally economy is achieved. Sometimes a big advantage is earned over other competitors particularly when there is a crisis in a particular service which is taken up. For example, when other competitors are suffering from power cuts, a producer having his own generating sets gets a clear advantage over others.

Forms : Generally the form of such kind of combination shall be strong. It is a kind of internal integration.

Conclusion — Integration of some form or other is common in big companies. Most of them have combination with some of the auxiliary or ancillary service units or power or raw material supply units. These subordinate power plants or raw material supplying units or mines are called 'captive' plants or 'captive' mines. More or less, these can be described as vertical integrations with backward movement.

EVOLUTION OF FORMS

For different purposes different types of combinations or integrations are formed by different business units engaged in either competitive or complementary business activities. Combinations are formed when their interests become common. In fact, the interests of the complementary business units are never conflicting but complementary. **Structurally, the combination can take different forms according to their durability and cohesion.** The combining units will form into strong, durable and complete combination when the interests have become permanently common. The units may even lose their respective identities. On the other hand, they will form into loose temporary and apparent combinations when their interests have become temporarily common. In such combinations, the combining units retain their respective identities and keep the door open for future separation. In short, **forms of combination depend on the degree of permanence of the common interests.** Competitive units generally form loose combinations which are mostly of horizontal type while complementary units generally form strong combinations which are mostly of other types.

Forms of combination have evolved out of circumstances and regulatory measures adopted by the Governments of different countries. Sometimes the same form bears different names in different countries. Broadly speaking, the forms are classified into three major groups and then each broad group has its own subdivisions. First of all there are **Simple combinations and Compound combinations.** Partnership form of business is a simple form of combination made of individual persons. A body corporate also may be a partner. Compound combinations mean combinations of business units, which are being discussed here. Therefore, classification of forms of combination will be concerned with compound combinations only. Accordingly, there are seven categories of combinations as detailed below :

A. Associations

1. Trade Association
2. Informal or Gentlemen's Agreements
3. Chambers of Commerce.

B. Federations

1. Pools
2. Cartels.

C. Partial Consolidation

(1) Trusts

(2) Community of Interest – (i) Common shareholding, (ii) Interlocking Directorate, (iii) Companies under same management.

(3) Holding company – (i) pure, (ii) operating, (iii) parent, (iv) offspring, (v) primary and (vi) intermediary.

D. Complete consolidation

(a) Amalgamation

(b) Merger or Absorption.

The arrangement is according to the degree of permanence.

A. ASSOCIATIONS

Businessmen often form into associations for some common purpose to safeguard or to augment their interests. The decisions taken by such associations are not binding on the members though they try to honour the decisions. Any directive given by the association cannot be enforced on any member. The employees or the workers also form such associations called trade unions. There is a Trade Union Act and any trade union formed under the Act has certain rights and obligations which can be enforced. There is, however, no such Act for the trade associations or the associations of the employers.

1. Trade Associations

Businessmen engaged in a particular line of business form a Trade Association of their own. Such associations are generally registered under the Societies Registration Act as a non-profit body with the following objects : (1) To look after the interest of a particular trade in the context of the society as a whole. (2) To safeguard and augment the interests of the trade as well as of the persons engaged in that trade. (3) To represent that trade before the Government and other bodies. (4) To prepare code of conduct of the members. (5) To assess the impact of the Government policies on that trade and to make representations. (6) To create better condition in the trade. (7) To protect the trade from adverse influences. (8) To maintain cooperation among the members. (9) To negotiate with the corresponding trade union. (10) To educate the members about the business to which they belong.

Such associations function through an Executive Committee consisting of office bearers periodically elected by the members. In a trade association of reasonable size there is a paid secretary. It may have a headquarters with regional and local branches. Usually a trade association is affiliated with a Chamber of Commerce (see below). Sometimes the entire office of a trade association is maintained by the Chamber.

A trade association holds meetings regularly on any topic concerning the trade or on general commercial matters. A library is maintained by a big association and bulletins or journals are published and distributed among the members. Circulars on trade matters, Government policies etc. are regularly circulated among the members. Members have to pay subscriptions regularly. Some important person in the society or in the Government is generally invited to address the annual general meeting of the association.

Historically, trade associations have evolved out of informal agreements among the businessmen.

The size and importance of such an association depends on the nature and importance of the trade itself. In India, there are some very powerful trade associations which cast influence on the Governmental policies and the general economy of the country. The Government takes such associations into confidence before taking any policy decision related to that trade or industry. For example, the Indian Jute Mills Association, the Tea Association of India, the Millowners' Association (the association of the cotton millowners), etc. There are about 1,000 such associations, big or small, in the country. There are associations of general character, not representing any particular line of business, e.g. All India Manufacturers Association. There may be separate associations for big and small units in the same industry.

2. Informal or Gentlemen's Agreements

Businessmen often enter into some understanding among themselves with regard to (a) the prices to be charged for the goods or services; (b) the terms of credit to be offered to the customers; (c) the discount to be offered to the retailers or agents; (d) the rates of wage payment, etc. These are all informal agreements without having any legal compulsion. But, as gentlemen, the business people honour these agreements and, therefore, they are also known as Gentlemen's Agreements. Such agreements, if made effective, do good to the trade. But there are occasions when some signatories make defaults and do not honour the agreements particularly when there is depression and market becomes down. Generally, the price agreed to is high enough to protect the most inefficient firm whose cost of production is the highest. This is definitely disadvantageous for the customers. Sometimes, members belonging to a trade association enter into such special agreements. Apparently, such agreements are in restraint of trade but according to the Law of Contract trade agreements are permissible unless it is anti-social and has a monopolistic or exploiting attitude.

3. Chambers of Commerce

Chambers of Commerce are associations of businessmen to work for the benefits of the business community as a whole of a particular region or businesses of particular size or even on the basis of pattern of ownership. These are bigger organisations than trade associations in respect of their constitution and function. Most of the trade associations are affiliated with some chamber. A trade association looks after the interests of individual members mostly while a chamber is concerned with the business **itself. A chamber can be described as an association of associations.** A chamber is often registered as a non-profit-making company. The members of a chamber are mainly institutional members, not merely individuals.

It is believed that businessmen formed into chambers as a counter–movement to trade unions. But, unlike trade unions, there are no legislations for chambers.

The functions of Chambers of Commerce are varied and can be : (1) To protect the interests of business and the business community as a whole. (2) To collect information, statistics etc. about business and to circulate them among the members. (3) To represent the business community before the Government to uphold their cause. (4) To promote, support or oppose legislations made or to be made by the Government affecting the interests of business and businessmen. (5) To hold seminars, conferences etc. to discuss on matters related to the economic issues. (6) To run libraries for the study of the members. (7) To publish booklets, journals, reports etc. for the members as well as for the public. (8) To carry out research on different aspects of the commercial world. (9) To send abroad or to receive from abroad trade delegations to foster trade and industry of the country. (10) To hold fairs and exhibitions for the development of trade and industry. (11) To arbitrate in the disputes among the members. (12) To take charge of trade associations affiliated with it. (13) To represent the business community by sending nominees on different types of official bodies like a Port Trust, Improvement Trust etc. (14) To issue certificates of origin for goods to be exported. (15) To participate in local or civic bodies or even in Parliaments.

Chambers are also found in socialist countries of East Europe. Their main function is to promote socialistic ideas in the fields of industry and commerce.

Types of Chamber — Broadly speaking there are two types of chamber : (1) In certain countries chambers **have Governmental support** and they are semi-official bodies as we find in France. There, the Government sends representatives in a chamber. Such a chamber may be entrusted with administering public undertaking or public utility services on behalf of the Government. (2) Most of the countries, however, have **non-official chambers** though the Government invites opinions or suggestions from the chambers on different issues affecting business. Big chambers invariably invite ministers to address their annual general meetings where the ministers spell out Government's commercial, industrial or fiscal policies. Further, chambers **can also be classified** according to region, character of the business represented by the members, etc. The whole picture can be well understood from India's case.

A case for India

In India the idea of chamber was brought by the British people as soon as they established business here. The first chamber was the Bengal Chamber of Commerce and Industry, established in Calcutta in 1834. The membership was exclusively for the white people and Indians were not allowed. Later on, during the Swadeshi Movement, to counter the colour bar instituted by the British rulers, the Indian Chamber of Commerce at Coconada in 1885 and Bengal National Chamber of Commerce and Industries in Calcutta in 1887 were established by Indian patriots. Since then, Chambers of Commerce have been established in different parts of the country, first in the important cities and then state-wise. At present, there are more than one hundred chambers in the country, big or small.

Another peculiar feature has been establishment of chambers on religion or race basis. For example, the Muslim Chamber of Commerce, the Marwari Chamber of Commerce etc. Now these parochial chambers have been re-constituted and re-named as Oriental Chamber of Commerce and Bharat Chamber of Commerce, respectively. On the other hand, the classification of chambers now stands on the scale of business represented by them. For example, Bengal National Chamber of Commerce represents more or less small and medium scale businesses. Bharat Chamber of Commerce is for medium scale and trading business. Bengal Chamber of Commerce representing British-predominated industries is now declining fast. Indian Chamber of Commerce is practically the main representative body for big industries in Eastern India. Federation of Associations of Small Industries in India has been formed to represent the small scale industries specially. Merchant Chamber of Commerce generally represents the small and medium scale traders. And so on. There is a Junior Chamber of Commerce for the young entrepreneurs.

During the European predominance in Indian business, the Associated Chambers of Commerce (ASSOCHAM) was formed in 1920 as a federal all-India body affiliating other chambers. It has lost its importance now. Instead, the Federation of Chambers of Commerce of India (FCCI), with its headquarters in New Delhi, has emerged as the supreme affiliating national chamber bringing under its affiliation all the other leading chambers in the country. It was established in 1927 and has now about 100 affiliated chambers.

International Chamber of Commerce — This institution was established in 1920 with its headquarters in Paris to promote the development of international trade, to bring down trade barriers and to foster better international commercial relations. It is governed by a Council of members elected by the member countries. There are about 50 members. Every country desirous of being a member must set up a National Committee for the purpose. India is a member and she has a National Committee for the purpose with its office in New Delhi.

B. FEDERATIONS

Federations are **loose types of external combinations** under which a few firms **join together on some specific points** and enter into some formal agreements but under no circumstances the internal autonomy of the firms is affected. It means that they combine on some aspect or aspects but competition among them continues in other aspects.

1. Pools

Pool — This is a common type of federation originated in USA. It looks like an informal price agreement but really it is quite different from that. There is an **agreement among the members on price** no doubt but there is **also some controlling element** with that so that the agreement can be enforced. Prof. Haney defines a pool as "a form of business agreement established through federation of business units whose members seek a degree of control over price by combining some factor in the price making process in a common aggregate and apportioning that aggregate among the units". From the definition, **the characteristics of a pool** come out to be as follows : (1) It is a federation or loose type of combination of business units. (2) The members of the pool want a degree of control over the price, i.e. there is an agreed price below which no member shall sell. (3) The members want to combine on some price-making process. The following factors come in the price-making process – the output and the market. (4) Apportionment of some common aggregate i.e. fixation of quota of output for each member or demarcation of the market area for each of them. Once these areas are apportioned, the agreement on price can be enforced. Therefore, **a pool is stronger than mere price agreement.** The combining units, however, do not lose their identities.

The following types of pools are found :

(1) **Output pool** — The members of the pool agree to control the output of every member according to the total demand of the product in the market and accordingly fix up the price. By checking possible over-production, the possibility of falling of price is also checked. In this way an aggregate pool* of supply is created. A quota is fixed for every member up to which he can produce. He has to submit a monthly report of his production. For fixation of output, hours of work in the factory may be fixed, number of shifts also may be minimised. If the forecasting on demand in the market is wrong then the whole scheme may upset. There may be controversy among the members with regard to the basis of fixing the quota. These are the occasions when a pool may break. But, anyway, no under-selling is possible. Total production may hamper and growth of the industry may be checked.

(2) **Market pool** — The price agreement can be maintained and controlled by **apportioning** among the members **the market share.** Market pools can be established in three ways :

* The word 'pool' has come from the gambling world. In a gambling, all the gamblers keep their stakes (money risked) at a common place on the gambling board, called 'pool'. The owner of the gambling den takes a percentage of the total stakes or pool as his commission.

(a) by territories, (b) by products and (c) by customers. Each member is allotted a definite market area within which he can sell his products. Or, when there are different types of products, each member is authorised to deal in some selected product, or products. Or, each member is authorised to cater to the needs of the particular class of customers. The territory may be divided into two parts : (a) the pool territory where the restriction applies and (b) the free territory which is outside the restriction. Some freedom is allowed to members for adjustments. If corresponding to market pool there is also output pool then the operation of the system becomes practicable, otherwise the members may try to evade.

(3) **Income or Profits Pool** — Output pool is adversely affected by wrong forecasting or over-production. Market pool is not liked by customers as their choice is restricted. An improved type of pool is Income or Profits pool. In this type a central agency is set up by agreement which will fix prices on contracts with the third parties. If a member can supply the goods to the central agency then there is an **income** of the central agency which **is pooled.** Or, if a member can increase the price by bidding with the customer, he makes an extra prof it which is pooled. This pooled income or profit is distributed among the members according to their productive capacities.

(4) **Other types** — There are other types of pools also. (a) Patent pool – The patent rights of different units are pooled and used in a manner beneficial to all members. (b) Traffic pool – Transport companies, particularly the Shipping Companies, through Shipping Conferences, restrict competition among themselves by dividing the territories among them.

Advantages of pool

(1) It is **easy to form** such combination.

(2) The combining units **do not lose their independent identity** and so can go out any time.

(3) As there is independence of the units, the capital is not blocked together and there is **no fear of over-capitalisation.**

(4) It is **a flexible system** and adjustments of the terms of agreement can be made time to time.

(5) **Imperfect competition** is controlled to some extent.

(6) It **does not affect the financial liability** of the members adversely.

Disadvantages of pool

(1) **It is unstable** because the separate identity of each member is retained and any one may break out.

(2) It **protects the inefficient units** and in the long run it may affect the business as a whole.

(3) It has a **monopolistic tendency** and leads to concentration of economic power.

(4) Through **restriction of production** the country's economic progress is hampered.

(5) **Customers' choice is restricted** causing dissatisfaction.

Evolution of Pool

Pools, originated in USA, became popular in the country leading to monopolistic combination. The courts in USA declared pools unlawful as against public policy. Therefore, pools disappeared being replaced by other devices of which formation of Selling Syndicate is one. Besides, Trusts came into existence (see below). Though pools were eliminated by law in USA, they emerged in other countries, specially in Germany in the form of Cartels having also characteristics of a Selling Syndicate (see below).

2. Cartels (or Syndicate)

Cartels or Syndicates are pools in different form as found in European countries. **Essentially, a cartel is a pool with a common selling agency.** Cartels or Kartells originated in

Germany, encouraged by the Government. Liefmann defines cartel as a "voluntary agreement between, or association of, independent enterprises of similar type to secure a monopoly of the market".

From the above definition the **following characteristics** of a cartel are found : (1) It is a voluntary agreement or association. (2) The enterprises remain independent and do not lose their identities through combining. (3) They are of similar type, and so a cartel is a horizontal type of integration. (4) The agreement is based on selling or the markets. (5) There is a motive for establishing a monopoly. The last characteristic is very significant. It is very strange that the Government of Germany encouraged cartels.

In such form of combination a number of producers form a company **(Cartel) to which every combining unit will deliver his products** with the exclusive right of selling them in the market. The cartel pays the combining units for their goods at agreed rates fixed on the basis of some standard price for a standard quality. **The cartel sells the goods as a discriminating monopolist** in the market on the principle of what the traffic can bear, i.e. charging different prices from different customers or in different areas and thereby maximising profits. **The profits are distributed among the members.** The cartel may also fix the limits of output by members according to the market conditions. The combining units concentrate on production only. Production and distribution are separated. Competition continues at production level.

Types of Cartel

(1) Ordinary — If cartels are considered as **counterpart of pools** in Europe then cartels can be (1) Price Cartel - by agreement the price is fixed at which every member unit is bound to sell his product. It is more or less a Price Agreement or Simple Association. (2) Output cartel — This is same as an output pool. (3) Market cartel - This is same as a market pool.

(2) **Proper** — A proper cartel is a cartel **with a selling agency.** It is what is known as Syndicate in USA.

(3) **International cartel** — Many German cartels assumed international character. International cartels were also formed in UK and USA on the German model. There were more than 150 international cartels even some with multinational ownership operating in the world before the Second World War. The mechanism of operation of an international cartel is as follows - (a) the domestic markets are reserved for the member units and (b) the foreign markets are divided among the members under a quota system agreed upon by them. Some leading international cartels are : the Dyestuff Cartel of I.G. Farben, the Unilever Organisation of which Hindustan Lever Ltd. is a subsidiary, the Standard Vacuum Oil Co., the Imperial Chemical Industries, the General Electric Company, etc.

Advantages of Cartel

(1) The **members are relieved** from the complications of distribution function.

(2) The members enjoy all the **economies of large scale marketing.** Common expenses of publicity, sales organisation, transportation etc. lead to economy.

(3) The members can concentrate in production and **can improve** the techniques of production and the quality of the products.

(4) The members **retain their independence** as separate units and may break out when they like.

(5) The members can enter into **international market** which independently might not be possible.

Disadvantages of Cartel

(1) Cartels are **unstable** and most of the pool type of cartels were ineffective.

(2) Cartels allow **inefficient firms to continue** which may ultimately affect the business adversely.

(3) Cartels have **monopoly motive** which is anti-social. Moreover, international cartels exploit underdeveloped countries through 'dumping' or charging very low prices so that those countries cannot develop the industries. Ultimately the Government takes control measures. The public also go against.

(4) It is very **difficult to make forecasting** for such wide markets and so imbalance between demand and supply occurs.

(5) All other **disadvantages of a pool** also apply.

Evolution of Cartel

Cartels (Kartells) originated in Germany as early as in 1860 as price cartels. By virtue of Government patronage during the Prime Ministership of Bismarck, cartels developed tremendously during the end of the nineteenth century. Certain industries, like coal, were fully cartelised. The Government wanted this for the development of the industry through economic marketing. There was a set– back during the First World War but after that there was a big thrust in the cartelisation process and a large number of industries came under it. Hitler used the cartels as tools for rapid industrial development in the country for war preparation.

After the Second World War and defeat of Germany, a policy of decartelisation was adopted. But the cartels are reappearing in Germany once the country has gained a tremendous momentum of economic growth.

Other types

Corners and Rings — When **a businessman holds all the available supplies of a commodity in the market there is cornering.** Forming corners is an age-old practice by businessmen. It existed in ancient times as well as in Middle Ages. A corner is not exactly a combination. But **when a number of businessmen form into a group to corner the market,** such a group is called a **Ring.** There is no agreement like a pool or cartel but it is purely a temporary affair. Generally, a ring is formed for speculative purposes. Cornering and ring formation are common in organised markets. A ring offers very high price to the producers to buy up the entire stock and charges still higher prices for making monopoly profit. The consumers have to suffer. The whole idea is anti-social.

Consortium — A purely short-term combination formed for a particular venture. The ISCON (Iron and Steel Consortium) was formed by some British firms for the Durgapur project.

Joint Ventures — A Joint venture takes place when two or more persons enter into a contract to do some business jointly either to complete a particular work or for a particular period. Joint ventures are not exactly combinations.

C. PARTIAL CONSOLIDATIONS

1. Trust — The word 'trust' in the economic world means **holding of other's property in confidence.** An individual or an institution like a bank or a group of individuals, collectively known as the Board of Trustees, hold the property of an individual or a group of individuals or an institution, called the beneficiary or the beneficiaries. Directors are trustees to the companies. There are many such trusts in the country. The Trustees have the right to buy and sell the property and to enjoy some benefits in exchange of their services. There is the Trust Act of 1888 to control trusts. There are many charitable trusts for making charities out of the income of the trust property. **Such trusts are known as common trusts.** But a trust, as a kind of partial consolidation of business units, is different though it has the same approach.

There is still another kind of trust called **investment trust.** Such trusts raise capital from the market by selling securities and invest the fund in other securities. The income from such investments are distributed among the holders of the trust securities after deducting running expenses. The Unit Trust of India is a very good example.

We are interested in that kind of trust which is **a form of partial consolidation of business units.** Such a trust can be formed in any of the two ways :

(1) **Assigning shares to a Board of Trustees** — The shareholders of the companies wanting consolidation, called beneficiaries, assign their shares to a Board of Trustees and get in exchange Trust Certificates. By such assignment – (a) the Board of Trustees gets the authority to control and manage all the companies under a common policy and to appoint the top executives for running the companies; (b) the shareholders, now trust certificate holders, have the right to get proportional shares in the profits. Thus, in a trust, there is a fusion of the internal and external interests of the combining units.

(2) **Voting trusts** — Under this system, instead of assigning the shares, the shareholders or the beneficiaries transfer their voting rights to the Board of Trustees by which they can exercise control over the combining companies. The shares of the companies are retained by the respective shareholders and they are also transferable by them. But the voting right is not transferable.

A trust is a kind of internal integration, though the outward separate entities of the combining units are retained. Generally, trusts are vertical combinations.

Advantages

(1) Trusts are **more dependable and stable** compared to the pools and cartels because there is partial fusion of the combining units.

(2) **Economies of integration,** because of unified control, can be enjoyed. It is specially true for vertical trusts.

(3) The Board of Trustees can be constituted with efficient men and thereby **efficiency in management** is ensured.

(4) It helps **accumulation of large capital** under unified control by which better utilisation of resources can be possible.

(5) **Standardisation of products or services** can be possible because of unified control of the companies which belong to the same kind of business.

Disadvantages

(1) It is **difficult to form** a trust because there are a large number of formalities.

(2) It is **less flexible** and, once formed, it is difficult to dissolve. A beneficiary cannot easily come out of it if it has any grievance.

(3) Because of heavy accumulation of capital under unified control there **may be over-capitalisation.**

(4) Generally a trust develops a **monopolistic tendency,** specially when it is a horizontal type, and makes a trust anti-social.

(5) **The Board of Trustees can misuse their power** for their personal gains.

Evolution

The concept of trust originated in USA as early as in 1879 when the Standard Oil Company was established. Trusts in USA became monopolistic and exploited the markets, both domestic and foreign. There was a great agitation led by Sherman and in 1890 an Anti-trust Act, known as Sherman Act, was passed making trusts by assignment of shares illegal. To avoid the legal restrictions, the idea of voting trust was introduced, the Pure Oil Company being the best example of it. Later on, the US Government declared that trusts formed in good faith and for economy and not for any anti-social motive would not be illegal.

2. Community of interest

This is a device by which without any formal agreement, either permanent or temporary, among the combining units but with a **commonness of interest of a community** or a group of persons in a large number of companies a combination is formed which goes by the name of community of interest. This can take place in the following ways :

(1) Same persons hold shares in a large number of companies doing the same type or different types of business, located in the same area or in different areas. This is very common in India. Generally a group of businessmen take interests in a number of companies. This is so because the investment-minded people are small in number.

(2) The same persons are directors of a number of companies and thereby determining the policies of the companies with joint or common objectives. This is known as **inter-locking directorate.** When the same number of persons hold controlling amount of shares in a number of companies they also become the common directors. This is also very common in India. The members of big industrial families hold the posts of directors of a number of companies. They are even promoters of a large number of companies.

In India, **the managing agents** created a peculiar form of combination through their common management of a large number of companies. They even captured the majority seats in the Boards of Directors of the managed companies. Now, of course, the managing agency system has been abolished. Various regulatory measures have been adopted against interlocking-directorate or companies under the same group.

Thus we find that community of interests can be achieved by three ways : (a) financial integration by holding of shares, (b) administrative integration through interlocking directorate and thereby controlling the policies, (c) managerial integration through contract of management as found in the managing agency system.

Advantages and disadvantages are more or less the same as of trusts. But, there is an additional advantage of having common directors who themselves are generally the biggest risk - takers. Additional disadvantage is that it leads invariably to concentration of economic powers in the hands of a few. A major characteristic of community of interest form is secrecy. Outwardly, nothing can be known what is happening behind the scene.

Evolution

The concept of community of interest was discovered in USA as a substitute to trusts which were declared illegal in general.

Companies under same management — The Companies Act takes special care of companies under the same management and impose various restrictions. Two bodies corporate shall be deemed to be under the same management if (1) the managing director or manager of one body corporate is the managing director or manager of the other body corporate, or (2) if the majority of directors of one body corporate constitute a majority of directors of the other body corporate, or (3) if one-third or more of the total voting power in each of the bodies corporate is exercised or controlled by the same individual or body corporate or (4) when the holding company of a body corporate is under the same management as is the other body corporate, or (5) if the directors of one body corporate themselves or with relations hold majority shares in that body corporate as well as of the other.

3. Holding Companies

The term holding company means **one company holding control over another company or companies.** It is a consolidation in the real sense and with a definite purpose and at the same time retaining the separate entities of all the companies concerned. The company which holds control is called the Holding Company and the company on which the control is exercised is called the Subsidiary Company. One holding company may hold a number of subsidiary companies.

Methods — Such **holding of control can be established in the following different ways :** (1) When the holding company holds majority, i.e. at least 51% of the nominal capital in the subsidiary company. (2) When the holding company holds the majority voting rights of the subsidiary company. This is possible in two ways : (a) When the subsidiary company does not have share capital. (b) When the subsidiary company has a good amount of preference shares with disproportionate voting rights, then holding of majority of the equity shares and thereby holding majority voting rights is enough though the holding company does not hold majority of shares in the subsidiary company. (3) When the holding company has the power to appoint the majority of directors of the subsidiary company. (4) When a holding company holds control over a subsidiary company which again holds control over another company (as its subsidiary), then the first company is a holding company and the last company is its subsidiary. By practice, the Boards of Directors of a holding company and its subsidiary company are the same. Therefore, a holding company is akin to an interlocking directorate.

It is a kind of internal integration as there is much closer inner relationship. It may be of any type – horizontal, vertical, lateral or diagonal.

Types — Holding companies themselves are of different types depending on the nature of the companies making the consolidation. They are :

(1) **Parent or primary holding company** — When an existing company establishes hold on any other existing company by any one of the above methods, then the holding company is called parent or father or primary holding company.

(2) **Offspring holding company** — When a new company is incorporated to establish hold on any other existing company or companies by any one of the above methods then the holding company is called offspring holding company.

(3) **Intermediary holding company** — When a holding company establishes hold on other company or companies but itself is subsidiary to a holding company, then such holding company is called intermediary holding company and the first holding company can be described as a grandfather holding company. In fact, the last subsidiary company is subsidiary of the grandfather holding company too.

(4) **Pure holding company** — When a holding company is just satisfied with holding majority shares or majority voting rights of a subsidiary or subsidiary companies without taking interest in the managment, then such a holding company is a pure holding company. **An Investment Company,** whose business is to invest funds in shares and securities of other companies, may hold majority shares of another company in the process but such an investment company cannot be called a holding company.

(5) **Mixed holding company** — Such a holding company not only establishes hold on subsidiary company or companies but also takes interest in the management. Most of the holding companies are of mixed type. A holding company, established by power of appointing majority directors of the subsidiary company or companies, is invariably a mixed holding company.

Finance Companies — Finance companies take interest in promotion of companies and marketing and underwriting of their shares. They do not have any controlling interest in such companies. Finance companies are, strictly, not holding companies.

Advantages

(1) It is **easy to form** such a combination. No formality, no agreement among the combining units, i.e. their shareholders, and no legal documentation are necessary. A company buying the controlling shares of another company gradually, or at a time, in the open market can achieve the purpose.

(2) **It is very flexible.** The holding company can hold the controlling number of shares in the subsidiary as long as it likes. Any time the holding company may discontinue it by disposing of the shares.

(3) Through a holding company, **economies of large scale production as well as the advantages of integration** (specially vertical integration) can be enjoyed.

(4) There is **no** public criticism because apparently there is no exposition of **monopolistic or exploiting tendency.**

(5) With **comparatively small investment,** by only buying controlling amount of shares, big companies with huge assets can be brought under control. This is called **pyramiding of finance.**

(6) **Complete secrecy** can be maintained of the whole affairs as the subsidiaries retain their independent identities. (This is, however, not practicable. According to the Companies Act a holding company has to disclose details of the accounts of its subsidiaries together with its own accounts).

(7) **The goodwill** of the holding company can be enjoyed by the subsidiary company and *vice versa* by which both are benefited.

(8) If any **subsidiary runs at a loss** the holding company can **leave control over it** and so the economy of the holding company is not affected.

Disadvantages

(1) A holding company develops **power** to control over subsidiaries **without corresponding responsibilities.**

(2) The **management of subsidiary becomes loose** and ineffective because it goes into remote hands.

(3) There may be too much accumulation of capital in the hands of the subsidiary **leading to over-capitalisation.**

(4) There is every possibility of **exploitation of the subsidiary company** by the holding company and then leaving it.

(5) A **secret monopoly** is created with **concentration of economic power** in the hands of a few.

(6) The whole affair with large operations, huge capital and greater risks may **become ultimately expensive and uneconomic** and the shareholders do not gain.

(7) It is true that the subsidiary retains its identity but for all practical purposes the **subsidiary becomes a non-entity.**

(8) By **window-dressing of accounts** real position of the subsidiary is kept concealed so that the real position of the holding company cannot be known.

Evolution

When trusts were declared illegal, the idea of forming holding companies developed in USA towards the end of nineteenth centtury as an alternative with no apparent monopolistic tendency. In India the managing agents enjoyed all the advantages of holding company by virtue of management contracts and not by holding majority shares. Interlocking directorate was also a common feature by manipulation and not through proper election of directors. At present, some big holding companies are found in the public sector, e.g. Steel Authority of India Limited (SAIL) and Coal India Limited (CIL).

D. COMPLETE CONSOLIDATION

Complete consolidation takes place when two or more business units **combine to fuse together losing their independent identities.** Such fusion can take place in different forms but there are two purposes behind them : (1) to gain economies of scale and (2) to obtain a larger share of the market. Prof. Haney has defined complete consolidation as "a form of business organisation which is established by the outright purchase of the properties of the constituent organisations and the merging or the amalgamating of such properties into a single business unit".

From the above definition the **following characteristics** of complete consolidation are found : (1) **There is some purchase.** Either, one unit purchases the other unit, or, a new unit purchases all the combining units. In the former case it is a merger because one unit merges into another. Merger is also known as absorption because one unit absorbs the other unit. In the latter case there is amalgamation. By the fusion of two units a third new unit is formed. (2) The fusion may be either in the form of a merger (absorption) or amalgamation. (3) A single business unit is formed.

It has to be noted that such consolidation may be of horizontal or vertical type and is an example of **internal integration.**

Amalgamation — Either two or a few companies of same size, strength and reputation or of different size, strength and reputation may amalgamate. A new name is given to the unit which may be altogether different or bearing the parts of names of each of the combining companies or name of one company may be accepted if it has a very big reputation or goodwill in the market. Suppose X Co. Ltd. and Y Co. Ltd. amalgamate. The name of the amalgamate may be Z Co. Ltd. or XY Co. Ltd. or X Co. Ltd. in case it has tremendous goodwill in the market. The purchase consideration is settled through exchange of shares between the new company and each of the combining companies.

Merger or absorption — One company enters into another, i.e. one company purchasing the other. The puchasing company's name is retained. The purchasing company gives to the shareholders of the purchased company shares in it or partly shares and partly cash as purchase consideration. From the purchase company's side it is a case of merger (as it merges). From the purchasing company's side it is a case of absorption (as it absorbs).

Take-over bid — Absorption is also known as take-over. The purchasing company makes a 'bid' or offer to the shareholders of the purchased company for purchasing their company. The Companies Act provides procedure how such take-over bid can be made. At least 90% of the shares should be offered to be purchased. If such shareholders agree to sell their shares, then the remaining 10% of the shareholders have no alternative left.

Advantages

(1) It **totally eliminates competition** among the combining units when there is horizontal consolidation.

(2) It brings **economies of scale and advantages of integration** in the fullest form. This is specially true when the type of consolidation is vertical.

(3) It is **most stable** and rather final form of combination because the question of future separation cannot arise.

(4) **Huge resources** can be pooled together for better utilisation. The credit-worthiness also increases.

(5) A big consolidated unit can afford **to carry on research** work for the further development of the techniques or nature of production.

(6) There is **no scope of imbalance** between power and responsibility.

(7) Since it is a fusion between companies **all the shareholders are equally affected,** leaving no majority group or minority group among the shareholders as in case of a holding company.

Disadvantages

(1) It requires a **complicated procedure** because the consent of all the shareholders has to be obtained.

(2) The fusing companies **lose their identities and goodwill** and these cannot be recovered again.

(3) If fusion is made without taking all the factors into account some **problems may arise in future difficult to settle.**

(4) **Management may become difficult** because of largeness in size and none of the people from the combining units may have the ability.

(5) **Problem to retain all the employees** of all the combining units is formidable. Retrenchment with compensation is equally difficult.

(6) There **can be over-capitalisation** leading to consequent diseconomy.

(7) **No secrecy** can be maintained.

Evolution

In fact, it is a further development of the concept of holding company. Sometimes it is created by order of the Court or the Central Government as we find in the Companies Act to avoid complete liquidation of some weak companies.

INTEGRATION

A. Internal and external

From the above discussion we find that integration can take place in many ways. There are three fundamental aspects in the whole process : (1) Who are combining ? (2) Why are they combining ? (3) How are they combining ?

Who are combining — Either some units doing the same business or some units doing different but inter-related business or some units doing different but not inter-related business may combine. In the first case the units are competitive and in the other two cases they are complementary or friendly.

Why are they combining — There are three broad purposes for combination : (1) For gaining economies of scale (which each individual unit could not by expansion). (2) For gaining advantages of integration. (3) For creating a monopolistic combination.

How are they combining — There are three basic ways : (1) Temporarily, by retaining separate identities (so that there can be separation in future). (2) Semi-permanently (partial consolidation) by not losing separate identities. (3) Permanently, by losing separate identities (and there is no chance of future separation).

Taking all these three questions together, it can be said that : (1) Units doing different but inter-related business generally have the purpose of gaining economies of scale and advantages of integration and so they may prefer to combine permanently (complete consolidation) or at least semi-permanently (partial consolidation). (2) Units doing similar type of business generally have the purpose of monopoly and prefer to combine temporarily (federation). (3) Units doing different but not inter-related business have the purpose of gaining advantages of integration and prefer to combine semi-permanently.

In the first case and partially in the third case there is **internal** integration while in the second case there is purely **external** integration.

B. National and international

When combination takes place among units belonging to the same country there is **national** integration. Such integration can be of different types, of different forms and for different purposes. By **nationalisation** of an industry the strongest type of national integration takes place. In India, after nationalisation of big banks, a peculiar situation has developed. Though the 20 big banks have been nationalised, each bank still retains its separate entity. Even, there is competition among the nationalised banks.

When business units belonging to different countries combine, there can be **international** combines. The multinational corporations can be cited as good examples. There are examples of a foreign company consolidating with a local company. In India, the Tatas and the Volkart Brothers have amalgamated into Voltas. The old Indo-Burma Petrol Co. Ltd. was a good example.

Foreign Collaboration — This is a good example of international integration. Any foreign company may collaborate with a local company, jointly promoting, financing and managing a company. Such collaboration can be on general basis or exclusively on technical know-how only, or on financing, or both. There are many examples of foreign collaboration in India both in the private and the public sectors.

Advantages and disadvantages

We have discussed the advantages and disadvantages of different types and forms of combinations separately. **On the whole,** integration or combination has some general advantages and disadvantages.

Advantages

(1) The main and obvious advantage of combination is that it **develops a spirit of cooperation** among the combining units. This is obvious if there is a combination among interrelated units and highly desirable in case of horizontal combination.

(2) It fosters **economies of large scale production.** There can be standardised mass production. Further economies are achieved by eliminating weak and inefficient units. The best technique of each unit is exploited and greater specialisation can be achieved. Ultimately, average cost is reduced leading to maximum profits.

(3) It helps achieving **economies of distribution.** The total distribution cost is reduced by centralising the sales force of each unit. Cost of publicity is reduced. Same can be said about the delivery expenses. Each customer gets the delivery of the goods from the nearest plant.

(4) It encourages **economies of integration** as a whole. For example, cost of purchasing of raw materials, machines, tools etc. can be centralised with reduction of expenses. The best things can be purchased as the ability to pay becomes higher.

(5) It improves **efficiency of management** too. The best managerial personnel can be appointed. The managerial skill and experience of the combining units can be pooled together.

(6) The **credit-worthiness is enhanced.** Because of largeness of size, the solvency of the combine is high and more assets can be offered as security. Therefore, getting credit becomes easier and the terms of credit also become favourable.

(7) A combine has **greater capability for research** and development and thereby achives greater efficiency and economy.

(8) The **customers are benefited** because they can get better quality goods and those at comparatively cheaper prices.

(9) The **society is benefited** because wasteful and futile competition is eliminated.

(10) There is **better adjustment** between demand and supply as the supply is very much regulated and controlled from one point .

Disadvantages

(1) **Combinations mostly lead to monopolies,** particularly when there are horizontal combinations. Being lured by maximisation of profits, the combine generally charges high prices and the customers and suppliers have to suffer. In practice, in most of the cases, by combination the customers and the suppliers do not get the benefit of large size.

(2) **Combinations mostly lead to concentration of economic power** in the hands of a few persons.

(3) There is every possibility of **over-exploitation** and its consequential bad effects.

(4) **Combinations may also lead to exploitation of labour.** As there is concentration of power in the hands of a few they become ruthless and exploit labour for further wealth.

(5) The **general management may deteriorate** because of largeness of size. The same men being directors of a number of companies, cannot devote much time for each.

(6) One obvious disadvantage is that it **is not so easy to enforce on** the members all the terms of the agreement.

COMBINATION MOVEMENT IN INDIA

A. **Evolution of the movement** — The combination movement in India has been **more sporadic than systematic,** at least at the early stage. The evolution can be divided into several phases :

(1) **The early phase,** i.e. up to the First World War period — **The movement was slow** and practically insignificant.

(2) **The middle phase,** i.e. between the First and Second World Wars — **Some development** could be seen, particularly because of the pre-eminence of the managing agents. But the nature and from of combinations were of special type, different from the Western models.

(3) **The modern phase,** i.e. the post-independence period. This period can be further subdivided into **two parts** : (a) the period of **existence of the managing agents** and their gradual Indianisation — This period has witnessed **fast growth** of the movement. A new feature has been establishment of joint enterprises with foreign collaboration. (b) The period **after the decline of the managing agency system** – During this period several measures have been taken by the Government to break the monopolies and concentration of economic power. As a result, combination movement has got a setback. On the other hand, **the Government itself is forming** some combinations, particularly in trading and commercial fields. Besides, a concept of joint sector has been introduced.

B. **Causes of slow and inconsistent growth** — of combination movement in India :

(1) **Industrialisation in India has been very slow** during the British rule, particularly up to the First World War period and so the chances of the growth of combinations were less.

(2) **By nature** Indians and so the Indian businessmen are **individualistic.** Therefore, they neither like nor they are capable of forming into combinations.

(3) **Industrial units in the country were scattered** all over the country suffering from poor communication which retarded the growth of combinations.

(4) **The Government did not encourage** the combination movement. The British Government wanted to safeguard the interests of the British export industries. In fact, the combination movement really **gained momentum** at the time of demand for protection of Indian industries against unfair foreign competition. Big combinations in India took shape **behind the policy of discriminating protection** adopted by the British Government in 1921.

(5) **The managing agency system** created a peculiar form of integration which **discouraged** formation of other types of combinations.

(6) Big industrial families were **happy with** their **common directorship** in large number of companies instead of forming into formal combinations.

C. **The pattern of growth of combinations** — The pattern of growth of combinations in India can be studied from **two aspects:** (1) The industries in which combinations have taken shape. (2) The form of combinations.

(1) Industry–wise study

Combinations have taken place in many major industries and commercial services in India. (a) **Jute Industry** — Jute industry is considered to be the most organised industry in the country. This is obvious because, until partition of the country prior to independence, India had monopoly in the world market for jute and jute products. The Indian Jute Mills Associati – on IJMA (formerly known as Indian Jute Manufacturers' Association), established in 1884, represents jute mills controlling about 90% of the total production in jute industry. After independence, the IJMA has established the Indian Jute Industries Research Association to carry on research on jute technology and diversification of products.

(b) **Sugar industry** — India is the inventor of sugar and has the largest acreage for sugar-cane cultivation. Therefore, it is a major industry of the country. The Indian Sugar Mills Syndicate was established in 1937 to control the large number of sugar mills cropping up under the coverage of protection granted to the industry in 1932. Taking advantage of local monopoly, the Syndicate indulged in activities against public interest and the Government banned it in 1950. It is replaced by Indian Sugar Mills' Association which is not of that monopolistic character.

(c) **Cement Industry** — The Associated Cement Company Ltd. (formerly known as Cement Marketing Company) which is an association of largest number of cement factories controlling about one-third of the total cement production in the country. There was a keen and cut-throat competition between the A.C.C. and the Dalmia group of industries for a long time causing much hardship to the consumers. Now cement factories have been established in the public sector too and the distribution of cement is controlled. The Cement Corporation of India Ltd. has been established by the Government for the purpose.

(d) **Iron and Steel industry** — There is no strong association in this industry but there are big consolidations and holding companies, both in the private and the public sectors. The Bengal Iron Co. Ltd. merged in the Indian Iron and Steel Co. Ltd. (IISCO) in 1936. In 1953 the Steel Corporation of Bengal Ltd. (SCOB) merged in IISCO. In 1953 Martin Co. Ltd. and Burn Co. Ltd. amalgamated into Martin Burn Ltd. The Steel Authority of India Ltd. (SAIL) has been established in 1974 as a holding company over all the public sector steel producing companies.

(e) **Banking service** — The United Bank of India was formed in 1952 by amalgamating a number of small banks like Comilla Union Bank Ltd., Comilla Banking Corporation Ltd., Bengal Central Bank Ltd. and Hooghly Bank Ltd. Had there been no such amalgamation none of these banks could continue their existence. Metropolitan Bank Ltd., Southern Bank Ltd. and Bank of Bankura Ltd. merged into United Industrial Bank Ltd. After the taking over of 14 big banks by the Government in 1969, followed by taking over of another 6 banks in 1980; there has been a big combine, though each of the 20 banks is having its separate identity and even competing with one another. Each bank has been allotted a special area with the responsibility of its developmental finance and in this way each bank is called the Lead Bank of that area. Indirectly every bank has been allotted an area where it has some monopolistic control. For example, the United Bank of India is the 'lead bank' for Calcutta. As the Government did not 'nationalise' the banks but only took over the banking business, the original banking companies have amalgamated with other companies. For example, the Central Bank of India (on which the Tatas had control) has merged in TELCO.

(f) **Insurance service** — The biggest combination through complete nationalisation has taken place in insurance business. Life insurance business, first taken over by an ordinance, was fully nationalised by the formation of the Life Insurance Corporation of India by a special statute in 1956. The entire business was brought under unified control. On the other hand, the general insurance business being nationalised in 1972 by formation of General Insurance Corpoation, is controlled by four major constituent companies: the National Insurance Co. of Calcutta, the Oriental Fire and General Insurance Co. of New Delhi, The New India Assurance Co. of Bombay and United India Insurance Co. of Madras.

(g) **Transport service** — Immediately after independence all the railway companies (mostly foreign) operating separately all over India were nationalised and brought under the unified system of Indian Railways and then divided gradually into nine decentralised zones for better administration. In 1952, Indian Cooperative Navigation and Trading Co. Ltd. and Ratnagar Steam Navigation Co. Ltd. merged with Bombay Steam Navigation Co. Ltd.

(h) **Other industries** — There are examples of combinations in other industries like paper, engineering, match, oil, mining etc. The Indian Paper Mills Association was started by the Titaghur Paper Mills Co. Ltd. with which other mills joined. Big engineering and allied industries companies, like Macneill and Barry Co. Ltd. and Williamson Magor Ltd., amalgamated into Macneill and Magor Ltd. A new company named Voltas Ltd. was formed with 55% of capital supplied by the Tatas and 45% by the Volkart Brothers to take over the latter foreign company. The biggest and virtually a monopolist in large scale match – making industry – Western India Match Co. (WIMCO), which is a subsidiary of a big Swedish multinational corporation—has a number of match-making units under it. The Burmah-Shell Co. Ltd. was formed by combining the interests of the Burmah Oil Co., the Royal Dutch Shell Co., the British Burmah Petroleum Co. and the Assam Oil Co. After nationalisation of Coal mining, a very big holding company named Coal India Ltd. (CIL) has been formed in the public sector.

Some of the managing agents used to hold majority and even entire shares of the managed companies engaged in different types of industries. For example, the Shaw Wallace Co. Ltd. (as managing agents) once held up to 99% shares of some tea gardens, cotton mills, flour mills, fertiliser manufacturing, coal mining etc. industries.

(2) The formwise study

All forms of combination can be found in the Indian business world out of which perhaps complete consolidations are more common. But, it has to be noted that India has her own special type of integration through the managing agency system.

(1) **Trade associations** — There are large number of trade associations in the country. Practically for each type of conceivable type of business activity, whether industry, trade or commerce, there is a trade association. Each trade association again is affiliated with some chamber of commerce. The offices of many trade associations are maintained by different Chambers. Approximately there are about 1,000 trade association in the country. There are some common trade associations not belonging to any particular line of business but for the employers in general. For example, All-India Manufactureres' Organisation established in 1940, All-India Organisation of Industrial Employers established in 1932, Employers' Federation of India established in 1933, etc. Out of the trade associations, perhaps the most powerful association is the Indian Jute Mills' Association and also the Millowners' Association (mill means here cotton mill). Big associations are found in sugar, paper, chemicals, glass, tea plantations and such other industries. Indian Banks Association is also a very powerful association which controls recruitments in banks.

(2) **Pools and Cartels** — We do not find much of pools but a number of cartels in the form of selling syndicates playing a big role in Indian economy though their importance is declining. The Indian Jute Mills Association can be indirectly called an output pool because the quotas of production of the jute mills are agreed upon. The Sugar Mills Syndicate was a strong type of cartel but now replaced by less powerful Indian Sugar Mills Association. The Indian Paper Mills Association fixes up prices for different categories of paper to be followed by the member mills. There was a big price cartel in petroleum distribution among the foreign companies operating in the country like the Esso, Burmah-Shell, Caltex etc. Now, of course, all these foreign companies have been nationalised. But different oil companies in the public sector like the Indian Oil, Hindusthan Petroleum, Bharat Petroleum etc. as a State policy, maintain a standard price and can be called a price cartel. The Cement Marketing Company of India was started as a cartel or selling Syndicate but without much success. It was followed by the formation of the Associated Cement Companies Limited by absorbing 11 cement companies.

(3) **Partial Consolidations** — (a) **Holding companies**— Holding Companies have not been much popular in the country because of the managing agency system. All the benefits of holding companies could be enjoyed through the managing agency system. In spite of this fact, some big holding companies can be found. The Associated Cement Co. purchased all shares of the Cement Marketing Co. Shaw Wallace Co. holds about 99% shares of some companies like the Atlas Fertilisers Ltd., Indo-Agri. Ltd. etc. Every big industrial house has under it one or more investment trusts through which they hold shares in other companies but not necessarily to form holding companies. Recently, however, holding companies are being formed in the public sector like the Steel Authority of India Ltd. (SAIL), under which there are 13 subsidiary companies, namely, Hindustan Steel Ltd., Bakaro Steel Ltd., Bhilai Steel Ltd., Rourkela Steel Ltd., Durgapur Alloy Steel Ltd., SAIL International Ltd. (engaged in exports), National Mineral Development Corporation Ltd., Metallurgical and Engineering Consultants (India) Ltd. Bharat Refractories Ltd., Hindustan Steel Works Construction Ltd., India Firebricks and Insulation Co. Ltd., Metal Scrap Trading Corporation Ltd. and Bolani Ores Ltd. It appears that SAIL wants to have economies of vertical integration as well as of horizontal integration. (The word 'Steel' is being increasingly replaced by the word 'Ispat' to Indianise the names.) SAIL is the biggest holding company in the country and is of world class. A very big holding company in the public sector is the Coal India Ltd. (CIL) with a number of subsidiaries like Eastern Coalfields, Western Coalfields, Central Coalfields, Bharat Coking Coal, etc.

(b) **Community of interest** — What is formally known as community of interest type of partial consolidation, can be found through the managing agency system. There are instances where one managing agent managed about 40 companies enjoying the benefits of all types of integration – vertical, horizontal, lateral and diagonal – though the cream of the benefits was enjoyed by the managing agent ownself. Obviously, **interlocking directorate,** with the common nominees of the managing agent filling up the Boards of directors of the different managed companies, was a regular feature. Big industrial houses have common directors in all the companies in which they are directly or indirectly interested. Of course, according to the Companies Act, one person cannot be director of more than 20 public companies at a time. Some renowned managing agency companies were Mackinnon and Mackenzie (with largest number of managed companies), McLeod, Balmer Lawerie, Andrew Yule, Bird, Martin-Burn, Birla Brothers, Tata and Sons, Duncan Brothers, etc.

(4) **Complete consolidation** — There are many cases of amalgamation and merger in engineering industry (Macneill Magor, Martin-Burn, Voltas etc.), in banking business (United Bank of India, United Industrial Bank Ltd.), in transport business (Indian Railways) etc. All have been described above. An important example of amalgamation is British India Corporation (BIC) which was established in 1920 taking over 6 separate companies producing different products. The Companies are : Cawnpore Woollen Mills Ltd., Cawnpore Cotton Mills Ltd., New Egerton Woollen Mills Ltd., North-West Tannery Co. Ltd., Cooper Allen and Co. Ltd. and Empire Engineering Co. Ltd. Later on, BIC took over Begg Sutherland and Co. Ltd. which had under its control 10 other companies. Associated Cement Co. Ltd. is another example of big amalgamation. Life Insurance Corporation of India is a formidable amalgamation in the public sector.

(5) **Joint enterprises or collaborations or alliances** — After independence, new type of combination came into existence called foreign collaborations or joint enterprises or alliances between Indian and foreign industrialists. Such collaborations are either in the field of finance or technocracy or both or floating companies jointly. The examples are Nuffield-Birla Motor Deal (for motor car manufacturing), Sen-Raleigh (for cycle manufacturing), Hindustan-Pilkington (for glass industry), Walchand Hirachand-Chrysler (for motor car), Voltas (for engineering), Tata-Benz (for trucks), Anand-Toshiba (for battery), etc. Collaboration also exists in the public sector as we find technical collaboration in the steel industry with the Russians at Bhilai, with the Germans at Rourkela and with the British at Durgapur.

Some foreign companies have re-registered themselves in India taking Indians with them. For example, the Peico (India) Ltd., the ICI (India) Ltd., etc.

THE POLICY OF THE GOVERNMENT

Policy towards combinations

The Government of India does not seem to have any definite policy towards combination. It has encouraged combination for the sake of economy. For example, the Government wanted merging of the Steel Corporation of Bengal (SCOB) in the Indian Iron and Steel Company (IISCO) in 1952. On the other hand, the Government disbanded the Indian Sugar Mills Syndicate in 1950 because of its anti-social activities. The Government encourages foreign collaboration subject to the Foreign Capital Policy, the Foreign Exchange Regulations Act, 1973, and other inter-related Acts. Recently the Government has announced that merging of a sick unit with a profitable unit will be highly desirable and the profitable unit will be allowed to set off the losses of the sick unit against its profits. The Government has, however, first restricted and then abolished the managing agency system which has been providing a form of integration. We have already seen how the Government has created combinations through nationalisation of certain businesses or by forming holding companies in the public sector.

Policy towards monopoly

The Government, however, has taken some positive steps to restrict growth of monopolies and to break concentration of economic power through restrictive trade practices.

The Mahalanobis Committee — As early as in 1960, the late Prime Minister Nehru announced the policy of **the Government to appoint a Committee** called 'Distribution of Income and Levels of Living Committee' under the chairmanship of Dr. P. C. Mahalanobis, the founder of the Indian Statistical Institute "to inquire into how the additional income generated in the First and Second Plan had been spread in the country". The Committee in its report submitted in 1964 held the opinion that by the end of two Plans there was a considerable inequality in the distribution of wealth and productive assets with a result of concentration of economic power in the hands of a few. The personal wealth amassed was more in the form of shares in companies than land or buildings. Inequality in wealth was greater than inequality in income. The growth of big companies, taking advantage of expanding and protected market has caused such inequality. According to the findings of the Committee, 15 big banks controlled 78% of the total deposits in all the 363 banks in the country. Further 20 leading business houses had interest in different forms in 983 companies with a total capital of Rs. 238 crores in 1951 which grew up to Rs. 352 crores in 1958. The Committee recommended for setting up a permanent agency to enquire into the matter in details and to suggest remedial measures.

The Monopolies Enquiry Commission — On the basis of the recommendation of the Mahalanobis Committee, the Government appointed a five-member Commission in 1964 with Sri K. C. Dasgupta, a retired judge of the Supreme Court, as its Chairman. The Commission **had a very wide term of reference** related to the functioning of the private sector and the financial institutions as a whole and the growth of monopolistic and restrictive trade practices and recommended remedial measures, legislative or otherwise.

The Commission submitted its report in 1965. In it, the Commission analysed the causes and extent of concentration of economic power. **The causes are :** (1) Taking advantage of corporate form of ownership, inwardly some people got hold of large number of shares in different companies. (2) Integration through the managing agency system and inter-company investment. (3) Purchasing of a number of foreign managing agency firms by some big Indian business houses. (4) Taking advantage of restriction to industrial licensing, as it was difficult for ordinary entrepreneurs to obtain. (5) Favours shown by banks to big business houses as each big business house had control over one or other bank. (6) Big business houses could take full advantage of the financial assistance offered by the financial institutions, whether state-sponsored or not. (7) Various exchange control measures restricting imports provided a safe and protected market for the Indian manufacturers.

The Commission analysed **the concentration from two aspects : (1) Productwise** — The productwise concentration was substantiated by the following facts : (a) The Commission examined the production pattern of 100 commodities out of which in 65 more than 75% share went to 3 top producers. (b) 17 out of 71 items of industrial machinery were produced by a single producer. A.V.B. Ltd. of Durgapur alone produced 88% of water tube boilers. Hindustan Motors alone produced 66.1% of the total motor cars. 82% of dry batteries were produced by Union Carbide. (2) **Groupwise** – Groupwise or countrywise concentration was substantiated by the following findings : (a) 75% big business groups were controlling 1,536 companies with total assets valued at Rs. 2,606 crores having a total paid-up capital of Rs. 646 crores. Their share in the total paid-up capital and the assets in the whole corporate sector was 44% and 47%, respectively. The details of the top ten groups* were :

Rank	Name of the Group	No. of Companies	Total Assets (in crores) Rs.
1	Tata	53	418
2	Birlas	151	293
3	Martin Burn	21	150
4	Bangur	81	78
5	A. C. C.	5	77
6	Thapar	43	72
7	Sahu Jain	26	68
8	Bird Heilgers	64	60
9	Singhanias	46	59
10	Soorajmul Nagarmull	76	57

Recommendations — The Commission recommended for both legislative and non-legislative measures. (1) **Legislative measure** — The Commission recommended for a suitable legislation to set up a permanent body to maintain constant vigilance and to take preventive measures. A Director of Investigation to be appointed. The body shall be empowered to take mecesary measures against monopolistic and restrictive trade practices.

(2) **Non-legislative measures** — (a) Prohibiting contribution by business houses to election funds of political parties. (b) Liberal granting of industrial licences to small industries. (c) Looking into consumers' interest while restricting import. (d) Expansion of the public sector as a counter – measure against big houses in the private sector. (e) Promotion of small and village industries for increasing supply of consumer goods and thereby breaking the monopoly of the big houses. (f) Encouragement for the formation of consumers' co-operative stores to control hoarding and artificial raising of prices.

The Government accepted the recommendations and passed the Monopolies Restrictive Trade Practices Act in 1969. This is known in short as the MRTP Act.

* Tatas and Birlas were engaged in a neck to neck race for supremacy among the 25 large industrial houses in the country as revealed from the figures of 1983 and informed by the Government in Parliament on 25.3.85. The net position is like this : Tatas – total turnover Rs. 3,069.38 crores, total assets Rs. 2,672.40 crores. Birlas – total turnover Rs. 2,765.04 crores, total assets Rs. 2,830.94 crores. Other industrial houses are – Mafatlal, J. K. Singhania, Thapar, ACC, Reliance Textiles, Sarabhai, Larsen and Toubro, Modi, Bajaj, Walchand, ICI, Kirloskar, TVS, Shriram, ITC, Bangur, Hindusthan Lever, Mahindra and Mahindra, Chowgula, Ashok Leyland, Dunlop, United Breweries and Khatau.

Apart from this Act there are other Acts which include various provisions for restricting monopolies or monopolistic combinations. They are : (1) The Companies Act, 1956, which contains various regulatory measures. (2) The Capital Isssue (Control) Act, 1947, indirectly verifies who are going to handle the funds of the public and how. (3) The Industries (Development and Regulation) Act, 1951, contains strict procedure for obtaining industrial licence. There is provision in the Act how and when the Government can take over any firm.

COMPARISON OF DIFFERENT COMBINATIONS

A. Types of combination

There are **four types** of combination : Horziontal, Vertical, Lateral and Diagonal. The first type is mainly for monopolistic purpose and the remaining three mainly for gaining economy. Diagonal combination is for managerial economy. Horizontal combination takes place among units doing same type of business while the other three are among dissimilar business units. Obviously, horizontal combination takes the form of federation, keeping the separate entity of each combining unit. The chance of breaking such a combination is very common. But other three types of combinations generally take the form of consolidation, either partial or complete. It has to be noted that lateral and diagonal types of combination are commonly found in the forms of a holding company or a community of interest. In India, lateral and diagonal types of combination could be found under the managing agency system. In fact, under holding company or managing agency system, we observe circular type of combination under holding company or managing agency system having the characteristics of all types of combination. The main purpose behind such combinations is economy.

B. Forms of combination

There are **broadly three forms of combination :** Associations, Federations and Consolidations. Each again has different subdivisions. Associations are not exactly integrations but loose types of combinations, mostly formal. Federations are loose forms where the combining units keep their separate entities intact. Generally, these are formed by competing firms and the type of combination is mainly horizontal. The purpose behind it is monopolistic tendency. Partial consolidations are stronger but the chances of their breaking are there. By releasing control on majority shares, a partial consolidation may be dislodged. A complete consolidation, however, is final and rigid. There is no chance of any separation in future. Consolidations usually belong to vertical, lateral and diagonal types of combinations and the main purpose behind consolidations is economy. In case of a horizontal consolidation, there is a tendency towards monopoly occasionally.

Summary

Combination — Different business units combine together and become a bigger unit. There must be some common purpose behind it. Combination is also known as integration. Besides, a number of business units may concentrate or centralise at one place. There can be concentration of economic power through ownership of a number of businesses by the same business group or house. A combination is generally a concentration but a concentration is not necessarily a combination. In a socialistic State, the Government controls all the economic activities and invariably there is concentration. Partnership is a combination of persons but this is not a combination. A real combination takes place when a few business units combine.

Cause of combination — There are many causes. **The root cause is defective competition.** Competition leads to combination. So long there is conflicting interest among the units, there is competition and when the interest becomes common, they combine. Competition leads to cut-throat competition and then the competing units combine. Generally, a business unit wants to grow in size. Either a firm itself grows or a few firms combine to be big in size. These are the following **causes of combination :** (a) to avoid wasteful competition. (b) To gain economies of scale. (c) Lust for power by being big. (d) Taking avantage of company form of organisation and exercising control by buying majority shares. (e) To take advantage of protection. (f) To tide over depression time in trade cycle. (g) Able organisers numbering small generally have control over a large number of units. (h) For rationalisation, a number of units combine. (i) Combination takes place when there is nationalisation. (j) Businessmen have respect and attraction for big size. (k) Sometimes the Government compels a few firms to combine for their safety.

Types of combination — Four types of combination : (a) **Horizontal** — Business units doing the same business combine. Purposes are – self-defence, economy, monopoly etc. Generally loose forms. (b) **Vertical** — Business units doing different types of business combine, either by forward or by backward movement. Purposes — economy, sure market, concentration of power etc. Generally strong forms. (c) **Lateral** — Business units doing dissimilar but allied business. Convergent type — dissimilar products or services but meant for same industry. Divergent type — dissimilar products but using same source of raw material. Purposes — sure market, improvement of quality, full capacity of plant etc. Loose form in case of convergent type and strong form in case of divergent type. (d) **Diagonal** — One business unit combining with another ancillary unit. Purposes — economy assurance of supply of some essential part, etc. Generally strong forms.

Forms — Structurally, there are different forms according to the durability of the combinations and their cohesion. Forms of combination have evolved out of circumstances and regulatory measures. There are simple combinations like partnership and compound combina – tions which are the proper combinations. Compound combinations are of the following types : A. **Associations** – Trade Associations, Informal or Gentlemen's Agreements, Chambers of Commerce. B. **Federations** — Pools, Cartels. C. **Partial Consolidations** – Trusts, Community of Interest – common shareholding, interlocking directorate, companies under same management. Holding Company – pure, operating, parent, offspring, primary and intermediary. D. **Complete consolidation** – amalgamation, merger or absorption.

Trade Associations — Businessmen doing the same business form into associations for protection of their interests. These are loose combinations and no legal binding. A trade association holds seminars, maintains libraries, issue circulars, does arbitration among members etc. **Informal or Gentlemen's Agreements** — Businessmen enter into some understanding with regard to price, discounts offered, terms of credit etc. There is no formal binding. **Chambers of Commerce** — These are associations of businessmen for the benefits of the business community. Generally, a trade association is affiliated to a Chamber of Commerce. A chamber holds seminars, conferences etc., represent the business community to the Government, to the other countries, etc., to promote, support or oppose legislations, to run libraries, to arbitrate in disputes among members, to make publications etc. In some countries, chambers have official status. There is one International Chamber of Commerce. India has a large number of chambers with the Federation of Indian Chambers of Commerce of India as the major all-India body.

Federations — **Pool** — An agreement among the combining units on price and there are some enforceable controlling elements – like on the output, on the area of market to be covered by a member etc. It is stronger than a mere price agreement. There are different types of pool – (a) Output pool – members produce according to the total demand. (b) Market pool – the total market is apportioned among the members. (c) Income or profits pool – A central agency to fix price with the third parties and any extra profit by any member is pooled for distribution among members. Pools originated in USA as an external form of integration. It has advantages and disadvantages. **Cartel** – Essentially a cartel or a syndicate is a pool with a common selling agency. Every member hands over his output to that agency for selling it jointly and apportion profits. The cartel sells the output as a discriminating monopolist for maximum profits. Cartels (Kartells) originated in Germany and then spread to other European countries. They are very often similar to pools and as such there are price cartels, output cartels and market cartels. But a proper cartel is a common selling agency. It is external type of combination. It has advantages and disadvantages. In Germany, the Government, and particularly that of Hitler, encouraged cartels. **Corners or Rings** – These are temporary understandings by suppliers of a commodity. A **consortium** is an extreme case of temporary combination where businessmen combine for a particular job. **Joint Ventures** are temporary agreements between persons for a particular venture or ventures.

Partial Consolidation — Trust — The shares of some companies are transferred to a Board of Trustees against trust certificates. The Board runs the companies. There is unified control. Either shares are transferred or voting rights are transferred to a Board of Trustees. Generally, they are vertical combinations of internal integration type. Trusts originated in USA but then declared unlawful for their monopolistic and antisocial activities. **Community of interest** – Same persons may hold shares in a number of companies and exercise control over them. When there are same directors in a number of companies, this is called interlocking directorate. India had a peculiar form of combination through management of a number of companies by a same managing agent. Community of interest can be through financial integration, administrative integration and managerial integration. In the Companies Act, there is a special provision for companies under same management. **Holding Companies** — One company may hold majority shares or majority voting rights or may have power of appointing the majority of directors, then this company is holding company and the other company is called its subsidiary. A holding company has a subsidiary company and that subsidiary company may be holding company of another company. Then the first company is the holding company of the last company. Holding company may be of different types – Parent or primary (an existing company holding another existing company), Intermediary (one holding company has a subsidiary but the holding company itself is a subsidiary of another holding company), Pure (the holding company does not have interest in the management of the subsidiary), Mixed (the holding company has interest in the management of the subsidiary). Finance companies buy shares in other companies but do not hold majority shares. A holding company has its advantages and disadvantages. The system originated in USA when trusts were declared unlawful. It is a case of internal integration.

Complete consolidation — It takes place when two or more firms combine losing their identities and forming into a new company. This is **amalgamation.** One company may absorb another company or one company merges into another. By this, one company's existence remains while the other disappears. This is **absorption** or **merger.** This is internal form of integration with full economies of large scale. It has advantages and disadvantages.

Actually, the whole classification is made on the basis – (1) Who are combining (units doing similar or dissimilar business) ? (2) Why are they combining (for gaining economy or for monopoly) ? (3) How are they combining (temporarily or permanently) ? There are national as well as international combinations. In India, we find foreign collaborations. There are multinationals which have businesses in different countries taking local people with them.

Combination movement in India — Combination movement in India has been more sporadic than systematic. At first the movement was slow. There are many causes for that : Industrialisation was slow, Indians are individualistic, industries are scattered, no encouragement by the Government, etc. The managing agency system created a new form of integration with interlocking-directorate and managerial integration. Combinations are found almost in all major industries like jute, sugar, cement, iron and steel, banking, insurance, paper etc. We find all forms of combinations in the country like trade associations, pools and cartels, holding companies, community of interest and complete consolidation. There are a number of chambers of commerce with all-India chambers. Besides, there are foreign collaborations.

The Government of India does not seem to have any definite policy towards combination. It has encouraged it for the sake of economy or through nationalisation. At the same time, it has banned combination when found to be anti-social.

CHAPTER SIX

SMALL BUSINESS

DEFINITION :

Size is a relative concept. A big business, when compared to a bigger one, may appear to be a small business. It is not, therefore, so easy to define a small business. We, however, have the definition of 'small industry'. A small business and a small industry are not identical. So, we are to find out a suitable definition of 'small business' keeping in mind the semantic and functional differences between a small industry and a small business.

Business is a comprehensive term and it embraces both industrial and commercial activities. We do not have any definition of a small commercial business. Had there been any definition we might have attempted to define a small business by combining and suitably modifying both the definitions.

We, therefore, attempt to define a small business on the basis of its characteristics. A small business is independently managed; the managers are usually the owners. Ownership and capital of a small business are held by an individual or by a small group. Being small compared to bigger units of the same industry, a small business operates within the locality mainly. A small business, for its expansion, depends mainly on reinvestment of earnings.

To sum up, we define a small business as **a business independently managed with ownership and capital confined to an individual or a group and the operational area is usually limited within a locality resting its dependence for its expansion mainly on re-investment of earnings. It may engage itself in trading, commercial or industrial activities.**

Features :

A Committee for Economic Development was set up to prepare an outline of qualitative characteristic of the American small business. These characteristics, according to some distinguished authors, are equally applicable to a small business in any country.

The features or the characteristics are as follows :

1. Independent management.
2. Management is usually in the hand of the owner.
3. Capital is generally contributed by the owner himself.
4. Ownership is usually individual.
5. Area of operation in a particular locality.
6. Relatively small size when compared to other business units of the same industry.
7. Expansion of the business is done generally by the re-investment of its own earnings.
8. Its output is generally for local consumption but international market, for the product of a small business unit, cannot be ruled out when it produces traditional items of art or modern products.

Role of small business

In any country, developed or developing, the role that the small business sector plays is significant. The survival of small business amidst large corporations is a sufficient proof of its inherent strength. There are certain spheres of business activities where, we should say, small business units have far important role to play and the nature and volumes of activities of small business units are more suitable in keeping with certain sectors of the economy of a country.

Small business enterprises help building up the economy in its developing stage and continue to play a very important role in certain sectors of the economy in its developed stage. Had this not been the case, the USA would have no small enterprises.

Small business alone can create large employment opportunities, can bring about balanced and diversified economic development, can secure equitable distribution of wealth and power, and can ensure proper growth of handicrafts.

Small business plays a very important role in the matter of caring for individual tastes. Changing fashions and widely fluctuating demand can only be met by small business enterprises. With shorter gestation period and greater motivation, a small enterprise secures an important position in the economy of a country.

Small business is eminently suitable and has a special role to play in certain circumstances viz., limited demand, changing tastes, local market, limited capital needs, limited managerial ability, limited risk of loss, special demand for quality of the product, for personal touch, attention and interest, shorter gestation period, reduced production lag etc.

As to the role of small business we can also add that it provides an effective shield to the big concerns by supplementing the activities of large firms, by providing a training ground for entrepreneurs, by playing an important role as ancillary units of large business and affording some guarantee against the emergence of new competition.

Small business has a very dominant and special role to play in an economy like ours in terms of employment and growth. In the various Industrial Policy Resolutions of India, specific role has been assigned to small business.

Problems of Small Business

The problem area of a business can be described as 'any phase of business operation that requires attention or decision'.

Problems are, therefore, at two stages – initial and later stages of operation.

At the initial stage, a small business may be confronted with the problem of determining the existence of a profitable business opportunity, choosing the right form of business ownership, selecting an economical location, procuring requisite physical facilities and inventories, designing and staffing the organisation and determining proper business plans and policy.

In its later operation, problems such as office management, technology, management control, production, marketing, personnel, finances, research and development, public relations etc. may crop up.

All the problems listed above may pose serious, but of them, certain problems are particularly disturbing for small business units. These problems centre round ownership, financing, marketing, staffing and technology.

A small business cannot afford to have professionalised management and it cannot be expected that the owner of a small business will be endowed with management acumen and ability. So, a small business may face the problem of management. Assuming that the owner of a small business possesses the requisite talents for good management, it becomes a problem for the business when his successor lacks in managerial efficiency.

Another serious problem that afflicts a small business is the problem of finance, both short-term and long-term. It is well nigh impossible for a small business entrepreneur to provide adeqaute finance for his business. For survival as well as for expansion, finance is a must and, therefore, the problem of finance is a serious problem. In our country, even today, the measures adopted by Government to finance small business are not satisfactory and various formalities that have to be observed in procuring finance from the Government are very difficult for a small entrepreneur to go through. Obtaining capital from friends, relatives and other private sources is usually at a very high cost of seriously damaging the management and capital-structure bases.

Management and financial problems having been encountered and overcome, a small business meets with the problems of marketing. It is a major problem area as a small unit finds it difficult to build an extensive network of distribution, faces stiff competition from big manufacturers, uncompetitive prices, Governmental regulations and such other problems. To find out ways and means to solve these problems is not easy for a small business, but what we actually feel is that these small business, by establishing contact with customers, can solve many problems which is not possible for a big organisation.

Personnel problems may not be so complicated in a small business but problems are there and these problems, once surfaced, need immediate solution. Small enterprises cannot afford expert personnel management to tackle complicated personnel problems and to face militant trade unions of modern times. Here also a small business solves various personnel problems by persuasion and by maintaining personal and close relation with the employees. Personnel problems may also be in the matter of recruitment, training and staffing. In its own way, a small business solves its personnel problems and in the matter of recruitment, training, promotion etc. it follows its convenient and crude methods.

In these days of giant business enterprises, when advanced technology is being used to increase production and productivity, a small business is obviously at a disadvantageous position and unless it is able to adapt itself to changing technique of production, to a certain extent at least, its very existence and survival is at stake.

Besides the problems listed above, a hostile political environment may play havoc with small enterprises. A clear–cut policy for small businesses can be of much help for small business in solving many of their problems.

Government policy towards small business :

The small business sector has a definite role to play in the economy of a country, be it a developed or a developing country.

In our country, it has been our 'State Policy' to give importance to small and cottage industries. In the various Industrial Policy Resolutions of India, the Government has accorded a special role to the small scale sector. In the Directive Principles of State Policy embodied in the Constitution of India, the development of this sector was also highlighted.

Various Committees and Commissions set up by the Government of India, and the "International Perspective Planning Team" in 1953-54 recognised the ever-increasing importance of the small scale sector.

Industrial Policy Resolution, 1948

This Policy Resolution of 1948 highlighted, 'Cottage and small scale industries has a very important role to play in the national economy in the spheres of individual entrepreneurship, Village and Co-operative enterprise and as a means for the rehabilitation of displaced persons. Essential consumer goods like food, cloth and agricultural implements can be made available in a better way through the small sector'. A Cottage Industries Board for the fostering of small scale industries and the creation of a suitable machinery to implement it, was recommended by the Industries Conference and Government accepted this recommendation in its Industrial Policy Resolution of 1948. A Cottage and Small Scale Industries Directorate was also set up.

Industrial Policy Resolution, 1956

This Policy Resolution spoke eloquently on the importance of the small scale sector. It stated, "They provide immediate large scale employment; they offer a method of ensuring a more equitable distribution of the natural income and they facilitate an effective mobilisation of resources of capital and skill which might otherwise remain unutilised. Some of the problems that unplanned urbanisation tends to create will be avoided by the establishment of small centres of industrial production all over the country".

It was made clear in the Industrial Policy Resolution, 1956, that the State had been following a policy of supporting Cottage and Village and Small Scale Industries restricting the volume of production in the large scale sector. The State Policy would be to ensure that the decentralised sector acquires sufficient vitality to be self–supporting and its development is integrated with that of large scale industry. The State will, therefore, concentrate on measures designed to improve the competitive strength of the small scale producer.

It was further stated in the Policy Resolution that to make good some serious deficiencies of the small scale sector, industrial estates and rural community workshops had been set up. Industrial co-operatives would be encouraged to give constant attention to the development of cottage and village and small scale industry. Industrial Policy Statement, 1973, outlined : "Government will continue to encourage competent small and medium entrepreneurs in all industries. They would be preferred to large houses and foreign investors. Production of ancillaries will be promoted in medium or small scale sectors. The area of reservation for small scale sector will continue and may be extended consistent with the potentialities and performance of these small industries".

Industrial Policy Statement, 1977

The Government in its Industrial Policy Statement declared that the emphasis of industrial policy had been so far mainly on large industries neglecting small industries to minor role. The Government was firm to change this approach. The main thrust of the new industrial policy (of the Janata Government) would be on effective promotion of cottage and small scale industries widely dispersed in rural areas and small towns. The Government policy would be to see that whatever can be produced by small and cottage industries must only be so produced. The Janata Government formulated various measures for the promotion of small industry.

Industrial Policy Statement, 1980

It was stated, "In order to promote the development of small scale industries and ensure their rapid growth, the Government has decided to increase the limit of investment". The new policy stated," While making all efforts towards integrated industrial development, it is proposed to promote the concept of economic federation with the setting up of a few nucleus plants in each district. These plants would work for upgrading the technology of small units".

The Industrial Policy (1990)

The investment ceiling for small scale industries would be raised to enable them to play an important role in the total export effort, such of the small units which undertakes to export at least 30 per cent of the annual production by the third year will be permitted to set up their investment in plant and machinery to Rs. 75 lakhs from Rs 60 lakhs. Investment ceiling in respect of tiny units would also be increased. More items would be reserved for exclusive manufacture in the small scale sector. A new scheme of Central Investment Subsidy exclusively for the small sector would be implemented. With a view to improving the competitiveness of the products manufactured in the small scale sector, programmes for modernisation and upgradation of technology would be implemented. To ensure adequate and timely flow of credit for the small scale sector a new apex bank known as SIDBI has already been established. Besides, commercial banks and financial institutions would channelise need-based, higher flow of credit, both by way of term loan and working capital, to the tiny industries. To provide sustained support to the units in the small sector the fiscal concessions would have to be reviewed.

The Industrial Policy (1990) so far as liberalisation and delicensing is concerned, echoed the former policy of the Congress Government.

Because of this policy, serious effects like driving out the small scale units from the market is likely to take place.

The Government policy towards small scale units is changing with the change of Government in our country. But one thing is now evident — liberalised industrial policy. This Policy may affect the small sector units.

CHAPTER SEVEN

ORGANISED MARKET

MARKET

Definition — In ordinary sense market means a place where the buyers and sellers meet for exchange of goods for price. In a city there are many markets. In a village there may be a small market place. But from the point of view of Economics, market is not really a place. It is not directed towards a place but **towards a commodity** and it recognises **existence of buyers and sellers** who shall meet. This meeting does not require a place. A buyer may meet a seller through correspondence or even over the telephone or through a middleman like a broker. According to Chapman, "Economically interpreted the term market refers, not to a place but to a commodity or commodities and buyers and sellers, who are in direct competition with one another." So, for market (a) there must be some commodity or commodities; (b) there must be buyers and sellers; and (c) there must be direct competition among buyers and sellers with one another. **There are three kinds of competition:** (1) Competition among the sellers to capture the market, each trying to have the largest share. (2) Competition among the buyers to get hold of some commodity when that commodity has restricted supply. (3) Competition among the buyers and the sellers. A seller wants to win over a buyer through publicity, salesmanship and such other techniques while a potential buyer tries not to be influenced by such techniques. In a socialistic country or under controlled economy such competition hardly exists. A market is commodity-oriented, viz, vegetable market, fish market, bullion market, share market, etc.

Firms and markets – The term business means repeated buying and selling of goods or services. Therefore, a market must exist. Markets do not exist for goods only but for services too, e.g. labour market, money market, etc. **Every goods** (or service) **is produced for its potential market.** If there is no potentiality of market, it is useless to produce the goods. Therefore, **the importance of market for every firm is very great.** In a sense, market for businessmen signifies a group of buyers. A firm is also interested in other types of market like the money market, capital market etc. Such markets are called organised markets (see below). To a firm, market also means a mechanism by which exchange takes place. Market is **an important social institution.** It is often said that our society is a 'market society'. Every firm must have some market of its own, i.e. a share in the total supply of the commodity or service. Collectively, an industry as a whole must have its market. **The main function of a businessman is to find out, to create, and protect the market** for his merchandise or service. This is more true when there is competition. He has to take recourse to various devices of publicity, salesmanship and sales promotion. The industry as a whole has to create and protect its market. For this purpose, Trade Associations are generally formed. According to Drucker, every firm must have some 'market standing'. This shall be the first objective of management. The marketing management is, therefore, the most critical function.

Characteristics of a good market

A good market shall have the following characteristics: (1) It shall be wide enough so that there is existence of a steady and continuous demand for the commodity under sale. If there is no steady demand there cannot be steady and continuous supply of the commodity. The suppliers can hold the stock when there is excess supply to adjust it with the demand.

(2) There shall be facilities for movement of the goods so that the supply of a commodity may reach the market easily, regularly and timely.

(3) The commodity must be capable of being identified and preferably be represented by sample or by description.

(4) The title to or ownership of goods must pass easily from the seller to the buyer with minimum formalities.

(5) There shall be freedom of entering into contracts by the buyers and the sellers among themselves for executing transactions of sale.

Classification of markets

Markets are of various types. The classification of markets can be envisaged from various viewpoints. Businessmen and economists differ in their approaches to the classification of markets. **Taking all the viewpoints together, the following types of markets are found:**

(1) **Geographical area** — From the viewpoint of area covered, a market can be **local, regional, national and international.** A local market has a very limited area and is generally for perishable daily necessary goods like fish, vegetables etc. A regional market covers a particular region of a country. Such regional classification is found in a large country. India, for example, is divided into four regions, east, west, north and south, for all practical purposes. A national market covers the entire country. An international market means extension of market in other countries.

(2) **Unit of sale** — Market is commonly classified on the basis of unit of sale. For example, **wholesale market and retail market.** The unit of sale in wholesale market is big while in retail market it is small and sometimes very small. The price of the same commodity differs in wholesale and retail markets.

(3) **Periodicity** — Economists classify markets from the view-point of time and, as such, there are **four types of markets.** (a) **Very short-period** - This is a market for perishable goods and the goods have to be sold out by the sellers in a short time. The supply cannot be adjusted with the demand. (b) **Short-period** - This is a market for goods with a limited stock. The supply can be adjusted with the demand to some extent but not fully. (c) **Long-period** - In such a market, the supply can be adjusted with the demand by changing the scale of production. (d) **Very long-period** — In such a market, the length of the period is so long that very big changes take place to affect the supply and the demand, e.g. change in technique of production, change in population, change in tastes etc.

(4) **Nature and degree of competition** — In a free economy country there is a competition in the market which may be either perfect or imperfect and, accordingly, we get **perfect** and **imperfect** markets. A market is perfect when some conditions are satisfied, e.g. (a) there are large number of sellers and buyers; (b) the products of the sellers are identical; (c) each buyer and each seller has perfect knowledge of the market; (d) each seller has equal access to the factors of production, etc. When one or more of the conditions are absent, the market is imperfect. Market can be further classified according to the degree of imperfection. The worst situation is when there is a monopoly (one seller) or a monopsony (one buyer).

(5) **Methods of transactions** — Generally, in a market there are 'spot' transactions. The main characteristic of a spot transaction is that the goods exist and the buyers and the sellers do the transactions on the basis of some agreed terms and conditions. A market where spot transactions take place is called an **ordinary market.** But there are some **organised markets** where 'future' transactions also take place. Under future transactions goods do not exist but transactions are made by samples and by descriptions or by both. Goods, which satisfy some conditions, can be bought under organised markets. There are different types of organised markets like money market, commodity market and capital market.

(6) **Position of sellers** — Markets can be further classified according to the position of sellers. Accordingly we find **primary, secondary and terminal markets.** The agricultural or industrial goods are sold by the producers to some middlemen, like wholesalers. This is the primary market. In the secondary market, the middlemen, like the wholesalers, sell the goods to another group of middlemen called the retailers. Ultimately, the goods are sold in the terminal market to the actual consumers.

ORGANISED MARKET

Market can be classified in many ways. One of the broad methods of classification is dividing markets into two categories: **Ordinary** and **Organised.** In general, in an ordinary market, 'spot' transactions take place while in an organised market 'future' transactions are very common. These two types of markets differ on many points and from that the characteristics of an organised market will come out. **The points of difference are :**

(1) In an ordinary market, **spot transactions take place** which means : (a) the goods exist and are displayed as we find in our daily markets in the cities or towns or villages. (b) The buyers make choice of goods. (c) The sellers try to impress upon the buyers with the help of publicity, salesmanship, sales promotion and such other techniques. (d) The terms of payment may be either cash or credit (either full or part, i.e. instalment system). (e) The mode and time of delivery of goods also depend upon the understanding between the buyer and the seller.

In an organised market **'future' transactions take place** which means; (a) The goods do not exist but there are expectations that the goods will be available. The goods are sold by sample or by description or by both. The **goods must satisfy the following conditions** to be included in future-transactions–(i) The goods have universal and continuous demand but they have seasonal or restricted supply like jute, cotton, shares etc. (ii) The goods can be graded and sampled so that they can be sold by samples and by description or by both. For example, jute, shares etc. (iii) The goods must be durable so that the stock can be held for the purpose of adjustment of supply with the demand. (iv) The unit of sale is big, e.g. hundreds of bales of jute at a time, hundreds of shares at a time, etc.

(2) In an ordinary market, any person can do transactions. There is no restriction for entering any such market.

In an organised market **only members can do transactions.** For every market there is an association, e.g. the East India Cotton Association, the Calcutta Stock Exchange Association, etc. The membership can be obtained according to the constitution and rules of that association. For example, admission fee and annual subscription may have to be paid as in the London Stock Exchange or a share has to be purchased as in case of the Calcutta Stock Exchange Association, which is a limited company. Obviously, the number of members has a limit.

(3) There are no definite rules and regulations for transactions in an ordinary market. There are, however, some customs and conventions and the laws related to contracts and sale of goods do apply.

In an organised market **there are definite rules and regulations** for transactions. Such rules and regulations are of two types: (a) Of the organisation itself — Since there is an association it has its constitution and bye-laws. (b) Statutory — The Government has enacted several laws to control the activities of the organised markets e.g. the Securities Contracts (Regulation) Act, 1956, controls the activities of the stock exchanges.

(4) In general, there are no specific classification of ordinary markets on the basis of commodities.

Organised markets, however, are further **classified on the basis of commodities** dealt in. Broadly speaking, there are three types of organised markets: (a) **Money market** — It consists of the banks of a country headed by its Central Bank. In India, the organised sector of the money market consists of the Reserve Bank of India at its top with other member banks under its control. There is specific Act called the Banking Regulations Act of 1949 to control the banking operations. Besides, there are other Acts like the Reserve Bank of India Act, 1948, the Companies Act, 1956, the Negotiable Instruments Act, 1881, etc. which also control the banking operations. (b) **Commodity market** — There are a large number of commodity markets based on different agricultural and non-agricultural commodities which satisfy all the conditions required to have organised markets (see above). For example, there are markets for jute, cotton, tea, gold, silver, wool, copper, spices, etc. The commodity markets which deal in argicultural commodities are also known as Produce Exchanges, e.g. jute, cotton etc. The Forward Contracts (Regulation) Act, 1952, controls the operations of commodity markets. (c) **Capital market** — It is a vast and complicated market for procuring long term funds both from inside and outside sources by bodies corporate as well as by the Government and other public bodies like Calcutta Corporation, a Port Trust etc. The individual investors, the bodies corporate, the financial institutions, the investment trusts, etc. supply the finance. The stock exchanges or the share markets constitute a part of the capital market where shares, debentures, etc. are bought and sold by the members and through the members by the general members of the public. The stock exchanges are controlled by the Securities Contracts (Regulation) Act, 1956. There are various Acts for the financial institutions like the Industrial Finance Corporation of India, the State Financial Corporations, the Unit Trust, the Life Insurance Corporation, etc.

Importance of market in business

The importance of market in business can be understood from **the following points :**

(1) Since a market is said to exist when buyers meet sellers, markets enable the buyers to obtain goods which are necessary for them for satisfaction of their wants and the sellers get their stocks exhausted. By this, both the buyers and the sellers are benefited.

(2) The existence of a market provides incentive to the producers to produce. Goods are produced for markets. To develop the markets, the producers take recourse to various measures. By all these efforts, employments are created.

(3) Markets generate demand for goods and services through publicity, salesmanship, sales promotion etc. and by that the standard of living of a community is raised and economic development takes place.

(4) The organised markets for industrial raw materials like jute, cotton, etc., which have seasonal supplies but daily demands, make adjustment between demands and supplies and stabilise their prices.

(5) The existence of the money market, i.e. the banking system, is essential for a country, otherwise heavy and long distance payments are not possible and particularly payments from one country to another in different currencies. Banks provide financial accommodation in various ways without which business transactions cannot be carried on in a large scale.

(6) The importance of capital market, of which the share market is a part, is equally great. People will face difficulties to find out outlets for investment of their savings if there is no share market. If there be no scope for investments, there shall be no employment and no production. On the other hand, companies can raise funds quickly by enlistment of their securities in stock exchanges.

(7) Markets themselves provide opportunities for different kinds of odd employments. There are various kinds of dealers, agents etc. and their staff to facilitate buying and selling.

(8) Markets provide an index for the economic situation of a country. When activities in markets are more and prices are high, it is a sign of economic advancement or prosperity for a country. Conversely, when the activities are less and prices are low, it is a sign of economic retardation or depression for a country.

CAPITAL MARKET

Definition — Capital market can be defined as **the market for long-term funds.** Long-term funds are required for business by the businessmen and also for developmental activities by the Government and other public bodies. These funds are supplied by the investors out of their savings, either directly or through institutions like insurance companies, investment trusts etc. Such savers or investors are of two types: (1) Individuals – either persons or artificial persons like bodies corporate. (2) Institutions – insurance companies, financial institutions, investment trusts, etc. Besides, supply of capital also comes from different created funds, e.g. Provident Funds, different types or redemption investment funds like debenture redemption investment funds.

The constituents — The capital market is a meeting point of borrowers and lenders. There are three types of borrowers: bodies corporate, the Government, and the public bodies like a municipality, a Port Trust, etc. There are basically two types of lenders – individuals and institutions. Individuals consist of persons and bodies corporate and institutions consist of insurance companies, industrial banks, financial institutions, investment trusts, redemption investment funds and Provident Funds (see above). Supply of long term capital comes in the form of securities either for permanent investment, e.g. shares, irredeemable or perpetual debentures, irredeemable Government Promissory Notes and units. Out of these, shares are most common. Further, there are long-term redeemable types of investments like Government Promissory Notes, debentures, public deposits and redeemable preference shares. Redeemable preference shares are uncommon. Investments of irredeemable type fetch dividends or share in the profits as returns while redeemable investments get interests.

Underwriting is a method of supplying funds. By this method, some institutions take the responsibility of marketing shares of companies. In the industrially advanced countries, there are specialised bodies called Issue Houses who underwrite subscription to shares of new companies and take heavy discount on the total value of shares guaranteed for sale by them. Through underwriting by renowned issue houses **companies can raise funds quickly.** In the case of a very large issue an issuing house distributes portions of the issue among sub-underwriters. Even some banks function as underwriters. The goodwill and the market value of shares of a company go high if some renowned underwriters take the responsibility of underwriting the shares. In India, the different financial institutions and, to some extent, commercial banks do underwriting. If an underwriter fails to market the securities, he himself shall hold the shares and pay for them. In this way, through underwriting, **bodies corporate become sure** about their sources of capital. The underwriters are important constituents of capital market.

Market does not always denote a place. Same is true for the capital market. But, **there are share markets** or stock exchanges which are organised markets and they have definite places where buyers and sellers of securities meet. Actually, **these markets are second-hand markets.** A share market or a stock exchange is a place where an existing shareholder tries to find out a buyer for the shares to whom the seller shall transfer the shares held by him. Similarly, a prospective buyer is in search of a probable seller inside the market.

COMPOSITION OF INDIAN CAPITAL MARKET

Background — Before independence, industrialisation did not take place in India and so **the capital market was not well organised.** Even immediately after independence, things did not change much though the Industrial Finance Corporation of India was established in 1948, sponsored by the Government, as the first institution for long term financial assistance. The First Five-Year Plan was launched in 1951 but that had a bias for agriculture. The Second Plan was introduced in 1956 with an emphasis on industrial development. In the same year, certain enabling measures were taken to create the objective conditions for industrial growth. **Since 1956, a capital market, in the true sense of the term, is developing in the country.** In the past, India did not have professional promoters (though the managing agents played the role to some extent), underwriting agencies, issue houses or such other financial intermediaries. At present, the managing agents do not exist but financial and promotional institutions have come into existence. Big business houses used to have investment trusts under their control to channelise their investments to those companies in which those respective business houses were interested. Such investment trusts still exist but the big business houses are taking maximum advantage of the State-sponsored financial institutions. One redeeming feature of the present capital market of India is **the predominance of the State in it.**

The different aspects of the capital market of India

(1) **The policies and enactments by the Government** — The Government announced its Industrial Policy in 1948, introducing mixed economy and emphasizing on the role of small and village industries. The policy was not liked by the business community because of threat of nationalisation to some major industries. The policy was revised in 1956 to remove the fears in the context of the Second Plan with industrial bias. The Government announced its Foreign Capital Policy in 1949 inviting foreign capital but that without foreign domination. It was rightly felt that foreign capital was necessary for the development of an underdeveloped country like India. In 1956, the Securities Contracts (Regulation) Act was passed to have a control over the constitution and operation of stock exchanges in the country, the major constituent of the capital market. In the same year, the Reserve Bank of India Act was heavily amended to have a more regulated money market. The Companies Act in its new form was passed in 1956. The Life Insurance Corporation of India was also established in 1956 to channelise savings of the people towards proper investments. In this way, 1956 proved to be a turning point in the economic history of the country. (Many other important economic events took place in the year, e.g. establishment of the State Trading Corporation, adoption of a policy of land reform by the ruling party, i.e. the Indian National Congress, etc.). Since then some other important legislations have come into being having regulatory effects on the capital market, e.g. the Capital Issues (Exemption) Order 1969, several amendments of the Companies Act, the Foreign Exchange Regulation Act, 1973, the Monopolies and Restrictive Trade Practices Act, 1969, etc.

It has to be noted that the Government assured, in its Industrial Policy, financial assistance to the private sector and the village and small-scale sectors in particular, for their development. A number of financial corporations, both at the Central and State levels, were established for the purpose. On the basis of the recommendations of the All India Rural Credit Survey Committee in 1952, the Government nationalised the Imperial Bank of India to establish the State Bank of India to implement the integrated credit scheme providing financial assistance for rural development and that mainly through the cooperatives.

(2) **Establishment of promotional institutions** — The Central Government established the National Industrial Development Corporation in 1954 for the promotion and development of industries in the country with a programme of balanced regional growth. It renders services both to the public and the private sectors. In the same pattern, Industrial Development Corporation have been set up from 1960 onwards in every State by the respective State Government. The Industrial Development Bank of India helps in promotion of big projects. All these institutions also provide financial help at the initial stage in addition to preparation of projects and acting as liaison with financial institutions. They also provide financial assistance for the modernisation of existing units by arranging purchase of machinery and equipment on hire-purchase basis. The National Small Industries Corporation, established in 1955, provide similar help to small industries. Different States also have established State Industrial Corporations for small industries.

(3) **Establishment of financial institutions** — The Central Government has established two big financial institutions to provide industrial finance to large scale industries, both in the public and the private sectors. They are : The Industrial Finance Corporation of India (1948) and the Industrial Development Bank of India (1964). Another institution, called the Industrial Reconstruction Bank of India (1971), has a special role to play to revitalise sick industries. The Central Government passed the State Financial Corporation Act in 1951 by virtue of which the State Governments can establish their own financial corporations with the assistance of the Central Government. There, are at, present 18 such State Financial Corporations in the country.

Apart from these state-sponsored financial institutions, the Industrial Credit and Investment Corporation of India was established in 1955 in the private sector with Government and foreign financial assistance.

A large number (about 600) of investment trusts or companies had been operating in the country in the private sector. The Central Government established in 1964 a giant investment trust in the public sector, called the Unit Trust of India. It has been already noted that the Life Insurance Corporation of India plays a formidable role in the field of industrial finance. The LIC is described as the single biggest investor in the country.

All these institutions do underwriting functions.

(4) **Role of banks** — Indian banks are traditionally commercial banks providing short-term financial accommodation. India does not have industrial banks. But recently the commercial banks are also providing term loans and doing underwriting functions. They often subscribe to the capital of the financial institutions. The State Bank has a big share in such capital. The situation is fast changing since the nationalisation of big banks. Now there is no fear of failure of banks and so banks can take such risks.

(5) **Funds** — Creation of provident funds for the employees of almost all establishments has become almost a compulsion by the Provident Fund Act, 1952. The huge funds so collected go for investments according to the rules stipulated in the Act. Provident fund collections are of three different types: (a) Funds of Government employees, both of the Central and State Governments. (b) Funds under the Employees' Provident Fund Scheme meant for specialised industrial establishments. (c) Funds in other establishments.

In India there are many properties held under trusts, dedicated to some 'gods' or 'goddesses' or otherwise, from which huge funds flow for investments, particularly for the Government Promissory Notes.

Lastly, general reserve funds, redemption investment funds etc. from companies also provide a big chunk to the capital market of the country.

(6) **Other sources** — Different registered societies including cooperative societies also have their surplus funds for investments. Housing societies are getting popular day by day in urban areas through ownership flats and thereby huge investments are taking place in buildings and constructions.

FINANCIAL AND DEVELOPMENTAL INSTITUTIONS IN INDIA

Need for such institutions — Financial and developmental institutions exist in many countries of the world. They have to play a significant role in underdeveloped countries for their economic development. This is particularly true for India. The need for such institutions was first pointed out by the Industrial Commission in 1918 appointed by the then British Government. The recommendations of the Commission, however, were not implemented. The need was further felt during the World War II, India engaging herself in industrial production on account of the impact of war.

The need for such institutions in India can be justified from the following viewpoints :

(1) **The rate of capital formation is low** because of low national income and low rate of savings. This is a common feature of all under-developed countries.

(2) **Capital in India is shy.** People of India hesitate to take risk of investment in industries. They believe in putting their savings in the forms of investment in land or in Government bonds.

(3) **The capital market of India** (until recently) **is not well organised.** The stock exchanges are mostly gambling dens.

(4) **The banks are almost wholly commercial banks** providing short-term accommodations. Limited attempts to start industrial banks met with failure.

(5) **Lack of industrial entrepreneurs** promoting companies attracting the people to invest is another drawback.

(6) Assistance of financial institutions is specially needed for (a) **developing small and medium scale industries** and (b) **modernisation and rehabilitation** of old and uneconomic units.

(7) Without such institutions investments, cannot be channelised **according to the requirements of the economic plans.**

Things, however, have vastly changed after independence. From 1948 onwards, a large number of institutions have been established in the country, mostly in the public sector, for financial and developmental assistance. The main institutions are as follows :

(A) Financial Institutions

(1) The Industrial Finance Corporation of India established by the Central Government.

(2) The Industrial Development Bank of India established by the Central Government as the biggest unit.

(3) The Industrial Credit and Investment Corporation of India established by the private sector.

(4) The Industrial Re-construction Corporation of India established by the Central Government for assisting sick and uneconomic units. Now it is renamed as Industrial Reconstruction Bank of India.

(5) The Unit Trust of India, established by the Central Government, is the biggest investment trust.

(6) The State Financial Corporations established by different State Governments.

(7) The Industrial Re-finance Corporation of India established by the Central Government to provide re-lending facilities to financial institutions. This has subsequently merged with the Industrial Development Bank of India.

Besides these, the Life Insurance Corporation of India and the General Insurance Corporation of India indirectly do financing functions through investments in the financial institutions. The State Bank of India also plays a similar role.

(B) Developmental Institutions

(1) The National Industrial Development Corporation established by the Central Government assisting industrial development through promotional activities.

(2) The State Industrial Development Corporations established by different State Governments in the line of the NIDC.

(3) The National Small Industries Corporations established by the Central Government for assisting small industries in developmental activities and indirect financing.

(4) The Small Industries Corporations started by some State Governments in the line of the NSIC.

A. The Industrial Finance Corporation of India

Incorporation — The Industrial Finance Corporation of India (IFCI) **was establised in July 1948 as a statutory corporation** by a special Act to provide **medium and long-term financial assistance** to any public limited company or co-operative society engaged in manufacturing or processing work or producing electricity or other kind of power, mining, shipping, hotel-keeping or preservation of goods. The IFCI is meant for **large-scale industrial concerns only.** By amending the Act in 1972,private limited companies have also been brought within the scope of the IFCI. This is the first financial corporation in the country.

Financial Resources – Share capital — The IFCI has an authorised capital of Rs. 20 crores. **The paid-up capital is Rs. 10 crores** of which 50% is held by the Industrial Development Bank of India. The IDBI established in 1964 took over the shares held by the Central Government and the Reserve Bank of India. The remaining 50% of the paid-up capital is held by the Life Insurance Corporation, scheduled banks and cooperative banks. **Bonds** – The IFCI can issue bonds up to the extent of its paid-up capital and reserves. **Deposits** – The IFCI can accept deposits from the public and from the State Governments as well as local authorities up to a limit of Rs. 10 crores. The public deposits are repayable after 5 years. Up to June 1974, the IFCI did not accept any public deposit. **Borrowings from abroad** — The IFCI can borrow in foreign currency from the World Bank against the guarantee by the Central Government. **Borrowing inland** – (1) The IFCI can borrow from the Reserve Bank of India in two ways : (a) medium-term with maturity within 18 months up to Rs. 3 crores and (b) short-term with maturity within 3 months without any limit. (2) The IFCI can borrow from the Central Government and the Industrial Development Bank of India.

The shares of the IFCI and a minimum dividend are guaranteed by the Central Government. A higher rate of dividend can be paid when the reserve fund becomes equal to the paid-up capital. The Central Government also guarantees repayment of the bonds and a fixed rate of interest.

Management — The IFCI is managed **by a Board of Directors** consisting of 13 members including a Chairman. The Composition of the Board of Directors is as follows : The Chairman and two Directors are appointed by the Central Government, four Directors are appointed by the Industrial Development Bank of India, and two Directors each are appointed by the Life Insurance Corporation of India, the Scheduled and Cooperative banks through election.

Functions — (1) **Financial assistance** — The main function of the IFCI is to provide medium and long-term financial assistance. According to Sec. 23 of the IFCI Act, it can transact the following business :

(a) To guarantee loans raised by industrial concerns from the market repayable within a period not exceeding 25 years.

(b) To underwrite issue of stock, shares, bonds or debentures by industrial concerns disposing them off within seven years.

(c) To grant loans or advances or subscribing to the debentures of industrial concerns repayable within a period not exceeding 25 years.

(d) To act as an agent for the Central Government and, with or without the approval of the Central Government, for the World Bank in respect of loans offered by them to industrial concerns.

(e) To guarantee deferred payments by Indian importers to foreign exporters.

(f) To guarantee loans raised by industrial concerns from scheduled or cooperative banks.

(g) To guarantee deferred payments by industrial concerns for capital goods manufactured in India.

(h) To guarantee loans, with the prior approval of the Central Government, raised by industrial concerns in foreign currencies from foreign banks or other financial institutions.

According to the amendment of the Companies Act, loans given by the IFCI can be converted into equity capital by the Govt.

(2) **Non-financial assistance** — In 1972, the IFCI has established the Management Development Institute to provide managerial training to new entrepreneurs or professional

managers. The Institute also imparts training to the staff of the IFCI at all levels and to the staff of other financial institutions at the Central or State levels. It has introduced merchant banking i.e. advising, for investments from July 1986.

Methods of operation — The operation of the IFCI has the following principles and procedures :

(1) Any large size enterprise desirous of having financial assistance **has to make an application** giving all the details about its capital, product, location and description of the factory, machinery, technical staff, market prospect, securities to be offered, etc. According to the recent change of policy, the IFCI can also receive application from any public sector undertaking or even from a medium or small size concern if it is of national interest.

(2) The officers of the IFCI **will carry out security and inspection** to verify the application and to be satisfied with the economic viability.

(3) The IFCI **will ask for security** with 50% margin. It can forego security if the assistance is required in national interest or if the loan is guaranteed by the Government, either Central or State, or by any Scheduled or Cooperative bank.

(4) The IFCI **charges interest** (at present) at the rate of 11.25% per annum on rupee loan and 11.50 on foreign loan. A rebate of $^1/_2$% is allowed if the interest or instalment repayment of capital are paid in due time.

(5) The borrower has to **submit periodic progress reports** on the performance of the concern to the satisfaction of the advisory committees appointed by the IFCI for different industries.

(6) The IFCI can grant loans **not exceeding Rs. 2 crores** to a single industrial concern.

(7) Though the IFCI can grant loan up to 25 years of time, in practice, however, it grants the loan **up to 12 years.** Repayment is demanded in equal or other gradual instalments, starting generally after two or three years of granting of the loan.

(8) Loans can be granted on **concessional terms** for setting up industries in backward districts of any State notified by the Central Government.

(9) Loans are granted **for the purposes of** establishing new industrial undertaking or for modernisation of existing plants or for diversification of existing production.

(10) The IFCI accords **special consideration** to applications made by **technocrats and professionally qualified persons** promoting new projects. Recently, the IFCI has been much active in this respect.

Working of the IFCI — The IFCI, by March 1989, had sanctioned financial assistance to the extent of Rs. 6,550 crores, the actual disbursement was Rs. 4,350 crores. Out of the sanctioned assistance, about one-third went for modernisation or diversification or expansion of existing units and two-third went for new projects and projects of high national priority. Total loans sanctioned in 1988-89 were Rs. 1,900 crores as against 1,050 crores in 1987-88. The disbursements of foreign currency loans were Rs. 85.32 crores.

Critical evaluation

The IFCI has rendered a great service in the field of industrial finance in the country as a pioneer. **At the early period, it did not function in business line** and there were complaints of favouritism. The Sucheta Kripalani Committee, appointed in 1953, made an enquiry and came to the conclusion that the complaints were largely substantial. Since then, **a number of attemps have been made to improve the operations** of the institution. The Mahalanobis Committee and the Dutta Committee (or Industrial Licensing Enquiry Committee) have commented that the benefits of financial assistance rendered by the IFCI had been mostly enjoyed by big industrial houses leading to concentration of economic power. Even then, it cannot be denied that the IFCI has filled in a vacuum created by absence of industrial banking in the country. However, the following points of criticism are generally raised against it :

(1) **The rates of interest charged by the IFCI are very high.** It is desirable that the rates should not be so high if it wanted to help new projects, since it is a public sector undertaking. But it may be mentioned that the rates of interest are not really very high keeping in view the rising cost of administration and the rates charged by banks.

(2) It is complained that **much time is taken** for processing any application for assistance. This is a valid criticism. The IFCI is very much influenced by the bureaucratic system of the Government, as is the case for any other public sector undertaking.

(3) It has so far given **larger assistance to consumer goods industries** than to capital goods industries although the object of the IFCI wanted it otherwise. Recently, however, a change in the policy of sanctioning loans has taken place.

(4) Assistance has been given **mostly to those concerns which are in a position to get financial assistance from other sources** by virtue of their goodwill and economic power. This is a serious complaint. The IFCI has been, no doubt, a victim of pressure groups. The IFCI has indirectly helped big industrial houses to earn more wealth with the help of public money.

(5) As it has helped the large scale enterprises, the **medium and small scale units** belonging to the same line of business **have been crushed.** But, in fact, the State Financial Corporations have been established to help the medium and small scale units.

(6) The statutory limit of the period of assistance is 25 years. But in practice, in most of the cases, the loan **has been granted for maximum 10 to 12 years** and in rare cases up to 15 years. This is a valid criticism but the sanctioning authorities might want full safety and reduction of risk.

(7) There are lots of **cases of favouritism and nepotism** in respect of granting of loans. But, unfortunately, these are now-a-days rampant in nearly all the different public undertakings.

(8) It has **not been very liberal towards industrial concerns in backward areas.** The possible counter-argument may be that financial assistance cannot be granted if other elements of infrastructure are not available.

(9) **Some States have taken away the lion's share.** It is revealed that 70% of the aid has been received by developed States, particularly that of Maharashtra. It is a fact that some States have greater political pull, which is not desirable. But, it is also true that some of the States are less enterprising.

Inspite of criticisms, it is no exaggeration to say that the IFCI has been performing commendable service for the last two decades.

B. The Industrial Development Bank of India

Incorporation — The Industrial Development Bank of India (IDBI) **was established in July 1964 under a special Act** as the biggest and highest organisation for long-term financial institution in the country. It was to provide a new direction in the field of long and medium-term financing. The IDBI has the **dual objects of promoting** very large enterprises by mobilising financial resources **and coordinating** as well as controlling the functions of other financial institutions. Such coordination is necessary to rationalise the functions of the financial institution in the context of growing industrialisation and diversification of the industrial sector, keeping in view the objectives of the Five-Year Plans. If necessary, it can take over any other financial institution (see below). The IDBI renders help both to the private and public sectors. It has been designed in the model of the Industrial Development Bank of Canada.

Financial resources — Share capital — The original authorised capital of the IDBI was Rs. 50 crores and by 1982 it had been increased to Rs. 500 crores. At the time of introduction, IDBI was a wholly-owned subsidiary of the Reserve Bank of India. In February 1976, it had been given an autonomous status by transferring all the shares held by the RBI to the Central Government. **Bonds, debentures and public deposits** – The IDBI can increase its capital by selling bonds and debentures with or without Government guarantee as well as can accept deposits from the public maturing after not less than one year. **Loan from the Central Government** – The IDBI is entitled to get interest-free loan from the Central Government to the extent of Rs. 10 crores repayable in fifteen equal instalments after the expiry of 15 years. In addition, it can get loans under usual terms and conditions from the Central Government. **Borrowings from the RBI** – The IDBI can borrow from the RBI for short periods up to 5 years against commercial bills and for long periods out of the National Industrial Credit (Long-term Operations) Fund established by the RBI in 1965. **Special Fund of the Central Government** — The IDBI can augment its capital by getting gifts and special grants from the Development Assistance Fund created by the Central Government. Such fund is necessary for financing special projects and time-consuming investments where rates of returns will be low and which are not financed by the existing financial institutions or banks.

Management — At the initial stage, it was a subsidiary of the RBI. But, after being delinked from the RBI, it **is managed by a Board of Directors** consisting of the representatives of other term-lending institutions like IFCI, ICICI, IRBI, LICI, and UTI. This is for maintaining coordination among the functions of these institutions.

Functions : The IDBI has been established to finance industries of all descriptions both in the private and public sectors and specially those which have priority in the Five-Year Plans. It also provides non-financial assistance.

(1) **Financial assistance** —– is rendered by the IDBI, either directly or indirectly, through other financial institutions. This is discussed in a classified manner :

(a) It can refinance term loans of 3 to 25 years given by the IFCI, SFC's and other notified financial institutions to industrial concerns. (b) It can refinance term loams of 3 to 10 years given by scheduled banks and state cooperative banks to industrial concerns. (c) It can refinance export credit of duration between 6 months and 10 years given by the financial institutions to exporting houses. (d) It can supplement the capital of the financial institutions themselves by subscribing to their shares and bonds. (e) Like any other financial institution, the IDBI can directly finance industrial concerns by granting loans (which can be converted into equity capital) or by subscribing to their shares or bonds or by underwriting their shares or bonds or by guaranteeing deferred payments or loans raised by the industrial concerns from the open market or scheduled banks or state cooperative banks. (f) The IDBI also can discount or rediscount bonafide commercial bills of industrial concerns.

There is no limit of financial assistance granted to a single unit.

(2) **Non-financial assistance** — The IDBI takes up promotional activities to establish new types of industries. It helps carrying out industrial survey and research, and market survey and research. It also provides managerial, technical and various consultancy services for establishment of new industries or for expansion and/or diversification of existing units. The IDBI is committed to fill up the gaps in the industrial structure of the country.

Working — Since its inception, the IDBI has done commendable job in promotional and financial activities in the industrial field. In 1988-89 it has sanctioned financial assistance of Rs. 7,010 crores and disbursed Rs. 4,630 crores. Up to March 1989, it has sanctioned financial assistance to the extent of Rs. 34,000 crores and disbursed a total amount of about Rs. 24,700 crores. The total amount of refinancing, as on the same date, stood at Rs. 15,400 crores. On the other hand, it has rationalised and restructured the industrial financing as a whole in the country. In 1964, the Refinance Corporation of India has merged with it. In 1976, it has taken up 50% of the shares of the Industrial Finance Corporation of India and the entire holdings of the RBI of the shares of different State Financial Corporations have been handed over to the IDBI. It has shown special favour to projects promoted by technocrats. IDBI provides two-thirds of the total assistance given by all all-India financial institutions.

Method of operation — Like other financial institutions, the IDBI also goes through the economic viability of projects and concerns before granting any assistance. Apart from this, the IDBI has set up two working groups with specialised functions – (1) The Informal Consultative Group and (2) the ad hoc Working Group consisting of representatives of the IDBI itself as well as of the banks concerned, the Export Credit Guarantee Corporation, and the two departments of the RBI – the Exchange Control Department and the Banking Operations and Development Department. These working groups facilitate coordinated decisions.

Critical evaluation — Out of all the financial institutions, the working of the IDBI has been so far the best. It has really opened new avenues of industrial development in the country. Its establishment can unhesitatingly be described as a "milestone in the country's journey to the institutional provision of industrial finance on a long and medium-term basis". There are two basic reasons (1) It has great freedom of operation. Since it has been delinked from the RBI, it is in a position to make prompt and independent decisions with a commercial bias. (2) It is exempted from income-tax and such other taxes. Many people are of the opinion that such freedom and exemption being granted, other financial institutions could have made better performance. The IDBI is functioning not only as a financing institution but also as a true development bank. It has already completed industrial survey of backward areas of the country in different States and Union Territories. Since a major part of its functions is akin to that of the National Industrial Development Corporation (see below), it is desirable that IDBI should take over the NIDC.

NABARD

In July 1982, the Government has established, by a special Act, the National Bank for Agricultural and Rural Development (NABARD), with a capital of Rs. 100 crores subscribed equally by the Central Government and the Reserve Bank of India. This is more or less like an Agricultural Development Bank, established according to the recommendations of the Committee to Review Arrangements for Institutional Credit for Agriculture and Rural Development (CRA-FICARD).

Functions : The NABARD will take over the functions of Argicultural Refinance and Development Corporation and the functions of the Reserve Bank in respect of agricultural credit and rural development.

Management : NABARD is managed by a Board of Directors consisting of (a) A Chairman, (b) Two directors as experts in rural economy, (c) Three directors of whom two have experience in cooperative banking and one in commercial banking. (d) Three directors from the directors of the RBI. (e) Three directors from the officials of the Central Government. (f) Two directors from the officials of the State Governments. (g) A Managing Director. (h) One or more wholetime Director(s) appointed by the Central Government.

C. The Industrial Credit and Investment Corporation of India

Incorporation — The Industrial Credit and Investment Corporation of India (ICICI) **was incorporated under the Companies Act in January 1955 in the private sector** with participation of foreign capital and interest-free loan from the Central Government. With the nationalisation of insurance companies in 1956, the shares held by some insurance companies (total 18%) have passed in the hands of the LIC, i.e., **the Government, which now is the single biggest shareholder.** The ICICI was established on the advice of the World Bank Mission and in the model of the Industrial and Commercial Finance Corporation of UK, to provide long and medium-term finance and to help the growth of industries in the private sector free from control by the Government.

Financial resources – Share capital — The authorised capital of the ICICI is Rs. 60 crores and the total paid-up capital is Rs. 22 crores, out of which 70% comes from Indian, 20% from British and 10% from American sources. **Borrowings** – It has a borrowed capital consisting of loans of Rs. 24.7 crores from the Central Government, from the IDBI, from the World Bank, from the Agency for Industrial Development (AID) of USA, from German Federal republic, from the UK Government and from the European Capital Market. **Debentures** – also issued debenture.

Management — The ICICI is managed by a Board of Directors consisting of 11 directors of whom 7 directors represent Indian investors, 2 represent the British and 1 represents the American. The eleventh director is a nominee of the Central Government. The number of directors may be raised to 15. It has a full-time Chairman and a General Manager.

Functions — The ICICI provides **two types of assistance** – financial and non-financial, as detailed below :

Financial assistance — (a) It provides secured loans in rupees up to 15 years. (b) It also provides loans in foreign currency up to 15 years to pay for imported capital goods and technical know-how. (c) It guarantees rupee loans procured from other sources. (d) It subscribes to shares directly as well as under-writing shares issued by companies in the private sector.

Non-financial assistance — (a) It helps in the establishment expansion and modernisation of industries. (b) It provides technical and managerial expertise. (c) It provides the service known as Merchant Banking, i.e. advice in respect of investment.

Working — The ICICI has been rendering services to a wide range of industries and even to medium and small-scale firms. Up to March 1989, it has sanctioned financial assistance to the extent of Rs. 3,400 crores. The amount consists of all kinds of assistance, direct and indirect, including subscription to shares, loans, guaranteeing for loans and underwriting. It has also cooperated with other financial institutions in financing and industrial surveying in backward areas.

Critical evaluation — The working of the ICICI has been so far highly commendable in fostering industrial development in the country. It has acted as the pioneer in the field of institutional underwriting of shares. In fact, it has contributed much for the qualitative improvement of the capital market of the country. Procurement of foreign currency for investment in industries in India is definitely a praiseworthy service rendered by the institution. It is the biggest supplier of foreign capital in the private sector.

D. Industrial Reconstruction Bank of India

Incorporation — The Industrial Reconstruction Corporation of India (IRCI) was **incorporated in April 1971 under the Companies Act,** financed by different financial institutions both in the public and the private sectors and the nationalised banks. It is not an ordinary type of financial institution. It provides financial, managerial and technical assistance to revitalise industrial concerns, of any size, which has become or going to be 'sick', i.e. unprofitable and uneconomic. The assistance is given by the period till it becomes economically viable. As the very name suggests, **it is meant for reconstruction of industrial units facing closure. The name has been changed** to Industrial Reconstruction Bank of India (IRBI) in 1984 to justify its financing character.

Financial resources — **Share Capital** — The authorised capital of the IRCI is Rs. 25 crores and the paid-up capital Rs. 5 crores, subscribed by the IDBI, LIC, ICICI, the State Bank and the nationalised banks. **Loan** – The Central Government has provided an interest-free loan of Rs. 10 crores, repayable in 15 equal instalments after the expiry of 14 years. **Borrowings** – It can make borrowings from the Reserve Bank, IDBI and the open market.

Management — It is managed by a Board of directors taking nominees of the subscribing units. There is a full-time Chairman and a General Manager.

Functions – Financial assistance – The IRBI grants soft loans i.e. loans not having much rigidness as regards securities offered, for a period from 4 to 12 years. The loans granted by the IRBI **have the following specialities :**

(a) The loans are granted for capital equipment and payment of most urgent liabilities to make the sick units capable of getting financial accommodation from banks and other financial institutions. (b) The loans are generally not given to meet current liabilities because that will not increase the productive capacity of the sick or closed units. (c) The loans can be granted to corporate as well as non-corporate bodies, though the IRBI will insist on the non-corporate bodies to be converted into corporate bodies. (d) The IRBI charges 8.5% interest per annum on large units and 7.5% on small units or units in backward areas. (e) The limit of the total reconstruction loan for a single unit is Rs. 50 lakhs. (f) The limit of the total reconstruction loan by the IRBI at a time is Rs. 50 crores.

Non-financial assistance — The IRBI also provides managerial guidance and technical assistance for the revitalisation of a sick unit. It helps in preparing reconstruction schemes and future projects which can be acceptable for banks to provide financial assistance which has been stopped.

Method of operation —The IRBI has its own procedure for granting financial assistance. The following **conditions have to be fulfilled** by the borrowing unit :

(a) The borrowing unit has to transfer 51% of its shares to the IRBI in case of a body corporate. The IRBI wants a control over the borrowing unit in a suitable way.

(b) It sends nominees in the Board of Directors of the borrowing company and keeps control on the appointment of managerial personnel in sales, purchase, accounting etc. The Chief Executive is appointed by the IRBI out of a panel of experts prepared and maintained by the IRBI.

(c) The borrowing unit has to submit progress reports periodically which are reviewed by the experts of the IRBI.

(d) The IRBI carries out regular inspection of the working of the assisted units.

Working — The IRBI started its operation in West Bengal and is now having its operation in other States. The IRBI has the responsibility of running those sick or closed units which have been taken over by the Government under Sec. 17 of the Industries (Development and Regulation) Act, 1951. It may be further noted that the IRBI has sanctioned Rs. 880 crores of term loan and hire-purchase assistance to as many as 201 sick units as on 31.3.89.

Critical evaluation — The IRBI has, no doubt, rendered valuable service for revitalisation of many sick and closed units. But it is being criticised because of heavy establishment expenses of the IRBI itself. So far, no cost-benefit analysis has been made of the financial assistance rendered by the IRBI to sick units. Many of them have again become sick. The IRBI has extended its help mostly to engineering and textile industries. IRBI has diversified its activities with consultancy services included in them. Various ancillary services such as merchant banking, equipment leasing etc. have been undertaken by IRBI as incidental to its task of rehabilitation of sick industrial units.

E. The Unit Trust of India

Incorporation — The Unit Trust of India (UTI) was established by the Government in 1963 under the Unit Trust of India Act, 1963. It started its operations from July 1964. The UTI **is a special type of financial institution,** rather a financial intermediary, **with two distinct types of objective :** (a) To augment savings, particularly small savings, so that people of small income can save and get opportunities to channelise their savings into lucrative and secured investments and to share in the prosperity resulting from the industrial growth of the country, which individually they could not do. (b) To augment capital formation through a portfolio of balanced investment in secured as well as growth-oriented stocks and other securities.

It has been formed in the line of the Unit Trust of England but **it has some special features:** (a) It is the first unit trust in public sector in the world; (b) It draws initial capital not from the investors or unit holders but from banks and financial institutions. (c) It does not make any separation between management of the concern and trusteeship of the investments. (d) It offers various tax advantages to the investors unlike any other unit trust of the world.

Financial resources — The UTI has two types of capital :

(1) **Initial Capital** — The UTI started with an initial capital of Rs. 5 crores with the following break-up: Reserve Bank of India – 2.5 crores; Life Insurance Corporation– .75 crores; State Bank of India with its subsidiaries– .75 crores; Scheduled Banks and other Financial Institutions – 1.00 crores.

(2) **Unit Capital** — The unit capital is obtained by selling 'units' of Rs. 10 each. Units are marketable securities and have great liquidity because the UTI is always ready to buy back the units from any unit-holder if he wants to sell them at any time. The sale price and re-purchase price of a 'unit' fluctuate in the capital market according to the market situation. The sale price is always higher (higher than the face value) than the repurchase price which proves the popularity of the unit scheme.

There are two types of 'unit scheme': (1) **The Unit Scheme of 1964**— The UTI started its operations by offering units for sale in the market, with the face value of Rs. 10. A person can buy units from the UTI or banks or post offices as its agents. The Government spends money for the publicity as a part of publicity to encourage small savings. There are private brokers also. There are registered agents in stock exchanges. Altogether, there are about 30,000 centres for selling units throughout the country. The sale price and repurchase price are published daily in newspapers and announced over the radio. One individual can buy any number of units. The UTI enjoys some tax and other concessions. Accordingly, the unit-holders also enjoy the following tax concessions: (a) Unit-holders need not pay income-tax on income earned exclusively from units, up to Rs. 2,000.00 in a year. Unit-holders need not pay super-tax on such income if his total income (excluding such income) does not come under super-tax. (b) No wealth tax is payable on units holding up to Rs. 25,000.

(2) **The Unit Scheme of 1971** — The UTI has introduced in 1971 a separate Unit Scheme called Unit-Linked Insurance Plan. The whole plan operates like this: A unit-holder makes a ten year contract with the UTI for a contribution of minimum Rs. 3,000 and maximum Rs.12,000 half-yearly. There shall be a total target amount to be contributed during the ten years. A small part of the contribution is transferred to the LIC as premium payment for a life insurance cover and the remaining part is invested in units. Dividends earned out of the investment are automatically re-invested in fresh units. On the completion of the contracted period of ten years, the saver can take a unit certificate for the total value of units invested so far or cash payment. In case of his earlier death, the legal representative of the deceased will get the full value of the units accumulated up to the date of death and the difference between the total target amount and this accumulated amount shall be payable by the LIC. This plan is applicable to those within the ages of 18 to 45 years. The saver shall get benefits of income-tax on his yearly contributions to this plan as he enjoys on insurance premium and provident fund contribution.

There are other types of schemes like unit scheme for charitable and religious trusts and the income unit scheme.

Management — The UTI is **managed by a Board of Trustees consisting of ten members.** The RBI appoints the Chairman, an Executive Trustee and four others taken from people having special knowledge or experience in commerce, industry, banking and finance. The LIC and SBI nominate one trustee each. Two other trustees are elected by the banks and financial institutions supplying the initial capital. The RBI practically dominates over the Board.

Functions — The UTI functions to fulfil its twin objectives as stated above. Its functions are exclusively financial. The funds collected from the two sources of capital are **invested in selected securities** which are safe as well as meant for industrial growth of the country. The UTI also does **underwriting function** for new companies. By an amendment of the UTI Act in 1985, the functions of UTI have been widened by including management of investments by non-residents, merchant banking, direct lending and bills discounting. It has also started participating in equity capital in private sector companies.

Methods of operation — The UTI operates according to a well-designed and definite investment policy. **The main features of the investment policy are:** (a) The investment must be safe as well as liquid. (b) There must be adequate return on the investments along with appreciation of the investment value. (c) In order to justify the above policy, the following rules for investment have to be followed: (i) Investment in one company by the UTI shall not exceed 5% of the total value of investments of the UTI or 10% of the total value of securities issued and outstanding of the company, whichever is less. (ii) Not more than 10% of the total investible funds of the UTI shall be invested in the initial issues of new industrial under-takings. (iii) The portfolio of investment of the UTI shall be a balanced one consisting of fixed-income-bearing securities and varying-income-yielding securities so that overall return on investments does not fall below 6% per annum.

According to the latest 'Mastershare' scheme, the members of public get the opportunity of investing "in a basket of many hard working and fast growing shares". Mastershares (Mutual Fund Unit) of Rs. 10 each will be sold to the public to the extent of Rs. 50 crores. The money will be managed by the Mutual Fund division of UTI which is a growth fund investing in shares of well-managed growing companies. Mastershares will be enlisted in stock exchanges.

Distribution of income — The Act provides rules as to how the income and expenses of the UTI shall be allocated between the Initial Capital and Unit Capital. After providing a fixed rate of return on the Initial Capital, the balance of the net income shall be distributed among the unit-holders. The Act provides a guarantee income of 90% of the total income to the unit-holders subject to expenses. The rate varies between 8 and 9% on the total value of Units.

Working — The UTI has made remarkable progress since its formation. Units have become popular among small investors. The Indian Trust Act, 1888, has been amended in 1975 facilitating investments by trusts in units. The minimum amount of investment that a trust can make in units has been fixed at Rs. 10,000.

Critical evaluation — It has to be admitted that the UTI has played a dominant and effective role in capital formation in the country by utilising the small savings of the people of small and medium income. It has given opportunities to the small savers to go for safe investments and share in the prosperity of big investments. Units have extreme liquidity as they can be repurchased by the UTI and the units provide first rate collateral security for bank accommodation. The UTI has been able so far to maintain a fair return on the units.

In spite of the above merits, **the UTI is criticised on the following grounds :**

(1) The expenses ratio of the UTI, (12%) is too high in comparison with the similar trusts in UK (about 6%) and in USA (about 8%).

(2) The unit-holders are deprived of voting rights like those of the shareholders of a company.

(3) The management of the financial portfolio of the UTI as well as the general administration, are in hands of the same Board of Trustees which is not proper.

(4) The units are popular in urban areas only, and specially in big cities. They must be made popular among the rural people for their benefits and mopping up small savings.

(5) The unit-holders do not get the benefit of capital appreciation.

(6) As there is a guarantee income of 90% to be distributed among the unit-holders, subject to expenses, there is very little scope of ploughing back of profit by the UTI itself.

(7) The UTI shall take more interest in the underwriting functions by investments in new issues for a faster industrial growth.

(8) Recent too much diversification of functions may not be ultimately economic.

F. State Financial Corporations

Incorporation — The Central Government passed the State Financial Corporation Act in 1951 to enable the State Governments to establish Financial Corporations in their respective States **with a view to providing long-term financial assistance to small and medium-sized industries** which do not come within the scope of operation of the Industrial Finance Corporation of India. By virtue of this Act, so far 18 State Financial Corporations have been set up including the Tamilnadu Industrial Investment Corporation Ltd. (established in 1949 under the Companies Act). In West Bengal we have the West Bengal Financial Corporation.

Special features — The State Financial Corporations have been set up more or less in the line of the Industrial Finance Corporation of India but the SFC's have **some special features** different from those of the IFCI. They are as follows :

(1) The definition of industrial concern is taken to be wider in scope, and it includes not only public limited companies but also private limited companies, partnership or sole-proprietorship firms.

(2) The shares of such Corporations can be purchased by the members of the public and non-scheduled banks up to the extent of 25% of the total capital. The shares can also be purchased by the IDBI and the State Governments.

(3) The corporations can make loans or give guarantee to loans for a maximum period of 20 years and not 25 years.

(4) The maximum amount of accommodation to a single unit by a Corporation is Rs. 20 lakhs or 10% of the paid-up capital of the Corporation, whichever is less, and up to Rs. 10 lakhs in case of a private limited company, partnership or sole-proprietorship firm.

(5) The State Government is to fix the share capital of a Corporation between Rs. 50 lakhs and Rs. 5 crores.

(6) The shares of the Corporations are not transferable except to the State Governments, the Reserve Bank of India or any financial institution recognised by the State Government.

(7) The State Governments guarantee repayment of the principal and a minimum rate of dividend (not exceeding 6% and in consultation with the Central Government).

(8) The Corporations can accept public deposits to an amount not exceeding the paid-up capital of the Corporations for a period not less than 5 years.

(9) The Corporations are not generally permitted to subscribe directly to the shares of a limited company but they can do under-writing.

Financial resources — Share Capital — Every State Financial Corporation has its own share capital. By the end of March 1976, all the State Financial Corporations had an aggregate paid-up capital of Rs. 39.6 crores. **Borrowings**— The State Financial Corporations can augment their funds by issuing bonds and debentures to a maximum of 5 times their paid-up capital and reserves. They also can accept public deposits for a minimum period of 5 years. They can also borrow from the Reserve Bank and State Governments. The repayment of bonds and debentures and payment of interests thereon are guaranteed by the State Government. **Refinancing** — The State Financial Corporations also enjoy the facilities of refinancing by the IDBI.

Management — Every State Financial Corporation is managed by a Board of Directors consisting of 10 members, of whom 3 are nominated by the State Government, one each by the IFCI and the IDBI, four are elected by the other shareholders and the remaining one, the Managing Director, is appointed by the State Government.

Functions — A State Financial Corporation **provides financial assistance in the following different ways :**

(1) Granting loans or advances or subscribing to debentures of industrial undertakings, repayable within 20 years.

(2) Guaranteeing loans to raise industrial units according to the terms and conditions mutually agreed upon but such loans must be repayable within 20 years.

(3) Underwriting shares and debentures issued by industrial companies which shall be finally disposed off within 7 years.

(4) Allowing up to 25% of the term loans to be used as working capital for a maximum period of 5 years in case no working capital is advanced by any commercial bank and provided the borrowing unit also brings some working capital of its own.

(5) Eight SFC's (Andhra Pradesh, Assam, Gujarat, Kerala, Maharashtra, Orissa, Rajasthan and Uttar Pradesh) function as agents for their respective State Governments for sanctioning or disbursing loans or doing both to small-scale industrial concerns under the State Aid to Industries Act.

The SFC's now can assist not only manufacturing but servicing industries too.

The rates of interest charged by the SFC's are as follows : 8 to 11% for small-scale industries, 8.5 to 12.5% for others, provided refinancing facility by IDBI is available, otherwise the rates vary between 8 and 14.5%. Besides, there is cost of registration, stamp duty etc., which work out to another 3%, approximately.

Working — With the development of industries and various incentives to entrepreneurship as well as shortage of finance for other reasons, the demand for financial assistance from SFC's is mounting up. Considering the demand and also considering the increase in the number of the SFC's, the working of the SFC's has not been very satisfactory. There are, however, various reasons for that (see below). During the last two decades, the amount of financial assistance sanctioned by the SFC's has increased by more than 16 times. It has to be noted, however, that the amount of outstanding loan is increasing at a faster rate than the rate of increase of sanctioned loans.

Critical evaluation — The functioning of the SFC's are criticised on the following grounds :

(1) The amount of financial assistance to small-scale and medium-scale industrial units is inadequate, keeping in view the Government's policy of developing them at a fast rate in the interest of the nation.

(2) The rate of interest together with other charges (see above) make the assistance too costly for a small or medium-size unit.

(3) The Corporations take too much time to examine the applications and actual disbursement is made after a long gap of time even after the loan is sanctioned.

(4) A larger number of applications are rejected than those which are accepted. The entrepreneurs get discouraged.

(5) The SFC's do not go for underwriting much and, as a result, new enterprises cannot be established. Small and medium-size units suffer from working capital very often but the SFC's generally provide long term loans.

It has to be admitted, however, that the **SFC's themselves suffer from various difficulties** and for that they are unable to show better performance. The difficulties are :

(1) It is very difficult to assess the credit-worthiness of the applicants. They generally do not supply all the information wanted. They very often hesitate to disclose many facts as they are afraid of greater Government control and higher taxes.

(2) The applicants cannot provide adequate security for the loans as demanded by the SFC's. This is more true for small partnership and sole-proprietorship firms. Very often the properties do not have 'clean' title.

(3) The applicants cannot make out the applications in proper form and with all the necessary information. Lack of education is a great problem.

(4) The SFC's themselves suffer from lack of funds. Many SFC's, therefore, act as agents for the State Governments in getting the loans advanced by the State Governments.

(5) The SFC's also do not get the services of experts who can make proper assessment of the applications and processing of the loans. The SFC's do not have the adequate staff.

In order to overcome the difficulties, several conferences have been held and Committees have been appointed from time to time. The IDBI has come to the help of the SFC's. In some States (including West Bengal) the State Bank has entered into some agreement with the SFC's to function as their agents, particularly in relation to the small-scale units negotiating with the SFC's.

G. The National Industrial Development Corporation

Incorporation — On the basis of a draft scheme presented by a group of industrialists the National Industrial Development Corporation was established in October 1954 **by the Central Government** under the Companies Act. The objects of the NIDC **as a purely promotional institution** are to investigate and prepare projects for those industries which are necessary to provide a base for a balanced and integrated industrial growth of the country and to promote those industries which cannot be promoted by the private industrialists because of requirement of heavy capital or specialised technical skill not available in the country. After being promoted by it, an industrial enterprise may be handed over to the private sector when the unit becomes economically mature.

Financial resources – Share Capital — The NIDC has an authorised capital of Rs. 1 crore but a paid-up capital of Rs. 10 lakhs. **Other sources** – The Government can increase its fund from time to time as and when required in the following ways : (a) annual grants to carry out investigation and research for new industries and technology and to build up a pool of technical and managerial personnel and (b) to grant loan for specific projects to be taken up by the Corporation.

Management — The management of the NIDC is in the hands of a Board of Directors consisting of 15 to 25 members, nominated by the Government. The Board is constituted with industrialists, engineers, technologists, economists and all such other experts.

Functions — The main function of the NIDC is to carry out research on industries and technology and to prepare and promote new types of projects. Further, it assists in finding out diversification plans of existing concerns either in the public or private sector.

The NIDC has set up the Technological Consultancy Bureau for rendering consultancy and engineering services to industrial enterprises, not only in this country but also abroad.

It can also function as an agent for the Government to provide financial assistance as special cases to any industry of national importance.

Working — The NIDC has made remarkable achievement, in the field of research works, particularly for industries related to manufacture of capital goods, synthetic rubber, dye-stuff, ball-bearings, alloy steel, forged products, aluminium, precision instruments, pumps, compressors etc. It has been carrying out such research work with foreign technical help in some cases.

It has been carrying out consultancy work in foreign countries under the auspices of the UNO or otherwise. It has done consultancy work for the development of a new capital city of Tanzania.

In 1975-76 it has rendered consultancy service whose value amounts to about Rs. 1 crore.

The NIDC has functioned as an agent for the Government in providing grants for modernisation of cotton and jute textile industries.

Critical evaluation — In a country like India, there is a great need for an institution like the NIDC. But, unfortunately, it has not been able to perform its best, mainly because of shortage of funds.

It has to be noted that many State Governments have established Industrial Development Corporations at State level. In West Bengal, we have the West Bengal Industrial Development Corporation.

H. National Small Industries Corporation

Incorporation — The National Small Industries Corporation (NSIC) **was incorporated as a private limited company in February 1955.** It was established on the basis of the recommendations of a team of experts on small industries under the Ford Foundation. **Its object is to render assistance to those small industries** which have a capital investment up to Rs. 10 lakhs (Rs. 15 lakhs in case of an ancillary to a large industry).

Financial resources — Share capital — It was established with an authorised capital of Rs. 10 lakhs which has been subsequently raised to Rs. 50 lakhs subscribed by the Government.

Management — It is managed by a Board of Directors consisting of members nominated by the Government.

Functions — The NSIC renders **both types of assistance, financial and non-financial.** The functions of the NSIC are as follows : (a) To arrange supply of machinery and other equipments on hire-purchase basis. (b) To procure orders from the Governments for supply of different goods produced by small firms. (c) To arrange supply of raw materials with central storing facilities. (d) To help developing markets for the products of small firms, particularly in rural areas. (e) To establish and run industrial training centres including the 'prototype' centres (such centres are established on some foreign or highly technical models).

The NSIC has set up four subsidiary Corporations in Calcutta, Delhi, Bombay and Madras to decentralise its activities and to establish liaison with other Government Agencies for industrial development.

The **Small Industries Service Institute,** with its headquarters in Delhi and branches all over India, has been established as a central organisation to function in perfect cooperation with the NSIC, to help small industries in the fields of production, marketing, exports, technical and managerial training. The SISI helps small units to get financial help from the NSIC and other financial agencies and banks.

For better working, the NSIC has set up several functional divisions : Hire-Purchase Division, Stores Purchase Division, Marketing Division, Industrial Estate Division and an Export Cell. Industrial Estates are established by the Government at selected areas where power and transport are made available with constructed sheds which can be utilised by small entrepreneurs.

A firm has to get its name registered with the NSIC for being eligible to get assistance.

Working — The NSIC has made considerable progress in its various activities. Besides providing employment to a large number of people in underdeveloped and backward areas, the Corporation opportunities in those areas.

It has to be noted that some State Governments have established Small Industries Corporations in their respective States, as in West Bengal.

THE SECURITIES MARKET : THE STOCK EXCHANGE

The Securities Market — The word security means an instrument in the form of a certificate or evidence for any property or debt. For example, a share certificate, a debenture bond, a Government Promissory Note, etc. A securities market comes into existence **when and where securities are bought and sold.** Not necessarily there shall be a definite place where such transactions shall take place. A Stock Exchange or a Share Market, however, is a definite place. Securities are transacted without having such definite place and merely through oral or written communication.

A 'securities market' consists of buyers and sellers of securities as well as different agencies and institutions including the share markets or stock exchanges. In such organised markets like share markets, there are specific rules and regulations for transactions on securities. The securities comprise of shares in, and debentures of, companies, Government papers, bonds issued by public or semi-public bodies like municipalities, port trusts etc. In general, a stock exchange deals with shares in, and debentures of, different public limited companies.

Types — Broadly speaking, there are **two types of securities markets** – (A) The new issues market and (B) the second-hand market (stock exchange).

A. The New Issues Market

A newly formed company has to issue shares or debentures for raising capital. An existing company may issue fresh shares or debentures for increasing its capital. All such **fresh or new issues make the New Issues Market.**

Issue of new shares or debentures can be made in **two distinct manners :** directly by the company or indirectly through intermediaries. Both the manners are described below :

(1) **Direct issue** — A widely held public company, immediately after its incorporation, **issues a Prospectus inviting the public to buy shares in, and debentures (if any) of, the company.** It is the most ordinary and less expensive method of selling securities. This is a risky method. The prospective investors are attracted through advertisements in the newspapers or by direct mailing. But there is no certainty that people will be attracted and come forward with offers for purchase. The company may not be able to sell sufficient volume of shares or debentures by this method.

When an existing company wants to increase its share capital it can do so **by issuing new shares or rights shares in some agreed proportion to the existing shareholders.** This is the provision laid down in the Companies Act. If the shareholders agree, then shares may be issued to outsiders. On the other hand, **reserve funds may be capitalised by issuing bonus shares** which are **allotted to the existing shareholders** on some agreed basis.

In private limited companies shares are issued among the friends or relations of the promoters.

In case of rights shares, an existing shareholder may or may not accept the invitation and he may transfer his rights to another person. In case of bonus shares, once the resolution is passed at a members' meeting in that respect, every existing shareholder is allotted proportionate number of shares through book adjustments only as no payment of price is required. In both cases the capital is increased. But when a shareholder transfers his shares, he gets the price and the capital of the company is not affected.

(2) **Indirectly through intermediaries** — Sale of shares or debentures through middlemen can be done in so many different ways as detailed below :

(a) **Offer for sale** — Under this method, a new company allots or agrees to allot shares or debentures to an issue house or financial institution with the condition that the latter will offer the securities for sale to the public at a higher price. The issue house or the financial institution publishes a document for inviting the public to buy the shares or debentures. This document is called 'offer for sale' and is treated in law as a prospectus. The issue house makes a profit out of this lower purchase price and higher selling price of the securities.

(b) **By placing of shares or debentures** — A new company does not really allot but actually places shares or debentures in favour of some issue houses which will sell out the shares or debentures to their clients privately. There is practically no public offer for sale of the shares or debentures. This is the cheapest method of selling shares or debentures but can be successful provided the issue houses have such clients who can take up the shares or debentures.

Sometimes a company appoints **managing brokers** who do not take any responsibility of selling the shares or debentures but assist the company in all other ways like drafting of prospectus, fixing up of prices of shares, rates of brokerage, helping in the procedure of enlistment of share in a recognised stock exchange, etc.

(c) **Through other intermediaries** — Marketing of securities of a company can also take place through financial institutions, banks, sharebrokers etc. who try to push the sale of the securities on commission or brokerage basis. But such intermediaries do not give any guarantee of sale.

(d) **Through underwriting** — By this method there is a guarantee of sale. The underwriters as brokers give a guarantee that they themselves shall take up the shares or debentures which will not be ordinarily sold out in the market. The underwriters are, however, not investors in real sense. They will sell out the securities gradually in the long run. They charge high rates of commission because of such guarantee.

B. The second-hand market or a Stock Exchange

A stock exchange means a **highly specialised and organised market where securities of all kinds are bought and sold.** The Securities Contracts (Regulation) Act, 1956, defines a stock exchange "as an association, organisation or body of individuals, whether incorporated or not, established for the purposes of assisting, regulating and controlling business in buying, selling and dealing in securities".

From the above definition the following **characteristics of a stock exchange** can be worked out :

(a) It is an association of persons. That association may or may not be incorporated as a company. For example, in India, the Calcutta Stock Exchange Association is a limited company with an authorised capital of Rs. 3 lakhs divided into 1,200 shares of Rs. 250 each, fully paid-up. As it is a non-profit-making company, the word Limited is dropped from its name.

(b) It has a number of purposes. In fact, it is not a mere centre for buying and selling of securities. It also controls and regulates the transactions. The Securities Contracts (Regulation) Act,1956, which controls the stock exchanges in India, provides various rules and regulations, as the very name suggests, for the purpose.

(c) It not only regulates the buying and selling of securities, it also regulates dealings in securities. According to the Act, only the members can deal in securities officially and that also under some strict rules and regulations.

The definition, as given above, is neither clear nor complete. Firstly, all types of securities are not transacted in a stock exchange recognised by the Act. A company has to enlist its shares and/debentures in a stock exchange. The Act provides elaborate rules for such enlistment. The enlistment is not certain. **Secondly,** a stock exchange itself has to be recognised by the Government by virtue of the Act. **Thirdly,** the definition does not clearly state that actually in a stock exchange securities are bought and sold by way of transfer. An existing holder of securities wants to dispose off his holdings to another individual who intends to buy them. In fact, no new investment is created, nor the capital structure of the company concerned is affected. What is investment for the transferee is disinvestment of the transferor. **Lastly**, the definition does not make clear that in a stock exchange securities are dealt in for dual purposes – investment and speculation.

Functions — The Stock exchange, as a vital organ of the capitalistic society, performs a large number of economic functions which are summarised below :

(1) **Provides ready market for securities** — Securities are marketable and generally transferable from one holder to another. This marketability is made practicable by the stock exchanges. Unless there is a common meeting place, transferability of securities cannot take place. Investors and speculators, through member brokers of a stock exchange, can buy and sell securities freely and easily. A holder can sell out his holdings when he is in need of cash or for re-investing the fund in other securities. On the other hand a saver, ready to invest, can get securities of existing concerns of his choice, which he can buy. This process adds liquidity to the securities making them more valuable as collateral security for loans and advances.

(2) **Proper valuation of securities** — Enlisted securities in a stock exchange get their prices determined according to the forces of demand and supply. The prices quoted officially in a stock exchange for the securities can be considered as true market value of them based on present and future income-yielding capacity. Prices of securities are quoted above, par or lower than face value according to market conditions. Any holder of securities may not go for selling them but can know the actual worth of his investments.

(3) **Channelisation of savings to correct investments** — From a stock exchange the position of different industries can be ascertained which helps investors to channelise their savings to correct investments, i.e. in the prospective businesses. Capital blocked in wasteful investments is released through disposing off the securities, even at a loss and then re-invested in prospective securities. Had there been no stock exchange, wasteful investments ultimately would have ended into total capital loss.

(4) **Helps capital formation** — The marketability and liquidity of enlisted securities attract the investors and, as a result, capital formation in the country as a whole becomes faster. Once an investing habit is generated, people go for other good investments too and, as a result, a habit of savings develops in the society. Thus, a stock exchange helps capital formation.

(5) **Indirect effect on company management** — Those companies whose securities are enlisted in a stock exchange have to observe several rules and regulations. This makes the management of such companies more regulated. Bad management is reflected in the market through fall of prices of the securities. This indirectly compels the management to be cautious and self-regulatory.

(6) **Protection to investors** — There are many rules and regulations as well as restrictive measures to be imposed on stock exchange operations by legislation. These are meant for protecting the interests of the investors as well as of the community as a whole. Such protection further encourages people to go for investment. A stock exchange in this way stimulates investments.

(7) **Provides scope for speculation** — Healthy speculation is always good and economic. A stock exchange allows and provides rules and regulations within which speculation in securities can be carried out. Such speculation brings out stability in prices by proper adjustment of demand and supply. The stock exchanges are subject to legislations which ban gamblings or unhealthy speculation.

Importance — The importance of stock exchanges is great in the capitalistic societies where there is freedom of enterprise through individual investments. To some lay man, a stock exchange is a place where one can become rich by magic, while to another it is a hell where one can turn out to be a pauper. In fact, neither of the feelings is true. A stock exchange has a vital role to play in the economy of a country. **It is rightly described as 'a business of all businesses'.** For every kind of business, capital is necessary. A stock exchange is an important part of the capital market. In a stock exchange, an investor finds out avenues of investment and investment leads to employment, employment to income. The study of economics is the study of income, how it is earned and how it is spent.

A stock exchange is often described as the **economic barometer** of a country. When the country is passing through a phase of economic prosperity there are more economic, i.e. income-generating, activities. There are more income and more savings and, obviously, there will be a greater tendency to investment resulting into higher demand for securities and higher prices for them. Conversely, during the phase of economic depression, price of securities will fall.

Importance of a stock exchange can be understood by analysing the services rendered by it, in a classified manner :

(1) Services to the investors

(a) The investors get a ready and continuous market for their investments. They can dispose off securities even at a loss because of high liquidity of enlisted securities.

(b) Because of high liquidity of enlisted securities they can be used as good collateral for obtaining loans or advances.

(c) The investors are protected by rules and regulations as well as legislations regulating and controlling transactions in a stock exchange. They can invest for safety.

(d) From the market operations they can know the correct market value of securities held by them or intended to be purchased by them.

(e) They get guidance, since a stock exchange is an economic barometer as to when to invest, where to invest as well as when to disinvest.

(2) Services to the Companies

(a) The goodwill of the companies, whose securities have been enlisted in a recognised stock exchange, is enhanced. Enlistment is allowed by the authorities of a stock exchange after thorough scrutiny of the company which applied for it.

(b) The market value of the real worth of the securities of a company can be properly ascertained. The face value as well as the intrinsic value of shares are not enough.

(c) The liquidity added to the securities make them more popular in the market and, as such, a company can get its securities easily and promptly sold when any fresh issue is made.

(d) Very often securities are quoted officially at a higher price than their face value. This becomes very useful when the merger or amalgamation of such a company comes up.

(e) When there are officially quoted prices for the securities, there cannot be wild fluctuations of the prices, nor there can be any erratic quotation in any transaction on such security.

(3) Services to the society

(a) The society is benefited because of existence of a regular capital market to attract the investors.

(b) Because of high liquidity and easy marketability of securities, investments become popular and capital formation becomes easier.

(c) It provides an index for prices of securities as an economic barometer which helps the Government to design its monetary and fiscal policies.

(d) By providing facilities and encouragement to investments and savings, it helps foster economic growth of the country.

Dis-services

A stock exchange **may indulge into some dis-services also.** Very often, speculation in a stock exchange degenerates into gambling. It is true that Government legislations, e.g., the Securities Contracts (Regulation) Act in India, control and regulate gamblings and even ban them altogether but even then gamblings carried on in private markets have their reactions on the genuine markets which cannot be controlled as same people are involved in both types of markets. The actions of Bulls and Bears cause artificial fluctuation of prices of securities. Total ban of all kinds of speculations cannot be a practical stand. Therefore, **some bad effects are sure to persist.** In socialistic countries, there is no scope for personal investments in business and so there is no existence of stock exchanges.

STOCK EXCHANGE OPERATIONS

Nature of operations

A stock exchange, as a part of capital market, shall be treated as an organised market and so **it has all the characteristics of an organised market. Firstly,** there must be an organisation or association of persons. The organisation can be either in the form of a registered society or a company. Membership has to be obtained either by paying admission fee and annual subscription or by buying a share or contributing to guarantee capital. **Secondly,** only members are allowed to enter the market hall to do the transactions. No outsiders are allowed. But any member of the public is generally allowed to do transactions through a member who will act as an agent or broker. In Indian stock exchanges, all the members function as brokers for outsiders. In some stock exchanges, as in London Stock Exchange, some members are broker-members while others are not. Those who are not are called jobbers, who do transactions among members only. **Thirdly,** there are some rules and regulations for transactions. Such rules and regulations are of two types : (a) of the organisation and (b) Statutory e.g. rules provided in the Securities Contracts (Regulation) Act, 1956, for Indian stock exchanges. **Fourthly,** transactions are done by bidding or auction. Members who want to buy quote their prices and members who want to sell also quote their prices. This is true for the securities on which speculation is allowed. **Fifthly,** speculation is allowed in such markets under restrictions but gamblings are banned by law (see below). There are various mechanisms or set procedures for speculative transactions. Those securities, out of the listed securities, on which speculation is allowed, are called cleared securities (or securities for 'hand delivery') and those securities on which speculation is not allowed are called non-cleared securities. Sometimes, securities enlisted in one stock exchange are permitted to be transacted by the members of another stock exchange where those securities are not listed. Such securities are called "permitted securities". **Sixthly,** transactions are done within some fixed hours of a working day and after that official prices of all the listed securities for the day are published which are reproduced in the newspapers, in a classified manner : Cleared and Non-cleared securities. Non-cleared securities are further classified industry or trade-wise. **Finally,** every stock exchange has a 'clearing house' or some clearing system just like the clearing house for banks for the settlement of accounts among members for speculative dealings.

Speculation

The term speculation comes from the Latin word 'speculate' which means to look from a distance. In other words, speculation is connected with anticipation of future trend of events. **Speculation is a very normal affair in business.** It means to buy now when the price is low, to sell when the price will become high in future, as anticipated, and to make profit out of price difference. Or, to sell in advance now when price is high to buy in future when price will become low as anticipated and to make profit out of price difference.

Every producer or trader is a speculator. A producer produces goods in anticipation of demand and ahead of it. That producer may be a manufacturer or an agriculturist. A trader holds stock of goods when the price is low and releases it when it is high. Such genuine speculation, called legitimate speculation, is good and economic because (i) it helps adjustment of supply with the demand, (ii) it prevents unusual fluctuation of prices and (iii) thereby it makes stabilisation of prices.

It is said that **two types of people visit stock exchanges** — investors and speculators. **Investors** are those who buy securities for long term investments and revenue gain. It means that the return on investment is expected by them in the forms of fluctuating rates of dividend (fixed in case of preference shares) or fixed rates of interest. They do not want immediate refund of their invested money. **Speculators** are those who buy securities not for holding them but selling them out at the earliest opportunity when the prices are high to make capital gain. It means they want to make immediate profit out of price difference.

Such classification between investors and speculators is purely theoretical. In fact, nobody is investor in its extreme sense. If any investor wants to hold his investments permanently, he shall never visit a stock exchange. It is quite likely that so called 'investor' will have a tendency to dispose off the securities when the price has become attractively high or when he is in urgent need of money or when he wants to divert his investment in some other direction which he thinks to be more profitable. He needs the help of a stock exchange if his holdings are listed ones. He is a speculator in a wider sense except when he disposes off his holdings for urgent need of money.

In the market parlance, a speculator is he who frequently buys and sells securities for making profit out of price difference. In a stock exchange there are various methods of forward transactions for this purpose. The members of a stock exchange generally do speculation out of their own or on behalf of their clients. In fact, the members of a stock exchange get themselves sharply divided into two groups of speculators, to carry out stock exchange operations and to add life to the market. A stock exchange cannot thrive on the occasional transactions of so called investors only.

Speculation and Gambling — When a person enters into a contract of either buying or selling some securities (or goods) with a genuine intention, then, as a buyer, he will pay the full price and take delivery of the securities (or goods) or, as a seller, he will deliver the securities (or goods) and take payment of full price. When there is no such intention of giving or taking of delivery or taking or giving of full payment of price, then there is speculation. Generally, people consider such speculative transactions as gamblings. In fact, they are not identical. **Speculation is done after intelligent study of the market situation,** with correct anticipation of future trend by virtue of foresight and with the help of collection of information. **Gambling means taking to chances without any intelligent study** of the market situation. Speculation, has therefore, a scientific basis. Emery, a great author on Stock exchange operations, defines speculation as : "speculation consists in buying and selling commodities or securities or other property, in the hope of a profit from anticipated changes of value." Speculation needs knowledge, expertise and competence. Gambling does not require them. Speculation has some ethical sense while gambling does not. It is rightly said that 'speculation begins where foresight enters and gambling begins where foresight leaves'. For successful speculation, some money is also required, otherwise the speculator will become insolvent at some time. For a gambler, it is all the same whether he has money or not. Speculation is based on pluck while gambling is based on luck. Certain kinds of speculation transactions are by nature of gambling type. Such speculations are banned by the Securities Contract (Regulation) Act in the stock exchanges. Gamblings are also banned in commodity markets. The Government is empowered by Law to ban other types of speculations which the Government can do as and when necessary.

The whole procedure of transactions, other than genuine investments, is of speculative type. The different types of transactions found in a stock exchange are described :

Ready delivery or forward delivery transactions

General procedure — For any transaction a prospective buyer or a seller of securities has to undergo a long-drawn procedure consisting of **several steps :**

(1) A member of the public cannot do transactions himself in a stock exchange. **He has to appoint a broker** who is a member of the stock exchange. A member will first enquire about the credit-worthiness of the person from his banker or other broker. This is so because, very often, the broker has to trust his client with his oral commitments.

(2) The next step **is to place an order.** An order is placed after studying the market condition and the financial position of the transactor. The client may have discussion with the broker for his expert advice. The order can be either to buy or to sell. **The order can be of different forms :** (a) **Fixed price order**— The client fixes up the price above which the broker cannot buy or below which the broker cannot sell. (b) **Limit price order** – The client fixes up two limits—beyond the upper limit the broker cannot buy and below the lower limit the broker cannot sell. (c) **Immediate or cancel order** – The client asks the broker to buy or sell immediately at the best possible price. If it is not immediately carried out, the order stands cancelled. (d) **Bargain price order** – The broker is instructed to use his discretion and to buy or sell at the best price. (e) **Stop-loss order** – When a client has already suffered a loss from a speculative transaction, he takes another risk of buying or selling to recover the loss and instructs his broker to do another transaction up to a certain amount of risk. Suppose he has already lost Rs. 1 per share by buying. He may instruct his broker to sell the holding immediately at a further loss up to Rs. 2 per share. He is afraid that price may fall further if there is delay. (f) **Open order** – The client is not in hurry. He instructs his broker to buy or to sell as and when the broker finds it most profitable. The order remains open until it is cancelled by the client. **A discretionary order** may be given to the broker asking him to do the transaction according to his discretion within a fixed period of time.

(3) The third step **is to make a contract.** In a stock exchange, securities are exchanged, i.e., existing holdings are transferred between persons. When a client asks his broker to buy some particular securities there must be a seller too (unknown to the buyer) who engages a broker to sell the shares held by him. Both the brokers meet in the stock exchange hall. There are separate posts or pits or wings for different kinds of securities. The buyers and sellers make bargains by quoting their respective prices by bidding, either to buy or to sell. The broker of a client will settle the terms with the broker of the other client and enter into a contract. The details of the terms are noted down by the brokers in their own note-books. Each will honour his commitment though no written contract is made. Each notes down the membership number of the other member for reference.

(4) The fourth step is **to make out a contract note** between the client and his broker. After the end of the working hours of the exchange, each broker or his authorised clerk (see below) will note down commitments at first in a temporary book called Kachha Sauda Book. This will be ultimately transferred to a permanent book called Pucca Sauda Book. On the basis of such noting, a contract note between the client and the broker is prepared. This is to be done both by the brokers of the buyer client and seller client from their respective sides.

(5) **The fifth step is the settlement of a transaction** — Now the account will be settled, i.e., the buying-selling transaction has to be executed. The settlement can be done in two distinct ways **depending on the nature of the contract :** ready delivery or forward delivery. The latter type of contract is concerned with speculative transaction and can be done with those securities which are specifically selected for the purpose by the authorities of the stock exchange. Such securities are the 'cleared securities' (see above).

(A) **Ready delivery contract** — These are genuine transactions. The share certificates or bonds are **physically transferred** after signing and endorsing the transfer needs on stamps of requisite value and **full payments** are made and received. Each stock exchange has its own rules with regard to number of days within which the transaction has to be completed, varying between 3 to 7 days. The Calcutta Stock Exchange allows 3 days only, some others, like the Madras Stock Exchange, allows 7 days.

(B) **Forward delivery contracts** — Such contracts are usually meant for speculative transactions. In many cases of genuine forward delivery contracts, the settlement is made on a future agreed date as stipulated in the rules of the exchange on physical delivery of the securities and full payment of price. Such transactions are common in commodity markets where industrial goods like jute, cotton, metals, etc. are traded. **In stock exchanges, forward delivery contracts are actually meant for speculation.** By an order on 27. 6. 69, the Government of India has banned such speculative transactions in stock exchanges. However, such speculative transactions are carried out unofficially. The different methods of settlement under speculative transaction are discussed below.

Speculative transactions

(1) **Differences settlement** — This is the most common form of speculative transaction known as **'fatka'**. Under this method neither actual delivery of securities nor full payment of price takes place. The account is settled **by payment of difference between the agreed price as decided on the date of contract and the market price on the date of settlement.** The market price changes on account of forces of demand and supply and other causes. If the market price is higher then the seller pays the difference to the buyer and suffers loss. If the market price is lower than the buyer pays the difference to the seller and suffers loss. Entries are made in the books of account of both the parties in the following manner: In the buyer's book : bought at the agreed price from the seller and sold back to the seller at the market price. In the seller's book : sold at the agreed price to the buyer and bought back from the buyer at the market price.

(2) **Carry over** — This is the second common method of speculation known as **'budla'.** If the rules of the exchange so permit then the settlement is not made **on the date of settlement** but **it is carried forward to another date,** generally after one fortnight. On the date of the settlement, the market price may be favourable to the buyer but unfavourable to the seller (when the price has become higher) or vice versa (when the price has become lower). The party to whom the price has become unfavourable wants to shift the date of settlement by a fortnight taking a chance and hoping that the price will move to his favour by that date. The other party will agree to shift the date provided **he gets the difference in price** (between the agreed price and the market price) **and an additional amount** called the 'budla' money. If the buyer wants to shift the date, he has to pay the difference *plus* **'Contango'** or 'sidha budla' to the seller. If the seller wants to shift the date, he has to pay the difference *plus* **'Backwardation'** or 'undha budla' to the buyer. On the changed date, account will be settled on payment of difference in price or it may be further carried forward. The rules of a particular exchange provides how many times carry over will be allowed in that exchange. The 'budla' amount is calculated on the following formula : the interest payable on the total value of the transaction at the market rate of interest for a fortnight (i.e. period of shifting). The stock exchange authorities fix the rate from time to time.

Special types of speculation

There are some special types of speculative transactions, **some of which are healthy and economic while others are of gambling nature.** Obviously, the healthy types are welcome but gambling types are banned. There are some **stimulants to gamblings** commonly found in organized markets. These are described below :

(1) **Hedging** — Hedging means 'an action to mitigate fluctuation in prices'. By this method of transactions, speculators try **to offset loss from one transaction by gain from other** transactions. One commitment to sell in future expecting fall in price in future may bring loss if the prices does not actually fall. Therefore, some spot or immediate purchase is made to cover up the possible loss. Thus, selling contracts followed by buying ones and *vice versa lead*

to stabilisation of price. Hedging is very commonly done in the organised markets of industrial materials like jute, cotton, metals etc. in order to keep the price steady. Otherwise cost of production cannot be standardised or correctly calculated. Hedging is economic and good.

(2) **Arbitrage** — Arbitrage means **buying the same security, or commodity in one market where the price is low and to sell it immediately in another market where the price is high.** By this the price in the former market will rise owing to higher demand and the price in the latter market will fall owing to larger supply and as a result there will be stabilisation and uniformity of price in both the markets. This is possible provided the commodity is dealt in both the markets and action is taken simultaneously. Arbitrage is very common in foreign exchange markets and is also practised in stock exchanges when the same securities are enlisted in more than one stock exchange. Some currency may have cheaper rate in one country and dearer in another country, e.g. when more goods are imported to India from USA, dollar is dearer here than in Germany where imports from USA are less. So, it may be profitable to buy dollars in Germany and sell them in India. This can be done by an exchange bank to earn profit. This type of speculation is healthy and economic.

(3) **Option dealings** — This type of speculation know as **'satta'** is purely of gambling type. Under this method, one speculator keeps some money deposited with another and buys 'option' or right to buy or to sell some securities at an agreed price on a future date. On that date the depositor may buy or sell. If he does not keep his promise then the other party forfeits the deposited amount. The depositor will not fulfil his promise if the price moves unfavourable to him (see below – types of speculators). There are three types of options. Put option (or 'mandi sauda') – the depositor buys an option to sell. Call option (or 'teji sauda') – the depositor buys an option to buy. Double option or straddle (or teji-mandi sauda) – the depositor buys the option either to buy or to sell. On the agreed date the depositor may settle the account on difference payment system if the prices moves to his favour.

(4) **Cornering** — Sometimes speculators try to create **artificial shortage of a certain security** in a stock exchange and thereby try to force the price up. They buy up the securities offered for sale and 'squeeze' the sellers. The genuine investors have to suffer. This is purely a temporary action. This is unhealthy and bad.

(5) **Rigging** — Rigging means **trying artificially to force the price of security up** in the market by making continuous demand for buying. When the price goes up, sudden sale is made at the topmost price to earn profit. This is unhealthy and bad.

(6) **Wash sales** — A speculator makes **fictitious transactions of selling some security and then buying it up** through his appointed broker. Actually there is no buying and selling but an impression is created in the market as if the security is in high demand and so the price of it actually goes up. Then the speculator actually sells out his holdings and makes profit. This is unhealthy and bad.

Stimulants to gamblings

Gambling means speculating without a proper study of the market and taking a chance. Though officially gambling is not allowed in a stock exchange (and also in a commodity exchange, and there are regulatory laws to control it, **gambling is very common in organised markets.** In a stock exchange, gambling **is encouraged by some systems** connected with transactions. These are described below :

(1) **Margin trading** — A member of the public has to appoint a member broker to do transactions in a stock exchange. The broker accepts the offer after being satisfied with the financial standing of the client (see above). Transactions are done by the broker in his own name on behalf of his client and **in most of the cases the instructions are issued verbally** by the client. Again, most of the transactions are settled by difference payments though in the books of account full entries of buying and selling are recorded (see above). Thus, a person staking a small amount of money (which he might have to pay as difference) can actually do transactions of higher value.

Suppose A wants to speculate on 100 shares in X Co. Ltd. of Rs. 100 each. When he buys the shares, the market price is Rs. 100 and he wants to sell when the price has gone up to Rs. 105. Apparently he has to spend Rs. 10,000 *plus* brokerage (say, Rs. 50) to buy the shares. When he sells he gets Rs. 10,500, less brokerage (say, Rs. 60) and thereby he makes a profit of (Rs. 10,500–Rs. 60) – (Rs. 10,000 + Rs. 50) = Rs. 390. In fact, such full payments are neither made at the time of purchase nor received at the time of sale. The transaction is closed by a difference payment. Whenever a client goes to **a broker,** the latter **asks from the client some Margin Deposit by way of security** so that in case there is a loss, the 'difference' amount can be safely paid by the broker from the client's deposit. When there is any profit, that is added to the deposit. When it is reduced by deductions, additional deposit is demanded.

The **margin system has apparently some advantages :** (1) From the broker's side, he is safe about his commitments in the market on behalf of his client. (2) From the client side, that is the limit within which he can take stake and thereby his speculative tendency is controlled. **But, in fact, the margin system stimulates gambling tendency.** In the above example, officially there is a profit of Rs. 390 on an investment of Rs. 10,050 but actually, it is not. It was enough for the client to keep a margin money of, say, Rs. 1,000. Actually, he is making a profit of Rs. 390 on an investment of Rs. 1,000.

Under the Securities Contracts (Regulation) Act, 1956, **every member of a stock exchange has to deposit a margin money with the stock exchange authorities** and on the amount of deposit depends what shall be the total volume of transactions on cleared securities that the member can do. If the total amount exceeds the limit, he is asked to deposit some further amount. This indirectly checks his volume of speculative transactions and his transactions mean transactions of his clients. Therefore, this margin system checks speculation in an indirect way. The margin system has been introduced by the Bombay, Calcutta, Delhi and Ahmedabad stock exchanges. In Calcutta, the minimum deposit is Rs. 20,000.

(2) **Blank transfer** — Transfer of shares means physical delivery to the transferee of shares certificates endorsed on transfer deed by the holder, duly stamped and authenticated by a public servant. The share transfer becomes effective when approved by the meeting of the Board of Directors of the company concerned. This is a time-consuming process. In a stock exchange, for quick transactions, share certificates are handed over by the holders after endorsement without waiting for the approval by the Board of Directors. **When the name of the transferee is not written, it is called blank transfer.** The advantage is that the transferee can transfer it to another person without any formality. In this way, **transfer may take place a number of times,** until a transferee gets his name recorded and finally gets the transfer approved by the Board of Directors. This **encourages speculation and even gambling** because of quick hand delivery of share scripts. There may not be any record of such transaction and thereby the seller, i.e., the transferor, may evade capital gain, tax and the Government also loses stamp duty. Further, the Members' Register of the company concerned remains defective and people holding the shares can influence the company in many ways though the company does not know them. Blank transfer, however, cannot be continued for a long time with the same share script because of strict rules with regard to transfer of shares under the Companies Act, 1956.

Different types of speculators

People of different attitudes visit a stock exchange. The members are permitted to do transactions inside a stock exchange but behind the broker-members there are a large number of clients. The clients reflect their attitudes in the market through the broker-members. Most of the people are supposed to be speculation-minded because through speculation, they think, easy earnings can be made. Such **earnings come out of price differences.** Therefore, **in a stock exchange there shall be price fluctuations.** The speculations are swayed by the fluctuations and also create them.

Price fluctuations occur owing to several causes : (1) **Demand and supply** — The prices of those securities will be high which have high demand and the prices of those securities will be low which have low demand. Securities of profitable and safe companies have high demand and high prices. (2) **Policies of the Government** — The industrial, fiscal, commercial, taxation, labour and such other policies of the Government have impacts on industry, trade and commerce and on the whole on the rates of return on investment. The bank rate has impact on the general interest rate and profitability. (3) **Political situation** – The poitical instability, war and such other things have their impact on the economy. (4) **Economic situation** – General economic condition, whether a period of prosperity or depression, has its reaction on industries and prices of securities. (5) **International situation** – Since the countries are inter-linked through trade, political relations, etc. any change in the international situation has its impact on the economy of a country and on the stock exchange. (6) **Action of speculators** – The speculators for their personal gains create artificial fluctuation of prices by various speculative activities. (7) **Others** – There are other causes too, e.g. global war, new discoveries, discovery of substitutes, power shortage etc.

There are **three types of price fluctuations** in a stock exchange. These are comparable to the three types of movements of river water. These are : (1) **Daily** fluctuations – Prices fluctuate daily mainly of speculative securities (just like ripples of river water). This happens mainly due to the actions of the speculators. (2) **Periodical** fluctuations—Fluctuations of prices are generally studied periodically, e.g. a week, a month, etc. (just like waves of river water). Daily fluctuations constitute the periodical fluctuations. These are caused by economic and political situation mainly. (3) **Cyclical** fluctuations – Such fluctuations are caused by trade cycles covering a period of eight to ten years (just like the tide in a river). These both have international causes and effects.

The speculators, therefore, have a big role to play in a stock exchange. There are different types of speculators named after animals because the temperaments of the different types of speculators have much similarity with those of the animals. **The same person as a speculator may behave differently under different situations and at different times.** The speculators move in groups. Thus, a speculator in a stock exchange belongs to some group at a given period of time. The **different types of speculators** are discussed below :

(1) **Bull** — A bull is a type of speculator **who expects that the price of securities will rise in future.** With that expectation he goes on buying the securities and sells them when the price has gone up. As he goes on purchasing the securities the price may slowly go up. On the average his buying price is lower than the price at which he sells. As a result he makes some profit. If his expectation proves to be wrong and the price falls, he will lose. He may 'carry over' the settlement a number of times to wait for his expectation to come to be true. He is an optimist. He is known as 'tejiwala'. He is called a bull because the bull has a tendency to throw up the enemy by the horns.

The speculators of the same temperament move in a group. By bidding, they very often force the price up to make their expectations come true.

(2) **Bear** — A bear is a type of speculator **who expects that the price of securities will fall in future.** With that expectation he goes on selling the securities and buys them when the price has fallen. As he goes on selling the securities the price may slowly go down. On the average, his selling price is higher than the price at which he buys them at the end. As a result he makes a profit. He may carry over the settlement date to see that ultimately the price falls. If his expectation comes to be wrong and the price does not fall, he loses. He is a pessimist. He is known as a 'mandiwala'. He is called a bear because a bear has a tendency to trample the enemy on the ground.

The speculators of the same temperament move in a group. By bidding, very often they pull the price down to make their expectations come true.

The mechanism of the operations of the bulls and the bears is as follows : We have already seen that in most of the cases the speculative transactions are settled by payment of price differences. Neither a bull is a real buyer who is ready to buy the securities on payment of price in full nor a bear is a real seller who possesses the securities and is in a position to deliver the securities against his commitments of sale. When a bear is unable to keep his commitments when he is asked to do so instead of settlement by payment of price difference he is called **a lame duck.** He struggles like a lame duck in a pool and hence the name.

Everyday and for a certain period of time, a stock exchange **is dominated either by a group of bulls or by a group of bears.** Accordingly the market is called **bullish** or 'teji' and **bearish** or "mandi'. When the bulls and the bears look equally powerful the market prices do not appear to be fluctuating much and the market is called **steady.** When both the bulls and the bears lose interest in the market, it is called **dull.** The bulls and the bears by virtue of their operations cause fluctuation of prices. The daily fluctuations of prices are generally caused by them.

(3) **Stag** — A stag is that type of speculator who is described as a premium hunter. He looks like a bull temperamentally but actually he does not buy securities. **A stag applies for new issues and** thereby creates a demand for them and he expects that price will go up. **When the price actually goes up he disposes off the securities at a premium immediately.** He does not really take much risk . He is called a stag because a stag is timid by nature.

It has to be noted that gamblings are carried out by the speculators outside the official market place. **There are many private markets called 'bucket or kerb markets' or 'katni bazars'.** Since **the same people operate** in the official as well as in the private markets, the actions in one type of market have reactions on the other. It is well neigh impossible to control the private markets.

Jobbers and Brokers — In London Stock Exchange, jobber members do transactions among members only while broker members do transaction on behalf of outside clients. A broker, after receiving an order from his client, either to buy or to sell, enters the Stock Exchange Hall and makes a contract with a jobber on behalf of his client. Different jobbers specialise in different kinds of securities. A jobber sells at a higher price and buys at a lower price and the difference, known as 'jobber's turn' is his profit.

STOCK EXCHANGES IN INDIA

Historical background — Stock exchanges cannot exist and flourish unless company form of organisation flourishes. In India, therefore, stock exchanges **have become popular only recently.** Stock exchanges appeared in the nineteenth century in Bombay (1875) and at Ahmedabad (1894) established as non-profit voluntary associations. Later on, the Calcutta Stock Exchange Association was established in 1908, followed by stock exchanges in other cities – in Madras (1928), at Indore (1930), at Hyderabad (1943) in Delhi (1937), at Bangalore (1957) and also at Cochin, Kanpur, Pune, Ludhiana and Guwahati.

At present — The different stock exchanges were established in different forms and with their own respective rules and regulations having no uniformity. With the passing of the Securities Contracts (Regulation) Act in 1956, which was made effective from 20.2.1957, standardisation of rules could be made to a great extent. Under the Act, only one stock exchange can function in one city which needs recognition of the Government under the Act. Out of the **13 recognised stock exchanges in India,** Bombay, Calcutta, Delhi, Ahmedabad and Madras have permanent recognition while others are recognised for 5 years at a time subject to renewal. The dates of recognition of some stock exchanges are as follows : The Bombay Stock Exchange – 31.8.57, the Ahmedabad Share and Stock - Brokers' Association – 16.9.57, the Calcutta Stock Exchange Association Ltd. – 10.10.57, the Madras Stock Exchange – 15.10.57, the Delhi Stock Exchange Association Ltd. – 9.12.57, the Hyderabad Stock Exchange Ltd. – 29.9.58, the Indore Share - Brokers' Association – 24.12.58, the Bangalore Stock Exchange – 16.2.63 and Guwahati Stock Exchange – 1.5.84.

The following associations have not been granted recognition and so they have become defunct – the Bombay Share and Stock - Brokers' Association; the Indian Stock Exchange, Bombay; the Bengal Share and Stock - Brokers' Association, Calcutta; the Gujarat Share and Stock Exchange, Ahmedabad and the Indian Share and General Exchange Association, Ahmedabad.

The composition, management, membership pattern and extent of operation of some of the stock exchanges are given below:

Composition — The Bombay Stock Exchange (old name – Native Share and Stock - Brokers' Association), the Ahmedabad Share and Stock – Brokers' Association and the Indore Share – Brokers' Association are like private clubs or voluntary associations. The Calcutta Stock Exchange Association Ltd. is a non-trading company limited by shares. (Originally, it was a voluntary association but later on incorporated in 1923). The Delhi Stock Exchange Association Ltd. is also a non-trading public company limited by shares. The Madras and the Hyderabad Stock Exchanges are non-trading public companies limited by guarantee. The Bangalore Stock Exchange is a non-trading private company limited by shares.

Thus we find that stock exchanges in India are either of voluntary association type or non-trading company type. The stock exchanges themselves do not do business but the members do business individually.

Membership — Membership in an Indian stock exchange can be acquired **either by paying subscription or by buying a share or by both.** Paying subscription is enough for voluntary associations but buying of share is essential for companies. Only a member can do transactions inside a stock exchange. He has to pay, in addition to price of a share or a membership card, an entrance fee, annual subscription and a margin deposit (see above). For example, in Calcutta, a member has to buy a share of Rs. 250 (the market value is several thousands of rupees), an entrance fee of Rs. 1,100, a deposit of Rs. 20,000 and a small annual subscription determined from time to time. On the whole, a member has to spend about Rs. 30,000 at the time of entry. For Bombay Stock Exchange, which is the biggest in India, a member has to bring initially about Rs. 40,000. It is very difficult to become a member. Unless any member voluntarily leaves membership or dies there is hardly any chance for a newcomer. In the past, membership could be obtained by a share - brokers' firm consisting of several partners. But at present an individual only can be a member in his own name. For a long time, the total number of members was 504. Recently, membership cards for 35 new membership have been sold, the value of each card being Rs. 7.51 lakhs including the value of 60 sq. ft. office area in the Stock Exchange building.

In India, all the members are broker members. In London Stock Exchange, members are divided into two groups – Jobbers (who do not do business on behalf of outsiders) and Brokers (who do business on behalf of outsiders). In Bombay Stock Exchange, members are grouped more or less in the same line. There are **'taravaniwalas'** (who do not do business on behalf of outsiders) and commission brokers. But the division is not very rigid. The taravaniwalas also do business as commission brokers from time to time. Taravaniwalas often cancel their original contracts with other members and come out in the market as brokers. Their role is very much criticised on this ground. They exploit their advantageous position to the best for making high profits. The Securities Contracts (Regulation) Act makes provisions to control their activities. In Bombay Stock Exchange, a full-fledged member appoints **'remisiers'** or sub-brokers who procure business from outside clients on behalf of the members. The members pay commission to the sub-brokers out of the commissions earned by the members from their clients.

Members of all stock exchanges can appoint **'authorised clerks'** or member assistants who are authorised to do transactions on behalf of their principals on the floors of the market. They cannot do business in their own names. Every stock exchange has its own rules as regards the maximum number of authorised clerks to be appointed by a member. In Calcutta, the number is the highest 8 while in Bombay it is 5. It is not possible for a member to cope with his growing activities. He also cannot advertise for his business. Therefore, there is need for appointing authorised clerks. The idea of appointing authorised clerks comes from

London Stock Exchange where an authorised clerk, after four years' service, becomes eligible to become a full-fledged member by virtue of his experience. In Indian stock exchanges, however, an authorised clerk does not have any such opportunity.

Size — By and large, the Bombay Stock Exchange is the biggest stock exchange in India followed by Calcutta, though Calcutta has a larger number of members. In Bombay Stock Exchange, the total number of members is around 500, the total number of enlisted companies is about 620, the total number of enlisted securities is about 1,140 and the total number of cleared securities (on which speculation is done) is 67. (All these figures fluctuate and so approximate figures are given.) Correspondingly, in Calcutta Stock Exchange, the figures are 1,120, 630, 1,070 and 47. The smallest stock exchange is the Indore Stock Exchange. The number of cleared securities changes from time to time. Altogether, about 1,650 of them have enlistment in 2, 3, 4, 5 stock exchanges. Calcutta and Bombay exchanges practically dominate Indian capital market. There is predominance of different industries in different exchanges. For example, in Calcutta, there is predominance of jute, plantation and engineering; in Bombay, cotton and chemicals; in Madras, plantation and cotton, etc.

Management — Every stock exchange is managed by some groups of people called either a Managing Committee or a Board of Governors etc. according to the constitution of the stock exchange. According to the Securities Contracts (Regulation) Act, there shall be nominees of the Government in the managing committee of every stock exchange. The Calcutta Stock Exchange has a Managing Committee with 19 members out of which 3 are nominees of the Government. Apart from the Managing Committee, there are many sub-committees to look after different activities. For example, the Listing Committee, the Arbitration Committee, the Defaulters' Committee etc.

Stock Exchange reforms — Because of rampant gamblings and other malpractices to exploit innocent investors obtaining in Indian stock exchanges, it was being felt even during the British rule that **some regulatory measures must be taken by the Government.** The urgency was specially felt during the all-time boom in stock exchanges during the Second World War. The then **British Government appointed a Committee** for the purpose and the responsibility was ultimately left on Dr. P. J. Thomas, the Economic Advisor to the Ministry of Finance. The report of Dr. Thomas, submitted in 1947, was examined by a high power Committee but, before any action could be taken, India became free and **the national Government subsequently appointed another Committee** in 1951 under the chairmanship of Sri A. D. Gorwala with 10 members representing the Government, the business community and the stock exchanges. On the basis of the findings of the Gorwala Committee, **the Securities Contracts (Regulation) Act was passed in 1956,** empowering the Government to have unitary control on all the stock exchanges. The purpose of the Act was to regulate stock exchange operations with a view to building up a healthy capital market for the economic development of the country.

The objects of the Act are : (1) To impose regulatory measures on security dealings except spot transactions under which delivery of securities has to be completed on the date of contract or on next day. Under exceptional situations the Government, however, can regulate spot delivery contracts too. (2) To declare all kerb markets or 'katni bazars' as illegal. By virtue of this the Katni Market of Calcutta and the Grey Market of Bombay were (officially) closed. (3) To impose that there should be only one stock exchange in one city. As a result, many unauthorised stock exchanges were closed (see above). (4) To introduce a system of Government recognition for every stock exchange. Such recognition may be permanent or for a fixed period, subject to renewal. Recognition can be granted provided the following conditions are fulfilled : (a) the rules and bye-laws of a stock exchange applying for recognition must be in conformity with the requirements under the Act; (b) the stock exchange must abide by the orders issued by the Government from time to time; (c) the stock exchange will serve the interests of the commercial world and of the public; (d) the applicant stock exchange shall accept Government nominees, not exceeding 3, on the Governing Body; (e) the members must maintain proper books of accounts which shall be audited by chartered accountants; (f) there shall be fixed qualifications for eligibility for membership; (g) the stock exchange shall submit all information about it as wanted by the Government; (5) To introduce a system of compulsory licensing of the sharebrokers to bring them under the control of the Government in the interests of those engaged in transactions on securities. (6) To introduce a procedure of enlistment of companies and their shares in a stock exchange and only those enlisted shares can be dealt in that stock exchange. (It has to be noted that there are corresponding provisions in the Companies Act, 1956.) (7) To impose control on speculative activities to eliminate gambling. (8) To empower the Government to make the Act effective and to exercise control on stock exchanges.

Application of the Act — The Securities Contract (Regulation) Act was made effective from 20.2.57. By virtue of the Act, a **great change has been brought about** in the composition, management and functioning of the stock exchanges in India.

Control on speculation — The option dealings have been declared illegal. The Government has been empowered to ban other types of speculation any time by public notification. In fact, all types of speculation has been banned by the Government by an order on 27.6.69. The Government can suspend all types of transactions in a stock exchange for 7 days. The Government may prohibit sale or purchase of any particular security if the Government feels that it may lead to gambling.

Control on general working — The bye-laws and rules of a recognised stock exchange must be approved by the Government before they are made effective. Such rules and bye-laws include : the working hours of the stock exchange; the conditions for making, effecting or cancelling contracts with clients; the rates and terms of margin requirement; the rates of brokerage; announcement of ceiling (highest) and floor (lowest) prices of securities for general information; settlements of all disputes through arbitration etc.

Control on management — The Act has empowered the Government to supersede the governing body or the managing committee of a stock exchange if the Government thinks it necessary. The Government may appoint any person to exercise the powers of the Governing Body. Besides, in the managing committee or governing body of every stock exchange there shall be nominees of the Government. All activities of a stock exchange can be suspended, for not exceeding 7 days, in the interests of public and trade.

Directorate of stock exchange — In order to enforce the provisions of the Act the Government has set up a Directorate of Stock Exchange in 1959 with its headquarters in Bombay and branch offices in Delhi and Calcutta. The functions of the Directorate are : (a) It maintains vigilance on the day-to-day working of the stock exchanges. (b) It demands returns from the members on their daily transactions. (c) It watches whether option dealings and kerb transactions are taking place or not. (d) It also observes whether rules in respect of listing of securities are strictly followed or not. (e) It is entrusted with the task of licensing of dealers in securities outside the jurisdiction of stock exchanges.

Critical evaluation — It has to be admitted that the Act has been able to remove many of the evils and malpractices abundantly found in Indian stock exchanges and has brought **far-reaching changes in the constitution and functioning** of them. It has provided enormous powers in the hands of the Government to control the stock exchanges and their operations. The Act itself is an outcome of detailed investigations, long discussions and compiled views and suggestions of experts. But even then **it is criticised on the following grounds :**

(1) There are **too many restrictions** with regard to the management and membership rules which destroy the autonomy of the stock exchanges. Had there been a greater autonomy, the stock exchanges could have functioned more freely in the interest of the investors.

(2) The Act **does not make categorisation of members** into jobbers and brokers as we find in London Stock Exchange. On the other hand, it permits the 'taravaniwala' type of members to exist creating a confusing situation.

(3) It **has not been successful in totally eliminating unhealthy speculation** by allowing carry-over and such other methods of trading. The Government, however, is empowered to ban them from time to time.

(4) The Act has not made any attempt to educate and encourage the investing public. In fact, **the investors are not directly benefited** by the Act so that they are attracted to stock exchanges.

Conclusion — India is on the road to industrialisation. Industries can flourish only through establishment of larger numbers of companies. Something has to be done so that people of small and middle income group, who have their small savings, can be attracted to corporate investment. **The stock exchanges have a great role to play to attract the small savers.** Investment facilities must not be confined to the rich class or the privileged few. So long mixed economy remains as the accepted economic policy and **so long the private sector is allowed to exist, the importance of the stock exchanges cannot be minimised.** The wrong idea that a stock exchange is a gambling den must be removed from the minds of the masses. The stock exchanges must gear up public relations. With greater public participation and education on investment methods, unhealthy speculation and malpractices shall be eradicated. The Central Government has appointed a Committee under the Chairmanship of Shri G. S. Patel (former chairman of UTI) to enquire into the functioning of the stock exchanges in India and to make recommendations for reform and amendment of the Act.

Listing of securities

Securities of all companies are not dealt in stock exchanges. **A company has to get its name and securities enlisted with a particular stock exchange** and then only the securities will be dealt there. A company can, however, enlist its name and securities in a number of stock exchanges. A company may have a variety of securities (e.g. different kinds of shares as well as debentures). It can enlist either all or some of the securities. Generally, a big widely-held public company can go for enlistment. Securities of small companies cannot be expected to be enlisted in any stock exchange. The Companies Act provides some rules with regard to allotment of shares which are proposed to be enlisted in a recognised stock exchange.

There cannot be any right nor there is any legal obligation of a company to have its securities enlisted in a stock exchange. **An application has to be made to a stock exchange** in a prescribed form with prescribed fees and subject to the rules provided in the Securities Contracts (Regulation) Act, 1956. The authorities of the **stock exchange may accept or reject the application.** The Government is empowered by the Act to compel a company to enlist its securities with a recognised stock exchange in the interests of the trade and the public. **There are many advantages of enlistments** which are enjoyed by the company and its members as well as the general investing public. Big companies, therefore, go for enlistment. Such enlistment can be done at the time of incorporation of the company or any time thereafter.

Before accepting an application from a company for enlistment the authorities (generally a special committee is appointed for the purpose) of a **stock exchange must examine the application thoroughly.** It has to be seen whether : (a) the company is properly constituted; (b) the management of the company is sound and in the hands of dependable persons; (c) the company is financially sound; (d) it is earning profit (in case of an existing company) or it has profit-earning capacity; and lastly (e) it has complied with all the rules of enlistment.

At present, shares of about 2,000 companies are enlisted in different stock exchanges in India which cover about 24% public limited companies in the country.

Rules and obligations for listing

There are two aspects in the process — Certain rules have to be observed by the applicant company and, after enlistment, the company will have some obligations in the future. The Securities Contracts (Regulation) Act, 1956, makes all the provisions.

Rules — The Company has to submit an application in a prescribed form with a fee of Rs.1,000, together with the following :

(1) Copies of Memorandum and Articles of Association, and Prospectus.

(2) Directors' Report, Balance Sheet, Profit and Loss Account up to last ten years, in case of an existing company.

(3) Specimen of Share Certificate, Debenture Bond etc. for preservation in the stock exchange.

(4) Particulars of dividends up to last ten years, in case of an existing company.

(5) A brief history of company's performance since its incorporation, in case of an existing company.

The authorities of stock exchange will verify :

(a) Whether the Articles contain the following provisions : (i) a common form of transfer shall be used. (ii) Calls paid in advance may carry interest but no dividend shall be payable on it. (iii) Fully paid shares shall be free from lien, etc.

(b) Whether at least 60% of each class of securities issued was offered to the public for subscription through newspapers at least for three days. Out of the 60% of each of the securities, 11% may be kept reserved for the financial institutions and other Government agencies.

(c) Whether the company is of fairly big size with a broad-based capital structure so that public may be interested in it.

It has to be noted that 40% of the securities may be held by the promoters or people wanting to have managerial control but there shall not be any concentration of power and the company must have a true public character so that the public may be interested.

Obligations — When the authorities of the stock exchange are satisfied they will ask the company to enter into an agreement. By that agreement, the company develops some future obligations, such as :

(a) To notify the stock exchange the date of the Board meeting where rates of dividend will be recommended.

(b) To submit to the stock exchange audited accounts as soon as they are issued.

(c) To notify the stock exchange any change in the nature of business or capital structure of the company.

(d) To notify the stock exchange before-hand when the company wants to issue rights shares, and bonus shares.

(e) To intimate the stock exchange any other information in which shareholders may be interested.

In case of a new company, the authorities of stock exchange will also see that allotment is fairly made. In case of over-subscription, the authorities of stock exchange will suggest on what basis allotment should be made.

Advantages of listing — A company intends to have enlistment of its securities in a stock exchange because of the following advantages :

(1) It increases the goodwill of the company and, by that, raising of finance becomes easier.

(2) The securities become more marketable and liquidity is increased. Prospective investors become attracted to such company.

(3) There is an indirect pressure to make the management efficient.

(4) In case of a new company, the allotment also becomes fair and equitable.

(5) The market value of the securities can be properly ascertained.

(6) The securities because of higher liquidity, acquire greater value as collateral and by that the status of the company becomes higher.

(7) From the stock exchange, all kinds of information about the company as well as specimen of the securities for verification can be known.

(8) There cannot be any fraud or other manipulations in the issue of the securities.

Limitations — There are the following limitations too :

(1) The securities may attract the attention of the speculators who may cause wild and artifical fluctuations in the prices of the securities, which may be harmful for the company and the genuine investors.

(2) The management of the company may be interested in speculating on the securities taking advantage of their inner knowledge of the affairs of the company.

(3) It may be harmful for the company to supply detailed information to the stock exchange under the listing agreement.

(4) Through cornering and other devices, a group of interested persons may encroach in the ownership and management of the company secretly.

MONEY MARKET

Definition — The money market can be defined as **a market for dealing in monetary assets, mainly of short-term character.** The borrowers are the 'buyers' of the monetary assets and the lenders are the 'sellers' and the interest is the 'price' payable by the borrowers to the lenders. The term 'monetary assets' require further classification. (The term has been used in the publications of the Reserve Bank of India). **Monetary assets mean short term loans,** either direct or indirect. Every businessman, every organisation, whether trading or non-trading, every public body, every individual and even the Government (whether State or Central) needs temporary **financial accommodation to bridge the gap between current expenditure and income.** Income may be delayed but expenses have to be continuously and immediately made. Such a situation can be overcome through temporary financial accommodation. That temporary period may be for several days or months or even years. But the main point is that a loan has to be repaid, sooner or later. It is not like capital which is invested without any obligation of being repaid. Monetary assets refer to all such types of repayable financial accommodations. These are supplied by the lenders consisting of bankers and moneylenders, who make the supply directly. Besides, financial accommodation can be obtained indirectly through deferred payments and negotiable instruments which will mature after some time.

Types — The money market can be of two types or may consist of two sectors – **organised and unorganised.**

The organised sector — The organised sector of the money market in a country is made of the banking system. In fact, whenever we think of a money market we mean the banking system. The components which make the system are : (a) **The Central Bank** of the country. Every developed or developing country has a central bank which is the banker of the Government and has the sole authority of creating the currency. (b) **The member banks** – All the other recognised banks are under the control of the central bank and are often called the member banks. The central bank controls the monetary system and the money market and it also controls all matters related to the conversion of the local currency into any other foreign currency. There can be different types of member banks specialising in different kinds of banking operations. **A bank is a dealer in debts.** A river erodes earth on one bank and piles it up on the other. A bank does the same with debts. A bank receives deposits (takes debts) from the depositors and makes loans (creates debts) to those who need them. The bank pays lower rate of interest to the depositors and charges higher rates of interest from the borrowers and thereby earns profit. Interest is the price in dealing in money. Thus, in the money market or in the banking system, we find all the characteristics of a market.

The unorganised sector — It is **constituted by different types of individual moneylenders** who are virtually free from any control by the laws related to the money market. The central bank of a country does not have any control on them. Such moneylenders are not strictly dealers in debts, like a bank. In India, we have a large number of individual moneylenders, specially in rural areas. The unorganised sector casts a great influence on the monetary system of the country and tends to foil monetary policies of the Government in many ways, as the Government has very little control on the unorganised sector.

Meaning of money — Physically, money is a commodity and, conceptually, money is a 'claim'. It is different from other commodities because money has a purchasing power which other commodities do not have. By money other commodities are purchased but money itself can neither be purchased nor sold. According to A. C. L. Day, an authority on monetary economics, "the real significance of money is that it is a claim which can be used by its owner to buy anything". Money, to create a claim, **can be owned in the forms of currency and bank deposits.** To an economist, money supply comes in the forms of currency and bank credit. In that sense a bank creates money. In practical life or business life, **money is handled in the forms of currency,** bank deposits, bank credit and money substitutes or the negotiable instruments. If money is a claim, the negotiable instruments are also actionable claims. As the size of the business becomes big, bank deposits and bank credits (collectively known as bank money) assumes great significance. Same can be said of the negotiable instruments. Handling of cash becomes less important except on specific occasions like payment of wages or salaries or for making unrecorded payments. The negotiable instruments are ultimately settled through bank. Therefore, **bank money has the greatest significance.** This is the real monetary asset as understood in the definition of the money market. In a restricted sense, money market denotes that market where loans of money can be obtained. Loans of money can be obtained in an organised manner from the banks headed and controlled by the central bank. Individual moneylenders also operate through banks in most of the cases. Unrecorded cash loans, however, are not taken into consideration in the legalised accounting world. But such unrecorded transactions exist as black money exists, causing much disturbance to the monetary system and policies.

Supply of money in the money market — Considering the money market in its accepted sense and, considering the organised part of it only, **the supply of money in a money market comes from the banks.** Banks are, however, of different types, as enumerated below :

(A) **The Central Bank** — Every developed and developing country has a central bank. In different countries, the central banks have different types of names. For example, in India it is called the Reserve Bank of India, in England it is called the Bank of England, in USA the name is the Federal Reserve Bank, in USSR it is known as the Gosbank, etc. **It supplies money in two ways :** (a) by creation of currency notes and (b) by giving long and short-term loans to the Government and to other member banks. The currency notes are created against some statutory minimum reserve of gold and foreign currency convertible into gold. (Since currency notes are mere papers without any intrinsic value, some reserve is maintained to add some solidarity or solvency.) When the Government of a country adopts a policy of deficit financing (i.e. meeting of commitments by the Government by printing of notes) huge quantity of currency notes are printed and issued by the central bank against same amount of reserve. Member banks have to rely on the central bank for accommodation, as a last resort, when there is a pressure of withdrawals from the banks and there is shortage of funds and all other sources of funds are exhausted.

(B) **The other banks** — There are different types of banks operating in a country which supply money by providing financial accommodation to their customers. Financial accommodation can be rendered in many ways. **The nature of accommodation largely depends on the nature of the bank.** The different types of banks are discussed below :

(1) **Commercial banks** — A commercial bank receives deposits, both short-term and long-term, and renders financial accommodation generally for short period to its customers. In recent times, commercial banks are also offering 'term' loans, i.e. fairly long-term loans. This is the most common type of bank.

(2) **Industrial banks** — An industrial bank receives deposits, both short-term and long-term, but provides long-term financial accommodation and that even by subscribing to the shares in, and debentures of, industrial companies. All countries do not have industrial banks. India does not have such banks.

(3) **Exchange banks** — These are like commercial banks but they specialise in transactions involving foreign trade. They take the responsibility of conversion of local currency into foreign currencies and provide financial accommodation for import-export transactions.

(4) **Cooperative banks** — These banks are organised on cooperative basis and also as cooperative credit societies to provide financial accommodation to members under special rules and regulations. They accept deposits from the members and charge low rates of interest from them.

(5) **Land Mortgage banks** — Such banks create negotiable bonds against land, building etc. These are sold in the market and bought by those who want safe investments. Such banks render financial accommodations, mostly for permanent improvements in agricultural lands. In India they are now called Land Development Banks.

(6) **Postal savings banks** — Many of the post offices run savings departments where small savers, specially those of rural areas, can deposit their savings. These are not lending banks.

Demand for money in the market — Demand for money comes out of need for financial accommodation by businessmen, individuals, public bodies and the Government. Generally, the need for financial accommodation by the businessmen is taken for major consideration.

The business community needs help from the money market for procuring short-term or working capital. The supply of the long-term or fixed capital comes from the capital market. Short-term (as well as medium term) capital is wanted to meet current expenses like continuing production, payment of wages and such other remuneration to the employees, to pay dividend etc. Money is also needed for heavy repairs or replacements of machines and machine parts. Sometimes, expansion or extension expenses are also included. Shortage of working capital is a very common feature in business. Credit sales are unavoidable and sometimes it takes a long time to realise the outstandings but current expenses have to be incurred. Failure of business for want of working capital is very common. More or less, every businessman has to keep arrangement with bank for the supply of working capital. Commercial banks (including those who deal in foreign exchange) supply the short-term capital and also term loans on special occasions.

The public bodies like municipalities, port trusts etc. also require short-term financial accommodation to meet current expenses. So does the Government. Even a bank takes temporary accommodation from another bank and this is shown in the balance sheet as 'call money' or 'money at short notice'. Such advances by one bank to another is purely temporary and for a very short period.

The businessmen get a large amount of **financial accommodation indirectly through various kinds of deferred payments.** Goods including raw materials, machine parts, tools, stock-in-trade, etc. can be procured on credit. Such credit is known as **trade credit or open-account credit.** The volume of such credit depends largely on the reputation of a firm as a pay–master. A businessman enjoys **consumer credit** through purchase of goods on instalment sale or hire-purchase basis. Credit can also be obtained through **use of negotiable instruments.** A promissory note or a bill of exchange may mature after some period of time. In the former case, a debtor takes the advantage by making out the note and in the latter case, a creditor allows a debtor to enjoy the advantage. But the creditor may get the instruments discounted in advance from banks.

The businessmen also enjoy indirect credit through **deferred payment of taxes and duties** as far as possible. Collection of sales tax from the buyers and belated payment of the taxes to the Government is a common method of increasing the working capital.

In addition to the different direct and indirect sources, a businessman has to approach his banker for short-term financing, i.e. for **bank credit.**

SHORT-TERM FINANCING

Meaning — Short-term financing is a major function of a bank. A bank is a dealer in debts. Therefore, a bank is always ready to provide financial assistance. Short-term financing means to devise ways and means by which a customer can make payments to his creditors although he does not have sufficient credit balance in his account with the bank. There are various methods by which a bank can create such situation.

Principles — In providing financial assistance, a bank must have in mind three cardinal principles :

(1) **Profitability** — A bank must earn income out of the transaction. A bank charges higher rate of interest from the borrowers than the rate it pays to the depositors. The bank also imposes some service charges in addition to the interest.

(2) **Solvency** — A bank cannot provide financial assistance without any security. The bank must have a remedy if the borrower fails to repay the money in time. Accepting **security has two aspects : (1) Primary security** – The primary security is the bond signed by the borrower. A bank always helps a customer who is a known person and has good relations with the bank. The signing of the bond by the customer may be enough if the customer has great reputation and very good relation with the bank. Besides, some other person shall stand as a guarantor. But, for safety, the bank asks for a secondary or collateral security from the borrower. (2) **Collateral security** – The collateral security must be tangible goods and can be either movable or immovable. In case of **movable goods** like land, building etc., it is called **mortgage.** The title deed of the property is kept with the bank until repayment is made. The bank may sell out the property to realise its dues if the borrower fails to repay. In case of **movable goods** such as stock-in-trade, raw materials, shares, gold ornaments, etc, the following situations may arise : (a) **Lien** – When the bank is already in possession of some movable goods, as a custodian, belonging to the borrower, then the bank will have the right to hold the goods until repayment is made by the borrower. (b) **Pledge** – It means that the borrower carries some movable goods to the bank and keeps under its possession, till repayment is made by the borrower. (c) **Hypothecation** – This is just opposite to pledge. Here, the goods remain in the possession of the borrower but under the control of the bank. The borrower uses the goods for making income by which repayment is maade. For example, a mini-bus hypothecated to a bank remains in possession of the owner-borrower. He runs the bus and repays loan to the bank by instalments along with the interest according to terms and conditions. The bank has **non-possessory lien** on the hypothecated goods and can take possession of the goods when the borrower fails to pay instalments. In each case of lien, pledge and hypothecation, the bank has the right to sell the goods as remedy to realise the dues when the borrower ultimately fails to repay.

While accepting a collateral security, a bank keeps a safe margin. It means that accommodation is provided up to certain percentage (say, 60%) of the value of the collateral security. The margin will be less if the security is highly liquid. In India, a bank has to maintain a statutory liquidity ratio of 34% at the minimum.

It has to be noted that when a bank makes advance by **discounting of bills** (see below), the bills themselves provide the collateral security.

(3) **Liquidity** — A financial accommodation by a bank must not only be backed by security which has solvency, but the security shall also be liquid or easily saleable. Liquidity is desirable because, if the borrower fails to make repayment and the bank is forced to sell the security, there shall not be any difficulty on the part of the bank to make the sale. A bank prefers movable to immovable goods as security because movable goods normally have greater liquidity. A very costly property is a very bad security in the eyes of a bank. It is rightly said that "a good banker is he who can distinguish between a bill of exchange and a mortgage". A bill of exchange drawn and accepted by reputable parties is highly dependable which has a definite date of maturity within a short period.

Types of bank accommodation

Broad classification — A bank can provide financial assistance broadly in **two ways :** (1) **Indirect** – Indirectly, a bank accommodates its customers by giving **guarantee** for financial transactions entered into by the customers with others. In case of foreign trade, the importer has to procure a **Letter of Credit** in his favour from his bank to be sent to the exporter. There are three things in a Letter of Credit, in short called L/C : (a) The description of the importer in whose favour the L/C is opened. (b) An amount up to which the bank gives the guarantee. (c) A period for which the L/C remains valid. There are different types of L/C : Revocable (i.e. withdrawable by the bank before the stated period is over), Irrevocable (i.e., not withdrawable), Revolving i.e., after the period is over it becomes again effective for another period) etc. No exporter will have confidence in the importer and send the goods to him unless an L/C is opened. Even in home trade also a consignor may demand an, L/C from the consignee. In ordinary trade, a seller wanting to sell goods on credit under usual trade custom demands **a bank reference** from the buyer.

(2) **Direct** — Directly, a bank can make advances to its customers in **four different ways** including loan. It has to be noted that the term loan has a special meaning in banking practice. **All advances are, strictly, not loans.** A loan can be given by a bank to a new customer but other kinds of direct accommodation can be made to a customer with whom the bank has close acquaintance. The four different ways of bank accommodation are discussed below. For the first three cases, a bank demands collateral security in most of the cases. But for discounting a bill, the bill itself is the collateral security (see above).

(a) **Overdraft** — Under this method, a bank allows the customer to overdraw, which means he **can withdraw more money than his actual credit balance** in the account with the bank. The bank fixes a limit up to which the overdraft will be allowed. This limit depends on many factors – the credit-worthiness of the customer, the security offered, the past performance of the customer, etc. The borrower can repay the overdrawn amount gradually in instalments. The **interest** at an agreed rate **is payable on the unrepaid balance only.** As part payment is made, the total volume of interest is reduced. Overdraft is a temporary arrangement.

(b) **Cash credit — It is like overdraft but for a longer duration.** There is an arrangement with the bank that all collections of the customer will be deposited with the bank and all payments by the customer to his parties shall be made by cheque. The customer, however, shall handle some imprest cash for petty expense. As the customer goes on making payment by cheques, there may be shortage of fund in the bank account but the banker will honour the cheques with the understanding that the customer will make the deposit at an early date to repay the advance made by the bank. Interest at an agreed rate shall be payable in the advance amount for the period until it is repaid.

(c) **Loan** — The term loan has a specific meaning. Loan means an agreed amount of money to be advanced by a bank to a borrower for an agreed period with an interest at an agreed rate. **The advanced money, together with the total calculated interest, shall have to be repaid** after the period of loan is over. There will be no reduction in the total value on interest; unless otherwise agreed, if part repayment of loan is made earlier. The bank will demand collateral security to cover the loan money fully. Loan can be given to a new customer who first time opens the account with a bank with the purpose of getting the facility and is ready with sufficient collateral security.

(d) **Discounting of bills — The drawer of a bill of exchange,** duly accepted by the drawee, **can get it discounted** from a bank before the date of maturity of the bill. The bank pays the money in advance after deducting some discount. On due, date the bank collects the full amount by presenting the bill to the acceptor of the bill. In foreign trade, the bills of exchange are regularly discounted by the exporters.

Extent of bank accommodation — A bank cannot provide financial assistance to its customers without any restriction. There are **so many factors** which determine to what extent a bank can accommodate its customers. They are :

(1) Firstly, there must be **demand for such accommodation** from the customer. The demand is less when the general business is dull and economy is at low key. Demand is artificially curtailed by raising of bank rate and increased by lowering it (see below).

(2) Secondly, a bank can provide financial accommodation if the borrower is ready to offer **sufficient collateral security** acceptable to the bank. The bank will also keep a safe margin.

(3) Thirdly, **the rate of interest must be economic** so that it will be profitable for the borrower to use the advance and make some earning. Generally, the rate of interest is round–about 18% and, in addition to that, there are nominal service charges. Unless a borrower can earn a profit of more than, say 25%, there is no sense in taking advance from bank.

(4) Fourthly, banks are **under strict control of the central bank** of the country which again operates under the control of the Government. When money has become cheap and banks make too much advance, the central bank raises the bank rate (the rate at which a member bank can take advance from the central bank) so that the banks have to raise their interest rates. The businessmen do not find it profitable to take bank accommodation at such a high bank rate. The total bank accommodation decreases. On the other hand, bank rate is lowered to make bank advances cheaper and attractive. To control credit, the central bank adopts various other policies like asking banks not to make advances against certain categories of security, asking the banks to transfer a high percentage of their total deposits to the central banks, etc. In India, the RBI compels the member banks to keep deposit of 6% of total deposits and 10% of incremental deposits since January 1977, with the RBI. In addition, a bank has to maintain a liquidity ratio of 34%.

(5) Lastly, a bank has to keep certain percentage of its total deposits as cash reserve. Generally it is 10%.

Loans create deposits

The source of a bank's loanable fund — A fundamental question arises as to what is the source of a bank's loanable fund. A large number of customers make deposits with a bank. Some of the deposits are demand deposits (Current Account) which are withdrawable at any time. Some of the deposits are time deposits (Savings Account, Fixed Deposit Account) which are not readily withdrawable. It is to be noted that all the demand deposits are not withdrawn immediately. A bank takes advantage of **the unwithdrawn deposits of some customers** to lend them to others. Further, the bank knows that every day some people will withdraw money while others will deposit money. There is a constant cash flow. But, for safety, every bank keeps some percentage (generally 10) of the total deposits as cash reserve to meet the contingency. If, unfortunately, there is heavy rush for withdrawals, a bank takes short-term loan called 'call money' or 'money at short notice' from other banks and finally as a last resort takes loan from the central bank (see above).

The above explanation is old and orthodox explanation. There is **a further source of a bank.** Whenever a bank makes financial accommodation to a customer, his account is credited to a larger artificial amount against which he draws cheques to make payment to his creditors. These cheques are deposited with other banks by those creditors in their accounts. (Some cheques may be deposited with the same lending bank.) Thus, **loans create deposits and against such deposits further advances can be made** by banks, after keeping cash reserves proportionately. In fact, all the advances made remain within the banking system as a whole except that part which is withdrawn as cash. Such cash may be ultimately deposited with banks, at least a part of it.

THE MONEY MARKET OF INDIA

Structure — The money market of India or the Indian banking system is **divided into two sectors :** the organised and the unorganised. **The organised sector** consists of the Reserve Bank of India (as the central bank), the nationalised Indian commercial banks, the non-nationalised Indian commercial banks, the non-nationalised foreign commercial banks (dealing in foreign exchange in all cases), the cooperative banks, the postal savings banks and the land development banks. The unorganised sector is constituted by the indigenous banks, i.e. private loan offices functioning in a traditional method with little regard to modern banking practice. It has to be noted, however, that the total banking activities in the country are shared equally by the two sectors. Therefore, **the importance of the unorganised sector cannot be ignored.** Details about the functioning of the unorganised sector are not available.

Recently, the Government has introduced a new type of bank called Regional Rural Bank. Such banks are opened in collaboration with the State Bank of India and the State Governments in rural areas to finance agricultural development. There are 87 such banks as on 31.3.80 in India, with 7 in West Bengal.

The organised sector — The **main features** of the organised sector of the Indian money market are as follows :

(1) There is **the Reserve Bank of India as the central bank** at the head of the banking system. It was established by the Reserve Bank of India Act, 1934, as a private shareholders' bank but after independence it has been nationalised by an Act in 1948 so that it can carry out the Government's developmental policies. It has the monopoly for creating currency. It controls other banks and all foreign exchange transactions. As the central bank of a developing country, it is engaged in other activities of economic development. So far, the RBI has managed Indian money market very well.

(2) There is **predominance of commercial banks.** Industrial banks are absent from the country. The void is filled up by the financial institutions like IFCI, IDBI etc.

(3) In India we have **Indian and (22) foreign banks.** The biggest foreign bank and the biggest bank in India, known as the Imperial Bank of India, was nationalised in 1955 and was renamed as the State Bank of India. When there was nationalisation of big banks in 1969, the foreign banks were exempted.

(4) The foreign banks function as foreign exchange banks. Some of the **leading Indian banks have started foreign exchange business.** 11 Indian commercial banks have, by December 1979, established 121 branches in foreign countries, including advanced countries. Some banks do foreign exchange banking through other foreign banks.

(5) Constitutionally, **Indian banks are joint stock companies** limited by shares. The nationalised banks have dropped the word 'Limited' from their names. Indian banks are regulated by the Companies Act, 1956, and Banking Regulations Act, 1949. Functionally, they are controlled by the Reserve Bank.

(6) Indian banks now-a-days are **classified into nationalised and non-nationalised.** In 1969, 14 big banks were nationalised. Besides, the State bank of India is there with its 7

subsidiaries (they are the banks of the erstwhile native states like Jodhpur, Bikanir, Travancore, Hyderabad, etc.). On 15.4.80 the Government has nationalised 6 banks by an Ordinance. Taken as a whole, there are 154 banks operating in the country out of which 20 are nationalised banks.

(7) Technically, banks are **classified into scheduled and non-scheduled.** A scheduled bank is that which has a paid-up capital and reserves aggregating not less than Rs. 5 lakhs, which is a joint stock company under the Companies Act and which strictly abide by the instructions of the RBI. By June 1980, India had 149 scheduled and 5 non-scheduled commercial banks.

(8) So far, Indian banks used to provide banking facilities, particularly advances to large-scale industries. Indian banks **used to ignore rural and small-scale sectors.** One of the reasons for nationalisation was compelling banks to help the so far neglected sectors which are now considered to be priority sectors. **Things have changed after nationalisation.**

(9) **Banking habit in India is not well developed.** Until recently, banks had their operations restricted to the urban areas and mostly cities and big towns. **Rural banking is developing now at a fast rate.** Even today, about 400 towns and 5 lakhs of villages are unbanked.

(10) **Bank deposits in India are covered by deposit insurance.** Traditionally, banking habit in India is not well–developed. A large scale of bank failures after the Second World War (1939–1945) made the depositors shaky. Deposit Insurance scheme was introduced in 1962.

(11) **Recently, banks are opening large number of branches** both in rural and urban areas. Out of 29,741 offices of banks by 30.6.80, 12,628 are in rural areas.

(12) There are some **new developments in the banking business.** Many commercial banks are allowing term loans to their customers. Merchant banking, i.e. giving business advice to customers, has been introduced by some banks. The 'lead bank scheme' has made much headway. Under the scheme each bank, both nationalised and non-nationalised, has been allotted by the RBI some specific district or districts where that particular bank has to take the responsibility of promoting economic development through intensive study of the potentialities and providing credit and other banking facilities.

Working of the banks — The **bank deposits in India have been rising very sharply** during last few years. Taking into consideration all the scheduled banks of the country, the total deposits have increased from Rs. 820 crores in 1950-51 to Rs. 5,910 crores in 1970-71 and to Rs. 36,149 crores by December 1980. The banks are also now providing credit facilities to industry, trade and commerce as well as to agriculture on much larger scale than before. Total bank credit has expanded from Rs. 3,616 crores by the end of December 1969 to Rs. 23,766 crores by the end of December 1980. The share or agricultural advances to the total credit by public sector banks has gone up by 12.6% by June 1978. All the districts have been brought under the 'lead bank' scheme. By September 1980, there are about 33,000 bank branches with one bank for each 17,000 persons in place of 65,000 persons as found in 1969. In the past, each big industrial house had control over a big bank (e.g. the Tatas had control over the Central Bank of India, the Birlas had over the United Commercial Bank, etc.). The banks were managed mainly to serve the interests of the respective houses. After the nationalisation of 20 big banks, with the State Bank of India already under State control, the management of banks is being professionalised to the advantage of the business community as a whole. The nationalised banks control 85% of the total banking functions in the country.

But there is a common complaint that **the services of banks to the customers have vastly deteriorated.** This is a normal result of nationalisation. Indiscipline has set in among the staff. A large percentage of advances remains unrealised threatening the solvency of the banks. The Banking Enquiry Commission made some valuable suggestions for bank reform in its report in 1972 but, strangely, the Government has not implemented many of the recommendations. It is all the more strange that the Government has not been able to decide how the nationalised banks will be restructured. The nationalised banks are still competing with one another without having any uniform policy. Six regional consultative committees have been constituted consisting of representatives of State Governments and Union Territories and Chairman of nationalised banks for better coordination among them. Too much branch-banking is against banking norm.

COMMODITY MARKET

Definition — A commodity market or a commodity exchange can be defined as **an organisation or association which has a place where trading in some selected commodity or commodities is carried on under some fixed rules and regulations and among members only.** The **characteristics** of a commodity exchange are : (1) It is an association of some individuals. There are rules and regulations for membership depending on the constitution of the association. (2) In an exchange, either one or more than one commodity can be dealt in, though the former is more common. (3) There are some fixed rules and regulations for trading which are determined by the association itself. Those rules permit future trading, including speculation. (4) Transactions can take place only among members. (5) It has great similarity with a stock exchange. On the whole, **a commodity market is a kind of organised market.**

Types : The commodity markets **are classified** according to the nature of the commodities.

(1) **General** – In such a market a number of type of commodities are traded. This is not common.

(2) **Special** — Only one special commodity is traded in such a market. This is the more common type. Commodity markets can be further classified into : (a) **Agricultural** – In such markets, agricultural commodities like jute, cotton, wheat, tea, oilseeds etc. are dealt in. In India, we have all three types of markets. Some of them are of international character, e.g. tea market in India. Commodity markets dealing in agricultural produces are also known as **Produce Exchanges.** (b) **Non-agricultural** — There are commodity markets for almost all kinds of important metals like gold (bullion market), silver, copper, iron etc. There are organised markets for manufactured, or semi-manufactured goods also, like cotton goods, jute goods, wool, hides and skins, sugar etc. In India, there is commodity market for only one kind of manufactured goods, i.e. jute goods. There are wholesale as well as terminal markets for all kinds of commodities but they are not exactly commodity markets because future transactions do not take place in all such markets. On the whole, **in India, there are** organised markets for wheat, cotton, jute, jute goods, tea and oilseeds.

According to the nature of their objects, commodity markets may be **profit-sharing** or **non-profit sharing** among their members. The leading commodity exchanges are non-profit-sharing ones.

Characteristics of commodities — Commodities which satisfy some basic conditions can be traded in an organised market. The characteristics of commodities to be traded in a commodity market are :

(1) **Homogeneity** — The units of the commodity must be homogeneous, i.e. they must have uniformity so that it can be dealt in by samples or by description and can be understood by different parties in the same manner.

(2) **Gradability** — The commodity shall be capable of being graded according to quality. Different grades may have different brand names. Since only members do transactions in the market, they are all accustomed with the grades and brand names. Grading also helps trading, by sample or by description.

(3) **Durability** — The commodities must be durable or non-perishable. This is so because of the following reasons : (i) There is a system of forward contracts. The delivery may have to be made after a long time which may cover several months. (ii) The commodities have to be stored for adjusting the supply with the changing demand.

(4) **Inelastic but unrestricted supply** — The supply of such commodities is generally inelastic and even seasonal (as in case of agricultural commodities). But the supply must not be restricted by the Government or by any monopolist. Sometimes, of course, various artificial restrictions are created by the speculators.

(5) **Unit and volume of transaction** — In every commodity market, there is a minimum unit of sale. For example, jute or cotton cannot be traded by kg. or maund. The unit is in terms of some bales (each bale containing several 100 kg. or several maunds). Each transaction again is of several bales at a time.

(6) **Continuous demand** — Though there is somewhat regulated or even seasonal supply of the commodities, there must be continuous and regular demand for them. The demand is of daily nature and at the same time it may be international.

(7) **Price fluctuations** — The commodities are under the influence of price fluctuations. This is so because of inelastic supply but continuous demand and also because of the action of the speculators.

Functions — The commodity exchanges render many useful functions to the business community as a whole and specially to the dealers in the specific commodities. The functions are :

(1) A commodity market provides **a definite place** where the traders can do their transactions under some standard rules and regulations.

(2) The commodity markets for different commodities **make the adjustment between the demand for and supply of** the respective commodities which is necessary in the interests of industries and trade.

(3) The markets **provide regular information** about the prices of the commodities prevailing in the markets as well as their future trends. These are essential for taking decisions in the business world.

(4) In every market, there are rules for transactions as well as rules for membership. All these lead to **uniformity in the dealings.**

(5) In every market, there is a separate committee **to settle disputes among the members** by arbitration.

(6) Those commodity markets which deal in commodities of international importance provide opportunities **for exportable markets.**

Importance — On account of their useful functions, the commodity markets **assume great importance** in the economy of a country. They have also international significance. The services rendered by commodity markets are as follows :

(1) To the business community

The services rendered to the business community as a whole are :

(a) The commodity markets provide **regular and continuous markets** for different commodities which are generally used as raw materials in different industries or used for general consumption by the people. In the former group come jute, cotton, metals etc. and in the latter come tea, wool, sugar etc. The markets become steady and unscrupulous middlemen cannot exploit them.

(b) The **burden of risks** of irregularities in supplies and violent price fluctuations are **shouldered by professional risk-bearers** who are the members of the different markets.

(c) The manufacturers who use the commodities as raw materials can make **proper planning of production and costing of their products.**

(d) **Bank advances can be procured more conveniently** as there is regularity of production and supply. Banks make advances against stock of raw materials, finished products, etc.

(e) The businessmen engaged in trading in commodity markets are also well **protected by rules and regulations** of the markets concerned.

(f) Various **helpful speculative' transactions** like hedging, arbitrage (see below etc. enable the traders in the markets to take more risks in their dealings.

(2) To the society

(a) The society is benefited in the long run as there is **steadiness in the markets** of some major commodities, either in the field of trade or industry.

(b) **Foreign exchanges can be earned** by exports of commodities dealt in commodity markets of international significance.

(c) The **producers** of agricultural commodities are **encouraged because of steady and continuous markets.**

Organisation of commodity markets

Constitution — Commodity markets are constituted **mainly as incorporated bodies.** There are, however, some other forms of organisations but they are less important and in many cases not recognised by the Government. Again, most of the organisations are **non-profit sharing** ones. The big organisations in India like the East India Cotton Association of Bombay or the East India Jute Association of Calcutta are non-profit-sharing organisations while the Indian Exchange Ltd. of Amritsar is a profit-sharing organisation.

Membership — The nature of membership depends on the constitution of the market. Membership may be by **buying of shares or payment of subscription or by both** and every organisation has restrictions to membership. The members, however, do transactions on behalf of the outsiders comprising of the producers, the manufacturers, the speculators or the foreign buyers. As we find in a stock exchange, the members may be classified into jobbers and brokers. Almost all the members are engaged in speculative transactions. Many of them indulge in gamblings (mostly unofficially).

Management — The system of management depends on the constitution of the organisation. There may be either **a Board of Directors or a Managing Committee.** The composition of such board or committee depends on the rules of the organisation. Different standing committees or sub-committees on Finance, Arbitration, Clearing House or such other subjects are set up for day-to-day functions.

Types of transactions

Broadly speaking, there are two types of transactions : Cash and Future. The commodity markets, therefore, have the characteristics of organised markets. In some commodity marke, only cash contracts are executed but generally commodity markets are future markets. The two types of contracts, cash and future, are detailed below :

(1) **Cash contracts** — Under cash contracts, there are genuine transactions of buying and selling with **full delivery of goods and full payment of price.** These are also known as physical contracts as physically the goods are delivered. Every market sets up rules as regards the time within which the delivery has to be completed. Generally, the delivery shall be ready within 8 days. The cash contracts are, therefore, also known as ready delivery contracts.

Cash contracts can be further classified into two categories : (a) **Spot contracts** – Under a spot contract, the buyer agrees to make payment and the seller agrees to make the delivery **immediately or on the spot.** It is an executed contract like any other contract of sale. Once the parties agree to such contract they cannot fall back. (b) **Forward contracts** — Under a forward contract, neither the payment nor the delivery is required to be made on the spot or immediately. The agreement is made in the spot market but the parties **fix up an agreed date** when actual execution of the contract will take place. This is the most common form of cash contract.

It has to be noted that cash contracts need not be executed inside the 'exchange hall' or the premises of the market. A large number of cash contracts are executed outside the premises.

(2) **Future contracts** — These contracts are of speculative nature. There is **no need of actual or physical delivery, nor there is need of actual payment.** Transactions take place by way of adjustments under the rules and regulations of the market.

The features of future contracts are : (1) Such contracts can be entered into among members only. Outsiders can do such transactions only through members acting as brokers.

(2) Transactions shall be done on the 'floor' or the exchange or in the 'ring'.

(3) Each transaction shall be on the basis of one fixed grade called the 'basic grade' or 'contract grade' as determined by the exchange itself. This is determined according to the condition of supply of the commodity in the market. Once the basis is fixed, no mentioning of the grade in the contract is necessary. If the supply of that grade is not available then an alternative or 'tenderable grade' may be used.

(4) Not only the grade but the 'unit' is also fixed and the members can do transactions in multiples of that unit. Suppose the 'unit' in jute market is fixed as 200 bales; then the transactions will be on 200, 400, 600 etc. bales. No fraction will be allowed.

(5) Each commodity exchange also fixes some trading months for the commodity in a year. The members have to settle their contracts within the trading months and not according to their choice. Generally, the contracts are settled within three or four trading months. Once one of the trading month is chosen, the seller can choose any one day of the month for delivery or settlement.

(6) Transactions have to be done according to the rules and regulations of the market. If there is any dispute, it is settled by arbitration and for that there is a special sub-committee in the exchange.

(7) Every member has to deposit a certain percentage of each contract with the authorities of the exchange as margin deposit same as in a stock exchange. The percentage is fixed by the authorities of the exchange. This is to guard against defaults made by members as the transactions are generally based on oral commitments.

Thus it is to be observed that there is a great **difference between forward contracts and future contracts.** The main points of difference are : (a) Forward contracts are more common and less restrictive than future contracts. Future contracts must be carried out among members on the floor of the exchange. (b) Under forward contracts, ultimately delivery has to be made though the date of settlement may be postponed. Under future contracts, there may not be any physical delivery of goods. (c) Forward contracts are meant for genuine transactions while future contracts are speculative in character.

Speculative transactions

As in a stock exchange, all types of speculative transactions like carry over or 'badla', options or 'satta', hedging, arbitrage etc. are carried out in commodity exchanges. There are operations of bulls and bears and there is a clearing house in each commodity exchange. Hedging is a very important type of transaction here. Besides, there is spreading or straddling. These are discussed below.

Spreading or straddling — Actually what is known as arbitraging in a stock exchange, is known as spreading in a commodity exchange and that is again called straddling in the cotton market. This is nothing but buying the commodity in one market where the price is low and selling it in another market where it is high. It helps in stabilising prices and regulating supplies.

Hedging — Hedging is not a speculative transaction in true sense because it is not done to earn profit but to protect against loss. There are two opposite transactions of buying and selling, of the same amount, one in the 'spot' market and the other in the 'future' market, so that probable loss is offset by the gain in another. If there is a spot sale it is followed by a future or hedge purchase. Conversely, a spot purchase is hedged by a future sale. Manufacturers using industrial raw materials, which are traded in commodity exchanges and have seasonal or variable supplies, like jute, cotton etc., have to do hedging operations to keep the price steady so that they can keep the cost of production reasonably steady.

It has to be remembered that spot price and future price of the same commodity move in the same direction or harmoniously. There cannot be big difference between the two. Future contracts can be converted into actual contracts, if necessary. But there are various external and non-controllable factors which may upset the expectations in the market. Suppose, there is a crop failure or sudden big fall in the demand for jute goods in the world market. The Government may make huge purchase of some commodity in the market, e.g. purchase of wheat for making stock for the army when an outbreak of war is feared.

The **importance of hedging**, however, is great. Manufacturers are benefited, as they can protect themselves against risks arising out of price fluctuations of raw materials and also of finished products. Middlemen or stockists are benefited because they can manipulate the supply position better. Middlemen engaged in hedging operations can get better credit facilities from banks because they are not mere speculators. Ultimately, consumers are benefited as they can get the goods at, more or less, steady and, preferably at, reduced prices.

There are **limitations** too. The benefits of hedging can be enjoyed only when some conditions are fulfilled. The movement of prices in the spot and the future markets must move in the same direction. In the spot market, goods of all grades are transacted but in future market only the 'contract' or 'basis' grade. This creates confusion. The prices of all grades cannot move in the same direction. Moreover, the 'unit' of transaction in both types of market may not be the same. The price of a manufactured product depends on many factors and not only on the price of the raw material. But hedging in commodity markets is concerned with raw materials only.

SOME ORGANISED COMMODITY MARKETS IN INDIA

(1) **The Calcutta Tea Traders' Association** — This is an auction market for tea in Calcutta. Major part of the business used to be controlled by non-Indian brokers but gradually their importance is declining. It is a spot market and future contracts are not carried out. Tea is sold by auction by showing samples, and delivery and payment have to be completed within seven days from the date of the auction. Auction takes place on two days – Monday for leaf tea and Wednesday for dust tea. Business is done for 10 months, June to March, as tea has a seasonal market. There are big air-conditioned warehouses specially meant for tea. Recently, a second exchange for tea has been opened at Cochin in Kerala. This exchange generally handles the South Indian tea.

(2) **The East India Jute and Hessian Exchange Ltd.** — This is a recognised exchange for jute and jute products to carry out spot and forward trading but the forward trading can be allowed only within the city of Calcutta. Forward tradings in jute in other parts of the country are banned. The rules and bye-laws of the Exchange have been approved by the Government for the purpose of forward tradings. There are three different products : raw jute, hessian cloth and sacking bags. The Exchange fixes the contract grades, margin deposits by members and maintains a clearing system.

(3) **The East India Cotton Association Ltd.** — This Association, situated in Bombay, is the organised market for raw cotton. This is recognised by the Government to carry out forward tradings in raw cotton. It has the rules and bye-laws approved by the Government for the purpose. The Association fixes contract grades, delivery months spread over the year and maintains a clearing system.

(4) **Others** — There are a number of recognised markets for oil and oilseeds. For example : The Bombay Oilseeds Exchange Ltd. (for castor seed), the Ahmebabad Seeds Merchants'

Association (for oil), the Saurashtra Oil and Oilseeds Association Ltd., Rajkot (for groundnut and groundnut oil), the Madras Oilseeds and Oils Exchange Ltd. (for groundnut oil), etc.

The Government has also granted the Central India Cotton Association Ltd. forward tradings in cotton and cotton seed for a limited period. The Association has two premises or 'rings' – one at Indore for cotton and the other at Ujjain for cotton seed.

Regulation of Commodity markets

Since various malpractices are indulged into by members of commodity exchanges it has long been felt that some regulatory measures for commodity exchanges are necessary for healthy growth of such markets and for effective hedging transactions. The malpractices done by unscrupulous traders are of many types : making false or fictitious transactions, spreading of false rumours, matched orders for false buying, wash sales, etc. A market is under a 'corner' when it is fully in the hands of manipulators or under 'squeeze' when there is partial control by them. The British Government did not take any such step till the Second World War when, by the Defence of India Rules, forward tradings in most of the commodities were banned in the interest of war. After the war ended, the restriction was continued under Essential Supplies (Temporary) Act, 1946.

After independence, immediately after the introduction of the First Five-Year Plan, which had a bias for agricultural development, the Government came forward with comprehensive measures to control commodity markets. The Forward Contracts (Regulation) Act was passed in 1952, which was made effective from August 24, 1953. In the same year the Forward Markets Commission was set up under the Act. The Act itself has been amended in 1953, 1957 and 1960. The main provisions of the Act are :

(1) One distinct feature of the Act is formation of a Forward Markets Commission. It is composed of two to four members appointed by the Central Government, one of whom acts as the Chairman. The Government is to carry out control over the commodity markets mainly through the agency of the Commission. The major functions of the Commission are : (a) To make recommendation on granting or withdrawing recognition of commodity markets engaged in forward dealings. (b) To observe the operations in the commodity markets to make recommendations from time to time to the Government for taking steps in respect of the markets. (c) To collect and publish various types of information related to the position of demand, supply and prices of commodities traded in commodity markets. (d) To inspect the accounts of the commodity markets and the nature of operations in the forward markets and to make recommendations for improvement. (e) To submit to the Government periodical reports on the functioning of the commodity markets and on the operation of the Act. (f) To discharge the responsibilities on behalf of the Government conferred upon the Commission in respect of making of rules for the markets, asking from the markets explanations on different matters, issuing directives to the markets and suspending business of any market, if necessary.

(2) Any commodity market where forward trading is to be carried out shall get recognised by the Government on the recommendation of the Commission. (There are hundreds of commodity markets in India out of which only about 26 markets are recognised.)

(3) For getting recognition, a commodity market must frame rules and bye-laws according to the provisions of the Act and get them approved by the Government. The bye-laws should include : (a) fortnightly clearing of the transactions; (b) establishment of a Clearing House for the purpose; (c) demanding margin deposits from members on futures contracts; (d) fixation of rates of brokerage; (e) penalty for violation of bye-laws, etc.

(4) The Act has exempted all non-transferable spot transactions from its purview. Such contracts are settled on due dates on the basis of actual delivery and actual payment. The day of settlement or the manner of settlement is fixed and so no control is necessary. But, if the Government so desires, regulatory measures can be imposed on such contracts by notification.

(5) The Act is applicable on all types of contracts other than non-transferable spot contracts like the ready delivery contracts and forward delivery contracts. The ready delivery contracts need settlement within a period not exceeding 11 days. Transferable spot contracts are transferable from one person to another. There shall be definite rules and regulations for final settlement between the first seller to the last buyer.

(6) The Act has banned option dealings in all commodities.

(7) The Act, by amendment of 1960, has prohibited all kinds of private dealings ('dabba' dealings) or kerb dealings, i.e. dealings outside office hours.

(8) The Government is empowered to nominate not more than 4 members on the Governing Body of a recognised commodity exchange. Further, each commodity exchange has to keep members in its Govering Body representing outside interests, not exceeding 3.

(9) The Government is empowered to withdraw recognition, to supersede the Governing Body and to suspend the business of any recognised exchange for up to 7 days.

(10) The Act provides a list of penalties including fines as well as imprisonments for violation of the provisions of the Act.

SUMMARY

Market — Market exists when there is a commodity (or service) and there are buyers of, and sellers for, it. In a market there is a competition among sellers, among buyers and among buyers and sellers. Every goods or service is produced for its potential market. Market is an important social organisation. **Characteristics** of a good market – Wide and steady demand. Facility for movement of the commodity. Identification of the commodity. Easy transfer of ownership. Freedom of contracts. Market can be **classified** on the basis of : (a) Area or geography. (b) Unit of sale (wholesale or retail). (c) Periodicity (long period, short period). (d) nature and degree of competition (perfect or imperfect). (e) Methods of transaction (ordinary or organised markets). (f) Position of sellers (primary, secondary and terminal). In an organised market futures transactions take place i.e. transactions take place on goods which do not exist but are expected. The goods must satisfy some conditions – universal or continuous demand but seasonal supply, can be graded and sampled, durable and traded in bulk. Only members can transact in an organised market and so there must be some organisation with rules and regulations of membership and transactions. Organised markets are classified according to the nature of goods transacted – share market, commodity markets (gold, silver, wool etc.). produce or agricultural commodity markets (jute, cotton, tea etc.). Besides, there is the money market or the banking system of the country and the capital market for securities meant for long term investment and the share market is a part of it. The different markets are regulated by different Acts.

The **importance** of the market can be justified on the following grounds : (a) It helps satisfaction of wants of the buyers and exhaustion of stocks of the sellers. (b) Production becomes fruitful. (c) It raises standard of living of the people. (d) Demand for and supply of goods are adjusted. (e) Without the money market business is not possible. (f) Without the capital market capital formation becomes difficult. (g) Markets provide employments. (h) Markets provide economic indicators.

Capital market can be defined as the market for long term funds. The borrowers are : bodies corporate, the Government and the public bodies. The lenders are : the individuals (persons and bodies corporate), the financial institutions, the banks, the insurance companies, the investment trusts and the various types of funds. The long term funds are available in the forms of shares, debentures, Government promissory notes, etc. There are specialised agents like underwriters and brokers who facilitate sale of securities. Before independence, in India, the capital market was not very organised. It is developing since independence and after the passing of the Securities Contracts (Regulation) Act, 1956, to control the share markets. The State now plays a predominant role through financial institutions, promotional institutions, nationalised banks and insurance companies. There has been a need for establishing financial and promotional or developmental institutions in the public sector because of the following reasons : (a) The rate of capital formation has been low. (b) Capital in India is shy. (c) The capital market in India is not well organised. (d) The banks are purely commercial banks. (e) There has been lack of industrial entrepreneurs. (f) Special assistance is necessary for small and medium scale industries. (h) Investments must be channelised to serve the objectives of Five-Year Plans. So far there are six **financial institutions** set up by the Central Goverment. In addition, there are State Financial Corporations : (1) The Industrial Finance Corporation of India (1948)) – Capital (including share capital, borrowings, bonds etc.) : About Rs. 220 crores. Objects : To grant long term loan up to 25 years, to guarantee loan and to underwrite shares and securities as well as assistance for management to large-scale industries. Working : So far granted financial assistance about Rs. 526 crores. (2) The Industrial Development Bank of India (1964) – Capital (including share capital, bonds borrowings etc.) : About Rs. 380 crores. Objects : To provide long term assistance to and promote large-scale enterprises and also to assist through refinancing or to direct financing as well as by taking over other financial institutions. Working : Total value of assistance stands at about Rs. 3,000 crores. (3) The Industrial Credit and Investment Corporation of India (1955) — Originally incorporated in the private sector, but now the Government is the single biggest shareholder. Capital (including shares, bonds, borrowings etc.) : About Rs. 340 crores. Objects: To provide financial (by way of granting and guaranteeing loans or by subscription) and non-financial (managerial and technical) assistance to large and medium and even to small-scale industries in the private sector. Working: Total value of assistance about Rs. 676 crores. (4) Industrial Re-construction Corporation of India (1971)—Capital (including shares, bonds, borrowings etc.): About Rs. 15 crores. Object: To provide financial and non-financial assistance to reconstruct sick industries. Working: Total direct financial assistance amounts to about Rs. 57 crores and indirect assistance about Rs. 62 crores. (5) Unit Trust of India (1963)–Capital (including shares capital and 'unit' capital): About Rs. 260 crores. Objects: Investing the unit capital collected from the public in selected securities. Working: Investment about Rs. 185 crores. (6) The Industrial Refinance Corporation of India – now merged into the Industrial Development Bank of India. (7) State Financial Corporation – So far there are 18 SFC's. Capital (including, shares, bonds, borrowings etc. of all the 18 SFC's): About Rs. 372 crores. Objects: To grant long-term loan or guarantee loanss to small and medium size industries. Working: Total assistance about Rs. 954 crores. So far there are two major **developmental institutions** established by the Central Government. In addition, different States have established similar institutions : (1) The National Industrial Development Corporation (1954) — Capital: Rs. 10 lakhs. Objects: To carry out research on industries and technology and to prepare projects. Working: Research and discovery of new types of products and technology. Consultancy work in India and abroad. (2) National Small Industries Corporation (1955) – Capital: Rs. 50 lakhs. Objects: To arrange supply of machines, raw materials etc. to run industrial training centres and to procure markets for small-scale industries. Working: Rendering service to about 21,000 units registered with it.

The Securities Market —It comes into existence **when and where different types of securities (shares, debentures, Govt. Promissory Notes etc.) are bought and sold. Two types:** (1) New Issues market – Market for shares and debentures of new companies or existing companies making new offers. Offers are made directly by the companies or indirectly through intermediaries like issue houses, managing brokers, underwriters etc. (2) Second-hand market or the Stock Exchange or the Share Market where securities are exchanged between existing holders and new holders. A **stock exchange** is an association of persons established for the purposes of assisting, regulating and controlling business of buying, selling and dealing in securities. It is an organ of capitalistic society with the following **functions:** (a) Provides ready market for securities . (b) Provides scope for proper valuation of securities.(c) Channelises savings to correct investments. (d) Helps capital formation. (e) Exerts influence on better company management. (f) Protects interests of investors. (g) Provides scope for speculation. The importance of stock exchange, therefore, is very great. It is the business of all businesses. **Services to the investors:** Ready market for securities. Liquidity or easy transferability. Protection by rules and regulations. Appraisal of the real value of the investments. Guidance as to when and where to invest. **Services to the companies:** Goodwill is increased. Appraisal of the real value of the shares. Popularity and appreciation of value of the securities. No erratic fluctuation of prices of shares. **Services to the society:** Regular capital market. Easy capital formation. Economic barometer, i.e. an index of economic condition. Fostering economic growth. **Dis-services** — Speculation often degenerates into gambling. It has harmful effects and it is difficult to control.

Nature of stock exchange operations: (1) It has all the characteristics of an organised market. (2) Transactions are done only by members under definite rules and regulations within fixed hours in a day. (3) Speculation is allowed on selected securities under restrictions. (4) Official quotations of prices are regularly published. (5) **Transactions** are done by bidding or auction. **Two types of people** visit stock exchanges: (1) Investors – they invest savings for dividends or interests. (2) Speculators – they buy and sell shares to earn profit out of price difference. Legitimate speculation is economic and good as it stops wild fluctuation of prices and adjusts supply with demand. But illegitimate speculation or gambling is bad and uneconomic and has to be controlled. **Speculation** is done after intelligent study of the market. **Gambling** is mere taking of chances. Gambling means settlement of transactions by various mechanisms without actual delivery of securities and payment of full prices. Gamblings are banned by the Securities Contracts (Regulation) Act of 1956 by which stock exchanges are controlled in India. **Procedure** of a stock exchange transaction: Any person wanting a transaction (either as a buyer or a seller) has to follow a definite procedure: (1) Appointment of a broker (who is a member of the Stock Exchange). (2) Placing an order with the broker. The order can be placed in different ways depending on whether the person is an investor or a speculator. (3) Making of a contract between the broker of the buyer and the broker of the seller. (4) Making of a contract between each broker with his client based on terms already settled and noted in 'note – books' of the brokers. (5) Settlement of the transaction depending on the nature of transaction: (a) ready delivery i.e. immediate delivery of the security and payment of price; (b) forward delivery, i.e. delivery, shall be made on a future agreed date when payment will be made; (c) difference settlement, i.e. on a future date the transaction will be settled by payment of difference between the agreed price and the price on that future date (no actual delivery and no full payment of price); (d) carry-over, i.e. on the future agreed date of settlement, no settlement is made but another date of settlement is fixed (the date is carried over) at the instance of the buyer or the seller and the party wanting to carry over has to pay some money to the other party to make him agree to the change of date. The last two methods of settlement are examples of speculation. The Govt. is empowered to ban speculative transactions. At present all are banned. There are some **special methods of speculation :** (a) Hedging – A speculator does simultaneously a transaction of sale and purchase, to offset loss from one transaction by gain in the other one. (b) Arbitrage — When the same security is dealt in different stock exchanges, it is bought in that exchange where the price is low and sold in that exchange where the price is high. (c) Option dealings – A speculator makes a promise to buy or sell a security with another speculator and keeps some deposit of money with the option that on the agreed future date he may or may not buy the security or may or may not sell the security. If he does not buy or sell, then the deposit money will be forfeited by the other party. This is pure gambling and is totally banned. (d) Other methods – cornering (causing artificial shortage of a security), rigging (forcing the price of a security up) and wash sales (fictitious transactions of selling and then buying). **Stimulants to gamblings** – There are certain mechanisms which encourage gamblings : (1) Margin trading – a client is asked by his broker to keep some deposit money just like a security. The broker does buying and selling on verbal instructions of the client. If the broker has to pay any difference money on behalf of the client, there is no fear as the margin money is there. The client is allowed to speculate on up to that amount so that the probable loss does not exceed the margin money. (2) Blank transfer – Share certificates are transferred from hand to hand without any endorsement. There is no record as to who is the transferee and thereby capital gains tax can be avoided. No stamp duty is paid. **Causes of price fluctuations :** Prices of securities fluctuate in a stock exchange because of the following reasons : (1) Demand and supply – Price fluctuate on account of the interplay of the forces of demand and supply. (2) The taxation, labour, import-export and such other policies of the Government cast influence of prices. (3) Political situation – Political instability lowers the prices. (4) Economic situation – Period of prosperity or period of depression forces the prices up or pulls the prices down, respectively. (5) International situation – It has also effects as the economies of countries are inter-linked. (6) Action of speculators – speculators deliberately cause price fluctuations to earn profit through price differences. Price fluctuations are of three types – daily, periodical and cyclical. **Types of speculators :** (1) Bull – A bull makes offers to buy and buy and thereby pushes the price up and then sells out to make profit through price difference. (2) Bear – A bear makes offers to sell and sell and thereby pulls the price down and then buys in to make profit out of price difference. (3) Stag – a stag makes applications for new issues creating demand and thereby raising the market price and sells out the allotment letters at a higher price. There are some other types.

Stock Exchanges in India — The first Stock Exchange in India was established in Bombay in 1875. At present, there are 13 recognised stock exchanges in the following cities – Bombay, Calcutta, Madras, Ahmedabad, Delhi, Hyderabad, Indore, Bangalore, Kanpur and Poona. Out of these Bombay, Calcutta, Delhi, Ahmedabad and Madras, have permanent recognition. The licence of operation has to be renewed from time to time by all other stock exchanges. There are some unrecognised markets. The composition, management, membership rules etc. are different for different stock exchanges. Some are limited companies (e.g. Calcutta Stock Exchange) while others are just associations (e.g. Bombay Stock Exchange). Membership may be by buying shares or paying subscription or both. All the members are broker members. In London Stock Exchange there are two types of members : **Jobbers** – They do transactions only with members. **Brokers** – They do transactions on behalf of outside clients on brokerage basis. In Bombay Stock Exchange there is a class of members called 'Tarvaniwalas' who are like jobbers. Members can appoint 'authorised clerks' to help them. The total number of members in Bombay Stock Exchange is about 500 and in Calcutta 1,120. The total number of companies whose shares are enlised in Calcutta is 630 (Bombay 620). The total number of securities enlisted in Calcutta is 1,070 (Bombay 1,140). The total number of cleared securities in Calcutta is 47 (Bombay 67). Speculation is done only on selected securities called cleared securities. Settlement of accounts is done through book entries through a Clearing House (just like banks). The Bombay Stock Exchange is the biggest one in India. **Stock Exchange reform** – Many times during British rule, attempts were made to control gamblings in stock exchange but without much effect. After independence, the Stock Exchange Contracts (Regulation) Act was passed in 1956, empowering the Government to grant recognition to stock exchanges, to ban gamblings, to regulate the procedure or transactions and to interfere in the management of stock exchanges. The Act also provides the procedure of enlistment of shares of a company in a stock exchange. A Directorate of Stock Exchange has been established for the purpose with its headquarters in Bombay. The Act is criticised as it fails to control (unofficial) gamblings. **The importance of stock exchange in India is declining** because of the emergence of the public sector. For listing of securities, a company has to make an application with a fee giving details of the company and its past performance (in case of an existing company) and assurance to supply copies of final accounts regularly and such other obligations. There are advantages and limitations of enlistment.

Money market — It ia a market for dealing in monetary assets mainly of short-term character. Monetary assets mean short-term loans to bridge the gap between current expenditure and income. Short-term means several days or months or even years. But the loan (unlike capital) has to be repaid sooner or later. Direct accommodation can be obtained from banks (the organised sector of the money market) or moneylenders (the unorganised sector of the money market). Indirect accommodation can be obtained through deferred payments (while buying machines etc.). The organised sector consists of : (a) The central bank at the apex (the Reserve Bank of India – in India). (b) The member banks under the control of the central bank. A bank is a dealer in debts. It takes loans (as deposits) from the depositors paying interest (on time deposits only like Savings Deposit and Fixed Deposit and not on demand deposit like Current Deposit) at a rate and it lends money to borrowers (the clients of the bank) at a higher rate of interest, thereby earning an income. Money includes currency notes and negotiable instruments like cheques. The central bank dictates how much accommodation can be given by member banks and to whom (the question of priority sectors) and on what terms. Banks are of the following types : Commercial banks (giving short-term accommodation), industrial banks (giving long-term accommodation – not found in India), exchange banks (doing foreign exchange transactions), cooperative banks, land development banks (giving agricultural credit against land as security) and postal savings banks. Commercial banks carry on business of lending on the following **principles** : (a) Profitability – Profit must be made through difference between rates of interest paid and charged. (b) Solvency – The accommodation must be secured by security offered by the borrowers. (c) Liquidity – The security must be easily saleable. **Types of accommodation :** Indirectly banks offer accommodation by issuing letter of credit or giving guarantee against loans. Banks offer accommodation directly through overdraft (allowing a client to overdraw up to certain limit for a certain period), eash credit (overdraft facility as a regular feature) loan (giving a lump sum money as advance) and discounting of bills (i.e. Bills of Exchange). The **extent of bank accommodation** depends on : (a) the demand for it; (b) the security offered; (c) the rate of interest; (d) directives of the central bank. Every loan creates fresh deposit as the borrower makes payment to his creditors (by cheque) and they deposit the money with their respective bank accounts. Banks also render various advisory functions to businessmen. This is called Merchant Banking.

Money market in India — In India, there are both unorganised and organised sectors in the money market. The unorganised sector has dominance in the rural areas. But the organised sector is developing and the banking habit is developing among the common people with the opening of large number of branches by banks, including in rural areas, since the nationalisation of 14 big banks in 1969 (followed by nationalisation of 6 more banks in April 1980). In the organised sector, there are nationalised and non-nationalised banks as well as some foreign banks. There is no industrial bank. Few banks do foreign exchange operations (mostly foreign banks do it). A new type of bank called Rural Bank has been introduced. The State Bank of India (with 7 subsidiaries – they were originally banks of native states) is the biggest bank. It was formed in 1955 by nationalising the Imperial Bank of India, the biggest foreign bank operating in the country. The Reserve Bank of India is the central bank and the bank of all other banks. It controls the money supply (both currency and credit) and foreign exchange operations. It is the bank of the Government. The State Bank of India also functions as bank of the Government. The Exim Bank, owned by the Central Government, looks after financing of export-import transactions. The nationalised banks control 85% of the total bank deposits. The number of branches of banks and the amount of deposits are rising very fast. Bank accommodation is now provided to so far neglected sectors like agriculture, small scale industries etc. which are now called priority sectors. Every bank is entrusted to see the development of a particular area and it is the Lead Bank of that area. But the quality of banking service, since nationalisation, has declined. The earnings of banks have also declined because of high operational costs.

Commodity market — A commodity market or a commodity exchange is an organisation or an association which has a place where trading in some selected commodity or commodities is carried on under some fixed rules and regulations and among members only. It satisfies all the characteristics of an organised market. **Types :** (1) General – a number of commodities are traded, e.g. spice market. (2) Special – only one commodity is traded, e.g. jute market. Commodity markets, where agricultural commodities are traded (like jute, cotton, wheat etc.) are also known as Produce Exchanges. Commodity markets may be profit-sharing among its members or non-profit-sharing. Goods traded in a commodity market must satisfy the following conditions : Homogeneity, gradability, durability, inelastic but unrestricted supply, trading in bulk, continuous demand and subject to price fluctuations. **Functions :** (1) A definite place for transactions. (2) Makes adjustment between inelastic supply and continuous demand. (3) Supplies regular information about commodities. (4) Enforces uniformity in transactions. (5) Settles disputes among members. (6) Provides opportunities for exports. **Importance** to the business community – Regular and continuous markets, risks shouldered by professional risk-bearers, proper planning possible for manufactures, easier bank advances, protected by rules of trading, good effects of speculation. Importance to the society – steadiness in the markets, opportunities of earning foreign exchange through organised exports, encouragement to production. **Organisation** – Organised either as profit-sharing or non-profit-sharing among members. Membership either by buying shares in case of limited companies or by paying subscription in case of ordinary associations. **Types of transactions –** (1) Cash contract – Settlement by full delivery and full payment of price. This can be done on the spot or on a future agreed date (forward contract). (2) Future contract – Same as in stock exchange with some additional special features. In India there are a number of commodity and produce exchanges of which three are important : Jute, Cotton and Tea. The commodity markets are controlled by the Forward Contracts (Regulation) Act of 1952. A Forward Markets Commission has been appointed to grant recognition to commodity markets and to regulate their activities.

CHAPTER EIGHT

Government And Business

SOCIAL CONTROL OF BUSINESS

Meaning — The term **business means repeated buying and selling of goods or services.** In fact, it covers all types of gainful or economic activities. The **term state means politically organised body of people usually occupying a definite territory.** In other words, the State comprises all the people within a political territory. It includes both the business and the non-business communities. A State has to be ruled or governed. In the old days there were kings. Today most of the countries have democratic form of government, i.e. a government by elected representatives of the people. There are totalitarian or communist states where a single political party has absolute power.

Whatever may be the nature of the State and whatever may be the political ideology followed by the powers to be, there is a common feature that **the State should and does exercise some control** on business either marginally or considerably or totally. Even under freedom of enterprise, some State control is necessary in the interest of the society and even for the benefit of the businessmen themselves. Laws are necessary to regulate human behaviour. The State has to maintain internal law and order and external security so that business can be carried on peacefully.

RELATIONSHIP BETWEEN GOVERNMENT AND BUSINESS

There is a very close relationship between Government and business. In the past, however, things were different. Most of the States believed in the principle of laissez *faire.* According to this principle, the State would not interfere in business but would engage itself in maintaining law and order and to protect the people from any external threat. It was believed that **through freedom of enterprise** there should be survival of the fittest and by that **the greatest good to be achieved to the greatest number of people.** But the State would enact various laws to regulate human behaviour in business as well as non-business life. Under this ideology, the capitalistic system of economy evolved. Under **the capitalistic system** there had been a fast economic growth but it was accompanied with economic inequality in the distribution of wealth. As a counter–measure to capitalism, **the socialistic system,** has been introduced. Under this system, the State has absolute control over the economic activities. Under the socialistic economy, the rate of economic growth is not so fast but there is equitable distribution of wealth. A *via-media* between the two systems is the system of **mixed economy** where both the public sector and the private sector co-exist and cooperate. This system is practised in most of the countries and is believed to be a better course for faster economic growth without much conflict or dissatisfaction. In India, a policy of mixed economy is practised with a view to establishing a socialistic pattern of society. At present, we have **democratic socialism** which means socialism without sacrificing individual freedom.

A CASE FOR INDIA

In the context of India, we observe **four types of relationship between Government and business.** They are as follows :

(1) **Regulation** — The State adopts various regulatory measures to exercise control over business. These measures are in different forms :

(a) **Planning** — The entire field of economic activities has been brought under economic planning and for that purpose the National Planning Commission has been set up. Business in the private sector can be established and carried out within the framework of the Five-year or One-year Plans as the case may be. The freedom of enterprise in our country today is, in a sense, limited freedom with regard to the choice of business. The **State reserves** certain business for itself.

(b) **Policies** — The Government (i.e., the State — here the terms State and Government are used in the same sense, though they are not the same) has different policies like the Industrial Policy, the Fiscal Policy, the Commercial Policy, the Industrial Licensing Policy, etc. which regulate business activities. Practically, the Government controls business by virtue of such policies.

(c) **Laws** — There are different kinds of commercial and labour laws to regulate contractual relationships in the business world among the business people themselves, among the buyers and the sellers and among the employers and employees. The last type of relationship is very important because on that production and productivity largely depend.

(d) **Taxation** — The State needs funds to maintain administration, to maintain the defence, and to expend on developmental activities. The State itself is in business and for that purpose it needs capital. The main source of the public revenue is tax. The people as a whole, and the business people in particular, have to pay a variety of taxes, both direct and indirect. New types of taxes are continuously introduced and the rates of existing taxes are enhanced. Such takings disturb business plans. Taxation can be called a kind of interference by the State. But progressive direct taxes are necessary to remove inequality of wealth in the interest of the people as a whole.

(e) **Controlling monopoly** — Under the policy of freedom of enterprise, competition grows. But, very soon, competition becomes unfair or among unequals. Those who succeed in competition acquire economic strength by virtue of which they consolidate their positions and gradually try to drive out others and establish monopoly. The Government has enacted the MRTP (Monopolies Restrictive Trade Practices) Act to stop concentration of economic power in the hands of a few. New licences for setting up industries are not given to the big industrial houses falling under the Act. The FERA (Foreign Exchange Regulation Act) has been passed to control foreign investments and domination in Indian business.

(f) **Healthy capital formation** — Business needs capital. In these days of large scale operations, a large amount of capital has to be invested. There is identification between investment and ownership. Further, investment comes from savings and, as in India the per capita income is low, the rates of savings and the amounts of individual savings are low. Unless there is safety and prospectiveness, such small savers cannot invest. Keeping such objective conditions in view, the Government has totally recast the Companies Act in 1956 to encourage investment in shares. The company form of organisation is undoubtedly the best form and so public companies must be made popular with a real 'public' character. Simultaneously, the Securities Contracts (Regulation) Act has been passed to control the securities market.

(g) **Checking speculation** — A large section of the business community has tendency to speculation and gambling which have harmful effects on the economy as a whole. Different legislations like the Securities Contracts (Regulation) Act and the Forward Contracts (Regulation) Act have been enacted to control unhealthy speculation and gambling in organised markets. The Gold Control Order is another significant example.

(h) **Checking hoarding, etc.** — Some businessmen have tendency to take recourse to hoarding, blackmarketing and such other malpractices to create artificial shortage of goods and raising of prices to make unusual profits. These are checked by passing the Essential Commodities Act. Time to time, emergency measures in the forms of Ordinances and Acts are taken for the purpose.

(i) **Nationalisation** — When regulatory measures fail to yield results or when some business unit or an industry as a whole becomes uneconomic, the Government takes it over or nationalises the industry as a whole in public interest. The Industries (Development and Regulation) Act empowers the Government to do so. If necessary, an Ordinance is passed for the purpose followed by comprehensive legislation. The insurance business as a whole, the banking business (substantial part), etc, have been taken over. In the same process, individual units like Indian Iron and Steel Company is now in the hands of the Government. The Government has established the State Trading Corporation (and its subsidiaries), the Food Corporation etc. to monopolise in the trade of some essential commodities either in the foreign or in local markets for ensuring equitable distribution as well as channelisation of exports. Sometimes the Government follows a **dual policy** as we see in case of distribution of sugar. There is a free market and at the same time the Government makes a 'levy' taking control over a part of the total production for public distribution. In big cities, foodgrains are completely under public distribution through rationing and in towns there is partial public distribution through modified rationing. Import-export business is completely under Government control through a system of compulsory licensing and restricted use of foreign exchange. Certain goods can be imported or exported only through Government Agencies. There is compulsory inspection for quality control of exportable goods. Heavy import duties and, to a great extent, export duties are indirect ways of restricting the operations. All these activities of the Government come under the over-all policies — Industrial, Fiscal, etc. (see above). It appears that the Government is more keen on regulating trading activities because the chances of malpractices by unscrupulous businessmen are more in this branch of business. But **how far the Government has sufficient and efficient machinery** to give effect to all these regulatory measures is a different question. The honesty and sincerity of the staff of the Government, including the high-ups, however, are not beyond doubts.

(2) **Assistance** — As declared by the Government in its Industrial Policy (see below), the Government assists, the business in the private sector in various ways for its faster and healthy development. Some of the ways are given below:

(a) **Building up the infra-structure** — In an underdeveloped country, it is the primary responsibility of the State to build up the infra-structure for the economic development of the country. In India, there has been no exception. Since independence, the country is continuously developing the infra-structure by virtue of its own resources and with the help of other developed countries as well as international organisations like the World Bank, the International Development Authority, etc. India today is no longer an under-developed country. She is now in the second list — the list of developing countries. The different aspects of infra-structure development are as follows:

(i) **Education** — This is perhaps the primary aspect. In India, all attempts are being made, though not sufficient yet, to develop general and technical including managerial education. A large number of schools, colleges and universities have been established for general education and primary education is being made free to motivate the people since low income prevents people from sending their children to schools. A large variety of institutions for technical education and technological research have been set up. A liberal policy is adopted for allowing individuals to go abroad for higher technical education.

(ii) **Capital** — Capital plays the vital role in business. A large number of financial institutions have been sponsored by the State to offer long-term financial accommodation to small, medium and large scale industries. Moreover, encouragement is given to different forms of small savings through buying of Savings Certificates, Units, etc. taking of life policies, tax concessions on earnings from small savings, etc. , all leading to capital formation. Control over securities market is another indirect way to encourage investment. Same can be said about the total revision of the company law and introduction of Provident Fund and such other laws.

(iii) **Power** — Without power, neither industries can run nor transport can move. Power generation needs formidable investment and comprehensive planning which are beyond the means of the private sector. Power is to be carried down to the remotest parts of the country. Since the introduction of economic planning, great emphasis has been laid on power generation from all the possible sources and specially from water. Quite rightly, it is completely under State control. Extensive and intensive efforts are made to find out sources of oil for substitution of imports. India is in the grip of power crisis, particularly in certain parts of the country, e.g. West Bengal. Such a crisis, however, could not be foreseen and might be for faulty planning or unplanned utilisation or simply a man-made situation.

(iv) **Transport** — The economy cannot move without transport. Importance of transport is all the more significant in a vast country like India with mountains, rivers, and forests standing in the way of easy movement. Development of transport means the development of the tracks, terminals and vehicles making industry and power generation. All these need technical education and capital as well as a comprehensive planning. Except road transport and partly water transport, railways and airways are completely under State control for a coordinated internal and external transport linkage. Transport has made tremendous progress during the Five Year Plans.

(b) **Indirect financing** — The Government helps the private sector business by providing indirect finance in the following ways :

(i) Making arrangement for hire-purchase of machinery or standing as a guarantor for such deferred payments.

(ii) Making arrangement for supply of raw materials with convenient provision for central storing. Such assistance is provided to the small industries through the National Small Industries Corporation. There are such corporations at State levels also.

(c) **Procuring market** — The National Small Industries Corporation also helps the small industries in finding out the market for their products. Orders are procured from different Government departments.

(d) **Preparing projects** — The National Industries Development Corporation has been set up to look after the growth of such industries which do not exist but there is a need for them. The Corporation prepares the projects of such new industries or new lines of production in existing industries. The Corporation itself promotes such industries either by itself or in collaboration with the private sector. The Central Government plays the role of the promoter.

There are such corporations at State levels also.

(e) **Helping export** — Products of small producers are exported through the State Trading Corporation.

(f) **Granting subsidy or bounty or protection** — Industries unable to stand on their own legs because of foreign competition or higher cost of production are helped by the Government in the following manner : (i) Bounty or a lump sum money is paid to such an industry to improve its scale of production and thereby to reduce the cost (ii) Regular subsidies are paid to fill up the gap between the actual cost of production and the competitive cost of production which should be paid until that lower level of cost is reached. (iii) Protection is granted to a developing industry by imposing high rates of import duty to save it from foreign competition. Such assistance is given particularly to those industries which have export potentiality.

(g) **Establishing Departments and Agencies** — The Government has its Department of Commercial Intelligence and Statistics to supply regularly statistics and other forms of information about different industries. The Publications Division publishes various journals useful for the business world like the Trade Journal, the Labour Journal, etc. Different Agencies have been established like the Small Investment Service Institute to provide all types of help, e.g. preparation of projects, linking with banks for getting finance, etc. to new and small entrepreneurs. Entrepreneurship Development Training is also carried out by it. Same training is also rendered by the Indian Investment Centre whose main function is to find out possibilities of foreign collaboration and to supply the foreign collaborations with information about India's business world. All these agencies have their own useful publications.

(3) **Cooperation** — The Government cooperates with the private sector in two broad manners :

(a) **Macro-level** — At the macro-level there is demarcation of industries into the public sector and the private sector. Both these are expected to cooperate with each other and are complementary in principle. Further, there are some industries where the existing units in private sector will continue but the Government will establish all the new units, e.g. the iron and steel industry. Sometimes the Government is allowing new units in the private sector, though, basically, the industry is in the public sector, e.g. fertiliser industry.

(b) **Micro-level** — With the introduction of Joint Sector there is an experiment of mixed economy at the micro-level. The Government controls the finance while private entrepreneurs control the management in a Joint Sector unit.

(4) **Others** — There are some other ways by which the Government helps the business world. The Government functions as an **arbitrator** through tribunals related to labour dispute, disputes on taxation as well as disputes on duties. The Government arranges **fairs and exhibitions** and the Government also participates in fairs and exhibitions held in other countries for the development of trade and industry. It has become a common practice that the Finance or Commerce or Industry Minister is invited to **inaugurate** the annual general meetings of different Chambers of Commerce. At such conferences, the views of the Government and the business community related to business are freely exchanged for better cooperation and guidance. The Government has set up **Export Promotion Councils** for types of products to encourage exports through publicity of those products in foreign countries and doing liaison work.

On the whole, it is **the duty of the State to maintain** law and order, to assure internal security, and to pursue a sound economic policy so that a **proper social and economic environment** is created where business activities can be carried out. Everystate is now a welfare State and it is wedded to the policy of doing welfare to the puple of the State. To achive the objective – the State should interfere in business activities through its Government. It regulates the economic policy of the country. The term economic policy is a wide term which can be broken down into Commercial Policy , Fiscal Policy etc.

COMMERCIAL POLICY

Meaning — In Business Organisation, the term Commerce means all the activities meant for the removal of hindrances standing in the way of trade, i.e. movement of goods from the place of production to the place of consumption. But the term Commercial Policy (also known as Trade Policy) in relation to a Government has a different and specific meaning. Commercial Policy means **the policy in respect of import and export.** Import and export are reciprocal terms and are collectively known as foreign trade. Each country cannot produce all types of goods needed by her people. On the principle of Comparative Costs (introduced by Ricardo, the great economist), a country will specialise in the production of that commodity (commodities) which it can produce at a cheaper cost in comparison with that of other countries and will exchange the surplus production with the surplus production of another country which that country can produce at a comparatively cheaper cost. **Foreign trade, therefore, arises out of geographical division of labour.**

The theory sounds very reasonable. **It appears that, through foreign trade, every country will be able to get the best product of every variety and that too at a cheaper cost.** It also appears that there is free movement of goods from one country to another. **In practice, however, such things do not happen.** The Government of no country allows free foreign trade. **Almost every Government controls the foreign trade** of its own country for the following reasons :

(a) If free trade is allowed there is every possibility that imports will be more than exports and so the country will be indebted to other countries. It is a situation of adverse balance of payments. **No Government allows adverse balance of payments.**

(b) Payments in foreign trade are involved with different currencies which are exchanged with one another. The basic exchange rate between any two currencies is fixed by the International Monetary Fund, an international organisation established in 1944 for the purpose of ensuring flow of trade among countries. The rate fluctuates with the changes in the volumes of imports and exports between two countries. If there is more export (there is favourable balance of payments), the rate goes in the favour of the exporting country. If there is more import (there is adverse or unfavourable balance of payments), the rate goes against the importing country, i.e. more money of that country is drained out. The Government wants to control foreign trade mainly because the balance of payments does not become adverse so that indebtedness is not increased and money is not drained out. Even a favourable rate of exchange is not good. Such a situation arises when there is more export which means goods go out of the country causing a short supply in the home market resulting into rise in price. More exports mean more money coming in which may ultimately cause inflation. Therefore, **every Government wants to maintain a stable rate of exchange.**

(c) If a liberal policy of imports is followed, then some home industries may suffer being unable to compete with foreign goods which may be of better quality or of cheaper price. This is more true if imports are made from a developed country to an underdeveloped country. In the past, imperialist countries used to exploit their colonial countries in this way. If such a situation arises, the Government of the importing country **has to grant protection to home industries by levying high import duties** on the imported goods and thereby, indirectly, stopping imports. The Government may restrict export of some raw materials so that the home industries can make better use of them.

(d) It is good to earn more foreign exchange but that foreign money should not be spent by purchasing foreign goods indiscriminately. **The Government may restrict the spending of foreign exchange** only for buying essential goods like machines or such other things which cannot be produced in the home country.

(e) The Government may, **on political or strategic reasons**, decide to have more trade with certain countries and to restrict trade with some others. Sometimes, through commercial relation, political relation may be established. Trade delegations at Government or even at the level of businessmen may play a vital role.

(f) On the whole, every Government **broadly wants to boost up exports** and curtail imports. Generally, an advanced country enjoys such privilege. A Government also wants **to have a big share** in the total volume of imports and exports carried out in the world trade as a whole. The USA enjoys both the types of privileges having the largest share in the world trade as a single country. Sometimes, the Government of a country, because of its political ideology, does not want to enter into foreign trade. Such a country is supposed to be surrounded by a 'iron curtain'. The USSR during the regime of Stalin believed in such philosophy.

CONTROL MEASURES

There are **various types of measures** taken by a Government to exercise control over the foreign trade. The main measures are :

Non-monetary measures

(1) **Tariffs** —The Government **imposes duties on imports and exports.** Duties are imposed for double purposes (a) to restrict imports and exports and (b) to earn revenue. In case of import duties the purpose is mainly restrictive. Because of high prices, imports fall. The Government does not earn revenue but as the home industries flourish, the revenue of the Government comes from them in various ways. When exports duties are charged, the prices of those goods become high in foreign markets and so exports are likely to fall. But the Government charges duties on those exportable goods in which the country has monopoly or

near-monopoly in foreign markets. The exports do not fall but the revenue of the Government goes up.

There is a **continuous dispute between supportes of free trade and of restrictive trade.** There are powerful arguments put forward by both the sides. In cannot be denied that free trade allows the citizens of each country to enjoy the best products of the world at the lowest prices. On the other hand, if protection is not granted, home industries may not prosper and the economic development, as a whole, of the country cannot take place. Defence industries must be developed in the home country at any cost. Protection is necessary to stop 'dumping', i.e. supply of goods at a very low price (even lower than, the cost of production) by an advanced country to a low developed country.

(2) **Licensing and Quota** — Every Government introduces a licensing system for imports and exports. It means that **either an importer or an exporter has to take a licence** from the Government before entering into a transaction of foreign trade. The Government maintains a department for granting licence and sets up rigid rules and regulations. Generally, **the Government announces its import and export policy** for the year at the beginning of the financial year, clearly notifying which goods can be imported and exported and what should be the rates of duties. In India, the Government announces such policy generally in the month of April.

The licence granted may be based on two principles : (a) O.G.L., i.e. Open General Licence – Under this principle the licence is given without much restriction and more or less like a formality. (b) Quota, i.e. licence is granted subject to some quota beyond which transaction cannot be done. Sometimes imports are allowed against earnings of foreign exchange through exports.

For the purpose of granting licence, **importers and exporters are classified**. There are two types of importers : (a) Established or merchant importers – They import goods as middlemen on behalf of others or as traders of the commodity. (b) Actual users – they are manufacturers using the imported goods, either capital goods or raw materials. There are two types of exporters : (a) Established exporters or shippers – they export goods produced by others. (b) Producers – They themselves produce or manufacture the goods, either capital goods or consumption goods.

(3) **Bilateral agreements** — Bilateral trade agreement (or Bilateralism) means an **agreement of export and import of goods between two countries exclusively**. Which goods and of what quality or quantity shall be exchanged between the two countries are specifically determined in advance for a fixed period of time. The rate of exchange between the two currencies is also fixed. As a result, there is no freedom with regard to choice of goods, choice of country and fixation of price. In the past, imperialist countries used to make such agreements with their colonies for exploitation. Now-a-days, the Communist countries which do trade directly through the Government of other countries do such bilateral agreements. Very often, a weak country becomes a loser. Sometimes, there is no alternative way.

(4) **State trading** — This is not actually a control measure but **an instance of State interference.** Under this method, the **State directly enters into import and export trade.** In socialist States, there is no other alternative and the State directly participates in foreign trade. In other countries, the State comes forward in the interest of the people importing essential goods including foodstuff and distributing them even at reduced prices adding subsidies for the benefit of the people. Products of small producers or handicrafts can be exported through this agency. Export is also handled by the State as a counter– measure when private traders fail to keep up their promises or indulge into malpractices for personal gain which is harmful and damaging for the country. Sometimes State trading becomes inevitable to meet the requirements of economic plans. At the time of emergency, e.g. war, even a staunch free economic country takes recourse to State trading. UK entered into State trading during the World War II. In Canada, the State directly imports goods necessary for the Defence Industry. India has the State Trading Corporation.

Rationale of Government Control :

(1) Sometimes it becomes necessary to have State monopoly over import or certain essential commodities e.g. foodgrains.

(2) It is the only method of trading by, or with, socialist countries.

(3) Bilateral trade agreements can be implemented mainly through State trading.

(4) It becomes necessary to implement economic plans.

(5) It is a weapon in the hands of the State to check profiteering tendencies of exporters and importers through invoice manipulation and other malpractices.

Arguments against State trading

(1) The Government officials do not have the technical knowledge and experience in the complicated procedure of foreign trade.

(2) There is lack of incentive on the part of the officials, unlike private traders.

(3) State monopoly in any form may not be ultimately beneficial to the people, particularly when the administration is weak.

(4) Dispute at trade level may result into bigger disputes between the countries as the State is involved.

Monetary measures

The control measures described above are not exhaustive. There are some monetary measures commonly adopted by the Government which, however, **do not strictly come under the Commercial Policy.**

The main monetary measures are :

(1) **Under-valuation or over-valuation of currency** — The rate of exchange between two currencies are basically fixed by IMF, but there are fluctuations within limits. Sometimes the currency of a country is deliberately under-valued so that home goods become cheaper in foreign markets and that encourages exports. This is called devaluation. This is the last counter-measure to adverse balance of payments. On the other hand, the currency may be overvalued to encourage imports. This is, of course, uncommon.

(2) **Adoption of multiple exchange rates** — Different rates of exchange are fixed for home currency for different purposes. By this method, import or export of certain goods are encouraged while those of others are discouraged. This method was followed by Germany before World War II. This is practically not possible since the acceptance of IMF rates. Sometimes, the currency is **'floated'** which means the rate of exchange is allowed to be settled according to the import-export position between two countries.

(3) **Exchange control** — It means **complete control by the Government over all transactions in foreign exchange,** either making or receiving payments. This is a common measure adopted by all countries. The Central Bank of every country is empowered to permit use of foreign exchange. Every exporter is compelled to surrender all foreign currency earnings to the Government. All transfers of securities are made subject to permission by the Government. Banks can deal in foreign exchange, subject to the control of the Central Bank. More restrictions are imposed for import of goods against 'hard' currency, i.e. a currency of that country which has more exports than imports, e.g. US dollar. Restrictions are less for 'soft' currency, i.e. a currency which is easily available.

A CASE FOR INDIA

Before independence, India's foreign trade was committed to British interests. In fact, there was no definite and national commercial or Trade Policy. After independence, it was realised that India should follow **a trade policy to achieve economic development with**

growing self-reliance. The main objectives of the Indian Trade Policy are : (a) to restrict imports to essential items only; (b) to encourage import substitution by developing our own industries; (c) to encourage export-oriented industries; (d) to ensure distribution of imported goods at fair prices in the home market.

The Trade Policy is in the process of evaluation and so far we find **four phases** in it. They are :

(1) **Phase I – 1947-48 to 1951-52** — Imports had to be made mainly from UK to adjust the accumulated Sterling Balance (India's dues from UK against war supplies). Exports had to be boosted to USA to adjust heavy adverse balance or the 'dollar gap'.

(2) **Phase II – 1952-53 to 1956-57** — A liberal policy of import and export was adopted. As a result, imports increased at a fast rate but not exports. There was a fall in our foreign exchange reserve.

(3) **Phase III – 1956-57 to 1965-66** — Restrictions were imposed on imports and, on the other hand, export promotion drive was launched with diversification of exportable goods from traditional to non-traditional. The scheme for import substitution was given priority.

(4) **Phase IV – Devaluation in 1966 and after** — With mounting adverse balance of payments on account of heavy imports of foodgrains, capital goods (for industrialisation starting from the Second Plan), defence goods (on account of the Chinese aggression in 1962 and the Pakistani attack in 1965) and consumer goods (to meet growing home demand), India had no other alternative than devaluation of rupee on 6.6.66, expecting that exports would be boosted up and imports would be curtailed. Imports came down because of high prices but exports did not move up according to expectations because other follow-up measures were not taken. Mere lowering of prices cannot increase the demand for home products in foreign markets. The Government liberalised imports so that industries can bring raw materials, spare parts, etc. to increase production in the priority sectors. In the long run, exports increased and a comfortable foreign exchange reserve was built up. Because of self-sufficiency in foodgrains, imports of foodgrains have stopped.

Since 1975-76, the Government is following, more or less, a liberal policy on imports being secured by the foreign exchange reserve. Recently, however, owing to greater imports than exports, the position has become critical again. The Janata Government adopted a liberal Trade Policy based on the principle of 'trust in trade'. Import was liberalised for better public consumption and for supporting Government's anti-smuggling measures. A system of automatic licensing was introduced for actual users. The present Government started with a stricter policy but very recently has again fallen back on liberalisation. The Government has agreed to take heavy loans from the IMF.

The highlights of India's import policy — (1) Imports should be restricted as far as possible to save foreign exchange. (2) The main aim of imports will be export promotion to wipe out adverse balance of payments. (3) Imports should help industrialisation of the country. (4) Import substitution should be vigorously carried out.

The highlights of India's export policy — (1) Exports must be so directed that maximum earnings of hard currency can be achieved (2) Exports should not create shortage in home markets causing sufferings to the people. (3) Exports should not cause rising of prices through shortage. (4) To develop export – consciousness by creation of Export Promotion Councils and such other agencies and by offering various incentives to export industries.

FISCAL POLICY

Meaning — Business is applied Economics. Economics deals with the earning and spending of man. Man has to earn money because he has to spend it to meet his wants. Income can be made through employment. A businessman or a professional man is self-employed. A service-holder or a wage-earner is employed by others. Therefore, **employment is essential for earning. Fiscal Policy** means the sum total of monetary and non-monetary policies **for gener-**

ating employment. In the narrow sense, fiscal policy denotes a policy towards taxation and public expenditure.

The economic standard and growth of a country are measured by its national income, i.e. the total income of all the people. National income can be increased by creating more and more employments. Employment is vital for an individual. It is the duty of the Government to follow various policies to reach **the target of full employment. In a capitalist country, it is alleged that unemployment remains.** In Economics, when we think of unemployment, we mean involuntary unemployment. In other words, unemployment exists if some people searching for employment do not get it. In a capitalist country, trade or business cycles occur. **There is cyclical unemployment** during the period of recession or depression. In a socialist country, all economic activities are controlled by the State. It is claimed that the State, through planned economy, provides employments for all. It is alleged that **in a totalitarian or communist country** a large number of people, who do not conform to the ideology of the ruling party, are **sent to the concentration camps**. Their numbers are not known. They cannot be called employed. There is a peculiar case of **disguised unemployment**. Apparently, people seem to do work but in fact they are not employed. For example, in an agricultural country with fast growing population, a large number of people (unnecessarily) work on the same plot of land. None of them get adequate return.

In practice, it is difficult to create a situation of full employment. Voluntary unemployment cannot be removed. Moreover, there are unemployable people, e.g. sick, disabled or very old persons.

Employment is created through investment or capital formation. People will go for investment when it appears to be remunerative and when surplus funds for investment are available. Investment creates employment – employment generates income – savings come out of income after deducting expenses for consumption and savings go for investment. There is an endless cycle. But more and more investments can be created by taking loans provided they are available on easy terms and at low rates of interest. **The Government of a country has to follow a sound Monetary Policy** so that loans are available under desired condition. A well-organised capital market is also necessary.

Fiscal Policy — Apart from the monetary policy, a Government has to adopt a sound Fiscal Policy. **It means a policy of taxation and public expenditure through construction of new public works and welfare activities.** Taxation includes duties of all kinds.

Taxation — A Government has to levy taxes to earn revenue for administrative, defence and developmental expenses. Taxes include duties like customs, excise, stamp etc. Taxes are of **two types** : (1) Direct – It means the impact (i.e. from whom the tax is collected) and incidence (i.e. on whom the burden ultimately falls) are on the same person. Example – Income-tax. (2) Indirect. It means the impact falls on one person but the incidence is shifted to another. Example – Sales Tax. The Government collects (impact) it from the seller (that is why it is called a Sales Tax) but actually it is paid by the buyer (incidence – it is really a Purchase Tax). Taxes are computed by **two methods:** (1) Proportional – The tax is calculated on some proportional or percentage basis. e.g. the Sales Tax is calculated at 5%, 7% etc. The same rate is payable by everybody, rich or poor. But high rates are charged on luxury goods which can be bought only by rich people. (2) Progressive – The tax is computed on a slab basis, e.g. the Income-tax is calculated at higher and higher rates for higher and higher income levels or slabs to reduce inequality. Wealthy and rich people have to pay other taxes like Wealth Tax on the total value of wealth i.e. property held.

It is desirable that the Government should charge taxes, particularly direct taxes, at reasonable rates so that people are not discouraged to invest and to earn higher profits. If there is more investments and more profits the revenue of the Government will go up in the aggregate. More investments by individuals will create more incomes and Government can spend its increased tax income for public works and welfare which again creates employments.

Public Works — Public Works mean **construction of roads, bridges, canals, dams, etc. for the benefit of the people.** Fresh employments are created when such construction works are taken up. But **the expenditure must be 'new' expenditure,** i.e. by creation of new money which was not available so far for investment. It has to be seen that Government expenditure does not in any way hamper private expenditure. Public expenditure, once started, **has a multiplier effect.** Those who get income shall spend it. This will create effective demand for different goods or services. The products of those goods and services shall try to produce more by expanding their scale of production which will again create new employments generating new income. From all such new incomes, new savings and new investments and, consequently, further employments will be created. The Fiscal Policy, therefore, has a great impact on business.

Welfare measures — The Government may take recourse to some welfare measures, e.g. relief grants, unemployment allowance, etc. These 'incomes' will create effective demand for goods and services, **ultimately creating new employments** in a circular way (see above). But there are dangers : (a) Once such grants are started, it is difficult to stop them and (b) the expenditure may be wasteful without generating new employment.

Management of public debt — **Management of public debt also comes** within the purview of fiscal policy. The term public debt means the debts or loans raised by the Government either from the people of the country or from other countries and outside specialised institutions. Public debts can be **productive unproductive.** When the funds are spent for constructive works which create income-yielding assets then definitely new employments are created. Further, the assets have their own income out of which the debts can be repaid. On the other hand, if the funds are spent for unproductive purposes, e.g. war, then the debt becomes a burden on the society.

According to economists, there are still other measures to create employments, such as keeping level of **wages** stable, encouragement to private investment, improvement of consumption standard of the people etc.

A perfect coordination among the different measures has to be maintained, otherwise expenditure may be wasteful, the revenue of the Government may fall, inflationary tendency may grow and ultimately the purpose is not served.

A CASE FOR INDIA

During the British Rule, there was no definite fiscal policy in India. **After independence, with the commitment of the country to economic planning, a well-defined fiscal policy** has been adopted with the following major objectives – rapid economic development, full employment, establishment of a welfare state, and setting up of a socialistic pattern of society. The budgets of the Central Government as well as of the State Governments have been directed towards development through economic planning.

The total revenue and expenditure, both on Revenue and Capital Accounts, has increased tremendously, particularly from the period of the Fourth Plan.

Looking at the budgets of all the State Governments we find that the States play comparatively a bigger role in the process of economic development.

Detailed analysis of the expenditure pattern of the Governments 'reveals that developmental expenditure and expenditure on social services have been more than non-developmental expenditure.' Deficits are mainly found on the Capital Account. Paradoxically however, at present non-developmental expenditure has exceeded developmental expenditure because of increased administrative and defence expenditure, as well as interests payable on public debts. Because of the deficits, India has to adopt **a policy of deficit financing,** i.e. printing of notes and to take recourse to bank borrowings to meet the budgetary gap. Since the Second Plan, deficit financing in India has assumed alarming proportions.

Deficit financing leads to inflation. In India there has been no exception. Prices are spiralling up at a very fast rate causing enormous hardship to the people.

Tax system — Indian tax system **consists of both direct and indirect taxes.** Direct taxes include income-tax, wealth tax, capital gain tax, gift tax, etc. Indirect taxes contain sales tax, excise duties, customs duties, octroi, etc. At present, indirect taxes predominate over direct taxes. While indirect taxes are indirectly paid by everybody, income-tax is paid by hardly 1% of the total population. Direct taxes are collected by the Central Government. Indirect taxes are collected (like excise duties) both by the Central and State Governments. The largest source of revenue of the Central Government is excise duty.

The **characteristics** of Indian tax system are : (a) It is **broad-based** because there are varieties of taxes, both direct and indirect.

(b) The total tax revenue is **not adequate** to meet the needs of economic development.

(c) The system is **regressive.** Since indirect taxes are main and payable by everybody, rich or poor, at the same rate, it is more of a burden on the poor.

(d) Not even 1% of the total population pays income-tax. From this point of view the **tax-base is narrow.**

(e) There is large–scale **evasion of taxes** because of inefficient administration and various malpractices adopted by the tax-prayers. Acceptance of bribe by officers concerned is a common complaint.

(f) As taxes are not collected in full, **inflation cannot be checked** by withdrawing excess money from the hands of the people.

(g) The entire system is **complicated and time-consuming.** It causes much harassment and leaves opportunities for malpractices.

Public debt — Independent India started with a heavy burden of public debts because almost **the entire burden of undivided India** had to be taken by India, Pakistan taking a very small share. Since then, the public debts are increasing at a very high rate because of increasing developmental and non-developmental expenditure, defence expenditure and payment of interests. Both the Central and the State Governments borrow money. The State Governments borrow from the Central Government in addition to others. The Central Government is the biggest creditor to the State Governments.

India's public debts are divided into **two groups : Internal and External.** Internal debts come from selling of Government Promissory Notes in the open market, compensation bonds, prize bonds etc. Besides, temporary loans are raised from the Reserve Bank, commercial banks etc. as well as through treasury bills. External debt comes from different international institutions and consortia like the World Bank, International Development Authority, International Monetary Fund, Aid India Club, etc. and also from advanced countries. Apart from the direct borrowings, **the Central Government has other liabilities** like refundable Compulsory Deposits, other refundable duties, reserve funds of the Railways and the Posts and Telegraph departments etc.

The **characteristics** of India's public debts are : (a) The debts are rising at a very fast rate.

(b) More than 70%, i.e. a big majority of the total debts, are internal.

(c) **The people being poor it is difficult** to raise loans quickly from the general public. But the bonds issued by the Government get subscribed quickly because of the **support of the institutions** like banks and insurance companies.

(d) The Government has to face **competition from the private sector ,** offering securities or inviting deposits at very attractive terms.

(e) A major part of the borrowed money is **invested in productive** i.e. income-yielding and assets-creating projects. Therefore, the position of debts is sound.

Public expenditure — Public expenditure increases at a very fast rate under a developing economy. In India, we notice a **phenomenal growth of public expenditure** since the planned economy has been introduced. The **reasons** for such phenomenal growth are :

(1) The main reason is the ever-increasing growth of expenditure to carry out various **development programmes** and provision of larger amounts for **social services**. This is true for both the Central and the State Governments.

(2) Another important reason is the increasing expenditure for the **defence** of the country. India has been involved in war three times once with China and twice with Pakistan. Moreover, India has to spend much for keeping watch at the Kashmir border.

(3) The expenditure for **civil administration** is also rising because of rising prices, better remuneration to the civil servants, more amenities to the civil servants, expanding activities of the Government, etc.

(4) The expenditure for **debt services,** i.e. payment of interests on the growing public borrowings, is also mounting up.

(5) The expenditure of the Central Government is increasing as it is offering more **grants** and **subsidies** to the States and, particularly, to the backward States or States suffering from some special problems, e.g. tribal welfare.

(6) There are some **other reasons** like larger expenses for elections which are more frequently held, extravagance by civil servants, higher costs for raising public debts, etc. Huge expenditure takes place to maintain many **losing public sector undertakings.**

Nature of public expenditure in India — (1) Public expenditure of both the Central and State Governments in India is divided into **two parts :** (a) **Capital expenditure** of the Central Government consists of developmental expenditure on capital account including investments in the public sector, defence expenditure on capital account including expenditure for construction work, establishment of factories for arms and ammunitions, etc. and loans made out by the Central Government to the States. The capital expenditure of the Central Government is on a steady rise. The State Governments also have to make capital expenditure by way of investments in their undertakings, construction of roads, irrigation projects, etc. Expenditure is also made through public bodies like 'panchayats'. (b) **Revenue expenditure** of the Central Government consists of administrative expenditure, defence expenditure etc. The State Governments, however, have administrative expenditure but no defence expenditure.

(2) The total expenditure is increasing at a fast rate but the different kinds of expenditure are not rising at the same rate. The **developmental expenditure is rising faster** than non-developmental expenditure. This is quite expected as the Government is committed to the principle of Welfare State. This is true for the State Governments also.

(3) **The largest single item** of expenditure is **defence.** There has been a phenomenal rise of defence expenditure over the last 40 years. For instance, the total defence expenditure in 1950-51 was Rs. 164 crores while it has gone over Rs. 3,000 crores by 1990.

(4) By far the **largest rate of increase** for Central Government expenditure has been in the matters of **grants-in-aid to State Governments.** Expenditure on this head has gone up by over 100 times.

(5) The entire public expenditure is guided by the dual policy of **defence and development.** Development expenditure is affected because of unavoidable rise in defence expenditure.

UNEMPLOYMENT

The problem of unemployment is a persistent problem in the economy of every country. **Unemployment is of many types.** Firstly, unemployment may be **voluntary** and **involuntary.**

There are people who do not want to work. For such **voluntary** unemployment, economists do not bother. But when people are willing to work and are in search of jobs but employment cannot be provided, there is involuntary unemployment and steps have to be taken for remedies. Involuntary unemployment means lowering of natural income and retardation of economic growth. Besides, there are some social evils too. **Involuntary unemployment** may be of the following types : (a) Frictional and seasonal – These are temporary unemployments caused by fall of demand for goods and services because of economic reasons or natural reasons of variation of seasons (e.g. agricultural seasons). Temporary structural unemployments are caused by technological change, e.g. introduction of new type of, or faster, machines. (b) Cyclical unemployment takes place because of operation of trade cycles. During depression there is unemployment. (c) Chronic unemployment occurs in under-developed countries where jobs cannot be created for want of adequate capital formation. (d) Disguised unemployment takes place primarily in an agricultural country where the population is large and growing. More people work on the same field, though not wanted and so, apparently, they are employed but, in fact, not. This is called disguised-unemployment or under - employment.

Frictional and cyclical unemployments occur in advanced countries. Some frictional unemployment and even structural unemployment (at least 1 to 2% among industrial labour) are unavoidable. Lord Keynes has prescribed his contra-cyclical fiscal policy, i.e. a policy of creating employments through public works by the Government. The problems of chronic and disguised unemployments are formidable and found in underdeveloped countries. Adoption of a comprehensive policy of economic planning is the remedy but highly difficult. **India,** an under – developed country at the time of independence, though now developing, **has to face these formidable problems.**

A CASE FOR INDIA

Nature of India's unemployment problems — (1) The problem of unemployment is assuming **alarming proportions** because of growing population and that inspite of adoption of a policy of planned economy and various remedial measures introduced by the Government.

(2) The **types of unemployment** in India are : **(a) Unemployment in the rural sector** — India, being an agricultural country with 72% of the people depending on agriculture and allied activities, this type of unemployment is critical. Rural unemployment again is of two types : (i) Seasonal – there is no work in the field when the rainy season is over. (ii) Chronic and disguised – with the growth of population more people are depending on the same land. (b) **Unemployment in the urban sector** — This again is divided into two types :(i) Unemployment among industrial labour – because of slow rate of industrial growth, establishment of capital-intensive rather than labour-intensive industries, non-utilisation of the full capacity of plants, too many strikes and lock-outs leading to closures, rationalisation (rather modernisation) of some industries, sickness in some industries, etc., this type of unemployment grows. (ii) Unemployment among the educated middle class – because of defective forms of education, lack of facilities for technical or vocational education, peculiar tendency to avoid manual labour, etc.– the number of unemployed among the educated middle class is growing at a very fast rate.

(3) According to the findings of the Bhagawati Committee nearly three-fourths of the total unemployed belong to **families** which are **below the poverty line** with an income level less than Rs. 200 per month.

(4) The same Committee reveals that an educated young man has to **wait for a long period** (from 11 to 17 months minimum) to get a job after completing his education (up to graduate level). Below graduate level the period varies from 25 to 27 months.

(5) The **Government** has taken, and continuously re-orienting, several measures to solve the problem. Some of the measures are :

(a) A **crash scheme** was introduced in 1971 for creating employments in the rural sector with an average of 1,000 employments in every district for a working period of 10 months in a year through road construction, minor irrigation work, expansion of primary education, etc.

(b) **Special construction programmes** in districts where generally droughts take place. This programme can provide employment for about 30,000 persons for every one crore rupees of expenditure. This programme was taken during the Fourth Plan.

(c) During the Fourth Plan period, a **special programme** was taken to create employments **for the educated unemployed** through expansion and development of primary education, establishment of agro-service centres, etc. and through self-employment schemes for the unemployed technical hands like engineers.

(d) According to the recommendations of a specialists' committee on unemployment, called the Bhagawati Committee, appointed in 1972, the Government took some **short-term schemes** like road construction, rural water supply, minor irrigation programmes, etc. to create about 40 lakh jobs including those for the educated unemployed, involving an expenditure of Rs. 2,000 crores.

(e) It has been the avowed policy of the Government to help in every possible respect **small scale and village industries** to create new jobs and particularly as a remedy against disguised and seasonal unemployments and to encourage self-employment through entrepreneurship development.

(f) Under the Sixth Plan, special massive programmes were introduced like the IRDP (Integrated Rural Development Programme), NREP (National Rural Employment Programme – a new form of Food for Work Programme under which foodgrains were offered by the Government in exchange of labour for constructive work) and TRYSEM (Training of Rural Youth for Self-Employment), to create employments, with an investment of more than Rs. 15,000 crores. The 20-Point Programme was virtually directed towards creation of employment and for eradication of poverty. Recently, a liberalised bank accommodation has been introduced known as Self-Employment Programme for Urban Poor (SEPUP) for the unemployed poor people living in towns.

For a long-term solution of the problem of unemployment, the Government should adopt the following steps : (a) Checking the growth rate of population. (b) Creation of labour-intensive industries. (c) Diversion of the rural people from agricultural occupation to other occupations. (d) Liberalisation of industrial licensing (see below) to encourage private investments. (e) Control of politicalised adventurism in the name of trade unionism discouraging private investment. (f) Entrepreneurship development through training.

INDUSTRIAL POLICY AND INDUSTRIAL LICENSING

Meaning — Industries play a significant role in the economy of a country. Industries cannot be allowed to grow in an unplanned manner leading to over-production or under-production, duplication or wastage, unhealthy competition or monopolistic concentration, etc. A country, therefore, needs a **definite and coordinated policy for the development of its industries.** For such a policy, different aspects of an industry have to be taken into consideration : location, ownership pattern, size, capacity, employment potential, pattern of distribution of products, labour relations, etc. Therefore, an industrial policy can be formulated **at the highest level of authority,** i.e. the State. The State is expected to make a **comprehensive approach** to this sector and issue directives based on some principles for the overall economic development.

Relationship between the two — Much depends on **the economic system obtaining in the country.** In a capitalist country, where there is freedom of enterprise, there is little scope for any comprehensive industrial policy by the Government. But even then there are various legislations and regulatory measures and the question of licences (trade, factory, etc.). The term licencing is used in a narrow and legal sense. Under socialistic economy, the state controls and performs all the economic activities and even there may not be any freedom of consumption. The entire economic world is based on some socialistic principles. A socialist State may become a communist or a totalitarian state with absolutely no freedom of the people in the true sense. The question of licensing does not arise in such circumstances. **In a country which adopts a policy of mixed economy**, there is a question of declaration of an industrial policy clearly showing the spheres of activities of the public and of the private sectors and of the joint sector, if any. The Government reserves the right of permitting any particular entrepreneur or group of entrepreneurs to start any particular form of industry or that at any particular place. Here rises the importance of industrial licensing too. **In India**, where mixed economy operates, there are the **importance and existence of both** — an industrial policy and industrial licensing. An industrial policy, as mentioned above, has a comprehensive approach to industrial development.

The Industrial Policy of the Government of India

Background — During the British rule, there was no definite and declared industrial policy of the Government. Immediately after the World War I (1914 – 1918) an Industrial Commission was appointed to devise some industrial policy, but without any affect. **After independence,** the national Government rightly adopted a policy of mixed economy for the economic development of the country in the quickest way and without much socio-economic disturbance. The independence dawned on the 15th of August 1947 and the Government announced its **first Industrial Policy** on the 6th of April 1948. This policy was followed by various **other policies** like the Fiscal Policy,* the Foreign Capital Policy and the Industrial Licensing Policy in 1949, 1950 and 1951, respectively. All these policies are interlinked. The Industrial Policy was revised considerably in 1956 (on the wake of the Second Plan) and marginally in 1973 (under some changed socio-economic situation).

The features of the first Industrial Policy — (1) **Basic objectives** — High rate of economic growth, adoption of a policy of mixed economy, growth and equitable distribution of national wealth, creation of employment opportunities, etc.

(2) **Classification of industries** — The industries were grouped into four groups, demarcating the spheres of the public and private sectors. The groups are : (a) **Exclusive State monopolies or the pure Public Sector** — Three industries – arms and ammunition, atomic energy, and railways – were brought under this group which must be developed by the Central Government as monopolies. (b) **State-controlled sphere** — This group included the following industries – iron and steel, mining, aircraft manufacturing, ship-building, mineral oils, etc.– which should be allowed to remain in the hands of the private sector for ten years but in the mean time the Government would set up new units. (c) **Subject to State regulation** — Industries like sugar, cotton textile, woollen textile, paper, cement, etc. should be allowed to remain in the private sector, subject to special control and regulation of the State. (d) **The remaining industries in the Private Sector** — The rest of the industries were allowed to remain in the private sector subject to general control of the State.

(3) **Management of State enterprises** — It was stated that the State enterprises should be operated in the form of statutory corporations.

(4) **Small and cottage industries** — The policy recognised the special role of small and cottage industries in Indian economy and emphasised the need of their integrated growth with large industries. Cooperatives should be encouraged for the purpose and there should be decentralisation of industries through them.

(5) **Industrial relations** — The policy stressed the need of better industrial or labour-capital relations for the smooth industrial progress in the country. The policy assured fair wages and labour participation in management.

* The term Fiscal Policy is used here to denote Tariff Policy or a policy of protection to Indian industries to overcome foreign competition and to develop exports.

(6) **Foreign capital** — The policy realised the need of foreign capital and technical know-how but foreign capital should be allowed without foreign domination and in national interest. Indians must have increased participation in enterprises having foreign capital.

The main aim of the Industrial Policy was to create an atmosphere **where the public and the private sector should cooperate** for a rapid economic growth of the country.

Evaluation — The Policy could satisfy neither the capitalists who did not like the dominance of the State, nor the socialists who expected greater thrust for nationalisation. The threat of nationalisation of some major industries as under the second group caused greatest dissatisfaction to the business community and retarded the growth of those industries.

The Industries (Development and Regulation) Act was passed in 1951 to empower the Government to implement some of the measures of the Industrial Policy and to introduce industrial licensing (see below). The Act was amended in 1955 and 1970.

The Features of the second Industrial Policy of 1956 — On the 30th of April 1956, the Government announced a **revised Industrial Policy**, necessitated by some of the major socio-economic developments during the years 1948-56. The main characteristics of such developments are : (a) Introduction of Five Year Plans from 1951 (and the successful implementation of the First Plan). (b) Adoption of the Constitution of India with 'Directives of State Policy' and recognition of 'Fundamental Rights'. (c) Faith in building up of a 'socialistic pattern of society'. (d) India's growing but non-committed relations with socialist countries. The **features of the revised Policy were :**

(1) **New classification of industries** — Industries were regrouped in three categories with a broader coverage and greater role of the State. There are now three Schedules : (a) **Schedule A** — Seventeen industries like arms and ammunition, atomic energy, iron and steel, heavy machinery, coal, oil, important minings, railways, aircraft, air transport, electricity generation, etc. which shall be exclusive **responsibility of the State.** (b) **Schedule B** — Twelve industries are named here like aluminium and non-ferrous metals, other minings, machine tools, antibiotics, heavy chemicals, drugs, fertilisers, etc. which shall be **progressively state-owned** and with setting up of new units by it, but the private sector shall be allowed to supplement the efforts of the State. (c) **Schedule C** — All the remaining industries shall be in the hands of **the private sector** in general but within the framework of socio-economic policy of the State. The divisions are not water-tight compartments. Any industry is transferable from one group to another.

(2) **Fair treatment to the private sector** — The State shall provide all assistance to the private sector so that they can develop confidently. Industrial and agricultural cooperatives shall be encouraged. The State should provide the infra-structure with the development of transport, power, etc. and setting up of financial institutions. In those spheres where both the public and private sectors should exist, the State shall extend fair treatment to the private sector without any discrimination.

(3) **Encouragement to village and small-scale enterprises** — The State should encourage cottage *(village) and small-scale enterprises by offering financial and technical help, restricting the production of big industries, rendering subsidies and tax relief.

(4) **Removal of regional disparity** — The Policy wants removal of regional disparity in the matter of industrial growth so that the whole country is benefited by industrialisation. There must be balanced and coordinated distribution of industries in the different regions.

(5) **Industrial peace** — The Policy aims at establishment of industrial peace through better employer-employee relations, recognition of labour as a partner in development through joint consultation and labour participation in management and ensuring better working conditions.

* In the past the term' cottage' was used what today is meant by the term 'village'.

(6) **Foreign capital** — There is no change in the matter of foreign capital from the First Policy.

(7) **Management of public sector** — Steps to be taken to train up managerial personnel and technical personnel for the efficient functioning of the public enterprises.

Evaluation — The new Policy increases the scope of the public sector and enhances the power and responsibility of the State for the development of industries. On the basis of the new Policy, the State has set up many new industries, particularly heavy industries, like iron and steel, machine-making, heavy chemicals, heavy electricals, ship-building, etc. **Yet criticisms** are made on the following points :

(1) The Government has failed to increase the rate of industrial growth as desired. (2) It has failed to control concentration of economic power (see below). (3) The public sector has not been able to play its coveted role. (4) Though the threat of nationalisation of some industries (as given in the First Policy) has been withdrawn, no definite policy of nationalisation has been mentioned, creating an uncertainty. (5) Many of the loopholes in the Policy have been exploited by interested business people. (6) Some critics say that the Policy "set out some of the principles of Nehru's philosophy". (7) The State wanted to assume big responsibility to develop industry without being sure whether it could discharge the responsibility.

The features of **the revised Industrial Policy of 1973** — Though the Government entered into a large variety of industries by the expansion of the public sector and by nationalisation of many private sector industries, **the performance of the Government in the field of industry was not very encouraging.** This was revealed by the Industrial Licensing Enquiry Committee. Because of the failure of the public sector, which was to control the basic and heavy industries, there was a steady decline in the industrial production, the private sector losing interest in investment. In order to improve the situation, the Government wanted to have a modification of the industrial policy by making a Statement in February 1973.

New Classification — According to this policy Statement and in the context of the Fifth Five Year Plan, a new approach was made to the classification of industries. The **'core' industries** and industries having linkage with the core industries and also **industries having export potential,** totalling 19, were brought under one list. The industries are metallurgical industries, electrical equipment, machine tools, scientific instruments, boilers, prime movers, synthetic rubber, drugs and pharmaceuticals, plate glass, ceramics, cement products etc. With regard to such industries the **following policy** was adopted :

(a) Larger industrial houses and foreign companies and branches of subsidiaries of foreign companies shall be permitted to participate in core industries provided the item of manufacture is not reserved for the public sector or the small-scale sector. Large houses and foreign companies will not be ordinarily permitted to enter into other industries, unless they are meant predominantly for export.

(b) A large industrial house means one which draws the attention of the MRTP Act, i.e. a house which, together with its subsidies, has total capital assets worth Rs. 100 crores or more.

(c) Other than large industrial houses, foreign companies shall be permitted to enter into these 19 types of industries.

(d) The Government will encourage the Joint Sector firms but large industrial houses and foreign companies shall not be allowed to enter into Joint Sector.

Small-scale and Cooperative Sectors — The Government will encourage small and medium-scale industrial units in all industries including the above-mentioned 19 industries. Cooperatives and small and medium entrepreneurs will be encouraged to produce mass-consumption goods.

The public sector — It shall participate more vigorously in the production and distribution of consumption goods.

Evaluation — The new approach of the Government **was welcome** from different quarters and particularly from the private sector. It improved the investment climate to a great extent. It ensured higher rate of growth with more effective enforcement of social objectives. **The large industrial houses became happy** to learn clearly in which industries they could participate. But they did not like the idea of disqualifying them to enter into the Joint Sector. A section of critics did not like the softening of attitude of the Government to the large industrial houses.

In October 1975, the Government also announced liberalisation of industrial licensing policy.

The Industrial Policy of the Janata Government — The entire political picture of India suddenly changed with the Janata Government coming into power with a crushing victory over the then Prime Minister, Smt. Indira Gandhi. In the opinion of the Janata Government, **the Industrial Policy, so far pursued, had created some 'distortions' in Indian economy,** such as growing unemployment, rural-urban disparities, widespread sickness of industries, heavy burden of losing public undertakings, etc. In order to do away with the distortions, the Janata Government adopted a new look at industrial policy **with the following features : (1) A greater emphasis on 'cottage and household' industries.** (2) A new sector was named as 'tiny sector' with machinery and equipment valued up to Rs. 1 lakh and situated in towns with a population of less than 50,000. (3) The Government wanted to assist the cottage industries, the tiny sector industries and the small-scale industries. (4) Altogether, 807 types of industries were brought under reservation (instead of 180 during the Congress rule) for the small-scale sector. (5) For the development of small industries, the Government wanted to set up a District Industries Centre in every district as the supreme Government Agency to help the small industries. (6) The Government wanted to extend the area of operation of the Khadi and Village Industries Commission. (7) The Government would not encourage large-scale sophisticated industries with eye-catching foreign technology. The large houses could expand with their self-generating resources. (8) The public sector should not only be the producer of basic and strategic goods but it should bring stability in economy and price level by maintaining steady supply of essential commodities. (9) The Government would allow foreign collaboration only when it was absolutely necessary. And, if necessary, the existing collaborations might not be renewed. (10) But the Government would invite high level and sophisticated technology to develop technological self-reliance in the country.

Evaluation — Unfortunately, the people could not have the experience of the effects of the new look at industrial policy as the Janata Government collapsed as suddenly as it had come into existence. But it can be said that the approach of the Government was **highly nationalistic in spirit and suited to the conditions of Indian economy.** One can see in it a blending of Gandhian and socialistic ideas. In many districts, the District Industries Centres are operating. The Government, however, did not ban the multinationals. How far the development of small-scale industries could be feasible was doubted by many as 2% of the total outlay under the Sixth Plan (prepared by the Janata Government) was allotted for it, the figure being less compared to the previous Plans. No positive measures were announced to curtail the powers of large industries or to change the socio-economic environment. The present Government is very keen to bring an era of high technology to lead India to the 21st century. Use of computer has become almost a craze. But nobody cares to know whether the infra-structure of India can withstand the modern technology. It is doubtful whether any advanced country will transfer the latest form of technology to India.

INDUSTRIAL LICENSING

Meaning — Under free economy, businessmen enjoy freedom of enterprise but they have to take different types of licences for doing business, e.g. a Trade Licence from the municipality or any other civic body, a licence under the Factories Act for running a factory, a licence for import or export business from the Controller of Imports and Exports, etc. Licence is a common thing in our everybody life. The term Industrial Licence means a licence or **a written permission to establish a large-scale production unit at any particular place.** The idea of Industrial Licence has been incorporated in the Industrial Policy. The Government wants economic development of the country not only through agriculture, which is the main occupation for the vast majority of the people, but also through establishment and expansion of industries. Industries need suitable locations. Every industry cannot be established at every place. On the whole, there are certain areas in a country where facilities for starting industries like availability of power, raw materials, and transport are found in plenty. Generally, there will be a tendency to establish industries there. In this way almost in every country we find some industrial belts. In India, for example, the belts are – Calcutta, Bombay, Kanpur, Bangalore etc. and their surroundings. Such **concentration is not always good** because it gives rise to the following **harmful effects :** (a) Disproportionate regional growth. (b) Inter-regional (inter-provincial) rivalry and jealousy. (c) Comprehensive destruction by enemy attack. (d) Too much pressure of population at selected areas. The Government, therefore, rightfully wants that before an industry (i.e., a production unit) is established by private entrepreneurs at any particular place, an industrial licence has to be obtained from the Government. The Government shall issue the licence, provided the Government is satisfied that **the location helps regional growth** and not duplication or unnecessary concentration. The Government will welcome such proposal from the private sector if the location is in a backward part of the country called 'zero industry district'. Even the Government is ready to offer some special favours and facilities (like reduced freight rates for railway transport) in such cases.

The Industries (Development and Regulation) Act of 1951 —This Act was passed **to implement the Industrial Policy of 1948.** The Act was made effective from May 6, 1952. The Act **has been amended** in 1955 to change the number of industries brought under it and again in 1970 to change some basic principles of licensing on the recommendations of the Industrial Licensing Policy Enquiry Committee.

The **main provisions** of the Act are :

(1) **A licence has to be obtained** from the Government before establishing **a new unit or expansion of an existing unit** for a number of industries as mentioned in a Schedule attached to the Act. Originally there were 37 industries; then the number has been increased in 1955 onwards and decreased in 1970. All **existing units** belonging to those industries had to be **registered** immediately after the Act was made effective. Industrial units with workers less than 100 and having fixed assets of less than Rs. 10 lakhs would not require licensing or registering under this Act. Subsequently, the exemption limit was raised up to Rs. 30 lakhs. But this limit did not apply to : (a) large industrial houses; (b) those units which require foreign capital of more than Rs. 10 lakhs or more than 10% of investment, whichever is less; 'dominant undertakings' as defined in the MRTP Act. (For latest position see below.) **The Government**, while granting licence, **may impose conditions** with regard to location, minimum size, etc.

(2) The Act empowers the **Government to make investigations** into some specified industries or undertakings with regard to quantum of production, quality of the products, mode of management etc. in public interest and **may issue directives.**

(3) The Government is further empowered **to take over under its own management** such undertakings which do not follow the directives of the Government as stated above. A large number of units have been taken over by the Government by this time and on many occasions on the demand of the employees.

(4) The Government is also empowered **to issue instructions** with regard to pricing, methods of production, channels of distribution, etc. for specified undertakings.

(5) By virtue of the Act the Government **sets up several bodies** to administer the law. The bodies are as follows :

(a) The **Central Advisory Council** has been set up to advise the Government to develop and regulate the industries scheduled in the Act.

(b) **A Development Council** is established **for each big industry or a group or industries.** Such Councils consist of representatives of employers, employees, and consumers. The Councils function as 'nurses for private enterprises' and as a bridge between the public and the private industries.

(c) For the coordination of the activities of the Development Councils and for the implementation of the economic and industrial development as a whole, **an apex body called the National Development Council** has been established. The Chief Ministers of different States, as well as economists, technologists, etc. on behalf of the Central Government, are members. The National Development Council also maintains coordination between the Central Advisory Council and the Development Councils.

(d) **A Licensing Committee** has been set up as the executive body to **issue the licences.** For expediting the licensing work, a Secretariat for Industrial Approvals has been established in 1973.

Evaluation — The Act has given **enormous powers in the hands of the Government** to regulate establishment of new units and expansion of existing units in the industrial world. The very name of the Act suggests that there are **dual purposes** behind the legislation. The Government wants to develop industries in a regulated way, so that the private sector behaves as desired by the Government through its economic planning. The implementation of the Act **has enabled the Government to have :** (a) a balanced regional growth of industries in the country; (b) proper utilisation of the natural resources of the country; (c) proper coordination between the growth of small and large scale industries; (d) control over concentration of economic power; (e) saving industrial units from ruination through improper management and thereby preventing unemployment and economic waste.

But the functioning of the whole licensing system has to face severe **criticisms** which are based on two reports. They are discussed below :

A. Findings of the Hazari Report (1967) :

In the Final Report on Industrial Planning and Licensing Policy, prepared by Dr. R. K. Hazari, the following observations have been made :

(1) Some big industrial houses made applications for a number of industries. It indirectly **checks entry of others** because so long one application for an industry is under consideration no new application in the same line cannot be accepted. For the purpose, new concerns were created.

(2) It is not a fact that by industrial licensing a balanced regional development has taken place to a great extent. **Some regions have taken advantage.**

(3) Once a licence is issued **no follow up measures** are generally taken by investigation by the Government. Various malpractices are adopted by the licencee afterwards. There is no provisions for revocation of licence once granted.

(B) Findings of the Industrial Licensing Policy Inquiry Committee or Dutta Committee (1969) :

On the basis of a discussion of the Hazari Report in Parliament, the Government of India appointed the Industrial Licensing Policy Enquiry Committee in 1969 under the chairmanship of Sri Subimal Dutt. In the Report, submitted in 1969, the Dutta Committee produced some astounding findings. **The Report is a landmark** in the history of industrial economy of India. **The findings are as follows :**

(1) The **large industrial houses managed to get the lion's share** in industrial licences. They captured 2,800 licences out of total 7,445 granted till the date of enquiry. Out of them again, foreign collaborations got a major share.

(2) There are 73 large industrial houses who controlled 55.5% of the total proposed investments and 60.4% of the total import of capital goods by the entire private corporate sector. Out of the **73 predominant industrial houses** , 20 had a major share.

(3) One of the most serious findings was granting **a number of licences to a single large industrial house**. The Licensing Committee totally ignored the principle of breaking the concentration of economic power. As a result, many of the licences remained unused and many important industries could not utilise their installed capacities in full.

(4) Industries reserved for the **public sector were made open to the private sector** on various grounds, for example, the full development of aluminium industry, which should be in the public sector, was handed over to the private sector. In drugs and pharmaceuticals industry, 184 licences were given to the private sector while only 12 were given to the public sector.

(5) There was discrimination to states with regard to granting of licences and with **total disregard to balanced regional development.** Maharashtra, West Bengal, Tamil Nadu and Gujarat got 62% of all the licences.

(6) Altogether, 720 licences were granted to **foreign collaborations** and out of them **70 licences were for consumer goods,** though it was not permissible under the Industrial Policy. It was argued by the Licensing Committee that the names of the foreign companies would add prestige to the products.

(7) Another damaging finding was that 44.4% of the total term assistance granted by financial institutions went to those 73 large industrial houses and 17% went to the bigger 20. In other words, money **flowed from public financial institutions to rich industrialists.***

Conclusion — The findings of the ILEPC are not startling but, in a sense, lamentable. It is evident that the bureaucracy was largely responsible for the malhandling of the licensing system. The ILEPC, however, did not blame it. But the ILEPC admitted that **mere licensing cannot prevent concentration of economic power**. In fact, the private sector has the strength to pressurise the Government. The ILEPC strongly recommended **encouragement to the Joint Sector.** The Government, after being guided by the findings of the ILEPC, made some modifications of the procedure of industrial licensing.

The Industrial Licensing Policy of 1970 — According to the policy adopted by the Government in respect of industrial licensing, the **industries are clearly divided into several categories** in order of preference. The different categories or sectors are :

(1) **Core Sector** — Industries were grouped into 9 categories, collectively known as the 'Core Sector' during the Fourth Plan. Taking that idea and being led by the findings of the ILEPC (see above) the Government has prepared a list of 19 basic, critical and strategic industries. This is the Core Sector. The private sector, including the large industrial houses and foreign companies, shall be granted licence for such industries excepting those reserved for the public sector (see above).

(2) **Heavy investment sector** — Heavy investment means investment over Rs. 5 crores. Licences can be issued to the private sector including large industrial houses and foreign companies for those industries which require heavy investment, excepting those reserved for the public sector.

(3) **Middle investment sector** — Middle investment means an investment between Rs. 1 crore and Rs. 5 crores. Licences will be granted without much restriction to the private sector

* This finding led the Government to amend the Companies Act by which, by order of the Government, loans given by any public financial institution to a company can be converted into equity capital, so that the institution can participate in the management of the company [Sec. 81 (4)].

but not to large industrial houses (unless it is for expansion for greater economy) and where foreign exchange problems are involved.

(4) **Small scale sector** — Licences will not be granted to other applicants for those industries which are reserved for the small scale sector.

(5) **Cooperative sector** — Cooperatives shall have preference for getting licences for agro-industries like sugar-cane or jute processing.

(6) **Export-oriented industries** — Export-oriented industries shall have top preference for getting licences. Small and medium sectors shall enjoy special favour in this respect. Even large industrial houses or foreign companies will get licence to start units in those areas where they are not ordinarily permitted, provided they agree to export 60% of the new production and even they may be permitted to enter into industries reserved for the small-scale sector provided they agree to export at least 75% of the new production.

(7) **De-licensed industries** — No licensing is necessary for any new undertaking or expansion up to investment of Rs. 1 crore. This exemption can be enjoyed by those concerns whose total value of assets is less than Rs. 5 crores and which do not belong to any large industrial house or are not a foreign company or a 'dominant undertaking' as understood by the MRTP Act. Since 1970, there have been revisions in the licensing policy in 1973, 1975, 1978 and in 1983 : In the licensing policy of 1983, The exemption limit for licensing has been raised from Rs. 3 crores to Rs. 5 crores in case of small and medium scale industries.

The Central Government announced in August 1980 a further licensing exemption on enhanced investments by only small and ancillary units which are not subsidiaries of or owned or controlled by any other undertaking. In this context, the Government has also **changed the limits of investments** by tiny, small and ancillary units.

The Union Finance Minister said in Rajya Sabha on 11.8.80 that the Government was thinking **to raise the credit limit for tiny units** to Rs. 20,000.00 for fixed and working capital. There would be no insistence on margin money from the tiny units and the rate of interest should not exceed 12.25%. The Minister admitted that the bigger units in the small sector had got a lion's share of the Institutional credit.

Industrial licensing has been further liberalised by the Central Government in 1991.

Government control of monopoly

The Government has, taken strong measures against monopolistic tendencies and concentration of economic power. The Mahalanobis Committee was appointed in 1960 to enquire into the distribution of income and wealth under the planned economy. The Committee reported on concentration of wealth in the hands of a few business houses. On the recommendations of the Mahalanobis Committee, the Monopolies Enquiry Commission was appointed in 1964 to find the extent of the concentration of economic power and to suggest remedies. According to the Commission, 75 big business houses had control over about half of the total assets of the corporate sector. On the basis of the Report and recommendations of the Commission the Monopolies Restrictive Trade Practices Act was passed in 1969. The Act has defined what is meant by dominant undertaking, monopolistic undertaking in which economic concentration has taken place and monopolistic as well as restrictive trade practices. Such undertakings require prior Government approval before expansion. All such undertakings must register their names. Normally, the Government shall not approve any expansion programme by a monopolistic undertaking. The Government may also order for division of such concerns into small parts or compulsory selling out of a part of its business. Agreements made by concerns leading to monopolistic or restrictive trade practice must registered which may be debarred by the Government from being effective. It is criticised and the Act is not adequate and the Government is empowered mostly to intervene when there has been some abuse of power instead of taking preventive measures.

Government as Promoter :

The promotion of business had hitherto been the exclusive job and privilege of private individuals. But with the farewell to the policy of laissez faire and with the realisation that a Government cannot be a passive onlooker to what has been happening in the economic and business spheres of the country, the Government has been active in promoting business. In a socialist economy it is the Government that alone owns, manages and control the means of production and in our country where we have been pursuing the policy of mixed economy, the Government has defined areas of operation and in these areas the Government is the promoter. The Industrial Policy of our Government has entrusted promotion and management of certain industries exclusively to the Government. Accordingly, in our country, the Central and State Governments are playing the role of promoters and many basic key industries and strategic industries are being promoted by the Government and side-by-side with the private entrepreneurs, Governments – Central and State – are promoting business enterprises. These units have been set up in different forms such as departmentally managed units, Government companies or statutory corporations. In the case of these units, the responsibility of promotion was shouldered by the Government alone. In the Joint Sector, the Government jointly promotes business enterprises.

As a promotee of business, the role of Government is very significant because Government promotes business enterprises, not being motivated by profit motive, but by consideration of greater economic well-being of the people of the country.

Government as Regulator of Business

Not only the Government promotes business enterprises but it also regulates them. Mere promotion of business by a Government cannot yield desired objectives, so after promotion comes the role of the Government as the regulator of business. The question of regulation of business enterprises becomes all the more important in case of private enterprises. In our country, where there is the existence of public and private sectors, there is the need for Government regulation of the private sector business. The regulations are aimed at controlling undesirable growth and undesirable activities of the business units in the private hands. Various legislations such as Industries (Development & Regulation) Act, 1951, MRTP (Monopolies and Restrictive Trade Practices) Act, Banking Regulation Act, etc. have been enacted in our country to regulate business by the Government. Executive measures like fixation of procurement prices of foodgrains and other agricultural produce, fixation of minimum wages etc. are instances of regulatory measures adopted by the Government in the sphere of business. Unbridled activities by private individuals are not allowed even in the capitalist countries. Every State is now a welfare State and it is wedded to the policy of doing welfare to the people of the country. This objective cannot be fulfilled if the Government does not regulate business. Primarily, profit–motivated businessmen may indulge in malpractices to earn excessive profit. So the Government keeps a vigilant watch over them through various regulatory measures.

Government as Arbitrator :

The Government today not only confines its activities in promoting and regulating business enterprises but also extends them in maintaining continuous flow of production in fields and factories. It acts as Arbitrator in cases of disputes between the employers and the employees. Industrial peace is a sine qua non for uninterrupted production and distribution and in order to ensure that various legislations have been enacted to bring about understanding and settlement between capital and labour through arbitration. The Industrial Disputes Act of 1947 provides for elaborate machinery for settlement of industrial disputes. In cases where the dispute between the employers and the employees does not attract the provisions of the Act, the Government takes initiative to arrange a tripartite conference with the disputing parties, itself acting as a benevolent arbitrator.

Not only in industrial disputes, but also in the matters concerning public interest where business activities are involved; say, in case of price-rise generating wide–spread public agitation, the Government sits in conference with the industrialists and traders to prevail upon them to reduce the prices. The need for Government arbitration also arises in cases when producers and manufacturers have genuine grievances on grounds of rising cost of production.

So, to ensure peaceful and congenial environment in the business world, the government comes forward as a referee or as an arbitrator or as a conciliator when it senses any smell of disturbance threatening to disrupt the economic balance of the country. In a world bereft with strifes, misunderstandings, disputes and conflicts, the role of the Government as an Arbitrator cannot be underestimated.

Government guidance and assistance to business :

Business today is not left to the whims and pleasures of the businessmen; it is now considered a vital function of any Government to be actively involved in business activities.

Depending upon the economic pattern of a country, the extent of guidance and assistance to business is considered. In our country, where the private sector and the public sector co-exist, it becomes all the more necessary for the Government to guide and assist the private sector business to ensure coordinated effort for the economic growth of the country. Ours is a planned economy and it is desired that the economy be directed towards achieving a common objective through the rigorous compliance with the economic disciplines envisaged in the Plan. This urges upon the Government to aid and guide the private sector to ensure a concerted effort of both the public and the private sectors to realise the plan objectives.

For instance, the Government guides the private sector in respect of :

(i) Selecting channels and direction of investment of fund,

(ii) direction and selection of items of exports and imports and

(iii) industries to be taken up, goods to be produced and selection of sites for setting up industrial units.

We have in our country a number of legislations such as The Securities Controls (Regulation) Act of 1956 to regulate and control investments of fund and it also lays down guidelines and imposes obligations in regard to investments. The Government has set up many organizations – Councils, Authorities and Committees to guide and assist business. The Small Scale Industries service Institute, National Industrial Development Corporation and the Directorates of Industries of State Governments etc. are meant for guiding and assisting business in all possible ways, right from the collection of raw materials up to the stage of distribution.

The Government assistance in the form of funds to business is also forthcoming. A number of financial institutions have been set up to finance trade, industry and commerce on short term, medium term and long term basis. The Government is also assisting business enterprises by providing them protection against loss, through insurance schemes.

The Government assistance to business is made available in various ways – in guiding, in providing financial assistance, in protecting against loss, disseminating business information etc. So, the Government now acts as a friend, philosopher and guide of business.

CHAPTER NINE

PRINCIPLES OF MANAGEMENT

NATURE AND SCOPE OF MANAGEMENT

A group of people working together to achieve some common objectives need a team spirit. To ensure this spirit a unified action with the common feeling for the realisation of the goals of the organisation is imperative. Coordinated effort under central directing and leadership is required to establish harmonious relationship of men, money and materials. The element that provides leadership and co-ordination is known as Management.

Management — Ordinarily, the term management means to make the best use of the available resources. For example, in these days of sharply rising prices we anyhow manage to make two ends meet. Every individual has to manage his individual and household problems. A business has to be managed. Every businessman manages his business even not knowing the technicalities of modern management thought. Since the end of the nineteenth century and more vigorously from the days of World War II, attempts are being made to ascribe some specific and scientific definition to **management** and it is being **treated as a separate discipline or branch of knowledge.** Different scholars studying management with this new outlook have given **different definitions** of management.

Perhaps **the most simple definition** of management has been developed by Lawrence Appley which states that, management means **"getting things done through the efforts of other people".** This is a **conceptual** or **notional definition.** It has two aspects : (a) There shall be certain 'things' to be done, i.e. some 'objectives' to be achieved. (b) There shall be some people, i.e. the human organisation. Therefore, without an organisation, management cannot exist.

Through change of time, approaches to management thought have changed from the old classical approach. Koontz defines management as 'the art of **getting things done through and with the people in formally organised groups'.** The addition of the word 'with' has great significance. It recognises the importance of human element and group relationship in an organisation.

Management is as old as human society. Since man started social life or group life, management started. But from the latter part of the nineteenth century different thinkers started the study of management as a separate branch of knowledge. (1) It is related to man and so it is treated as a social science. In order to understand the nature of management, this point has to be realised first.

(2) Management is a **philosophical subject.** It is a kind of mental **attitude. Like every kind of philosophical subject, management raises questions** and new types of questions come up with the growing complexities of human organisation.

(3) It helps a manager to have a **mental preparedness** before he enters into any organisational work. It means any work should start with a plan and shall end with control.

(4) Management is in the **process of evolution.** It is comparatively a new branch of knowledge and uptil now definite meaning of different terms used in this subject have not been decidedly accepted by all. Different experts have **different views.**

(5) It is considered as something **relating to human behaviour.** Therefore, management has to be studied from two aspects : individual aspect and group aspect. Since **human behaviour is unpredictable,** a manager should know that the same man may react differently to the same situation under different circumstances or different persons will react differently to the same situation.

(6) Though there are different approaches to management by different thinkers, it is admitted that **management has some basic principles.** Henri Fayol, for the first time, set out some basic or universal principles.

(7) Management is applicable to all forms of human organisation. So **it has an universality** of application that does not matter whether the organisation is profit-making or non-profit-making. For non-profit-making organisation, the term administration is preferably used in place of management.

(8) Perhaps the most important point with regard to the nature of management is whether it is **a science or an art.** F. W. Taylor wanted to establish that management is a science when he wrote his famous book 'The Principles of Scientific Management'. But according to Fayol, the basic principles of management have to be applied differently in different organisations and under different circumstances or environments. "Science advances by knowledge, proves, predicts, defines and measures. Art advances by practice, feels, guesses, describes and opines." By a close observation of the characteristics of both science and art we can say that management has some common characteristics of both. Management principles, like the theories of science, are not applicable in the same manner at all times and at all places. Management is concerned with human behaviour which is unpredictable. **It is a philosophy and philosophy is a meeting point of science and art.** It is rightly said that management is the oldest art but the youngest science. **It is the oldest art** because man knowingly or unknowingly has been managing his group life since the dawn of society. **It is the youngest science** because the study of management as a science — social science (precisely a behavioural science), has started only in this century. A social science has its own theories but the theories of a social science (like political science) are not as rigid and universal as those of a natural science (like physics). At best it can be said that management is an art based on some scientific principles. Brech criticises Taylor, saying that management cannot be 'scientific' in the real sense but there can be 'scientific approach' to management. George Terry aptly remarks, "In essence, a manager is as much an artist as a scientist. In certain sense it can be said that **the art of management begins where the science of management stops."**

(9) Management is very **closely connected with other branches of science** like sociology, psychology, political since, anthropology, etc. Besides, in modern times, quantitative sciences like mathematics and statistics are frequently used in the management process and particularly for decision-making.

(10) In modern times management **has become a profession. With** the separation of management from ownership through the growth and development of corporate form of organisation, importance of professional management has become great. Managers are now-a-days trained in management training institutes just like other types of technical training institutes. **Professional management satisfies all the norms and characteristics of a profession.** Professional management is common in public enterprises.

The term 'management', unlike philosophy and religion, defies precise definition. Every writer has tried to explain the term in his own way but none has been able to offer such a definition as would contain all the ingredients of management. Brech has said, "exactly what the term means is not always clear and not always agreed".

The basic reason for the difference of opinion as to the concept of management lies in the fact that some writers consider management as a group of managerial personnel while others think that management is functional in nature and it involves a process of planning, organising, staffing, directing, coordinating and controlling. There is another school of opinion where management is looked upon as a body of knowledge and practice. Some writers also hold the view that management is an economic resource or a factor of production. Still others feel that management is a system of authority or a class or elite group.

To some authors, Management is a technique of leadership or a means of coordination.

George R. Terry in his 'Principles of Management' observes : "Management is extensive and formulating a comprehensive definition of it poses certain difficulties". **Taylor,** the father of scientific Management, described management as the art of 'knowing what you want to do' and then seeing that, it is done in the best and cheapest way. A better definition of management was offered by **Henri Fayol,** according to whom 'to manage is to forecast and to plan, to organise, to command, to coordinate and to control.' This is a functional definition of management which has sought to explain the concept of management from a functional angle in an appropriate manner. **Peter Drucker** has also justified this functional approach to the definition of management because management is an organ; organs can be described and defined only through their functions.

To define management purely as human administrative or management of people is not correct either. Human aspect is only one, of course a very important, aspect of management. According to **Rrech,** "The true character of management must be seen as **process** or skill compound of several essential elements many of which are steeped in the traditional technologies and each of which has its own contribution to make to the effective working of that process as a whole". Brech has defined Management as a social process.

A few definitions of Management

"A multi-purpose organ that manages a business and manages managers and manages workers and work." — Peter F. Drucker

"Management is the process by which a co-operative group directs actions towards common goals." — Joseph L. Massie

"Management is that function of an enterprise which concerns itself with the direction and control of the various activities to attain the business objectives." — William R. Spriegel.

"Management is principally the task of planning, co-ordinating, motivating and controlling the efforts of others towards specific objectives." — J. L. Lundy

"Management consists of getting things done through others. Manager is one who accomplishes the objectives by directing the efforts of others." — C. S. George

As we see, the term **Management** has been interpreted by different authors in different ways. But, if management has to develop as a science, it should be defined in one sense only. The same word should not be used to describe both status and function. L. Urwick pleaded that management, to be effective, must get rid of its multiple meanings.

(1) Every human group activity consists of some objectives. Management is an intangible but **distinct process** by which such objectives are realised.

(2) Management itself has **objectives.** Drucker says that management must not be by crisis and drive but it shall be by objectives. It means that it is not proper to think that whenever there is a crisis or problem it requires to be solved or managed but **management shall exist all through** to satisfy the need of all the people connected with an organisation and of the organisation itself.

(3) There are some **basic principles of management** applicable to all types of organisation. Henri Fayol, for the first time, has given 14 principles of management.

(4) Management is a **separate branch of knowledge** which can be acquired and transferred from person to person, activity to activity and from organisation to organisation.

(5) It is a **developing concept.** With the change of time and gathering of experience, the concept of management is changing and developing.

(6) Management has a **number of functions** and all these are necessary to make human efforts in an organisation effective.

Significance — The significance or importance of management in modern society is very great. (1) By proper management the existing **resources** of the society **can be fully utilised,** productivity can be increased and the society as a whole prospers. Countries with limited resources and natural disadvantages like Japan, Switzerland, etc. have been able to prosper by virtue of efficient management of the available resources. (2) Management in economic sense **can be treated as a factor of production** which makes better use of other factors of production. (3) People in management are small in number but the **managerial people hold a dominant position** in the society. The owners of the business are not necessarily the managers in modern times. There are **professional managers.** In socialist countries, managers of state-controlled organisations have formidable powers. (4) The significance or importance is justified as **every kind of human group activity needs management.** Drucker says that management can be described as the "most powerful engine for human betterment and social justice."

Management, however, has its **limitations.** (1) Management creates a **powerful class** similar to the bureaucrats. The professional managers develop a peculiar type of **self-interest** and try to create a kind of importance for them above the organisation. (2) C. N. Parkinson, a retired British army officer, has written a number of interesting books describing the inner defects of modern management. According to him, modern professional managers **unnecessarily create problems** to increase their importance and also create a number of subordinate posts so that the managers can do better bossing. (3) The management is a developing concept. Different authors are **interpreting managerial terms differently.** Many theories are being presented. Koontz and O'Donnell rightly say that we are in a 'jungle of management theory'.

Whatever may be the limitations of and criticisms against management, it has to be admitted that **management plays a vital role** in modern society. Knowingly or unknowingly, we are involved in management process in our everyday life.

Management and Administration

Scholars are not unanimous as to the relationship between management and administration. Their views can be divided into three categories —

(a) Management and administration are synonymous.

(b) Management and administration are two separate functions.

(c) Management is a wider term including administration.

Management and Administration are synonymous :

Henri Fayol, Terry, Allen, Koontz and O'Donnell and some other authors do not like a distinction between management and administration. According to them, what is administration in government departments goes by the name of management in business. **Newman** defined management or administration as the guidance, leadership and control of the efforts of a group of individuals towards some common goal and according to Allen, administration is the total of planning, organising, co-ordinating, motivating, controlling and operating work.

So, the terms Management and Administration are interchangeable.

Management and Administration are two separate functions :

In his 'The Philosophy of Management,' **Oliver Sheldon** brought a distinction, perhaps for the first time, between management and administration. According to him, management is the industrial function relating to the execution of policy within the limits set up by administration whereas administration is that function in industry which determines corporate policy, co-ordinates finance, production and distribution, settles the compass of the organisation and ultimately controls the executive.

Nature & Scope

According to this school of opinion, administration determines the organisation and management uses it. Administration determines the goal, management strives towards it. Management uses the organisation tool to achieve the goals set up by administration.

According to **McFarland**, "Administration refers to the determination of major aims and policies, whereas management refers to the carrying out of operations designed to accomplish the aims and effectuate the policies."

So, administration is policy determining and management is executive function.

Management is wider than administration

The English School of thought, led by **Brech,** propounds that management is a wider term that covers both administration and execution. The American writers consider administration as a policy-making function and management as an executive function. They think that administration is a top level function and management is a lower level activity.

The British author Brech says that management is the generic (all-inclusive) term for the total process of executive control involving responsibility for effective planning and guidance of the operations of an enterprise. According to this view, management is principally concerned with the determination of over-all policy while administration involves execution of such policy.

In practice, however, their distinction is neither possible nor logical. We can rather say, Administrative management and Operating management to mean determining objectives and policies by the former and the execution **of plans by** the latter.

Functions of Management

Different authorities have given different names for the key functions of management.

The following seven functions are described below in brief :

1. Decision making, 2. Organising, 3. Staffing, 4. Planning, 5. Controlling, 6. Communication, 7. Directing.

These functions are inter-related. But management being a process, the functions of management should be treated separately.

Decision-making

An executive is a man who decides; sometimes he decides right, but always he decides (J. H. Pottersen).

A manager makes decisions and actions are carried out by others. He can be considered a specialist in the art of decision-making. Decision can be defined as a course of action consciously chosen from available alternatives for the purpose of achieving a desired result. It is a rational process. The decision taken by an individual affects him but the decisions taken by a manager influence the actions of others. The ability to make correct decision and that, too, without wasting much time makes a manager an effective one and leads the organisation to desired goals.

Decision-making is a process : It involves :

1. Consciousness about the factors that set the stage for the decision.
2. Recognition of the right problem.
3. Search for and analysis of available alternatives.
4. Selection of the solution.
5. Making the decision acceptable to the organisation.

Decision-making is the essence of management. Management can be rightly called the art and science of decision-making. It is a common silken thread running through the entire process of management culminating in the ultimate realisation of the objectives of the organisation. Decision has to be made at every stage or level of management; it is, therefore, pervasive in nature and covers the entire gamut of organisations. In essence, management is simply the process of decision-making and control over the action of human beings, thus it is the heart of the managerial job.

Organising :

To organise is to create a harmonious structure of authority-responsibility relationships and order and system by bringing together different elements. An organisation is built up for the people so that they can work effectively to achieve the common objectives of the enterprise.

In the words of Koontz and O'Donnell, Organising involves the establishment of an intentional structure of roles through determination and enumeration of the activities required to achieve the goals of the enterprise, the grouping of these activities, the assignment of such groups of activities to a manager, the delegation of authority to carry them out and provision for co-ordination of authority relationships horizontally and vertically in the organisational structure.

Organisation is a conscious co-ordination of people towards a common goal. It is one of the basic functions of management the proper implementation of which leads the enterprise to success. An organisation strongly built upon sound principles can ensure a coherent effort on the part of its people to reach the pre-determined goal.

To serve its purpose, certain principles should be adhered to while organising. Principles are :

1. Unity of objective, 2. Principle of efficiency, 3. Principle of division of work, 4. Principle of span of control, 5. The Scalar principle, 6. Principle of delegation, 7. Principle of correspondence, 8. Principle of absoluteness of responsibility, 9. Principle of commensuration, 10. Principle of Unity of command, 11.Principle of Balance, 12. Exception principle, 13. Principle of co-ordination, 14. Principle of flexibility, 15. Principle of continuity.

This is not an exhaustive list. These principles are, however, truths of general application. They are not like laws of pure science. They are rather guides and broad generalisations to be pursued to instal a sound organisation.

Organisation theory is developing rapidly. It is being viewed as a system of human interactions.

To quote Allen — Sound organisation can contribute greatly to the continuity and success of the enterprise.

Peter Drucker states : Good organisation structure does not by itself produce good performance but a poor organisation structure makes good performance impossible, no matter how good the individuals may be. The right organisational structure is the necessary foundation; without it the best performance in all other areas of management will be ineffectual and frustrated.

Staffing :

The Staffing function of Management relates to selection of competent personnel. To find out the right man, to place him to the right job at the right time are the activities of the staffing function. The management experts believe that more important than production genius, more important than having sufficient money in the bank, is having the right kind of people in the organisation. It is a function performed by managers at all levels.

Staffing or Manning function is assuming more and more importance with the growing importance of human factor in business. Staffing was a part of organising function; now it is treated as a separate function of management and is given considerable weight as a dominating factor of production. It has developed as an important functional area known as Personnel Management. Staffing is a continuous function as the work force is subject to constant change.

Planning :

The concept of planning as a part of management process has been a part of all management thought. It was the first of the seven administrative processes in Luther Gulick's famous POSDCORB. Planning precedes all other functions. According to Terry "Planning is the selecting and relating of facts and the making and using of assumptions regarding the future in the visualization and formulation of proposed activities believed necessary to achieve desired results."

Various authors have defined planning, one saying planning is anticipating, another saying a plan is a trap to capture the future and the third one saying that planning is, in essence, the exercise of foresight.

Planning is looking ahead and deciding in advance what is to be done, when and where it is to be done, how it is to be done and by whom. A plan is essentially today's design for tomorrow's action.

The process of planning consists of determination of objectives, forecasting; search for and evaluation of alternative courses of action and selection of a suitable course of action; formulation of policies and programmes; preparation of schedules and budgets; laying down of procedures and standards of performance, etc.

Planning may be long term, short term, formal or informal. But it is always an intellectual or mental process.

According to Niles, "Planning is the conscious process of selecting and developing the best course of action to accomplish an objective. It is the basis from which future management decisions spring."

A Plan is, therefore, a detailed method or scheme, formulated before-hand, for doing or making something.

Controlling :

Controlling is a process of making sure that performance takes place in conformity with plans. Management control system is the technique by which executives measure actual performance and guide it towards the achievement of pre-determined goals.

Control as a of method administration has been in existence from times immemorial. The essence of control is that it must be positive and constructive, designed to help, rather then hinder the achievement of plans.

The chief characteristics of management control are —

(a) It is a manager's function,

(b) It is a circular movement — starts with planning, the determination of objectives — ends with planning function again to determine how performance can be improved,

(c) It is forward-looking — A manager can take corrective action only in regard to future operations,

(d) It is exercised at all levels of management,

(e) It is a continuing process involving constant analysis of the validity of the policies,

(f) It has both positive and negative aspects. In its positive aspect, it secures and maintains acceptable productivity and in its negative aspect it prevents and reduces unacceptable and incorrect performance.

A control system has five basic elements —

1. The detection element, 2. The evaluation element, 3. The specification element, 4. The notification element, 5. The correction element.

To be effective, a control system must be prompt, positive, continuous and self-regulating.

Communicating :

"Communicating is the process to which ideas are transmitted to others for the purpose of effecting a desired result" (Massia). It is one of the most important functions of management. Its importance was highlighted by the president of the American Management Association, when he said : "The No. I management problem today is communication". Communication has been defined as any behaviour that results in an exchange of meaning, the act of making one's ideas and opinions known to others.

The media of communication are words, pictures and actions. These different media have their respective merits and demerits. Any medium is resorted to on the merit of the circumstances.

Communication may be both upward and downward flowing from subordinate to the superior or vice versa.

The main purpose of communication is to change someone, some group or something or to head off unfavourable trends.

There are certain barriers to communication such as unsound objectives, organisation of blocks, semantic blocks and human relations problem.

"Communication is at the very heart of the process of organizing" (Dale Yoder). An area where communication can produce tremendous results is in the avoidance of industrial disputes, which pose a serious problem to modern management.

More detailed descriptions of some functions of management are given below :

Planning :

Planning is the core of management functions. Whatever the management does is preceded by planning. Planning is mainly a mental exercise which is not an exclusive function of the management area of business only. In everyday life, every one plans consciously or unconsciously and the day passes off smoothly : Planning for the day or planning for the whole life — whatever it may be — planning is there. A good planning makes a life successful; a bad planning leads it to failure.

The significance of planning cannot be over-emphasised. In business, planning lays the foundation on which the edifice of business stands. The concept of planning as a part of management process has been a part of all management thought. In early twentieth century, Henri Fayol identified five functions of management. The first was "to forecast and plan". Frederick Taylor considered planning as one of the major functions of management. It was the first of the seven administrative processes in Luther Gulick's famous POSDCORB. Indeed, even the most modern thinkers and teachers follow the lead of Fayol by sub-dividing management generally into the more specific management processes of planning and control. Decision-making and communicating are regarded as underlying processes entering into planning.

In this age of rapid technological changes, the importance of planning has tremendously increased. It has become a key managerial function to cope with a complex, dynamic and everchanging business environment.

Be it formally or informally — in a single crude fashion or in a scientific, sophisticated manner, planning is a must when a business concern is confronted with alternative courses of action. Without proper planning, disorder and chaos must arise. Koontz and O'Donnell state, "Without planning, business becomes random in nature and decisions become meaningless **ad hoc** choices." So to provide purpose and direction to the member of an organisation, planning is imperative.

The **benefits** of planning are —

(1) Better utilisation of resources, (2) Minimisation of Cost, (3) Improvement of competitive strength, (4) Minimisation of uncertainty, (5) Encouragement and improvement of motivation, (6) Facilities for control, (7) Better co-ordination, (8) Facility for better delegation of authority, (9) Creation of forward looking attitude in Management, (10) Prevention of hasty judgement, (11) Anticipation of crises, (12) Better communication throughout the organisation and (13) Better training ground for future managers.

Planning premises :

Planning premises are basic assumptions for and upon which the planning process proceeds. So, planning premises actually mean the environment or the background or the framework within which a firm works. These premises not only imply assumptions but also predictions.

Effective planning is, therefore, largely dependent upon the knowledge and accurate choice of planning premises. It is the opinion of a renowned author of Management that in order to plan for the future, the manager needs these planning premises for his own foundation of planning.

Planning premises can be classified as follows : (1) External and Internal premises (2) Tangible and Intangible premises (3) Controllable, Semi-controllable and Uncontrollable premises and (4) Foreseeable and Unforeseeable premises.

External and Internal premises signify the business climate prevailing outside and inside a business. The general business climate relates to external premise and the inside business climate such as sales forecast, capital investment in plant and equipment, policies, major programmes already undertaken are all internal premises. Political, social, economic and technological conditions in general determine external premises. To formulate plans, both these premises have significant roles to play in business.

Tangible and Intangible premises mean quantifiable and unquantifiable premises. A firm's reputation, for example, is an unquantifiable intangible premise, the importance of which can very well be understood in formulating plans and for final decisions.

Controllable, Semi-controllable and Uncontrollable premises — There are planning premises which are well within the control and value of management such as policy framing, drawing up of programmes and laying down of rules, etc. Premises such as war, strikes, natural calamities, population trends over which a firm has absolutely no control fall within the category of uncontrollable premises and premises over which management has partial control are semi-controllable premises.

Foreseeable and Unforeseeable premises are premises which can be foreseen and which cannot be foreseen. Foreseeable premises can be controlled but unforeseeable premises largely remain uncontrollable.

On the nature of planning premises, the nature of planning and the effectiveness of planning depend and thus the significance of planning premises to planners is worth reckoning.

Steps in Planning :

Planning is a process. It involves a number of steps. According to Koontz and O'Donnell, planning in a business organisation usually involves the following steps — (1) Establishment of objectives, (2) Establishment of planning premises, (3) Search for and examination of alternative courses of action, (4) Evaluation of alternative courses of action, (5) Selection of a course or courses of action and (6) Formulation of necessary derivative plans.

1) Establishment of objectives

This is the first step in the planning process. The objectives must be established at the very outset and, accordingly, planning has to be made. A plan, to be meaningful, must have some goal which will give the key as to what basically to do, where to place the primary emphasis and what to accomplish by the network of policies, procedures, budgets and programmes.

2) Establishment of planning premises :

The establishment of planning premises comes as the second step. These premises are planning assumptions and they are the future setting against which all planning takes place. To establish planning premises is to spell out as clearly as possible the assumptions under which plans are to operate.

3) Search for and examination of alternative courses of action :

Next comes the third step to search for and examine alternative courses of action. Every plan made cannot be such as there can be no alternatives to that. There always remain alternative courses of action; so constant endeavour must be made to examine alternative courses of action suitable for the organisation.

4) Evaluation of alternative courses of action :

Simply finding out the alternative course or courses of action cannot make a plan a sound one. One has to be sure that the alternative courses of action found out are really worth pursuing; this needs evaluation of alternative courses of action involving various factors — their relative merits and demerits.

5) Selection of a course or courses of action :

Last but one step in the process of planning is the selection of a course or courses of action to be undertaken. "This is the point at which the plan is adopted — the point of decision-making". Evaluation of alternative may disclose that two or more alternatives are advisable and the management may decide to pursue a number of alternatives than the best one.

6) Formulation of necessary derivative plans :

The basic plan to be effective needs some derivative plans to support it. So, while preparing a plan, derivative plans must be constructed and a derivative programme may be necessary to develop new policies and procedures for effecting the plan.

As to the steps in planning, it has also been stated that the planning should follow the following steps —

(1) Deciding in general terms what has to be done.

(2) Taking a look at what one has to work with.

(3) Determining what will happen if an exceptional action is taken.

(4) Deciding very specifically what is to be accomplished.

(5) Figuring out also very specifically how to get the planned results.

(6) Following up with an effective programme of reporting and analysis of performance.

Types of Planning :

Time, management and subject form the basis on which planning may be classified.

There may be long term planning and short term planning on the basis of time span.

On the basis of nature, planning may be **Strategic** or **Operational.**

Again, planning may be standing plans or single use plans on the basis of frequency.

According to subject matter, planning may be organisation, production, marketing, manpower, financial or profit planning.

Elements or Components of planning :

(1) **Objectives** — First of all there shall be some definite objectives which have to be fulfilled. The immediate or short term objective of an enterprise is to achieve customers' satisfaction and then only it can survive. Ultimate or long term objective is to achieve maximum profitability. There are common objectives of the organisation as a whole as well as objectives for different groups or sub-groups inside the organisation. There is a hierarchy or objectives from the lower to higher levels. A balancing of objectives is necessary.

(2) **Policy** — Objectives decide what is to be done. It is followed by policy which decides how it is to done. It is the framework within which decisions have to be taken.

(3) **Procedures** — Procedures are definite tasks arranged according to time sequence which have to be followed step by step to complete a job. Procedures are definite and specific. For example, the procedure of purchasing raw materials shall consist of the following steps : tender, quotation, placement of order, receiving the goods, checking, storing etc.

(4) **Programmes** — Once the objectives, the policies and the procedures are finalised, they are integrated in orderly manner which are called programmes which have to be executed.

The human element — Primarily it relates to the managerial staff.

(5) **Budgets** — Budgets are numerical expressions of the objectives to be fulfilled. They are called the targets. A budget has two aspects: (a) Physical — It deals with the quantum of work which has to be done. For example, production budget or how much quantity to be produced. (b) Financial — It is the monetary value of the job. For example, the cost of production of the physical quantity. Once a budget is prepared and accepted, it has to be followed and there shall be no deviation. Therefore, a budget is also a tool of control.

(6) **Strategies** — In a competitive market, a manager has to apply some artful devices to win over the competition which are called strategies. Strategies are used by generals in the battlefields against enemy action. The same idea is applicable to business. Time-to-time adjustment of policies has to be done because of changing situations and to counteract the action of competitors. Through spying, managers try to learn the policies and techniques used by competitors and accordingly mould their strategies. According to modern management thinkers, every organisation must have some master strategy by which it excels in the competitive market. A manufacturer may have a marketing policy of not allowing any credit sale. The total sales may fall. In order to increase the sales, the strategy adopted will be offering cash discount.

(7) **Rules** — In planning, rules should be framed to specify what is to be done and not to be done in a given situation without deviation. Rules reflect what a manager expects of his subordinates. Rules help in maintaining and enhancing efficiency. They are specific guides to action and permits no discretion or judgement.

(8) **Projects** — A project is a distinct cluster of function and facilities for a definite purpose. It is a part of a general programme. Projects help simplify co-ordination and control by identifying an integrated work package.

Limitations of Planning :

Planning is not a panacea for all ills. Planning also suffers from certain limitations. Limitations can broadly be divided into two parts — **internal** and **external.**

Internal limitation may be —

(a) Internal inflexibility, (b) Expenses, (c) Time-consuming, (d) Sudden emergencies, (e) Stifling of initiative, (f) Investment pattern, (g) Frustrating work, (h) Mental ability and (i) Resistance to change.

External limitations — There are planning limitations over which the planners have no control, such as environmental forces, the general national and international climate.

Directing :

Directing determines the scope, gives order and instructions and provides the dynamic leadership. It is the heart of administration.

To direct sub-ordinates, a manager must motivate, communicate and lead. In the words of Earnest Dale, "direction is telling people what to do and seeing that they do it to the best of their ability."

"Directing is a complex function. That includes all those activities which are designed to encourage sub-ordinates to work effectively both in the short and the long run." (Koontz and O'Donnell). Directing is a process around which all performance revolves. It is the essence of operation and co-ordination is a necessary by–product of good managerial directing.

The importance of directing can well be understood if we believe that management is to get things done by others. Management being a team–work the leader — the director – has a special role to play. Faulty direction can nullify an efficient planning.

An inefficient director of a film fails to make the best use of even the best actors.

Characteristics of directing :

(1) It is dynamic in nature,

(2) It provides a link among different functions,

(3) Its essence is performance,

(4) It is universally applicable — no matter to which level a particular manager belongs to,

(5) It is concerned with human relationship.

Principles of Direction :

A manager, to be an effective director, should follow certain principles. Direction is a complex function; so some principles rigidly followed may lead the directing function to success.

The principles are :

(i) Harmony of objectives, (ii) Unity of command, (iii) Individual contribution, (iv) Direct supervisions, (v) Appropriate techniques, (vi) Managerial communication, (vii) Comprehension, (viii) Principle of follow–through, (ix) Strategic use of informal organisation and (x) Effective leadership.

Role of leadership in Management :

Leadership is the main vehicle to convey direction. To lead is to guide, direct, integrate and energise the efforts of people towards a common goal. A good leader knows that if he develops his associates, he will be even stronger.

Business leadership is the function of organising and directing business enterprises, making the decisions which determine the course of a firm's activities.

The role of leadership in management can be better described by the function that a leader is expected to perform.

A leader sets the goals and acts as a guide and teacher of his followers to achieve the desired goals.

The leader organises; he creates and moulds the organisation by assigning roles appropriate to individual abilities. He shapes the character of the group and leads them towards goals with proper direction.

A leader co-ordinates individual and common objectives. In infusing mutual understanding, the leader has a very vital role to play.

It is the leader who motivates, creates and sustains enthusiasm among his followers. He establishes a motivational system that enables people to meet both organisational and personal goals.

The leader controls. He controls internal conflicts. In the words of Drucker, "The first test of management's competence is its ability to keep people working with minimum of disruption and the maximum of effectiveness". A leader is essentially a controller of human behaviour.

The leader has a representative role to play. He represents the group to his superiors. A leader develops and maintains morale by evoking confidence and by building zeal and enthusiasm among his followers.

No organisation can function without an effective leader. In spite of all the factors being favourable, there are numerous instances where the organisation has not succeeded in attaining its goals because of the lack of leadership. "Leadership is the cohesive force which holds the group intact, the disciplinary power that keeps the group working towards the goal, the electric current that energises human action, the force that transforms chaos into order, the insight that converts despair into hope and changes half-hearted endeavours into superior performance. In fact, there is no substitute for good leadership".

Organising :

"All that organisation means is the correlation of the activities of men and women for a common purpose." It is the process of so combining the work which individuals or groups have to perform with the facilities necessary for its execution, that the duties so performed provide the best channels for the efficient, systematic, positive and co-ordinated application of the available effort.

Organisation is considered as a function of management. It creates harmonious authority -responsibility relationships between different parts of an enterprise. Organising defines the role each individual is to play and establishes relationships between them. Human organisations are treated as systems of interdependent human relationships directed towards common goals.

"Two functions of management, organising and staffing, are so closely related that they are discussed together. Organising focuses attention on the structure and process of allocating jobs so that common objectives can be achieved; staffing pertains to the people in the jobs. In other words, organising is job-oriented; staffing is worker-oriented." (Massie)

The need for organisation arises when two or more persons work together for a common goal. "It is the objective of organisation to establish an activity–authority environment in which people can perform most effectively". (Koontz and O'Donnell). An organisation is the framework within which people can work in co-operation. So organisation, grow out of the human need for co-operation. Organisation is the means by which management blends human and material resources. It is also the mechanism for the direction, co-ordination and control of individual efforts. Defective organisation structure renders management difficult and ineffective.

Organisation, according to Allen, is indispensable for the following reasons —

(1) It facilitates administration, (2) It makes growth and diversification possible, (3) It permits optimum use of resources, (4) It encourages good human relations, (5) It stimulates initiative and creativity.

Andrew Carnegie, the great American industrialist, once said, "Take away our factory, our trade, our avenues of transportation, our money, leave us nothing but our organisation and in four years, we shall have re-established ourselves". Such is the importance and significance of organisation and organising in an effective manner is thus a very important task of the management.

Steps in organisation :

Organisation is a process and this process consists of the following **Steps** :

1. Determination and division of work :

The organising function starts in determining the tasks to be performed in the accomplishment of the business objectives. Once the tasks are determined, there arises the need for the division of the tasks into appropriate groups or functions. This division of total work forms the foundation of the organisation. In a modern business, these functions are generally divided into manufacturing, marketing, finance and personnel and they are known as functional areas of business.

2. Grouping of activities :

In the second step of the process of organisation, the various functions determined and identified are classified into appropriate departments according to similarity and common purposes. This organisational function of grouping of activities is known as "Departmentation". The departmentation may be based on function, products, territories, customs etc. or on the basis of most use, most interest, competition, co-ordination and policy control. This grouping or departmentation is done with a view to achieving specialisation and the grouping may be carried still further and sub-units may be organised to create a logical structure.

3. Assignment of duties :

The next step or the third step in the process of organisation is to man every department with suitable individuals. Specific duties are allotted to the departmental heads to ensure efficiency of performance. Duties are so assigned as to avoid duplication of work and overlapping of efforts.

4. Delegation of authority :

Assignment of duties necessarily leads to delegation of authority. A manager cannot be burdened with duties and responsibilities only, he must be armed with authority and that authority he cannot retain with him alone. However competent and efficient a manager may be, he cannot be expected to do everything personally. He needs the assistance of others and there arises the need for delegation of authority. This delegation of authority, being the last step in the process of organisation, must be made to ensure that the delegation be effective and there is a balance between authority and responsibility.

These steps in organisation are necessary to create a logical structure of authority — responsibility — relationships.

Organisational Formats

Organisational format or structure may be formal or informal. There are several forms of formal structure — Line, Functional or Staff, Line and Staff, Matrix and Project.

Line Organisation — Refers to direct lines of authority flowing from top to the bottom of the organisational hierarchy. Authority and responsibility flow vertically in an unbroken straight line from one level to another, hence the name-line or scalar organisation. It is the traditional type of organisation. Every superior has complete command over his subordinates and every subordinate is directly accountable to only one superior immediately above him. There is unity of command, each department is self-contained. This form is usually found in Government departments. This is the oldest and the simplest form of organisation.

This form of organisation is simple, flexible. It helps executive development, encourages quick decisions and effective co-ordination. Responsibility can easily be fixed and proper discipline can be maintained. It is also economical.

But from disadvantages such as overburdening, instability, lack of specialisation, autocratic leadership and also difficulty in staffing, large-scale organisations, because of these disadvantages, discard this form of organisation.

Staff Organisation

Staff service in organisation means the service of advice or counsel. It is an organisation which provides for advisory staff. The main function of staff is to help the line so that the latter may be able to perform its duties efficiently. Staff service has three phases — the information, the advisory and the supervisory.

Staff activities can be classified into four categories — control agencies, service agencies, co-ordinator agencies and advisory agencies.

The major responsibilities of staff division are five — (a) formulation of policy, (b) programme planning, (c) constant review and appraisal, (d) consultation and (e) services to the operating line.

Staff organisation offers **advantage** of specialisation, easy staffing, democratic control, better supervision and scope for expansion.

Disadvantages accruing from staff organisation are —

(a) poor discipline, (b) divided responsibility, (c) low morale, (d) lack of executive development, (e) lack of coordination, (f) delayed decisions and (g) uneconomical.

This type of organisation as was developed by Taylor is rarely used in its pure form. It is now used in modified form.

Line and Staff Organisation

To overcome the defects of both line and staff types of organisation, the blending of the two types has been envisaged. Too much concentration of control in line organisation and too much division of control in staff organisation had to be removed; so came line & staff organisation.

It seeks to combine the advantage of division of work with unity of command. The line portion serves to maintain unity of command and discipline whereas the staff portion concentrates on providing expert knowledge and advice in the solution of managerial problems.

Through this organisation format are achieved the following advantages :

(1) planned specialisation, (2) discipline, (3) staffing and development, (4) balanced decision, (5) flexibility and (6) undivided responsibility.

But as against these advantages, the following drawbacks have to be admitted in this type of organisation :

(1) conflicts, (2) lack of co-ordination, (3) ineffectiveness of staff, (4) lack of creativity and (5) expensiveness.

In practice, this is the most common type of organisational format.

Matrix organisation

The line and staff type of organisation, too, in course of time, was not found suitable to cope with the complex problem of a firm. So another type was devised known as **Matrix organisation.** This type difers sharply from the typical one–boss command structures based on the principle of unity of command.

Matrix organisation has been defined as "any organisation that employs a multiple command and system that includes not only a multiple command structure but also related support mechanisms and an associated organisational structure and behaviour pattern" (Davis & Lawrence). Thus, the matrix organisation confines functional departmentation with product or programme structure. The matrix structure is used in big projects which have to be completed within a stipulated time period. Here, the individuals working on a project have a continuing dual assignment to the project and to their base department. This is a major departure from the usual line staff structure.

The matrix structure is designed to give the strength of both the line and staff organisation while avoiding their weakness.

The **benefits** derived from this structure are : (a) specialisation, (b) lateral coordination, (c) encouragement to team work, (d) flexibility, and (e) improvement of communication.

Limitations

(1) Role conflict arising out of the violation of the principle of unity of command or due to the multiple flows of authority.

(2) This organisation is not a homogeneous and compact group. The multiplicity of vertical and horizontal relationships impairs organisational efficiency.

(3) Employee performance appraisal becomes difficult for the functional heads because of the placement of the specialists from functional departments to projects.

Project Organisation

Matrix and project organisations are often used as interchangeable terms. Project or programme organisation is oriented towards the completion of specific projects. It results in bringing specialists from several different parts of the organisation together to work on a particular project.

Project organisation focuses concentrated attention to a complex project. Highly talented professionals are better employed under project organisation since they can give their best, being a part of a team of skilled professionals and this acts as a powerful motivator. A large project with definite beginning and end can be better managed in this type of organisation. It cuts the manager's job to a reasonable level, spreads decision-making and facilitates communications through lateral relationships.

Though the concept of project organisation is sound, it suffers from certain drawbacks; (a) It violates the principles of unity of command. (b) The project manager with total authority requires resources to accomplish his project goals and as such budgets, man-power and authority are always problems in project management. (c) This type of management organisation lacks in the specificity of line and staff as it is not clear who is to do what. (d) There is the scope for feeling of insecurity and worry among the project staff on the completion of a project as to their reassignment.

Committee Management

Formation of committees has become a usual and common feature in modern management organisation. A committee is a group of persons who function collectively and perform some specified functions. "It is the characteristic of group action that sets the committee apart from other organisational devices." Committee management, strictly speaking, is a supplement that can be used in any structure of organisation. A committee may be line or staff depending upon the function assigned to it.

Committees are formed to pool knowledge and experience, to ensure democratic management and to represent different interests. Committee management helps development of the executive talent by providing opportunities for having experience in different aspects of various problems. Co-ordination, communication, initiative and creativity can also be better assured in the committee form of management. Through committee management, better motivation and morale and consolidation of authority can be expected.

Limitations are found in respect of indecisiveness, controversy, diffused responsibility and domination by a few. The committee form is also expensive.

Delegation of Authority

According to Allen, delegation is "the process a manager follows in dividing the work assigned to him so that he performs that part which only he, because of his unique organisational placement, can perform effectively and so that he can get others to help him with what remains."

Authority refers to that relationship which exists between two individuals — one superior and the other subordinate. Henri Fayol thinks authority is "the right to give orders and the power to exact obedience".

The need for delegation arises from the fact that the chief executive cannot do all alone all the work assigned to him. The process of granting authority to subordinates and exacting responsibility from them starts to accomplish work in an organisation to achieve its desired goals.

Elements of delegation

The process of delegation involves the following steps :

1. Assignment of duties

The process of delegation starts with the allocation of duties to subordinates. A superior defines the work to be done by the subordinates and then he assigns the job to them.

2. Granting Authority

Assignment of duties cannot yield results unless and until the assignee or delegatee is granted authority or power. So, authority is granted to perform the part of the duty assigned to a subordinate.

3. Exacting responsibility

The process of delegation to be effective cannot stop just after assignment of duties and granting of authorities. The duties or responsibilities assigned must have to be exacted, otherwise the whole exercise is a futile one. The subordinates must be held accountable for the work assigned to them. Duty, authority and accountability go hand-in-hand in the process of delegation.

Principles of delegation

For an effective delegation, certain principles are to be adhered to. They can be enumerated as follows :

1. Defining the functions

The functions to be performed by a subordinate should be clearly defined and there should remain no scope for ambiguity as to the interpretation of the work assigned to a particular subordinate. The entire work in an organisation should be grouped according to enterprise functions.

2. Scalar principle

From a single source, the authority should flow. Every one must know from whom he gets authority and to whom matters beyond his authority must be referred. Authority should flow to various positions in clear lines.

3. Authority Level Principle

This principle in delegation emphasises that only those decisions that cannot be made at a given level of authority should be referred to the higher level. The executive should resist his temptation to take any decision on matters that should reasonably be referred to the higher authority.

4. Unity of Command

The command should come from one and single individual at a time and not from many. This is unity of command. A subordinate should be made responsible to only one superior at a time. Dual subordination results in conflicts, division of loyalty and lack of personal responsibility for results.

5. Delegation by results expected

Delegation should be made according to the results expected from subordinates. This means the superior must see that the volume of work delegated to be performed by the sub-ordinate is justified and is likely to be accomplished with efficiency.

6. Absoluteness of responsibility

Responsibility cannot be delegated. A superior cannot be relieved of his obligation to his superior simply by delegating it to his subordinate. He rather increases his responsibility as he becomes accountable for the results and actions of the subordinates in addition to his own actions.

7. Parity of authority and responsibility

This is a basic principle of delegation that not only authority and responsibility should go together but there must be parity between authority and responsibility. They must be co-extensive and co-terminus. A man having no authority over something cannot be held responsible for that thing. There need not be mathematical equality between authority and responsibility but it is desired that they should be well - balanced. A person authorised to do something must be made responsible for its non-compliance and a person held responsible for some non-compliance must have been given the authority to do it. This is what is wanted in this **principle.**

Importance of delegation

There can be no organisation without delegation. The absence of delegation means one-man operation. So, delegation of authority is the key to organisation. It is quite understandable that however efficient an executive may be, he needs the assistance of others to accomplish his job. Here is the need for delegation. With the increase in the size of business organisations, the importance of delegation of authority is also increasing. By delegating his job, the manager or the superior creates a chain of command. It is said that the cement that holds formal organisation together is made up of delegation and resulting relationship between the organisation members. "Many stories of management indicate that a principle reason for the failure of managers is in their inability to delegate authority" (Koontz and O'Donnell).

Delegation of authority does not actually mean assignment or allocation of the entire job of the manager to his subordinate. It actually means that routine work has to be delegated and the more important tasks of planning, organising, leading and controlling would be the job of the manager and the manager alone. This ensures efficiency in organisation, a better management of affairs and a more scientific approach to reach the desired goals of the enterprise. Delegation helps development of initiative and self– reliance among subordinates.

Delegation has been described as the dynamics of management; without delegation one cannot get things done through others. Delegation helps the manager to multiply himself. It is through delegation that the manager acts as a team. It is a means by which the strength and ability of the subordinates are properly utilised. It also leads to faster decisions as authority lies near the point of action.

The complexity of modern business has all the more made delegation necessary. It is well, nigh impossible for the manager to be conversant with all the aspects of management of an enterprise; delegation helps him to solve this problem and enables him to lead the organisation to successful attainment of its goals through the united efforts of all — the delegatees. Delegation can be one of managements best technique for satisfying needs and for motivating subordinates to better performance. Delegation is not a defence mechanism to lessen pressure of the top management but it is an aggressive move to secure the benefits of direct and indirect decision-making.

Co-ordination

It is considered as the essence of management organisation. The task of co-ordination is essentially a matter of seeing that activities are performed in the proper sequence and at the proper time. In the words of Terry, "Co-ordination deals with the task of blending efforts in order to ensure successful attainment of an objective." Luther Gulick has rightly stated "If sub-division of work is inescapable, co-ordination becomes mandatory."

Basic features of co-ordination are :

1. It is a continuous process
2. It is the function of an executive
3. It is orderly arrangement of group effort
4. It secures unity of action
5. Its object is to achieve a common purpose.

Co-ordination is a matter of co-operation but there are differences between the two :

Co-operation is a vehicle for attaining co-ordination. Co-ordination has a number of elements; co-operation is one of them. So, it is a far more inclusive term embracing the idea of co-operation.

Co-operation comes out of the voluntary attitudes of the people in an organisation, but co-ordination cannot be generated out of such voluntary attitudes. It is brought about by the executive through deliberate action on his part. Co-operation is essential for co-ordination but it cannot be a substitute for co-ordination. Co-operation without co-ordination and vice-versa is fatal for management organisation. "Co-operation will usually be ineffective — will not reach its goal, whatever the intention of participants — in the absence of co-ordination" (Simon).

Principles of Co-ordination

According to Mary Parker Follett, there are four broad rules or principles of co-ordination :

1. The principle of direct contact, 2. Co-ordination in early stages, 3. Reciprocal relation of all the factors, 4. Co-ordination as a continuous process.

The principle of direct contact

Direct contact and communication constitute the basic principle of co-ordination. Co-ordination can be best achieved when the persons involved in an effort to attain certain goals are in direct and personal contact with one another. A direct horizontal relationship is essential for co-ordination.

The principle of co-ordination as to its start

Co-ordination should be started in early stages of planning and policy making. A project to be fruitful and the teamwork of all the men employed to implement the project to be effective, a direct involvement with co-operation and identity of minds is necessary and this can only be achieved through co-ordination from the very beginning of the planning. There should remain cross-relations between heads of departments instead of up and down the line through the chief executive.

Reciprocal relation of all the factors

Miss Follett believes that all factors in a situation are reciprocally related. One is influenced by other while working together and both are influenced by all persons in the total situation. According to Urwick, this principle is an application to the dynamic aspect of organisation of the same psychological truth as forms the basis of the principle of span of control.

done through the scalar chain. Over-all control is a kind of remote control. On the other hand, each departmental or functional area manager has to control his own area only. It is a kind of close control.

Terry says, "Controlling over-all performance is advantageous in that it encourages a manager **to see the forest and not simply the trees."** The 'trees' in the 'forest' of an enterprise are : different plants, different branches, different functional departments, different selling centres, etc. depending on the nature and size of the enterprise. It is also enough if control is maintained on strategic or critical areas only. All the different partial control measures may not be equally effective. An integrated approach to control **covers up the deficiencies of partial control measures.** It leads to greater co-ordination.

Techniques or methods — There are various techniques or methods of controlling overall performance : (1) **Final Accounts** — The most common and simple method is preparation and audit of the final accounts. (2) **Written reports** — Written reports from different units, branches, departments, etc. are called for, compared and integrated. (3) **Budget summaries** — Individual budgets of different units, branches,and departments are collected together and summarised into an integrated form called Master Budget or Balance Sheet Budget, as tool for over-all control. (4) **Management self-audit** — Instead of, or in addition to, appointment – of professional auditors from outside, internal and continuous audit can be carried out by trained and qualified managers. Such audit is centralised for all units, branches, departments, etc. (5) **Close and over-all** — Close control means the direct control of the subordinates by their immediate superior. Over-all control means the control by the top-level management, like the Board of Directors, over the entire organisation through the scalar chain.

Moder control techniques — (1) Programme Evaluation and Review Technique (PERT), Critical Path Method (CPM), Time Net Work Analysis, Operation's Research (OR), Logisties etc.

Tools :

There are several tools in the hands of the management to exercise control. Many of the tools are highly technical, using quantitative sciences like mathematics and statistics. Some of the tools are :

(1) **Written reports** — Each superior prepares reports on the performance of his subordinates and submits them to his higher authority. In this way, departmental managers submit reports to the General Manager. Ultimately, the Board of Directors have to submit an Annual Report to the members of the company, the virtual owners and the highest authority.

(2) **Budget** — The budget, which is a component of planning, is itself a tool of control. The budget predetermines the extent of expenditure which cannot be normally exceeded. The budget estimates the income which has to be earned. Similarly, non-financial budget determines the limits of production, employment etc. A budget means projected results which are expected to be achieved. Budgetary control is accepted to be one of the most common tools of control.

(3) **Key ratios** — Control of over-all performance can be exercised through some 'key ratios' of which Return On Investment (ROI) is very common. There are some expected returns on certain categories of investments. Those percentages must be achieved. Ratios between total assets and total liabilities, between turnover and investment, etc. are other kinds of key ratios.

(4) **Accounting techniques** — Various new kinds of audit, like cost audit and management audit, are now-a-days being introduced for better control. Management Accounting, which is not merely based on double-entry book-keeping but is concerned with resource-utilisation as a whole, is a powerful tool of control.

(5) **Statistical Quality Control and Inventory Control** — SQC is a scientific technique of controlling quelity of products through the use of statistical tools. It helps in identifying the

causes of defects in the manufacturing process and in measuring the extent of deibations from standards, through the techniques of control charts and Acceptance Sampling, this control device operates. Inventory control is exercised by production management in regard to raw materials, factore supplies etc.

BUDGETARY CONTROL

Budgetary control — Budget is a numerical expression of some objectives in the form of targets. This is called the physical or non-financial budget. But financial budget is more common and popular. It means estimation of probable expenditure and probable income for some definite period of time in relation to some activity or activities. Such estimation is not possible with theoretical knowledge only. Budget is influenced by internal, as well as external (socio-economic and political), factors. **It provides a comprehensive and projected picture** of the financial structure of an organisation. By budget the limits of expenses are fixed and those cannot be normally exceeded. This **provides a check** and is a means of control. Similarly, if the income falls short of estimation, then explanations are asked for, causes are ascertained and steps are taken. This provides a check or control on the lack of efforts, if any, for collection. Budget can be prepared for the organisation as a whole as well as for its every department. **Costing is an essential function** of financial budgeting. Non-financial budgeting takes place for production, purchase, sales and manpower. **Budget, therefore, exists in every area of management.** Every non-financial budget has impact on financial budget. Therefore, **financial and non-financial budgeting go together.**

Different aspects of budgeting — (1) **A budget has to be prepared.** It is based on facts, data and information. Budgets of different departments have to be prepared one by one. These are inter-linked. These can be called **derivative budgets. The master budget** will be prepared by aggregating all the derivative budgets. The master budget contains some more items and amounts for over-all activities of the organisation. (2) A budget **has to be approved.** Generally the top-level management has the authority of such approval. In case of a company, the Board of Directors has this authority. (3) Budgeting is a technical function and so the **assistance or staff people or specialists** is necessary. It is a combined function of line and staff. (4) A budget **has to be implemented.** At the stage of implementation it becomes a **tool of control.** Implementation of budget means disallowing deviation or variation. As soon as a period's actual operations are completed, operating results and cost data are prepared and sent to the higher level management. The report contains columns for actual, budget, amount of favourable variance and amount of unfavourable variance. All these are necessary for verification and control. The management must then determine which variances are important, discover their causes and try to find out remedial measures to avoid recurrence. This is the **process of budgetary control.**

Zero-based budgeting — Budget is prepared for every financial period (usually one year) and budgets of different financial periods are compared for studying the variances. Zero-based budgeting is a technique by which budgeting is started at base zero and costs are calculated afresh for each budget period.

Advantages of budgetary control — (1) It provides an **over-all picture** for each department which is essential for successful management. (2) It **fosters co-ordination** because all the derivative budgets are aggregated to make the master budget. (3) It keeps every department under control and so **over-all performance becomes best.** (4) **It entrusts responsibility** on every department to keep the activities confined within the budget. (5) It provides an automatic **check on wastage** and thus **creates economy.**

Disadvantages or limitations of budgetary control — (1) It indirectly **destroys initiatives** in the minds of the people as every action is within check. (2) The departmental managers **distort their requirements,** either keeping them low so that the department will have less work-load on keeping them high to exert the importance of the department. The purpose of control is lost. (3) It is **difficult to make co-ordination** or adjustments among the budgets of different departments. (4) There is a **wrong notion** to consider budgetary control as a substitute for management itself.

How to make budgetary control effective — In many big concerns there is a specially empowered person called budget director or budget controller to enforce budgetary control. **Budgetary control is a hard task.** After all, budgetary control is a tool of management. Koontz and O'Donnell give the warning — "Like any tools they have limitations and must be tailored to the job to be done." The **conditions** to be satisfied for budgetary control are : (1) The **objectives and the policies** of the organisation **must be clearly defined** because budgets largely depend on their nature. (2) The tool shall be used in **conformity with the authority.** Top-level people shall use the tool from financial aspect while lower level people shall use it from quantitative aspect, e.g., number of units produced or sold. (3) The budgetary **estimates must be balanced,** moderate and practicable. The estimates shall not be too high nor too low. (4) The budget itself must have **flexibility.** Scope for adjustment or **revision** must be there. (5) There shall be **reasonable period** for the budget depending on the nature of the activity. The capital budget shall be for a long period or years while production or sales budget shall be for a short period or one year. (6) If there is any necessity for any unbudgeted **action, approval** from higher authority has to be immediately obtained.

Steps of control :

There are in practice four steps of control (1) **Determination of the standard of performance** — Determination of standard of output is a vital step because if the standard is wrongly determined, nothing can be achieved. The standard has four aspects : quantity, quality, cost and time. Certain desirable quantity of work with a minimum quality has to be completed within a stipulated time but the cost must not be uneconomic. In case of mental work like the management work itself, it is not possible to ascertain the quantity.

(2) **Evaluation of the performance** — After the performance is over the actual performance has to be evaluated in terms of quantity, quality, cost and time. It is difficult to 'measure' mental work.

(3) **Verification** — The actual performance must be verified with the standard already determined. In the meantime, however, anticipatory control (see above) has been operating.

(4) **Correcting deviation, if any** — If there is any deviation, then the reasons for that have to be found out and then corrective measures have to be suggested for future planning and action. "Effective control", says Terry," cannot tolerate needless delays, excuses, endless compromises or excessive exceptions". Therefore, corrective measures are essential.

Importance or advantages

Importance of control is supreme for successful running of an organisation because of the following **advantages** : (1) **Protection against deviation** — An organisation may deviate from its predetermined line of action. It is control that brings it back to the track. (2) **Test of managerial efficiency** — Management will fail if it cannot maintain control over the activities of the organisation at all levels. (3) **Extension of decentralisation** — Decentralisation is not possible if there is absence of control. How far decentralisation can be carried out depends on whether control can be maintained. (4) **Fostering co-ordination** — By keeping all the functions of an enterprise on a right track, controls facilitate co-ordination. By fostering co-ordination control helps achievement of the common objectives. (5) **Provisions for future planning** — Control over present performances provides sufficient materials to prepare future planning or replanning.

Limitations or disadvantages

(1) **All performances cannot be standardised.** Activities which are of intellectual and advisory types cannot be standardised. The human behaviour as a whole cannot be put into any set standard. (2) **No effects on external situation** — There are various external factors which cast influence on the functioning of an organisation. These external factors cannot be

controlled. (3) **Adverse human reactions** — Control affects human elements directly and they may react adversely. It is rightly said that control cannot be imposed. Self-control is the best control. (4) **Difficulties in finding out corrective measures** — Sometimes corrective measures for errors cannot be found because of situation beyond control. This situation arises when there is excessive external influence or the person responsible for error cannot be identified or taken to task for unavoidable reasons. Minor mistakes have to be overlooked. Sometimes corrective measures cannot be introduced because of practical difficulties.

How to make control effective — (1) First of all **there must be an organisation and its activities** which have to be controlled. Control cannot exist in vacuum. (2) **There must be some planning.** Planning and controlling are twin functions of management. If there is no plan there cannot be any control because control means verification of the actual performance with the standard. Plan sets out the standard. (3) **All the pre-requisites for effective control must exist.** The standard itself shall be practicable to be performed. The people must have faith in the standard. There must be proper superior-subordinate relationship through two-way communication. (4) **Span of control shall not be too big.** Span of control means the number of subordinates which one superior can control. The number shall not be very big. At the higher level, the number can be between three and six. At the lower level, however, the number can be bigger. (5) **The principle of unity of command has to be respected.** It means that one subordinate shall be accountable to only one superior, otherwise there will be confusion. (6) **A part-authority has to be delegated.** The superior never delegates full authority to his subordinate. By keeping the remaining part reserved, the superior can exercise control over the subordinates. (7) **The steps of control have to be systematically followed.** (8) **Proper tools of control have to be used** at different situations and on different activities of persons.

LEVELS OF MANAGEMENT

Meaning — An organisation is vertically divided on the basis of levels of authority. Such **levels of authority are otherwise known as levels of management** because authority means power of taking decision and making order on others to carry out the decisions. This is the managerial function. **Generally, three levels of management** are found in an organisation — top, middle, and lower. In very large organisations, as we find in USA and such other advanced countries, four levels of management are thought of — top, intermediate, middle, and supervisory. The level or the hierarchy of management are described below :

(1) **Top management** — It lies at the head of the organisation whose function is to make overall decisions to be carried out by the organisation as a whole functioning at different levels. The top level management decides what 'things' are to be done and why. **It determines the objectives of the organisation and sets out the policies or guidelines to action.** The top level management controls the management process as a whole.

Generally, **the owner or owners of an organisation is/are at this level.** In case of sole-proprietorship, the proprietor himself holds the position. In case of a partnership firm the partners are the top management people. In a Joint Hindu Family business the **'Karta'** alone holds the supreme post. In any corporate form of organisation, the elected body, either the Board of Directors or the Managing Committee, occupies the position. This is also known as management by 'plural executives'. In the public sector, much depends on the form of organisation. In a departmental undertaking, the Minister concerned is the final decision-maker. In other corporate or autonomous forms there is a Board of Directors or a Committee. The members are, however, nominated by the Government, mainly from the civil servants but also from outside. Professional managers hardly occupy the top level in Indian companies but things are changing. **Professional managers are coming up,** particularly in the public sector. The Government is experimenting by offering the highest managerial positions to retired army officers in public undertakings to ensure discipline.

Generally, **the topmost position is held by the Chairman** of the Board of Directors who is followed by the Managing Director (or Manager), if any, and the executive directors. A

culture of that country and as such its socio-economic and cultural significance can not be overestimated.

Management — Science, Art and Profession

A question is often raised as to whether management is a science, art or a profession. The proper answers to these questions depend first upon a clear understanding of the meaning of the three key terms : science, art and profession.

Science involves seeking new knowledge through the use of a rigorous method of collecting data, classifying and measuring it, setting up hypotheses and testing those hypotheses. Science establishes a relationship between cause and effect and explains 'why' of human behaviour or nature. Science explains the phenomena, the events and situations. Management is a science, something more than common sense. There is now a systematic body of principles, theories and techniques in management. In every functional area of management, principles are applied to increase the effectiveness of the manager. The principles of delegation of authority, the techniques of budgeting, ratio analysis, PERT, Critical Path Method — all these help in the better management of resources. Management is a social science as it deals with people and their behaviour. F. W. Taylor applied scientific methods in management. Being a social science, management cannot be as perfect as Physics or Chemistry. To predict human behaviour with complete accuracy is not possible, nor is it possible to forecast with cent per cent certainty the future of a business as its conditions frequently change. Management is an applied science; it is inter-disciplinary in nature as it draws freely on Economics, Mathematics, Sociology etc. Being an applied science, it lacks a coherent body of knowledge but it greatly improves the quality of management practice. Truly speaking, management is a "soft" science in which no hard and fast rules can be expected.

An art is an application of skills and knowledge and accomplishing an end through deliberate efforts. If this idea of art is applied to managerial activity, management becomes an art. Art is essentially creative and the success of art is the result it achieves. The process of Management involves the use of knowledge and skills to achieve concrete results. Management is a creative art as it makes things happen and converts resources into output. Management has been elevated to the status of an art as it involves judgment and experience in decision-making. Every manager practises his own style of managing the affairs of the organisation — this is, the art of managing. Like all other arts, management makes use of underlying knowledge to gain desired practical results. Today, society needs group action and in that case management is the most important art.

Whether management is a profession is a complicated question to answer. Since management is a broad subject, parts of the subject may have professional characteristics and other parts may not. A profession is based on specialised knowledge. It is always in quest of new ideas and it emphasises services to others. Entrance into a profession is usually restricted by standards established by an association. Judging by these ideas, management may not be strictly a profession. The place of management, however, has forced a new look at its professional status. The moral and social climate, today, has created new challenges for management and to answer these challenges, managers need more intellectual training and search for new ideas. As in profession, management is now to consider ethics and service of society and managers must organise associations with definite standards for membership. So, we can say, though management cannot be termed as profession similar to the medical or legal profession but the professional overtones are present in management.

Professionalisation of management is far from complete. There is no prescribed qualification for entry into management. There are no universal standards of competence and evaluation. A uniform and binding code of professional conduct has not yet been developed. There is neither sense of mission nor dedication of service, nor is there any autonomy of decision-making.

But it is a fact that management is fast moving towards professionalisation, though it is not as yet a full-fledged profession. Even in a country like ours several institutions have been set up to impart management education.

It will not be out of context to mention here that man like Drucker did not consider management as a profession. He apprehended that the attempt to professionalise management would harm economy and society.

Turning to India, we find that Tata Iron & Steel Co. Ltd. has the tradition of professional type of organisation. The creation of Tata Management Service and the establishment of the Mafatlal Services Private Ltd. have, among others, accelerated the trend towards professionalization of management. Hindusthan Levers has professional management and many others, even conservative ones, are moving towards professional management, though most of them are controlled by families and groups.

However, it is encouraging to note that the second generation of industrialists are more keen to have a realistic approach to managerial problems and they are becoming increasingly aware of their limitations. They are, therefore, much more receptive to professional advice.

Principles of Management

Principles signify general truths leading to thoughts or actions. They provide general propositions applicable to the series of phenomena under consideration to provide a guide of thought. Management has its own principles which act as guidelines to provide efficient management to any organisation. These principles have developed through experience, through trials and errors; they are dynamic in nature. With the passage of time, new thoughts are being developed and new principles are enriching the realm of management. As Brech has put it — "A principle means a fundamental truth as the basis of reasoning, a primary element, a general law." So, the principles grown and developed through decades in the world of management – out of the practical experience and constant endeavours of the managers – form the foundation on which is built up the management structure in an organisation.

Management principles, as it is claimed, are true generally, regardless of time, place, organisation or level within an organisation. These principles are not, however, immutable, for there is nothing rigid or absolute in management. These principles are meant for the managers to take decisions on their basis, as they are tested generalisations. The Management principles are rightly called "diagnostic guides". According to Henri Fayol, they are flexible and capable of adaptation. Certain factors, such as cultural traditions, the stage of economic development and the philosophy of the Government, affect the application of the principles of management and they are adapted to the conditions prevalent in an organisation. The flexibility of the principles of management does not make them less important. They are of crucial importance, as has been said by Terry. According to him, "Principles of management are to a manager as a table of strengths of materials is to a civil engineer". Koontz and O'Donnell emphasise the need for management principles. According to them, the need arises to increase managerial efficiency, to crystallize the nature of management, to improve research and to attain social goals.

Nothing is an unmixed blessing in this world. The principles of management cannot be an exception. Criticisms have been levelled against these principles such as they are "unscientific", "dogmatic", etc.

It is criticized that the management principles 'force executives into a strait-jacket'.

Henri Fayol, who for the first time stated a set of principles of management, used the term "principles" for his well-known 14 statements. Later writers viewed these principles as universal and unchangeable although Fayol never claimed such. Principles of management, it may be reiterated, are guide-posts which will help a manager to take right decisions. They are not absolute laws suitable for application blindly in similar situations. "They are", according to Terry, "capsules of selected management wisdom to be used carefully and discreetly."

Henri Fayol divided industrial activities in **two parts : Operational and managerial.** The operational part depends on the nature of the industry while for the managerial part he enunciated some basic principles which are **applicable to all types of organisation.** There are fourteen such principles which are discussed below :

(1) **Division of work** — With the growth of complexities in human organisation, it is no longer possible that one person shall perform a number of activities. So there is necessity of division of work. **Each person shall be assigned a particular task.**

(2) **Authority and responsibility** — Authority means the power of taking decisions and making order on others to carry out the decisions. Every person shall be given some definite amount of authority. As much authority a person shall have, exactly the same amount of responsibility he has to shoulder. Responsibility means a sense of duty to use authority properly. **There must be parity between authority and responsibility.** If there is disparity, then there will be either wastage or misuse of authority.

(3) **Discipline** — Discipline means obedience to certain rules and norms, outward mark of respect to the higher authority and controlled behaviour. **The managers shall have to create and preserve discipline** in the organisation. This can be done provided there is good relation between the superiors and the subordinates.

(4) **Unity of command** — It means one individual should get his command or **order to do some work from only one superior.** If orders are given by more than one superior then there will be confusion and discipline will be broken.

(5) **Unity of direction** — Every organisation must have some common objectives. Each action to be done and each person doing some action inside the organisation must be directed towards the common objectives. **Unity of direction means oneness of purpose.** All depends on the leadership of the managers. If there is no unity of direction the organisation cannot function as an integrated unit.

(6) **Subordination of individual interest to general interest** — In an organisation, there are individuals and a number of big or small functional groups. Each individual or each group has his or its own interest. But all these **individual and group interests shall have to be surrendered to the general or common interest** of the organisation as a whole. Then only an organisation can function as an integrated unit. A 'sense of belonging' will be developed.

(7) **Remuneration** — Remuneration is the 'price' offered to the personnel for the services rendered by them. The rates of remuneration shall be **fair and satisfactory to both the employers and the employees.** The rates of remuneration depend on various internal factors like cost of other factors, skill of the personnel, etc. and also on external factors like trade union pressure, Government policy, etc. A reconciliation of all the factors has to be achieved.

(8) **Centralisation** — As, in a human body, all the sensations in different parts of the body converge in the brain through the nerves, in an organisation, **all the forces or functions must be centralised through communication.** Communication means exchange of views between persons belonging to different levels or to same level of an organisation. Such centralisation through communication shall have to be achieved by the top level management. This will cause unity of direction and the organisation shall function as an integrated unit. Smaller the organisation, easier is the centralisation.

(9) **Scalar chain** — The entire organisation is divided into some levels creating **a superior-subordinate relationship in a chain. It is a scalar chain because there is a level of scale of authority.** Higher the level, greater is the authority (and responsibility). There shall be perfect communication among the persons in the scalar chain, downward and upward or top

to bottom. It starts from the topmost level and ends at the bottom or lowest level. Persons at the same level, called 'peers', are joined by a plank called 'gangplank'. The whole thing looks like a ladder looking like a triangle as represented by the G-A-Q diagram. If section F has to be put into contact with section P, then the ladder has to be climbed from F to A and then to come down from A to P. Again there shall be climbing from P to A and stepping down from A to F. It is easier and quicker to reach directly from F to P or P to F by the use of FP 'gangplank', provided E and O authorise F and P, respectively, to have direct connection and F and P inform E and O, respectively, after they have communicated.

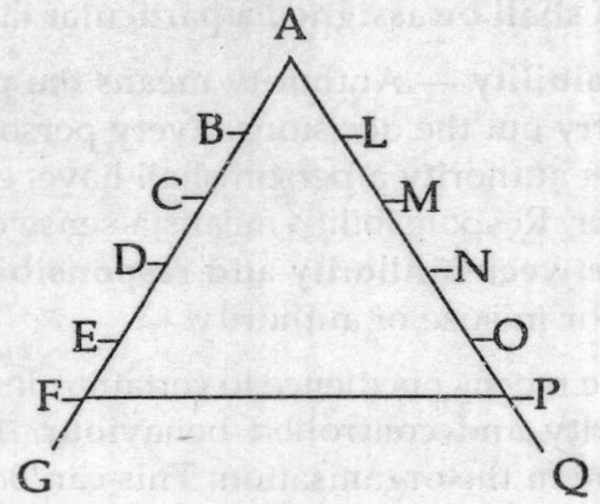

(10) Order — Inside an organisation, there must be 'a place for everything and everything in its place'. Similarly, a right man shall be at the right place. If **everything or every person is at its or his right** place, the organisation can function efficiently. It needs proper choice of man, material and place in each case.

(11) Equity — Equity means combination of equality and justice. **Nobody should feel that he is ignored.** A sense of equity should prevail in the entire organisation.

(12) Stability of tenure of personnel — An employee needs time to get accustomed to the environment in which he is employed. Once he has settled down and he is sure of his stay, he can show his efficiency. Such **stability will inspire confidence** in the minds of the personnel.

(13) Initiative — A person gets motivated and zeal and energy to do work are developed in him only if he has freedom to plan and to execute it. Everybody wants **some freedom within the limits of his position.** Such freedom creates initiative.

(14) Esprit de corps — **Teamwork is essential** for the success of an organisation. Such a team-spirit can be developed through better communication and motivation. Management is concerned with human organisation and so every human element has to be motivated, leading to development of team-spirit, because everybody is directed to the general interest of the organisation.

Universality of Management

Universality of management implies that the principles of management are of universal application. Regardless of their place in the organisation structure or nature of the organisation, managers perform the same functions. Irrespective of the size and location of the organisation, the basic principles of management can be applied in all managerial situations. As a management expert observes " the principles of management are universal. They are applicable to any kind of enterprise wherever there is the co-ordinated effort of human beings. The type of enterprise is not significant. This universality aspect of management has been stoutly proclaimed by F. W. Taylor in his Scientific Management where he said that management principles are applicable to all kinds of human activities, from our simplest individual acts to the work of our great corporations. Henri Fayol fully propounded the universality aspect of management. Since the organic functions of management are deemed to be the same at all levels of management and in all organisations, the universality of management is accepted. Harbison and Myers, after studying management practices in twenty= three countries, came to the conclusion that "there is a general logic of management development which has applicability both to advanced and industrialising countries in the modern world".

Megginson and Mc Cann write : The universality of management concept is not restricted to certain nations or societies of the world. The functions and principles are constant though execution of the organic functions of management varies from culture to culture. An example of a universally true principle of management is the division of labour or specialisation. This principle applies everywhere whether the organisation is big or small or it is a religious or educational organisation. The principle of standardisation is also such a principle whose applicability is universal. All the principles of management may not be of universal application; for example, the principle of span of control. But, in general, management is universal.

Qualities and skills required of a manager

Management, today, is a very complex job and to discharge management functions effectively, a manager must be well – equipped with various qualities and skills. The skills of management have been classified into three categories — technical, human and conceptual.

Technical Skills : The methods of production and the equipment and techniques used in production or in a job are its technical aspect. A manager who knows this technical aspect of his job can be said to have technical skills. These skills are more concerned with things than with men. To cite an instance, we can say, a manager having the knowledge of how to operate a computer may be said to possess technical skills. To be equipped with technical skills, no general instruction can be prescribed. A manager, to be technically skilled, must know which skills should be employed in his particular enterprise and be familiar enough with their potentiality to ask discerning questions of his technical advisers. He must also understand both the role of each skill employed and the interrelationships between skills.

Human skills : The ability to work effectively with people and the capacity to build work teams can be called human skills. A modern manager must possess human skills along with other skills because of growing importance of the human factor in management. To acquire these skills what is needed is a heart filled with warmth and compassion, love and affection for the fellow-workers. A manager must be a man first, then a manager. His dealings with his superiors and subordinates and also with his equals will be appropriate, humane and of such quality that can be expected of a man of refined culture. A manager in making must keep it in his mind that the acquisition of the qualities and human skills starts with his career and continues unabated and it becomes a part of his orientation and a constant endeavour should be there by the manager, throughout his career, to develop the human skills.

Conceptual skills : The ability to see the whole enterprise as an unit of operation is a conceptual skill. Conceptual skills enable the manager to diagnose the different facts of a problem in relation to its total environment and to apply the best methods to solve the problems. These skills are helpful in decision-making. Conceptual skills deal primarily with ideas and, in higher levels of management, managers become increasingly involved in conceptual skills. All the three types of skill – technical, human and conceptual — are interrelated but their significance tends to differ at various levels of management.

Different types of skills make qualitative difference between a manager and a manager. These skills are all-important, no doubt, but conceptual skills are very important for top management in formulating policies. Human skills are important at all levels of management since management, is a process of getting things done through people. Technical skills, on the other hand, are especially important at a the supervisory level, where very intimate understanding of techniques is often necessary.

Managers' skills can be transferred from one enterprise to another and from one occupation to the other. A successful manager, it has been observed, is an all-purpose manager, a man suited to any type of organisation. But the transferability of skills suffers from limitations from business to non-business situations. Human and conceptual skills are more easily transferable but technical skills cannot be so easily transferred.

Skills are acquired but qualities are more or less in- born. Improvement upon the qualities which a manager already possesses is possible but qualities that did never exist cannot be made to grow, what to speak of their improvement. A manager should have qualities such as personality, feeling for others, vision, intellect and, to crown all, the most uncommon quality – a strong common sense.